REFUGEES' ROLES *in* RESOLVING DISPLACEMENT *and* BUILDING PEACE

REFUGEES' ROLES
in RESOLVING
DISPLACEMENT
and BUILDING PEACE

Beyond Beneficiaries

MEGAN BRADLEY
JAMES MILNER
BLAIR PERUNIAK
Editors

Georgetown University Press
Washington, DC

Library of Congress Cataloging-in-Publication Data

Names: Bradley, Megan, 1980- editor. | Milner, James (James H. S.), editor. | Peruniak, Blair, editor.
Title: Refugees' Roles in Resolving Displacement and Building Peace : Beyond Beneficiaries / Megan Bradley, James Milner, and Blair Peruniak, editors.
Description: Washington, DC : Georgetown University Press, 2019. | Includes bibliographical references and index.
Identifiers: LCCN 2018038734 (print) | LCCN 2018045298 (ebook) | ISBN 9781626166769 (ebook) | ISBN 9781626166745 | ISBN 9781626166745 (hardcover : alk. paper) | ISBN 9781626166752 (pbk. : alk. paper) | ISBN 9781626166769 (ebook)
Subjects: LCSH: Refugees—Political activity. | Emigration and immigration—Political aspects. | Peace-building.
Classification: LCC JV6346 (ebook) | LCC JV6346 .R447 2019 (print) | DDC 362.87—dc23
LC record available at https://lccn.loc.gov/2018038734

♾ This book is printed on acid-free paper meeting the requirements of the American National Standard for Permanence in Paper for Printed Library Materials.

20 19   9 8 7 6 5 4 3 2 First printing

Printed in the United States of America.
Cover design by Will Brown.
Cover image courtesy of flickr: A street scene in Altos de Cazucá in Soacha, the area where the 'Círculos de aprendizaje' (Learning circles) functions with the aid of UNHCR Colombia./ UNHCR / P. Smith

Contents

Conclusion: Where Do We Go from Here?   267
JAMES MILNER, MEGAN BRADLEY, AND BLAIR PERUNIAK

Foreword

Throughout history, refugees, internally displaced persons (IDPs) and other migrants have, for the most part, had to find their own solutions to the problems they have encountered. Only in recent times have public mechanisms allowed for some groups of refugees and migrants to come and start new lives in the Global North or supported the pursuit of "durable solutions" to displacement in the Global South.

In recent years hundreds of thousands of refugees and migrants have taken it on themselves to move toward Europe, often using smuggling rings. Had they been offered viable options, such as resettlement programs or residence visas, most would have come as documented immigrants. But the Global North offered little or nothing for several years, and refugees and migrants realized they could count on only their own agency and resourcefulness.

The Global North does not want to acknowledge that migrants will come, no matter what. As long as the drivers of migration—essentially, violence and poverty as push factors, and labor needs as pull factors—will remain, people will move, documented if possible, undocumented if need be. Resisting mobility is inefficient and costly in the long term. Organizing it is a better option.

We need to change our collective mind-set. Prohibitions and repressive policies, without regular migration channels for asylum seekers and much-needed low-wage migrants, do not change push and pull factors and only entrench smuggling operations and underground labor markets, resulting in more deaths at sea and more human rights violations. There is ample testimony of the toxic, counterproductive, and unsustainable nature of most of the repressive measures when no appropriate mobility option is offered by the authorities. Prohibition is part of the problem, not the solution.

As long as persons in need of mobility are not offered official mobility solutions, underground mobility solutions will be provided by opportunistic smuggling rings. The only way to reduce smuggling is to take over the mobility market by offering regular, safe, accessible, and affordable mobility solutions, with all the security checks that efficient visa and nonvisa mobility regimes can provide.

As Kenneth Roth, head of Human Rights Watch, said in April 2016, "If there is a crisis, it is one of politics, not capacity." We are facing a crisis of political leadership. All around the world, many politicians are fanning the flames of xenophobia, racism, scapegoating, exclusion, and discrimination, pitting "them" against "us."

There is no getting out of a crisis unless one provides a post-crisis vision. There will be no tackling the present migration "crisis" (in Europe and elsewhere) unless politicians delineate a long-term, human rights-based strategic mobility and diversity policy vision that will give meaning and direction to the actions presently taken.

The main axis of this long-term vision should be the elimination of precariousness in the statuses of migrants so they are empowered to establish their own mobility strategies, devise their own family solutions, and fight for their own rights, whatever the context: labor market, housing, health care, education, or antiterrorism.

For refugees, long-term, substantial, and collectively shared resettlement policies would go a long way toward responding to their needs, alleviating the responsibilities undertaken by transit countries, and reassuring populations in host countries that this migration is properly governed.

For migrant workers, countries should recognize their real labor needs and open regular migration channels for labor at all wage levels. The idea is not to diminish border controls. On the contrary, it is to increase them and make them more effective. Offering most foreigners easier access to appropriate travel documents, such as refugee status and resettlement visas, visitor visas, family reunification visas, work visas, or student visas would allow states to concentrate their intelligence and deterrence efforts on the minute percentage of foreigners who really need to be identified for exclusion.

Key conditions remain, however, and political leadership will be expected. We need a sharp increase in respect for labor conditions in favor of *all* workers, regardless of status, and the repression of exploitative employers and recruiters. We also need a convincing mainstream discourse on diversity as a central and dynamic feature of most contemporary societies. The challenges facing those displaced within their own countries also need more careful, focused attention.

Ultimately, we need to bank on the agency, resourcefulness, and creativity of migrants, refugees, and IDPs—on their ability to find their own productive place in our societies—just as we have banked on the ability of rural migrants to find their place in our cities during the rural exodus. We adapted then to help them thrive. We can adapt now to help migrants, refugees, and IDPs thrive. For their benefit and ours.

This is not wishful thinking. I would argue that the wishful thinking is on the side of those who claim that migration can be stopped, that there is a technical solution to such issues, that we can continue to live peacefully with millions of disenfranchised migrant youths, that we can deport millions of migrants and "seal" the borders while respecting human rights.

Many silver linings suggest that greater openness will come eventually: the present ground work of civil society, the increasing vigilance of the judiciary, the much-improved reporting of the media, the welcoming policies of cities, the appetite of the business community for diversity and mobility, the much more open attitudes of the youth toward mobility and diversity as well as the United Nations *Global Compact on Migration*, which sends a clear message that states need to "facilitate" mobility.

As the contributors to this volume make clear, the diverse strategies employed by migrants, refugees, and IDPs to build peace and resolve displacement also provide reasons for optimism. The challenge for states and international institutions is to join and empower migrants, refugees, and IDPs in building constructive solutions, as opposed to the tragic and recurring consequences of working against them.

François Crépeau, O.C., F.R.S.C., Ad.E.
Trudeau Fellow
Hans & Tamar Oppenheimer Professor in Public International Law
McGill University
April 13, 2018

Acknowledgments

This book emerged from a workshop, "From Beneficiaries to Actors: Understanding Displaced Persons' Roles in Resolution Processes," convened at McGill University in December 2015. Earlier versions of these chapters were all presented and discussed at the workshop, and we are grateful for the contributors' sustained engagement to bring this collection to press. The workshop and this volume were supported by the Social Sciences and Humanities Research Council of Canada (SSHRC). We would like to express our appreciation to SSHRC as well as to the other institutions and individuals who supported the project, including McGill's Institute for the Study of International Development, the Hans & Tamar Oppenheimer Chair in Public International Law, the Centre for Human Rights and Legal Pluralism, the Yan Lin Centre Research Group on Global Justice, and Carleton University. On the individual level, we would like to thank François Crépeau, Catherine Lu, Lorenz Lüthi, Iain Blair, Sonia Laszlo, Laura Madokoro, and Catherine-Lune Grayson.

Our sincere gratitude goes to Ecem Oskay for her adept organization of the workshop and her intellectual contributions to the project. Our thanks are also due to Margaret June Mills, Shiva Mazrouei-Seidani, and Victoria Spiteri for their research assistance.

At Georgetown University Press, we would like to thank Don Jacobs for his warm, consistent, and insightful support. We are also grateful to the two anonymous reviewers for their thoughtful feedback.

As editors, we would like to dedicate our work on this project to Matthew Gibney. We all had the good fortune to complete our doctoral studies under Matthew's supervision and continue to be influenced, each in our own way, by his work and his commitment to grappling with hard questions surrounding refugees' dispossession—physical, social, and political. We are grateful to Matt for his support as we joined in exploring these hard questions and for his humor along the way.

Introduction

Shaping the Struggles of Their Times: Refugees, Peacebuilding, and Resolving Displacement

Megan Bradley, James Milner,
and Blair Peruniak

In September 2015, as global displacement rates continued to climb, the image of a three-year-old refugee boy who had washed up on a Turkish beach galvanized international attention. In many ways the depiction of Alan Kurdi reflected conventional assumptions about refugees as hapless, helpless victims. Yet a closer look at the Kurdi family's history reveals a more complex picture of the struggle to find solutions, however imperfect, to the loss of home. The Kurdi family was displaced several times within Syria before fleeing to Turkey with the aim of reuniting with Alan's aunt in Canada. After their application was denied for technical reasons by Canadian authorities, Alan's father arranged for the family to be smuggled by sea from Turkey to Greece in the hope of finding shelter in the European Union. After their boat hit high waves, Alan, his mother, and brother were drowned. At every step, the family's story exposes tensions between agency and constraint, compulsion and cruel choices. These tensions are at the heart of displacement experiences worldwide, whether in the context of conflict, persecution, or natural disasters.

By official counts there are now more people uprooted by conflict than at any time since World War II; millions more are displaced every year in disasters (UNHCR 2018). With record numbers of refugees and internally displaced persons (IDPs) has come increased interest in obstacles to the resolution of forced migration that have made displacement situations more protracted than ever: in the early 1990s, refugee situations typically lasted nine years, compared to the contemporary average of approximately twenty years (UNHCR 2012). Those uprooted within their own countries face a similarly bleak dynamic. Lack of access to "durable solutions" to displacement—whether voluntary return, local integration, or resettlement elsewhere—is in part a consequence of the failure to resolve and build peace following the conflicts that generate many forced migration crises. International norms and standards that have emerged in recent decades routinely call for the active engagement of refugees and IDPs in peacebuilding, postconflict development and reconstruction processes, and in efforts to resolve displacement, rooting the need for participation and consultation in international human rights principles (see, e.g., IASC 2010; UNHCR 2004). Yet states, humanitarian agencies, and other international actors routinely fail to actively incorporate displaced persons in these processes or to recognize the ways in which they are nonetheless independently shaped by forced migrants themselves. Instead, institutional actors often employ rhetoric suggesting that refugees and IDPs are merely the "beneficiaries"—to use a common humanitarian term—of durable solutions that are simply provided once the conditions that uprooted them have been resolved and that states and international organizations are best positioned to interpret the preferability of different solutions. This approach effaces the active and significant roles refugees and IDPs play in the complex political processes surrounding efforts to resolve conflict and the predicament of displacement itself.

Alongside rising displacement rates, forced migration studies has evolved into a large, dynamic, interdisciplinary field. As in many other interdisciplinary fields, forced migration scholars from different backgrounds sometimes struggle with "speaking past" one another, employing diverse and often unreconciled concepts and approaches to identify and explain how forced migrants shape the pursuit of peace and solutions to displacement, from interpersonal to national and transnational levels. The resilience and resourcefulness of displaced populations is recognized (at least rhetorically) by many researchers and practitioners, and a wide range of scholars have called for greater attention to and careful theorization of the ways in which refugees and IDPs understand and exert themselves as agents (see, e.g., Bradley 2014; Chatty 2010; Essed, Frerks, and Schrijvers 2004; Moulin 2012; Perera 2013). However, these dynamics remain largely peripheral to policy responses to displacement and peacebuilding. Similarly, scholarship on the global politics of forced migration has focused primarily on macro-level structural dynamics and institutional actors, such as states and international organizations, and either has not addressed or has struggled to comprehend the active roles of displaced individuals and communities in peacebuilding and the resolution of forced migration. Ethnographic examinations of forced migration have yielded considerable insight into the myriad ways in which displaced individuals and communities maneuver in the face of diverse socioeconomic, cultural, legal, political, and institutional constraints and shape the structures that condition their experiences and opportunities (see, e.g., Allan 2014; Horst 2006c; Malkki 1995a). Yet these findings are rarely integrated into policy and academic analyses of more macro-level challenges surrounding attempts to build peace and resolve displacement. Indeed, despite increased academic and policy interest in durable solutions to displacement and the links between forced migration and peace, there is still little work that applies interdisciplinary approaches to explore these processes across cases, and the normative implications of displaced persons' involvement in these processes remain underexamined.

Accordingly, this collection draws on interdisciplinary perspectives—including political science, anthropology, philosophy, law, and sociology—to more systematically analyze where and how displaced populations contribute to interrelated political "resolution" processes and the empirical and normative significance of these engagements. While refugees and IDPs are still often portrayed as simply the "beneficiaries" of assistance and solutions determined by national and international actors, this book probes how displaced persons themselves conceptualize and advance solutions to their predicament. Displaced persons' efforts often sit in tension, implicitly or explicitly, with the approaches promoted by powerful institutions and bring into question the assumption that institutionally favored solutions truly help their supposed beneficiaries. Indeed, in focusing on the vital yet still too often neglected processes of peacebuilding and the pursuit of durable solutions to displacement, we recognize that in many cases the "solutions" crafted by refugees and IDPs themselves may necessitate critical reconsideration of these very constructs. Beyond exploring an underexamined but pivotal challenge, this book aims to advance the study of forced migration by probing the dichotomies and links between different levels of analysis and action, and the tools used to understand them, and by using refugees' engagement in resolution processes as an opportunity to contribute to debates on the different meanings and expressions of refugees' agency. The volume also seeks to speak to the broader community of peacebuilding, humanitarian and human rights scholars concerned with the nature and dynamics of agency in contentious political contexts, and to identify insights that may help inform policy and practice.

The book proceeds in three parts. Part 1 draws on disciplinary perspectives from political science, anthropology, philosophy, and law—four fields that have significantly shaped refugee and forced migration studies—to broach some of the critical questions surrounding efforts to understand how refugees shape resolution processes: How do refugees politically mobilize to affect peacebuilding and displacement resolution processes? How are these processes shaped by refugees' "everyday" practices and life experiences? What are refugees' responsibilities, and what does it mean to recognize and respect refugees as *moral* agents in these processes? How might the law strengthen (or hinder) refugees' efforts to build peace and resolve displacement? Part 2 provides a more focused examination of refugees' roles in pursuing peace and social reconstruction, while part 3 concentrates on efforts to resolve displacement within and beyond traditional durable solutions frameworks. The conclusion draws out some of the implications of this discussion for future research, policy, and practice. This introduction lays the ground for this work by exploring the contested concepts that underpin the project, considering some of the methodological challenges associated with analyzing refugees' roles in resolution processes, and highlighting some of the key ways in which refugees and IDPs have shaped complex political "resolution processes." It elucidates the need to develop more robust accounts of these processes and their implications for theory, policy, and practice, and it reflects on some of the central themes that emerge within and across the following chapters, particularly the notion of agency.

Conceptualizing Displacement, Durable Solutions, Peacebuilding, and Agency

This section examines several concepts pivotal to this discussion: refugees, durable solutions, peacebuilding, resolution processes, and agency. First, international laws and frameworks establish various technical definitions of terms such as "refugees" and "IDPs."[1] Yet debates on displaced populations as actors in resolution processes cannot be isolated from analyses of how these labels are constructed, applied, contested, and claimed over time, leading to new concerns about what it means to act *as* a refugee or an IDP and to participate in efforts to build peace and resolve displacement (Zetter 1991; Feldman 2012a). Being displaced internally versus across borders can raise distinctive challenges and concerns, particularly in the context of peacebuilding and the pursuit of durable solutions. However, like many of the contributors to this volume, we use the term "refugee" broadly to refer to an individual who not only has "lost the protection of her basic rights" but who has in important ways been "deprived of her social world" (Gibney 2015, 13). From this perspective, to be a refugee is "to be someone who has been displaced from the communities, associations, relationships and cultural context that have shaped one's identity and around which one's life plan has hitherto been organized" (Gibney 2015, 13). This is not to say that refugees do not actively construct new relationships, sustain links with their countries and communities of origin, and participate in politics. Indeed, for the growing number of people who are born and spend their lives as refugees, in many ways experiences of exile constitute their "social world." However, this conceptualization helpfully underscores the link between displacement and the disruption of the ability to make and pursue life plans, whether individual, communal, or even intergenerational (Horst and Grabska 2015). When conceived from this perspective, as Erin Baines demonstrates in this volume, the resolution of displacement can be understood as a struggle to overcome social exile as much as physical exile by reclaiming membership in humanity and in particular communities.

In humanitarian parlance, "durable solutions" refer to the three traditional routes for resolving displacement: voluntary return, local integration in the country or community in which the displaced person has sought shelter, and resettlement elsewhere. Discussions of durable solutions for legally recognized refugees typically focus on restoring (or freshly establishing) their ability to make effective citizenship claims, whether through the reassertion of citizenship rights in the country of origin upon return or through the acquisition of new citizenship rights in a host or resettlement state. In contrast, because IDPs are typically citizens of the state in which they are uprooted, international standards suggest that durable solutions have been achieved when IDPs are back on equal footing with their conationals—that is, when they "no longer have any specific assistance and protection needs that are linked to their displacement and can enjoy their human rights without discrimination on account of their displacement" (IASC 2010, 5). While Amanda Coffie's contribution focuses on how displaced populations have resisted customary durable solutions, particularly local integration and voluntary repatriation, other contributors, including Loren Landau, Angela Sherwood, and Elena Fiddian-Qasmiyeh, question this traditional trinity of durable solutions and its sedentary, individualistic bias, deepening discussion of the role of mobility in the resolution of displacement and the need to deconstruct the traditional categories of durable solutions and the commitments at their foundations.

The notion of peacebuilding has a long pedigree but came to prominence with the 1992 UN secretary-general's *Agenda for Peace*, which defined peacebuilding as "action to identify and support structures which will tend to strengthen and solidify peace in order to avoid a relapse into conflict," recognizing that this may involve "rebuilding the institutions and infrastructures of nations torn by civil war and strife; and building bonds of peaceful mutual benefit among nations formerly at war" (UNSG 1992, 4–5). Over the course of the 1990s and first decades of the twenty-first century, internationally supported peacebuilding initiatives were implemented in several cases characterized by large-scale forced migration, yet divisions within the UN system and at the domestic level between actors responsible for peacebuilding and postconflict development and those responsible for displacement undercut integrated institutional responses to these challenges. In 2009 the secretary-general issued a report stressing the important links between durable solutions and peacebuilding and in 2011 instructed UN agencies to pilot a framework intended to foster more coordinated approaches to advancing peacebuilding and displacement resolution goals (UNSG 2009, 2011). The relationship between displacement, peacebuilding, and broader development processes is also central to the 2016 New York Declaration on Refugees and Migrants and to the ensuing Global Compact on Refugees. Despite these initiatives, sustained efforts to fully engage the links between these issues remain limited, and internationally backed peacebuilding processes have been widely critiqued as uncoordinated, inappropriately short term, externally driven, overly focused on notions of liberal peace and negative over positive peace, insufficiently attentive to regional dynamics, and illegitimate in light of inadequate consultation with affected populations (Milner 2009, 2015). Notwithstanding such shortcomings, there are repeated examples—including from Mozambique and Uganda, explored here in contributions from James Milner and Baines—of displaced populations engaging in and affecting peacebuilding and social reconstruction processes in diverse ways and with diverse consequences that challenge assumptions about who builds peace and within what geographic, thematic, and temporal parameters.

Our focus on peacebuilding is attributable in part to forced migration studies' predominant concern with uprootings associated with violence and persecution. Yet every year even more people are displaced in the context of natural disasters. Disasters are often assumed to be "easier," "less political" situations in which conflict is minimal and displacement can be more rapidly resolved. However, closer examination reveals significant similarities between peacebuilding and postdisaster reconstruction processes in terms of, for example, political contestation over the nature and characteristics of the state and its citizenry, claims to public and private space, the marginalization of particular socioeconomic groups, the influence of informal governance systems, and disconnects between international priorities and the strategies employed by displaced populations to address their foremost concerns. Sherwood's chapter on post-earthquake Haiti disrupts assumptions about the relative simplicity of postdisaster displacement and demonstrates the central if often overlooked roles that displaced persons play in shaping not only peacebuilding but also postdisaster reconstruction.

Throughout this volume, the term "resolution processes" is used to denote contested political "problem-solving" efforts shaped by diverse actors, interests, and constraints. Our focus on durable solutions, peacebuilding, and, to a more limited extent, postdisaster reconstruction is not to suggest that these are the only resolution processes in which displaced populations play considerable roles. For example, as Anna Purkey's contribution underscores, refugees also shape transitional and "transformative" justice and reconciliation processes, which may be seen as resolution processes in their own right (Bradley 2013a; 2015; Duthie 2012b). More broadly, development may be understood as a process of resolving poverty and inequality—although some internationally supported approaches to development arguably do more to entrench these conditions than alleviate them. The complex relationship between forced migration, durable solutions, conflict, and development has been a long-standing concern for researchers, policymakers, and practitioners alike, with debates on the "root causes" of refugee flows going back decades. Growing rates of forced migration and the increasingly protracted nature of displacement have led to resurgent interest in the links between development and displacement.[2] Although this volume does not explicitly concentrate on development per se, development challenges are interwoven throughout as integral aspects of peacebuilding and the resolution of displacement. For instance, Fiddian-Qasmiyeh explores how access to education shapes the strategies of Palestinian and Sahrawi refugees for whom neither peace nor traditional solutions are on the horizon, while Landau and Sherwood consider the significance of urbanization processes and cultivating livelihoods in informal urban economies.

Given this book's concern with the roles of refugees and IDPs in complex resolution processes, the notion of agency is central to many of the chapters, whether explicitly or implicitly. Agency is of course a long-standing concern in forced migration scholarship. Many concertedly push back against stereotypical characterizations of refugees as helpless and vulnerable, pointing to the fact that uprooted populations have often led revolutions, run governments-in-exile, and even instigated invasions to demonstrate that refugees are potentially powerful actors. Yet in much of the field, agency arguably remains something of a theoretical "black box."[3] Scholars' approaches to the question of refugee agency are informed to varying degrees by broader, ongoing debates in a range of disciplines.[4] But, perhaps counterintuitively in light of the intricacy and breadth of these debates, there is a tendency in some forced migration scholarship to reduce the question to the simple recognition or nonrecognition of refugees as agents, implying that "listening to refugee voices" is a straightforward solution to thorny practical and theoretical problems.[5] Policymakers and practitioners often pay lip service to consulting with displaced populations and including them in programmatic decision-making, but forced migrants' varying interests and perspectives commonly take a back seat to those of institutional actors who often fail to recognize and account for the myriad ways in which refugees shape resolution processes beyond the confines of formal consultation and participation processes.

While there is no definitive way to conceptualize "refugee agency" or its relation to agency more generally, displacement may be associated with a range of distinctive concerns and dynamics vis-à-vis agency. For example, being uprooted from one's home or outside one's country of origin may entail a range of potentially negative implications for agency, including increased precariousness associated with fragile legal status and limitations on particular forms of agency such as speech, formal political participation, and certain kinds of economic activity. Refugees' agency may be directed toward particular goals or claims that are closely associated with displacement, such as obtaining asylum, securing resettlement opportunities, or returning home. Displacement may also put refugees and IDPs in a position to (have to) address their claims to a particularly wide variety of actors and authorities, including host states and communities, countries and communities of origin, and international organizations such as the Office of the United Nations High Commissioner for Refugees (UNHCR) and the International Organization for Migration, although their liminal political and socioeconomic status may significantly reduce the likelihood of their claims being heard and addressed. The subjugation associated with displacement may additionally have an "inadvertently enabling power," with experiences of forced migration catalyzing new forms of organization, mobilization, protest, and claims-making (Butler 1997, 94).

Notwithstanding the potentially distinctive aspects of refugee agency, it is essential not to lose sight of the variation within and between displaced populations, and in the conditions and structures they encounter, from camps in Kenya and informal settlements in Haiti to detention centers in Canada, which shape and are shaped by displaced persons' agency. Equally, discussions of refugee agency cannot be divorced from broader discussions of human agency: everyone encounters limitations to the exercise of their agency, and these limitations have varying legitimacy.[6] While displaced individuals and populations often face particular and pronounced constraints on their ability to act, including in the context of resolution processes, these constraints may be closely related to those faced by other groups, such as poor and otherwise marginalized populations. These constraints can shift over time and in terms of their significance for different individuals and groups within a displaced population.

Bearing these issues in mind, we use the term "refugee agency" as an imperfect shorthand for the ability of displaced individuals (and, in some cases, communities) to make and enact choices that potentially affect outcomes, particularly of resolution processes, recognizing that the extent to which displaced persons can exercise agency generally and in particular circumstances will depend on complex, shifting political, socioeconomic, cultural, historical, and institutional structures. In their examinations of how refugees shape peacebuilding processes and the resolution of displacement, the contributors to this collection engage in different ways and to different degrees with notions of agency.

Researching Refugees' Roles in Resolution Processes: Methodological Considerations

One can acknowledge that "refugees were (and are) regularly forced to live in extreme conditions, without necessarily being deprived of their capacity to exercise a degree of control over their own lives" or the capacity to influence resolution processes on different levels (Gatrell 2013, 8). This recognition underpins this volume and raises significant methodological questions about how to explore and understand the fluid contours of refugees' roles.

The contributors to this collection take a pluralistic approach, adopting methods and methodologies that suit the orientation and ambitions of their investigations. Certain methodological approaches sit in tension with one another—for example, in the extent to which they value and aim for empirical generalizability or normative universalizability. However, the volume's pluralist approach is in keeping with and seeks to deepen forced migration studies' commitment to interdisciplinary exchange. It looks to capitalize on the potential complementarities between approaches that focus attention on different units and levels of analysis, from the macro to the micro, and challenge the tokenistic use of "refugee voices." Such pluralism is appropriate as the collection's aim is not to generate and test a single, comprehensive theory of refugees' roles in resolution processes but to provide insight into the complex empirical and normative dynamics surrounding this issue. Accordingly, most of the case studies developed in this volume are not intended to produce generalizable claims but to problematize assumptions, reveal pressures, illuminate strategies, and expose tensions in ways that are attentive to the specificities of circumstances but may also raise valuable questions and insights when considered comparatively.

The empirical chapters bring into focus certain methodological challenges associated with spanning different levels and units of analysis and with understanding the ways in which refugees' roles and perspectives evolve and relate to wider identities and social contexts. Many chapters are especially attuned to the importance of beginning analysis from the perspective of experiences in the Global South, where the vast majority of the world's displaced persons remain, rather than unquestioningly privileging experiences, perspectives, and processes associated with international institutions and Northern states and structures. For instance, in chapter 1, Karen

Jacobsen synthesizes the findings of a wide range of scholarship on refugee mobilization in the Global South, particularly Africa, to develop a typology of non–armed political action by refugees, as individuals and in groups, bringing into focus the classes and potential costs of such efforts. In a related effort, Coffie (chapter 12) explores Liberian refugees' mobilization in opposition to the imposition of "solutions" at odds with their aspirations and concerns.

Building on this interest in rooting explanations of refugees' roles in resolution processes in Southern realities, various contributions consider refugees' agency in resolution processes on a range of levels, including individual, family, communal, national, regional, and international levels. Employing influential philosophical theories of shared action, Blair Peruniak (chapter 3) probes some of the tensions associated with recognizing and respecting refugees as moral agents in the context of large-scale displacement resolution processes that typically require the coordinated participation of thousands of actors—from institutions to individuals—with often dramatically different goals, interests, and capacities. In addition to navigating such thorny theoretical questions, applying classificatory divisions or levels of analysis to displacement situations underscores the need to acknowledge and clarify assumptions about the relationships between social structures and action (whether individual or communal) in varying cultural contexts and often unstable socioeconomic circumstances. For example, Fiddian-Qasmiyeh (chapter 13) examines Palestinian and Sahrawi refugees' participation in international education programs as "rhizomatic strategies" to address displacement-related challenges in the absence of prospects for traditional durable solutions. This analysis demonstrates how long-standing assumptions about the confluence of individual, family, and communal/national interests may fray as displacement becomes protracted, with refugees using educational opportunities in ways that are beneficial on individual and family levels but not necessarily in relation to the assumed interests of the refugee community and national struggles.

As they explore the dynamics of refugee engagement in resolution processes on different levels, the chapters reflect the need for continuous critical awareness of the often drastic power imbalances between actors. They also stress the need to understand the precariousness that shapes refugees' lives and their involvement in resolution processes in relation to the broader precarity of conflict, postconflict, and postdisaster spaces. This entails unpacking how, even before the outbreak of conflict or disaster, uncertainty and inequality influence decision-making and efforts to advance life plans. In other words, analyses cannot unquestioningly begin at the point in time at which national elites or international actors declare a conflict to be over or the pursuit of durable solutions to have started, as these processes are definitively shaped by dynamics that precede and outlast such finite moments. In this connection the methods applied to examine refugees' roles in resolution processes must be adaptable to the fact that refugees' views, plans, and roles, including in relation to resolution processes, are not static but evolve over time. Longitudinal and historically informed studies—including those that draw on narrative interviews, long-term ethnographic work, and archival research—are particularly well suited to capturing refugees' evolving strategies and contributions and their short, medium, and long-term consequences. In her contribution, Cindy Horst (chapter 2) draws on refugees' life histories to consider the relationship between "everyday" civic engagement and resolution processes such as peacebuilding. As Horst reflects, such an approach does not necessarily "bridge the divide between micro and macro, between voluntarism and determinism, or individuals and larger structures." Rather, it can "show the limitations these analytical distinctions present" and underscore how "the radical uncertainty that refugees are faced with often shapes their engagements in dramatic ways: experiences of violent conflict and human rights abuses do not just disproportionately affect but also further create political subjects." Purkey (chapter 4) continues this exploration of the emergence of new forms of political subjectivity in contexts of radical uncertainty by analyzing how legal "conscientization" among refugees from countries such as Burma (Myanmar) may open up opportunities for transformative justice and refugees' active participation in peacebuilding and reconciliation processes.[7]

Questions of social positioning, autonomy, and (inter)dependence lie at the heart of efforts to meaningfully recognize and respond to the varying ways in which refugees engage in resolution processes. These themes are also prominent in feminist analyses of and methodologies for examining forced migration, which implicitly or explicitly inform various chapters in this collection. In the context of state-dominated responses to protracted refugee situations, feminized refugees who "wait patiently" for a state-sanctioned solution are often perceived by powerful institutional actors as more honest and deserving than those who seek to realize solutions on their own terms (Hyndman and Giles 2011). This is evident in responses to undocumented movements, and the forms of "land grabbing" Sherwood (chapter 9) explores in her analysis of how those uprooted by the 2010 earthquake in Haiti have attempted to seize their own solutions, however imperfect, in the broader context of systemic inequality, deep poverty, and a rapidly changing urban landscape.

Examinations of refugees' roles in resolution processes may be deepened through intersectional analysis—that is, by exploring "intersecting constellation[s] of power relationships that produce unequal material realities and distinctive social experiences for individuals and groups positioned within them" (Collins and Chepp 2013, 58–59). Attending to the shifting relationships between constructs such as gender, class, race, sexuality, ethnicity, ability, and age can help illuminate how "individuals and groups can *simultaneously* experience privilege and disadvantage," including in the context of efforts to build peace and resolve displacement (Collins and Chepp 2013, 60; see also Crenshaw 1991). Intersectionality has particularly important implications for analyzing how varying interests, needs, conditions, and identities shape engagement in resolution processes. In this connection, Clark-Kazak and Thomson's (chapter 11) application of intersectional analysis illuminates how Congolese refugees in Uganda and Tanzania have strategically navigated the resettlement process in ways obscured by UNHCR's static resettlement categories. Julieta Lemaitre and Kristin Bergtora Sandvik (chapter 10) also explore the intersections between displacement and other identities in the context of the durable solutions process, considering how gender, membership in indigenous nations, and the emergence of the "victim" discourse in relation to the national transitional justice process have interacted, influencing ideas of what constitutes a solution for IDPs.

Refugees as Agents in Resolution Processes

In her influential account of refugeehood in *The Origins of Totalitarianism*, Hannah Arendt (2004, 343, 382) depicts the refugee as stateless, rightless "scum of the earth," deprived of "political status in the struggle of his time." Overly simplistic readings of Arendt's work have fostered assumptions about refugees as impotent pawns of politics and history, a conceptualization that forced migration scholars have both perpetuated and refuted. This section provides an introductory examination of refugees' diverse roles in resolution processes—in other words, the ways they have shaped the struggles of their times.

Overall, the field of forced migration is characterized by a divide: on the one hand, there is now widespread recognition of the striking ways in which refugees exercise agency, including in the context of resolution processes, despite significant constraints. Refugees are, for example, acknowledged to have shaped resolution processes through protests, political mobilization in exile, and involvement in justice campaigns as well as through more "everyday" actions from economic cooperation to the peaceful mediation of local disputes and the rekindling of interpersonal relationships.[8] On the other hand, images, rhetoric, and assumptions persist about refugees as powerless, vulnerable victims utterly deprived of meaningful choices and the capacity to influence resolution processes.[9] This divide persists for reasons ranging from paternalism, ignorance, discrimination, and manipulation to strategic over-simplification for the purposes of delivering more "compelling" advocacy messages. (Because refugees' particular claims to protection and assistance are, normatively speaking, tied to the notion that they were *forced* to flee and cannot return, refugee advocates may be hesitant to openly recognize the ways refugees make choices and exert power, even in their highly constrained circumstances, out of fear that this may undermine the perceived legitimacy of their claims.) To the extent that opportunities for refugees to participate in resolution processes are limited, there may be disagreement over whether these limitations are morally concerning or even required. Thwarting the intention of exiled Hutu *génocidaires* in the Democratic Republic of Congo (formerly Zaire) to return to Rwanda and complete the extermination of the Tutsi is clearly a different kind of issue than that of the government of Bhutan thwarting the desire of displaced Lhotshampas to return peacefully to their homes, pointing to the need for careful, context-specific analysis of the legitimacy of refugees' claims and limits to their realization.

With growing displacement rates and resurgent political interest in refugees, this is an opportune time to advance the discussion through more nuanced examinations of how refugees influence resolution processes and with what normative and empirical implications across different levels of analysis. This entails moving beyond the "solitudes" of forced migration studies, which limit conversation between those focused on the lived experiences of displaced communities, and those concerned with more macro-level regime dynamics and theoretical and legal debates. As several contributors to this book suggest, it also entails moving beyond the predominant focus on major institutional actors such as states, UN agencies, and international nongovernmental organizations to consider the ways in which other, more shadowy forces such as gangs, land cartels, and informal economic systems also shape the ways in which refugees perceive, experience, and influence the pursuit of peace and efforts to resolve the predicament of displacement itself. (On these dynamics, see, for example, the chapters by Sherwood and Landau.)

The Roles of Displaced Persons in Peacebuilding

Displaced persons' roles in resolution processes, especially peacebuilding, are mediated by factors including histories and cultures of social mobilization; the strength of exile leadership and power structures; "enabling conditions" for organization and advocacy in host communities, including access to resources, international networks, and ethnic, religious, and political affinities between displaced and host populations; socially constructed gender and generational roles; awareness of and ability to frame concerns in relation to international rhetoric on rights, development, peace, and security; and the nature of the relationship between displaced populations and national and international authorities. These factors have shaped the engagement of displaced persons in various aspects of postconflict peacebuilding, including security establishment, institutional reform, economic revitalization, basic service provision, and political processes such as party formation and electioneering. Despite the massive scale of displacement in many conflict situations, a broad trend toward the inclusion of provisions on displacement in peace agreements, and popular assumptions about the centrality of return movements and participation in postconflict elections to successful peacebuilding, the inclusion of the displaced in peacebuilding processes continues to be seen as secondary to core peacebuilding objectives, and of peripheral importance to conventionally powerful peacebuilding actors.[10] Discussions of the role and contributions of displaced populations in peacebuilding are notably absent in various recent anthologies and handbooks in peace, conflict, and security studies, reflecting the persistent chasm between security studies and refugee studies (Morris and Stedman 2008).

To the limited extent that the relationship between displacement and peacebuilding has been addressed in research and practice, the focus is usually on grassroots empowerment among members of displaced communities. Relatively little attention has been paid to refugees as key transnational actors seeking to influence global governance or internationally mediated peace processes from below, although some have explored the relationship between powerful elites and displaced populations who attempt to access or shape political mechanisms, especially through transnational advocacy networks (see, e.g., North and Simmons 1999; Stølen 2007). Reflecting this gap, Snyder (2011, 194) argues that "further research is needed on how grassroots efforts might be linked to political participation at the top level." Others suggest that although regional transnational interests may play important and largely underappreciated roles in contributing to meaningful democratic processes of political change in postconflict states, refugees and other displaced persons remain unlikely to be systematically included in such processes because positions of power are typically occupied by nondisplaced elites (Stewart 2014). Still others question such characterizations, pointing out that in many conflicts, elites flee, preserve, or recreate governing institutions in exile, and subsequently return to power in the postconflict context.

Although displaced elites may retain significant power, enabling them to actively participate in peace negotiations and peacebuilding processes more broadly, prospects for the increased participation of non-elite refugees and IDPs in formal peacebuilding processes remain dim. Against this backdrop, understanding refugees' varying, informal roles in peacebuilding processes requires attention to intersecting experiences and identities, as discussed above, and examination of their implications for involvement in peacebuilding at different levels. For example, as the "refugee warrior" phenomenon makes abundantly clear, the experience of being a combatant may intersect with the experience of displacement; both may be transformative of personal and political identities and circumstances (see, e.g., Perera 2013).[11] Beyond directly shaping conflicts by taking up arms—perhaps one of the most overt examples of refugee agency—refugee warriors may also shape peacebuilding processes through their support for and participation in demobilization and peace movements (Milner 2011, 262; Clark 2014). Baines (chapter 5) advances this conversation by drawing on detailed life histories and extensive ethnographic work to elucidate the role of complex victims—that is, those implicated in the "violence to which they are also subject"—in social reconstruction following the war in northern Uganda.[12] As Baines shows, "displacement is both physical and social. Resolutions involve not only holding the most responsible to account but also reweaving the social fabric." How one can engage in such reweaving—and, in so doing, remedy social displacement—is delimited by what one lost as well as the losses one is seen to have caused for others in war.

Milner (chapter 6) similarly focuses on grassroots experiences of displacement and peacebuilding in sub-Saharan Africa, turning to the case of Mozambique in the early 1990s to explore the disconnect between international institutional perspectives, policies, and practices, particularly on the part of UNHCR, and the informal but highly active role returning refugees played in the country's celebrated peace process. Drawing on UN archives and notions of paternalism, Milner traces how UNHCR discounted refugees' potential and actual contributions and nonetheless took credit for a peaceful return process that was largely of the refugees' making. While Milner's analysis points to how returnees' own efforts can be transformed into a symbol of bureaucratic success, Patrik Johansson (chapter 7) demonstrates how displaced populations can become symbols of grievance, using the cases of forced migration in Nagorno-Karabakh and Israel/Palestine to trace the often troubling implications of this dynamic for efforts to build peace and uphold individual rights while also attending to collective claims to regain lost homes and lands.

Shaping the Search for Solutions to Displacement

Formal durable solutions to displacement are now rare. This is partially attributable to the decreased availability of large-scale resettlement to Western countries and the use of temporary protection modalities in lieu of extending citizenship to refugees who obtain asylum in the Global North. Yet, historically and presently, the vast majority of the world's refugees and IDPs live in and pursue solutions to their predicaments in the Global South, where the scarcity of solutions to displacement is tied to the failure of peacebuilding and reconstruction processes. These failures are themselves often attributed at least in part to the persistence of displacement—a conundrum that cannot be unpacked in isolation from broader analyses of the macro- and micro-level effects of (international) political economies, structural inequalities, and governance systems. In chapter 10, Lemaitre and Sandvik explore this tangled relationship between building peace and resolving displacement in the case of Colombia, tracing how IDPs have organized to influence the peace process and how these organizations and their members' identities and visions for the resolution process have in turn been influenced by shifting policy and legal frameworks.

Institutions such as UNHCR often use language that suggests that durable solutions are "provided" to refugees and IDPs, overlooking the central role uprooted persons play in styling their own routes out of displacement and the disconnects between experiences of forced migration and the abstract, bureaucratic concept of durable solutions. At the same time, they also emphasize the importance of "resilience" and self-reliance, suggesting that "self-reliant refugees are more likely to achieve durable solutions" (UNHCR 2005, iv). Self-reliance policies and the discourse of resilience have attracted criticism as thinly disguised reactions to budgetary pressures and scaled-back protection and assistance efforts. The emphasis on self-reliance has, however, found support among those who are troubled by the dominance of large-scale institutional or international approaches to liberal peacebuilding and efforts to resolve displacement crises. Marc Vincent and Birgitte Refslund Sørensen claim, for instance, that more attention must be paid to IDPs' own adaptive strategies, correcting the inaccurate "perception that the international stage is the only venue for action" (2001, 1).

Certain aspects of refugees' involvement in realizing the three "traditional" durable solutions to displacement have been examined in detail, while other facets of the issue remain largely unexplored. For example, the question of durable solutions features quite prominently in the growing body of work on refugee protests, as a significant proportion of refugee protests focus on concerns such as access to resettlement and camp closures as a precursor to returns (Moulin 2012; Moulin and Nyers 2007). Coffie (chapter 12) advances this conversation through her examination of protests launched by Liberian refugee women in Ghana in 2008. Challenging characterizations of these protests as a failure for their inability to significantly shift durable solutions structures, such as access to resettlement, Coffie demonstrates their role in incrementally expanding refugees' ability to influence and exercise choice in the return process. In this way, Coffie's chapter bridges the literature on refugee protests and the now considerable body of work exploring the (in)voluntariness of return movements and refugees' decision-making processes in the context of repatriation (see, e.g., Allen 1994; Omata 2013; Koser 1997). There is also a growing body of work on how displaced populations participate in and shape reconciliation and transitional justice processes, including property restitution, and how these processes in turn affect the pursuit of durable solutions (see, e.g., Bradley 2015; Duthie 2012b; Smit 2012). But there is still a need for deeper understanding of how individual, family, and community decisions factor into more macro-level norm implementation and policy-making efforts.

Theoretically, achieving a durable solution helps to overcome the liminality imposed by displacement, expanding refugees' autonomy by redressing the barriers and subjugations that accompany exile, such as limited political participation and employment rights. Accessing a durable solution may mean reduced or rescinded access to particular "benefits," such as targeted assistance in refugee camps; in the logic of the refugee regime, however, it is assumed that "resolving" displacement increases the range of choices available to those who are uprooted. However, as several contributions to this volume stress, in many ways the durable solutions process as conceived and advanced by national and international actors can be *dis*empowering, especially in the short and medium terms. This is epitomized by the predicament of refugees who, in the absence of other options, repatriate only to become IDPs. Even resettlement, the purported "golden ticket" of durable solutions, can be disempowering, as reflected in the experiences of Palestinian refugees who were met, upon their resettlement to Brazil, with the expectation that their gratitude for having been resettled would eclipse unresolved rights claims that they continued to carry (Moulin 2012; see also Clark-Kazak and Thomson's chapter in this volume). Debates on whether de facto (rather than de jure) local integration may represent a true durable solution to displacement similarly reflect a concern that it may be disempowering to declare a refugee situation resolved when those who were uprooted still lack full and effective citizenship rights. While they may presently be able to live, move, and work freely in their host country, in the absence of full citizenship rights, changes in political dynamics may leave de facto integrated refugees open to risk of exploitation and may undercut their long-term ability to advance their aspirations. That said, such concerns must be situated in relation to broader state practices that routinely deny or fail to meaningfully uphold the rights of even long-standing nondisplaced citizens. Cognizant of this reality, Landau (chapter 8) offers an analysis of how refugees and other migrants, particularly in Southern African cities, tactically shun solidary, theoretically durable solutions in favor of continued mobility, even in precarious conditions. In this way, Landau brings into question the presumption that achieving durable solutions is the most immediately desirable outcome for the displaced and that solutions serve to "replicate, or at least approximate the status quo ante through the provision of legal rights and the reconstruction of place-bound socialities."

In opening part 3, "Seeking 'Solutions' to Displacement within and beyond Traditional Frameworks," with Landau and Sherwood's destabilizing discussions of solutions and mobility in dynamic urban environments and in closing it with Fiddian-Qasmiyeh's reflections on the educational strategies employed by displaced populations for whom there are simply no solutions in sight, this volume aims to expand conversations on the limits and risks surrounding the pursuit of durable solutions to displacement and the relationship between mobility and attempts to resolve forced migration.[13] As Sherwood and Landau (among others) highlight, displaced persons' self-styled strategies to resolve displacement or grapple with the challenges and opportunities it presents often unfold under the radar of states and humanitarian agencies' managerial efforts. In such circumstances, being identified as displaced and becoming the target of interventions intended to "resolve" displacement, particularly through the end of mobility, may work counter to the purported beneficiaries' conceptions of their own interests. In these cases, bringing refugees' agency and efforts into focus presents something of a catch-22: increased understanding of these dynamics is essential for improved policy and practice, but in the absence of such elusive improvements, making refugees' resolution efforts visible may counterproductively limit the spaces in which they can maneuver or transform limbo conditions to their advantage. This points to the importance of continually asking "Who are durable solutions *for?*" and being alert to the possibility that in some cases benefit may primarily accrue to states and other institutions keen to "close the books" on particular "caseloads."

Even when return, local integration, and resettlement do open up new opportunities and yield greater autonomy for refugees and IDPs, it is a fallacy to equate achieving durable solutions with "ending displacement," because experiences of exile continue to shape individual and family identities, narratives, and choices long after institutional actors close the books on particular "populations of concern." Equally, it is a fallacy to assume that durable solutions entail the end of mobility. Labeling mobility a "fourth solution" is disingenuous when those on the move want to settle but have no viable option to do so. However, for many current and former refugees and IDPs, mobility (whether in the context of nomadism, labor migration, transnational family connections, or other movements) is a long-standing part of their cultures and survival strategies (Horst 2006a, 2006b). Former refugee families may continue to be highly mobile while also participating in more traditional "durable solutions" to displacement—the difference being that such mobility would in theory be undertaken as a free choice rather than as a stopgap measure employed because of a lack of other viable options.

Conclusion

Beyond simply asserting that refugees are not merely beneficiaries but actors in peacebuilding and crafting durable solutions to displacement, this collection seeks to better understand *how* refugees and IDPs perceive, engage, and influence these processes, and to understand the implications of such engagements for theory, future research, policy, and practice. A more complex understanding of the empirical dynamics and normative stakes surrounding refugees' roles in resolution processes makes it all the more challenging to distill insights from research for policy and practice. Nonetheless, the conclusion to this volume opens up this discussion while also reflecting on the significance of this work for future research on refugees and resolution processes and for the field of refugee and forced migration studies more broadly.

Notes

1. See, for example, the definitions in the 1951 Convention Relating to the Status of Refugees.

2. The World Bank has become a particularly active player in these renewed conversations. While recognizing the links between development, peacebuilding, and durable solutions, much of the recent debate and investments by institutions such as the World Bank have not focused on the *resolution* of displacement. Rather, the focus has been on how strategic development interventions may help preserve asylum space by alleviating pressures new arrivals place on already overstretched public systems and services. See World Bank (2017).

3. This is not to say that scholars have not engaged influential theories of agency to explore particular cases of forced migration. (See, for example, Clark-Kazak 2014; Horst 2006c; Healey 2006.)

4. See, for example, Nyers (2006b) and Owens (2009) (political science/political theory); Levinson (2010) and Rabinowitz (2010) (philosophy); Cooper (2007) (sociology); Malkki (1995a, 1995b) (anthropology); and Vecchio (2015) and Sanyal (2011) (architecture and urban studies).

5. This is not, of course, to discount the importance of taking the diverse perspectives of displaced persons seriously in both scholarship and practice.

6. In emergency contexts, for example, otherwise unacceptable limitations may arguably be legitimately imposed on consultation and deliberative processes. See Rubenstein (2013).

7. Purkey's chapter sits in tension with several others in this volume (e.g., Sherwood's chapter) in terms of the extent to which the law is, or could be, a source of empowerment for refugees in searching out solutions to displacement.

8. For examination of protests by refugees and other noncitizens, see Nyers and Rygiel (2012); Clark-Kazak (2010); Allan (2014). On political mobilization in exile, see, e.g., Sznajder and Roniger (2009;) Betts and Jones (2016).

9. For challenges to such representations, see, for example, Malkki 1996; Horst (2006c).

10. With few exceptions, displaced persons are not actively involved in negotiating the provisions in peace agreements pertaining to their predicament, although technical advice has been prepared to facilitate their participation. See McHugh (2010).

11. Some contend that individuals who bear arms should not be considered refugees (traditionally a civilian category); even if these individuals are not formally refugees, their lives may be shaped by experiences of displacement.

12. For further discussion of cases involving complex victims, see also Lemaitre and Sandvik (chapter 10).

13. This conversation is particularly salient in light of the exposure of refugees and IDPs in protracted situations to repeated displacement. For instance, thousands of Palestinian refugees in Syria have been forced from the camps where they have lived for generations, raising underexamined questions about what states, humanitarian actors, and refugees themselves could and should seek to achieve by way of "solutions" in such circumstances.

Part I

Refugees and Resolution Processes

Disciplinary Perspectives

1

Durable Solutions and the Political Action of Refugees

Karen Jacobsen

Integrating the issue of displacement into peace processes has been widely called for by scholars and peacemaking agencies (Koser 2007; Harpviken 2008; Kälin 2015), who believe that resolving displacement can significantly contribute to achieving a lasting peace and that the return of internally displaced persons (IDPs) and refugees is a sign of a successful peace process.[1] Similarly, the active involvement of refugees and IDPs both in peace processes and in forging their own solutions to displacement is seen as an important ingredient to resolving protracted situations by those who advocate for the "politics of presence" (Phillips 1995). Given the numbers of displaced people in and from conflict-affected countries, their involvement—including as spoilers—in peace processes is an important piece of the problem (Stedman 1997; Milner 2011). Refugees' involvement in peace processes points to their broader political activities, particularly in countries of first asylum, where their activities and motivations are diverse, complex, and riven with contradictory and competing interests, including their interests in peace and other political processes such as repatriation and resettlement (Krznaric 1997). As Rex Brynen suggests, "forced exile frequently implies a broader context of war, foreign occupation, dictatorship and resistance, or civil strife—circumstances in which refugees may be both victims and participants. As a result, strong political or national grievances may exist, sustaining in turn high levels of mass politicization" (Brynen 1990). This politicization is not always aligned with the preferences of aid agencies and host governments, particularly when it comes to so-called durable solutions of repatriation, local integration, or third-country resettlement. As in the 1980s, with the Eritrean repatriation from Sudan, today it is still the case that "donor-managed repatriations, coordinated as they are by governments and associations of governments, are not always in concert with, nor reflective of, the desires of refugees themselves" (Hendrie 1991). In sum, refugees' political aspirations and grievances can make it difficult to conflate the goals of peace and formal displacement resolution processes. To date, refugees and peacebuilding programs have not been systematically linked in policy and practice, and "the prolonged presence of refugees in neighboring countries poses both challenges and opportunities for peacebuilding in the country of origin" (Milner 2011, 1).

This chapter contributes to theory building about refugee political action by exploring the forms of refugee political engagement that take place beyond arenas of formal consultation and institutionalized processes. A large body of scholarship focuses on refugee militarization (Lischer 2000; Muggah 2006; Harpviken 2008; Lebson 2013), and there are plentiful examples, including Afghan refugees in Pakistan; the Rwandan Patriotic Front in Uganda; Darfur rebel groups in Chad and elsewhere.[2] However, our understanding of how and why displaced people engage in nonmilitarized forms of political action—often at great risk to themselves—is less well studied. In an effort to broaden and supplement our understanding of refugee militarization as a form of political action, this chapter provides a typology of nonarmed political action by refugee individuals or groups. Nonarmed political action includes all forms of direct engagement—activities in which refugees have "skin in the game"—that is, they are willing to contribute their own time and resources and to confront the risks that often come with political action. It also includes more strategic forms of political action, such as the mobilization of nonrefugee advocacy groups like religious organizations and engagement by the refugee diaspora to pressure host countries (Van Hear 1998; Betts and Jones 2016). By focusing on nonarmed political action, the chapter expands our analytical understanding of the categories and costs of political action by refugees.

The chapter focuses on the largest subset of the global refugee population—those in developing countries of first asylum, that is, the low- and middle-income countries that are not members of the Organisation for Economic Co-operation and Development, where 86 percent of the world's refugees live (UNHCR 2015).[3] The chapter focuses particularly on Africa, where "the problem of protracted refugee problems has assumed the most serious dimensions" (Slaughter and Crisp 2009), but also considers the highly illustrative case of Guatemalan refugees in Mexico in the 1990s.[4] In most countries of first asylum, the government admits refugees under some form of temporary protection, either as prima facie refugees or under some other temporary status. This status generally means refugees are excluded from formal political institutions and the political rights that come with citizenship; thus, few refugees are able to participate in their host country's formal political systems.[5] Nonetheless, refugees do engage in a wide range of political action, as this chapter explores.

The research and literature on the political mobilization and action of refugees is well established, particularly concerning diasporas and refugees in North America and Europe (van Bochove and Rusinovic 2008; Wald 2008; Lindley 2009), in keeping with a general bias in migration research toward studies of destination countries and of immigrants within receiving nations (Beauchemin 2014). However, studies of refugee political action in countries of first asylum are relatively scant. Most research on refugees in countries of first asylum focuses on refugees' socioeconomic experiences and livelihood strategies (Zetter and Ruaudel 2016; Bellamy et al. 2017). Existing scholarship on how and why refugees get involved in political processes; how political engagement differs for men and women; what their diverse interests, strategies, and tactics are; and how the structural and contextual factors constrain their ability to mobilize and organize tends to be regionally or case-study based.[6] Efforts to theorize more generally are still emerging.[7] Much of this literature is located in the humanitarian discourse of crisis and emergency response, where refugees' action is often described in terms of "coping strategies."[8] Andrea Purdeková's critique of this scholarship argues for moving "beyond a crisis-centric, humanitarian perspective to understand the longer-term political dimensions underpinning people's decisions to move or stay" (2016, 1). Other recent scholarship, particularly by scholars of urban societies in Africa, has challenged this humanitarian discourse and sought to place the actions of refugees in a wider political context.[9]

The Goals of Refugee Political Action

Refugee political action is similar to the political action of other migrants in that the goals are broadly related to the host (asylum) or home (origin) countries (Østergaard Nielsen 2003) or to mobility within and between host and home countries. Four categories of political goals are described below: immigrant politics (focused on the host country), homeland politics (focused on the home country), self-government, and mobility politics. These categories are shaped into a typology of migrant political action. The typology is intended as a heuristic framework that can help organize the literature and serve as a basis for more systematic and comparative research.

Immigrant politics are political actions undertaken by immigrants and refugees to improve their situation in the host country, including to obtain political, social, and economic rights or to fight against maltreatment and discrimination. There is substantial scholarship on this topic covering immigrant politics in destination countries (Givens and Maxwell 2012; Rubio-Marin 2000; Schulz 2003; Zapata-Barrero et al. 2013) but less research in transit countries and countries of first asylum (as further discussed below), except when it comes to Palestinians (Brynen 1990; Schulz 2003; Doraï 2010). In these countries, refugees' political goals are aimed at securing increased assistance, the right to work, access to documentation, and so forth, and to ameliorating poverty. An important goal is the right to freedom of movement or mobility, including the right to resist being relocated (e.g., sent back to camps). Immigrant/refugee political action aimed at the host country is motivated by the desire to pursue livelihoods and education for their children and by grievances about treatment by host government authorities, the public, or international humanitarian agencies. This grievous treatment can include inadequate food, education, shelter, and other services as well as harassment, discrimination, and other issues related to dignity. The targets of political action include the national host government, local authorities or civil society, and aid agencies, particularly the United Nations High Commissioner for Refugees (UNHCR), which, as the international organization mandated to protect refugees, is seen by refugees as bearing the responsibility for their welfare.

Homeland politics are the political actions of immigrants, including the so-called the diaspora channel (Burgess 2014), that seek to oppose or support the political regime in the origin country. Immigrant actions can be aimed at the homeland regime itself or at its foreign policy or other policies including return movements and treatment of returnees. In countries of first asylum, one type of refugee political action aimed at home countries is the formation of and recruitment to "refugee warrior" groups aimed at overthrowing the home country government. As discussed above, this area is fairly well studied, and this chapter focuses on more peaceful (but not necessarily less risky) forms of political action. Refugees also engage in peacemaking processes and seek to shape the postconflict political situation in the homeland through influencing processes of repatriation: "Refugees . . . may use the repatriation process as an opportunity to renegotiate their relationship with their state of origin by asserting their rights claims and challenging the state's prerogative in deciding which citizens can participate in the political community of the state" (Bradley 2014, 117).

A third type of political action by refugees and immigrants concerns self-government, in which refugees organize themselves through elections and the formation of self-governance bodies in order to manage the affairs of their community.[10] These activities include dispensing community justice (da

Costa 2006), developing self-help organizations such as schools for children, or pressuring UNHCR or the host government for services. Another reason for self-government can be that nationalist movements embedded in the refugee population get "a chance to practice the forms of governance and social organisation they would establish following independence," as is the case in the Polisario Front–controlled camps of Western Sahara (Mundy 2007). This development of a "state in exile" is more likely where refugees have been in protracted situations, that is, where their stay in a country of first asylum has been longer than three years (Crawford et al. 2015).

An important cross-cutting theme concerns mobility, including between host and home countries and within the host country. For refugees, freedom of movement can mean security (to escape threats) and livelihoods (to find work or education or to conduct trade) (Horst and Nur 2016). But refugees also resist imposed movement, such as when the host government or UNHCR tries to encourage relocation (e.g., to camps) or repatriation in the interests of "durable solutions." Resistance to being relocated within the host country or to being repatriated is a long-standing theme in refugee protest. In 1976 representatives of Ethiopian refugees from the Wad El Heleiw camp in Sudan sent several petitions to UNHCR to protest the decision of the Sudanese authorities to transfer them to camps further from the border with Ethiopia (Karadawi 1999, 121).[11]

Forms of Refugee Political Participation

In pursuing their political goals, refugees engage in both conventional and nonconventional forms of political action. Conventional forms of political participation include voting in or standing for elections; promoting referenda; participating in advisory councils and arenas of dialogue; joining political parties, pressure groups, and political organizations; lobbying activities; attending political meetings; and generally contributing time and money for political activities (Zapata-Barrero et al. 2013). Conventional forms of political participation are the prerogative of refugees with permanent residence and citizenship. These include those few (less than 1 percent of the world's refugees) who have been resettled in third countries (such as the US or Canada) or those who have been given citizenship in first-asylum countries (such as Burundian refugees in Tanzania; Milner 2014a; Kuch 2016). However, refugees with temporary status who lack formal political rights nevertheless engage in conventional forms of participation such as elections, as described below.

Nonconventional and extraparliamentary forms of political participation include protests, demonstrations, sit-ins, political strikes, hunger strikes, civil disobedience, and boycotts. These forms of political participation often involve greater risk, especially for refugees and immigrants who lack documentation and are in a "legal limbo"; the lack of documents increases a refugee's exposure to the authorities of the host country (Kihato 2011).

Table 1.1 outlines a typology of the goals and types of direct political action by refugees. The typology is not definitive; it is intended as an analytical tool to think about the political action of forced migrants. The rest of this chapter explores this typology in selected camp and noncamp settings to see whether the type of settlement influences political activity.

The Difference an Encampment Policy Makes

Countries of first asylum can be divided into those where the government tries to impose encampment policies and those where the government permits refugees to live among the host population. In countries with encampment policies, the government requires refugees to live in formal camps and seeks to make the international humanitarian community provide most of the assistance (and local communities provide the land). Globally in 2015, there were 196 countries hosting refugees (UNHCR 2015).[12] Of the 108 countries hosting more than 1,000 refugees, 36 (36 percent) countries required refugees to live in camps, with African countries having encampment policies more often than other regions.[13] However, in most countries with encampment policies, not all (or even most) refugees live in camps, and those who do tend to move in and out of the camps on a regular basis (Jansen 2015).[14] For example, in 2017 Jordan hosted over 656,000 registered Syrian refugees, of whom 21 percent lived in three refugee camps and the rest lived in Jordan's urban settings.[15]

In countries without encampment policies, refugees live among the host population, from whom they rent or share housing and land. Especially in the Middle East, many refugees move into towns or informal settlements adjacent to towns. These informal settlements can resemble camps, but they fall outside designated UN-administered and government-recognized official camps and are neglected by the UN, the state, aid agencies, and (for Palestinians) even the Palestinian Authority. For example, many Palestinians—and increasingly many Syrian refugees—live in informal tented settlements in Jordan and Lebanon.[16]

Whether refugees live in camps, informal settlements, or among the host population is an important dimension of refugees' political life. Type of settlement is potentially both an enabler and disabler of political action, providing opportunities for action (for example, access to social capital and resource mobilization) and imposing constraints. Some scholars suggest that, because

Table 1.1 A Typology of Refugee Political Action

Goals of Political Action (directed at)	Forms of Political Mobilization	
	Conventional	*Nonconventional*
Self-Governance:		
Managing refugee affairs (community justice)	Participating in elections and running for office	
"Practicing to be a state" (states in exile)	Forming and participating in self-governing bodies (leadership councils, nongovernmental organizations)	
Host Country:		
Grievances about lack of mobility, including resettlement	Meetings with UNHCR and government authorities	Protests, demonstrations, sit-ins, political strikes/boycotts, hunger strikes
Resistance to being relocated or repatriated ("entrenchment")	Participation in advisory councils and arenas of dialogue with UNHCR and host government	Civil disobedience and illicit self-help activities (such as tapping into water or electricity systems)
Grievances about treatment, including lack of services, right to work	Formation of non-governmental organizations and lobbying activities	
Durable solutions—pursuing political membership through local integration		
Home Country:		
Ending the war (peace processes)	Formation of exile political parties	Protests, demonstrations, sit-ins outside embassy
Actions or lack of action about durable solutions concerning repatriation	Negotiating to gain formal participation in peace processes	Formation of militant or jihadist movements
Changing the government or government policies	Social media advocacy aimed at host country government	
Demanding and asserting rights claims, challenging the state's prerogative in deciding which citizens can participate in the political community of the state	Leveraging rights accorded to them under international law to negotiate the conditions of their return with their states of origin	

of the "exceptional" status of camp life, the political actions of refugees in camps are unusual or "experimental" (Turner 2015; Lecadet 2016). Another argument, however, is that camp politics is simply a form of "normal" politics—that is, actions designed to attain a purpose through the use of political power or political channels—except that the power dynamics in camps are different, so the targets of political action differ too.[17] Long-standing (protracted) refugee camps are increasingly seen and studied as places where forms of governance and justice, order and organization, emerge over time (da Costa 2006; McConnachie 2014; Holzer 2015).

An additional dimension to the settlement aspect is the policy context and particularly whether host countries have and enforce encampment policies. In countries with encampment policies, refugees who live outside camps are potentially more vulnerable to crackdowns, harassment, and forced relocation than those who live in countries without encampment policies. However, even in host countries without encampment policies, such as South Africa and Egypt, refugees are harassed by the authorities, such as police demands for documents followed by shakedowns; discriminated against by employers, shop owners, and landlords; and experience discrimination and racism on the streets. The difficulties refugees confront with the state and civil society are likely to have a chilling effect on their political engagement.

The rest of the chapter examines refugee political action in selected host countries with and without encampment policies to see how political activities play out in countries with different patterns of settlement. The countries listed in table 1.2 were selected based on their relative prominence in the literature, either in terms of the frequency of their discussion or because they have recently received attention by scholars. In table 1.2, "Encampment policies" refers to host countries in which there are formal camps, even if not all refugees reside in them. "No encampment policies" refers to countries without formal camps, even if some refugees live in informal settlements that resemble camps, for example, Palestinian camps in Lebanon.

Political Action in Camps

Refugees' political action in camps encompasses all types of goals and both conventional and nonconventional forms outlined in the typology in table 1.1. Political actions "reflect the diverse preoccupations at the heart of camp life; they are concerned with the most basic aspects of camp organization— the quality and quantity of food rations, the materials used for shelter—but also with the protection afforded by UNHCR and with that most crucial of all questions: the decision to keep refugees in their camp or to repatriate them" (Lecadet 2016).

Table 1.2   Selected Countries with and without Encampment Policies

Region	Encampment Policies	No Encampment Policies
Africa	Kenya (Kakuma, Dadaab) Tanzania (Kigoma) Zambia (Meheba) Ghana (Buduburam) Benin (Kpomassè) Algeria (Tindouf)	South Africa Egypt
Middle East	Jordan	Lebanon
Central America	Mexico (1990s)	
Asia	Thailand Bangladesh	Malaysia India

SELF-GOVERNANCE

Examples of self-government in camps are widespread. In Africa, well-documented examples come from Ghana (Holzer 2012), Benin (Lecadet 2016); Kenya (both Kakuma camp [(Jansen 2008) and Dadaab (Horst 2006c; Hyndman 2000), and the Sahrawi camps in Algeria (Mundy 2007)]. Self-government takes different forms, reflecting different levels of political mobilization and control of the camps by refugees. In some camps, such as Buduburam (for Liberian refugees in Ghana), leadership councils were created in order to interact with UNHCR. According to Elizabeth Holzer (2012, 260–61), "a web of group affiliations linked politically active people throughout the camp," and community leadership organizations operated under the authority of the Liberian Refugee Welfare Council. The welfare council was a means "for UNHCR to disseminate information to refugees, provide camp authorities with the refugee perspective, hear interpersonal grievances, and implement the food distribution programme," and camp authorities appointed the people serving on it. Other Liberian collective bodies emerged in the camps, including rival nongovernmental organization networks and organizations. By contrast, the Sahrawi camps near Tindouf, Algeria, are fully self-managed and controlled by the Polisario nationalist liberation movement, with elected leaders managing aid distribution (Mundy 2007, 286). Elections in camps can resemble electoral processes in democratic states, as in the Agamè camp in Benin: "The plan to elect a president of the refugees was in all respects a copy of electoral processes in democratic states. The way in which the organization of the refugees followed established electoral models showed that the politicization of camps cannot be reduced to the level of mere protest, but equally involves the creation of an appropriate political structure" (Lecadet 2016).

THE HOST COUNTRY

In camps, political action targeted at the host government and UNHCR mainly concern poverty, lack of security, and relocation. Protests are reported in almost all camps, large and small. In Kenya, the Dadaab complex has seen protests by Somali refugees over the conditions of the camp, and in Kakuma, Somali refugees organized a protest in 2012 demanding security and protection over increased killings and insecurity (KANERE 2012). In smaller camps such as Kpomassè camp (Benin), Togolese women refugees organized a strike in 2003 and traveled to the UNHCR offices in Cotonou to protest the poverty and violence of camp conditions (Lecadet 2016).

One of the main goals of refugees' political action aimed at host countries is resistance to relocation within the country or repatriation to their country of origin. A typical example was the women's protest that occurred in 2007–8 in Buduburam camp in Ghana. This case, fully discussed in Amanda Coffie's chapter in this volume, illustrates many of the problems and refugee responses that arise in camps around the implementation of durable solutions. The Liberian protests arose from the lack of realistic repatriation to war-ravaged Liberia or the possibility of third-country resettlement. The refugees demanded larger financial grants for repatriation or resettlement to a Western country, and they also were opposed to local integration based on their experience in Ghana (Holzer 2012). The political action, mainly conducted by a refugee women's organization called Concerned Women, included marches, letters to UNHCR, a hunger strike, and sit-down protests over a six-month period. The protest was ultimately unsuccessful; it was forcibly ended by Ghanaian security forces, who conducted raids against the protesters, detained over six hundred women and children in a remote detention camp, and deported a small number of Liberians as a result of the protests (Holzer 2012, 268; see also Coffie's chapter, this volume). The protest led to the involvement of the Liberian government, tensions and threats aimed at Ghanaians living in Liberia, and eventually the signing of a tripartite agreement between Liberia, Ghana, and UNHCR that required Liberians to leave Ghana within six months. The political actions by the Buduburam women concerning resistance to durable solutions are mirrored in many other camps settings, as are the outcomes.

THE HOME COUNTRY

Political action in camps focuses on the home country in different ways. Refugees' segregation in camps can serve refugee leaders' efforts to shape refugee attitudes, including toward repatriation or naturalization. For example, in Tanzania in 2008, the church and refugee leadership strongly advocated against the naturalization option being offered by the Tanzanian government

(Malkki 1995a; Milner 2013). Camps provide opportunities to engage in formal institutionalized peace processes. A classic example of refugees participating in a "track-one" process occurred in 1987, when Guatemalan refugees in Mexico organized themselves into Permanent Commissions, dedicated to achieving a "collective and organized return" to Guatemala (Krznaric 1997; Blue 2005; Holzer 2012; Bradley 2014). In 1992, after protracted negotiations (and with UNHCR's help), the government of Guatemala and the refugee Permanent Commissions signed the October 8 Accord, which guaranteed compliance with existing constitutional rights and ensured specific benefits, exemptions, and mechanisms for returnees to acquire land. The first collective return took place in January 1993, largely organized by the Permanent Commissions. The negotiations, including consultations with refugee and IDP organizations, achieved separate peace accords over the next three years. The case is unusual because many refugees were from poor, marginalized, and excluded groups; they spoke multiple languages and were not always fluent in Spanish. In addition, women refugees were active in the movement (Blue 2005).

Political Action Outside Camps in Countries with and without Encampment Policies

As noted above, except in Africa, most host countries do not have encampment policies, and refugees live among local populations. Even in host countries that do have encampment policies, many refugees avoid the camps and often reside in towns and cities where they lack authorization to live and "become virtually invisible, falling out of UNHCR annual reports."[18] The number and proportion of refugees living outside camps in countries with encampment policies varies. For refugees from middle-income countries such as Syria, the majority do not live in camps. In some host countries, refugees of the same nationality live in different dwelling situations, with some ethnic groups going to camps and others staying out of them. For example, in Thailand, Burmese refugees in camps are mostly Karen and Karenni, while Shan, Chin, Kachin, and Burman ethnic groups are more likely to live as undocumented migrants in the villages and towns along the Thai–Burma border (McConnachie 2014).

Refugees who live outside camps, whether they are permitted to or not, struggle to pursue livelihoods and find affordable housing, particularly in cities. In countries with encampment policies, refugees who live outside camps without permission are vulnerable to arrest and forced removal to camps. These threats make political activity highly risky for refugees, so we would not expect to find widespread refugee mobilization. However, studies reveal a surprising amount of political involvement and risk-taking, often focused on resistance to being relocated to camps or other areas of the country. For example, in Zambia, the government and UNHCR implemented a new urban residency policy in 2001 that required refugees living in Lusaka who did not meet the strict urban residency requirements to move to the rural refugee settlement in Meheba.[19] Many refugees, especially those from urban backgrounds and professionals or entrepreneurs established in Lusaka, refused to move to the settlement, despite the efforts of the state. Those without proper documentation faced arrest and forced relocation to the camps (Frischkorn 2015).

Refusal to move to camps, coupled with repeated returns to the city when forcibly relocated, is a common act of political defiance by refugees in urban settings. Nairobi is well known for the substantial presence of Somali refugees, despite Kenya's encampment policy that requires Somalis to live in Dadaab and Kakuma (Campbell 2006; Lindley 2007; Jansen 2015). In urban settings, refugees form their own organizations, either according to their ethnic or national groups, as in Cairo (Pascucci 2016), or simply by identifying as refugees and working together, often with advocacy associations and civil society allies such as human rights or religious agencies. (Frischkorn 2015).

In countries without encampment policies—where refugees are permitted to live among the host population—refugees might conceivably have more freedom to be politically engaged. However, in these countries as in countries with encampment policies, refugees are subject to surveillance, raids, and imprisonment or other penalties subject to the state's population control mechanisms, often enforced through biometric or digital means. In addition, a culture of xenophobia and harassment often emerges that serves to silence refugee protest. This means that urban refugees take risks when they become politically active. One of the most dramatic examples—in which some refugees paid with their lives—is the Sudanese refugee protest that occurred at Mustafa Mahmoud Park in Cairo, from September to December 2005. During these three months, up to two thousand Sudanese refugees conducted a sit-in, many living in the park.[20] The protest was originally intended to draw international attention to the plight of Sudanese refugees in Cairo, including the lack of adequate food and housing and racist attitudes by Egyptians. Prior to 1995, the Wadi El Nil Treaty between Sudan and Egypt had allowed Sudanese nationals to live in Egypt with almost all the rights of citizens, and there was a large, fairly well-integrated Sudanese population in Cairo, not all of them refugees, and many with successful careers and long-term living situations. In 1995, after a Sudanese extremist attempted to assassinate the Egyptian president, Egypt ended the Wadi El Nil Treaty and the Sudanese situation became much more difficult, especially after a new influx of refugees arrived from Darfur. The Egyptian government imposed new employment restrictions and required Sudanese to obtain refugee status (giving that responsibility to UNHCR). Sudanese refugees now struggled to find work and a way out of poverty. They had minimal access to basic education and health services, and most could not obtain rent-controlled housing. These practical difficulties were compounded by the anti-immigrant racism of Egyptians, many of whom were also poor and saw immigrants as competitors for jobs and resources. In 2004 UNHCR suspended refugee-status determination because of the peace agreement in Sudan, putting a hold on resettlement prospects.[21] This move had elicited an earlier protest in August 2004, when Sudanese refugees had gathered in front of the UNHCR's offices to protest the agency's change in policy and the reduction in assistance to refugees. This protest had ended in "an open riot" with UNHCR premises damaged and dozens of protesters and ten police officers injured, while the concerns of the protesters were not addressed. Likewise, in 2005 the park protest ended when Egyptian police violently dispersed the protest, killing some twenty-seven Sudanese and arresting over six hundred. Both Sudanese protests in Cairo demonstrated the desperation of refugees and their courage, but little was achieved. Instead relations deteriorated between the Sudanese, UNHCR, and the Egyptian government, and today the Sudanese in Egypt face the same challenges, heightened by the regional turmoil and additional refugees arriving in Cairo.

Conclusion

The types of political action described in this chapter, in both camp and non-camp (usually urban) settings, reveal that when the goals of the action are to improve conditions in the host country or to resist imposed movement, such as relocation to camps or repatriation, the actions have mostly ended in government crackdowns, and refugees have not attained the goals for which they fought. More successful are efforts aimed at shaping peace processes in the host country that often include agreed-on repatriation movements, as in the case of the Guatemalans returning to Mexico. However, refugee scholarship lacks many documented cases of such political activity, and it would be useful to identify more such cases.

This chapter explored, in a highly selective way, whether living in or outside camps influences political action and what role, if any, the encampment policy context plays. The few cases explored here indicate that refugees pursue all three of the typology's political goals—self-government, improving their situation in the host country (including resisting efforts to be relocated or repatriated), and trying to address outcomes in their home country—

whether they are in or outside camps. In countries with encampment policies, we would expect refugees living outside of camps to be more cautious about engaging in political action such as protests and demonstrations, and perhaps to be more likely to work through partner organizations that can represent them. However, refugees are willing to take political risks, whether in countries where they are required to be in camps, such as Mexico, Ghana, Kenya, and Zambia, or in countries without encampment policies, such as Egypt and South Africa. Often this political engagement results only in harm and the failure to achieve their objectives. But there are significant examples of success, as with the Guatemalans negotiating their return from Mexico.

This exploration is by no means exhaustive but intends to outline a typology of political action and use it to analyze the spatial or dwelling dimension. Further research on the political lives of refugees could flesh out—or completely revise—this typology and thereby sharpen this analytical tool. In general, we encourage future research and study of the political actions of refugees as a necessary complement to the extensive research on livelihoods and self-sufficiency. While detailed case studies are always welcome, we lack comparative analyses of how refugees in different host countries and policy contexts engage politically. Understanding refugees' political motivations and whether and when they choose to become politically active are important underpinnings of refugee theory.

Notes

1. "The new UN Peacebuilding Commission represents a unique institutional opportunity to mainstream IDPs and their priorities in peace-building efforts worldwide" (Koser 2007).

2. For example, Mike Lebson proposes "a comprehensive theory of refugee militarization including political factors endogenous to refugee groups, which will help explain the motivation of refugees to militarize and the framing used by militancy entrepreneurs to mobilize them" (2013, 133). Kristian Berg Harpviken (2008) estimates that militarization is significant in some 15–20 percent of all refugee situations globally.

3. It would be ideal to include IDPs in such an analysis, but for the sake of analytical clarity and because of space constraints, the chapter focuses on refugees.

4. The countries were selected based on their relative prominence in the literature, either in terms of the frequency of their discussion or because they have recently received attention by scholars.

5. Internally displaced people, as citizens of their countries, are entitled to citizenship-based political rights, but many IDPs are denied their rights when they become displaced. For example, in Sri Lanka during the war, IDPs who moved from one state to another were denied state transfers because they were not registered as residents and were not "local citizens" (Brun 2003).

6. For example, there is rich literature on the Guatemalan refugees' efforts to influence their return from Mexico and the peace process in Guatemala. See Bradley (2014).

7. A recent notable exception is Holzer (2015). The editors of this volume note several scholars who have engaged theories of agency to explore certain cases of forced migration. (See, for example, Clark-Kazak 2014; Horst 2006c; Healey 2006.)

8. In this critique, I include my own work, which has often focused on understanding how refugees pursue livelihoods without considering their wider political aims and orientation, and has thereby depoliticized our understanding of displaced livelihoods. See, for example, Jacobsen and Fratzke (2016).

9. For example, Caroline Kihato's work on African women migrants and refugees in Johannesburg (2011).

10. While representatives are often elected by refugees, in some cases the structures of governance are constructed and imposed by external actors such as UNHCR. See Slaughter and Crisp (2009).

11. Early examples of entrenchment—the resistance to being relocated—also can be found with IDPs, including those who are caught up in disasters. Anthony Oliver-Smith (2010) writes about the fierce and ultimately successful grassroots resistance to being uprooted on the part of Peruvians whose town (Yungay) was destroyed by an earthquake and avalanche in 1970.

12. For more on the distribution of countries with and without camps and on the relative numbers of refugees living in and outside them, see Jacobsen (2017).

13. In 2015, of Africa's twenty-five host countries with more than ten thousand refugees, nineteen (75 percent) had camps. See Jacobsen (2017).

14. For a discussion of Syrians trying to avoid the Jordan camps, see Bellamy et al. 2017.

15. "Syria Regional Refugee Response," UNHCR Operational Portal Refugee Situations, last updated July 29, 2018, http://data.unhcr.org/syrianrefugees/country.php?id=107.

16. In Lebanon these are known as "gatherings." See Yassin, Stel, and Rassie 2016.

17. For discussions of the "exceptionalism" versus "normalization" perspectives on camps, see Fresia and Von Känel (2016); Turner (2015). The "normalization" idea follows David Turton, who in 2003 urged us "to think of forced migrants as 'ordinary people', or 'purposive actors', embedded in particular social, political and historical situations" (2).

18. For example, in a 2007 analysis of the gaps in refugee protection in Zambia, the UNHCR acknowledged that approximately ten thousand refugees were living in Lusaka illegally, but the exact composition of this group is unknown. (See Frischkorn 2015, 215; UNHCR 2007.)

19. At the end of 2001, the UNHCR reported assisting 14,368 recognized urban refugees, mostly in Lusaka. After the new policy began in 2002, only some 4,000 urban refugees were issued electronic cards permitting urban residence (Frischkorn 2015).

20. The following account is taken from a carefully investigated and detailed report by the American University of Cairo. See Azzam (2006).

21. The cease-fire declared in early 2004 between the government of Sudan and the Sudan People's Liberation Army led the UNHCR to suspend refugee status determination procedures for all Sudanese asylum seekers. Instead, the UNHCR provided all applicants with asylum-seeker cards, which offer temporary protection against refoulement (forced repatriation). The rationale was that, given the potential for peace in Sudan, temporary asylum offered better protection than the rejection of a large number of applicants on the basis of a fundamental change of circumstances in the country of origin, which would undermine the reasons for granting refugee status. The decision was subsequently reviewed and renewed every six months (Azzam 2006, 10).

2

Refugees, Peacebuilding, and the Anthropology of the Good

Cindy Horst

Are refugees impotent pawns of politics and history, or do they exercise agency in relation to resolution processes that affect their lives?[1] This is a central question running through this edited volume, and it sums up an important divide within forced migration studies and practice. The common understanding that refugees and internally displaced persons (IDPs) are simply "provided" a durable solution does not contribute to increased insights into refugee agency (Bradley, Milner, and Peruniak, introduction to this volume). Thus, exploring the important roles refugees and IDPs play in resolution processes—while recognizing that their levels of influence and choice are affected by a complex range of structural factors—is a good way to bridge the divide. I would like to go one step further, though, by arguing for a broadened understanding of how and where resolution processes take place. Important societal transformations like peacebuilding processes are often understood as orchestrated "from above" by local and international politicoeconomic powerholders. Thus, the participation of a range of "minority groups"—including displaced people and women (Horst and Doeland 2016)—in such peacebuilding processes is seen as a means toward more inclusive and thus sustainable conflict resolution and reconstruction. While macropolitical decisions indeed can impact the lives of millions in profound ways, and while being "at the decision-making table" is important, sustainable peacebuilding rarely takes place in such arenas.

In this chapter I argue that the civil-political acts of refugees are important to study as part of the "everyday politics" that are central to inclusion and resolution processes. Michael Gardiner (2000) argues for a critical approach to the study of the everyday, exploring the potential held by individual and collective agency to transform existing social conditions. The decades-old feminist claim that the personal is political, as Hirschmann and Di Stefano (1996, 6) point to, has offered a "radical challenge to the notion of politics itself and has instigated a redefinition of politics to include things that 'mainstream' theory considers completely non-political, such as the body and sexuality, the family and interpersonal relationships." Studying resolution processes in the everyday, through the civic engagement of refugees, does not so much bridge the divide between micro and macro, between voluntarism and determinism, or individuals and larger structures. Rather, by presenting individual refugee engagement in the context of excerpts of their life histories, I aim to show the limitations these analytical distinctions present. I build on well-established positions on the importance of the everyday, developed in feminist studies through its critique of the private/public dichotomy, which now have a wide reach, including in international relations and peace studies (Chandler 2015; Enloe 2011; Highmore 2002; Jennings and Bøas 2015).

The experiences that refugees undergo often shape their civic engagements and lead them to be active political subjects in a range of local and transnational contexts. While the fact that the life histories of individuals impact their civic virtues and motivations is not unique to refugees, the radical uncertainty that refugees are faced with often shapes their engagements in dramatic ways: experiences of violent conflict and human rights abuses do not just disproportionately affect but also further create political subjects. I am particularly interested in exploring the fact that, for many of the refugees we interviewed, their political subjectivities led them to be strongly inspired by a vision of society based on justice and equality while they were also occupied with their own roles and responsibilities in contributing to this vision. As such, the focus of this chapter is inspired by the anthropology of the good (Robbins 2013). This anthropology builds on three recent strands within the discipline: First, the anthropology of morality (Fassin 2012), which studies the cultural construction of the good or the way that people in different contexts understand the good; second, the anthropology of care and empathy (Held 2006; Throop and Hollan 2008), which explores how people enact "the good" in social relationships;[2] and, third, the anthropology of hope (Crapanzano 2004; Mattingly 2010), which analyzes the future-orientedness of such acts: how people believe they can create a good beyond what is present in their lives.

While drawing on the anthropology of the good, this chapter is not based on a naïve assumption that refugee experiences always lead to morally motivated acts or that "the good" is unambiguous. This chapter simply sets out to explore the processes through which some individuals facing radical uncertainty develop a strong sense of political responsibility in the shape of a forward-looking, nonblameworthy responsibility to participate in collective action for change and against what they see as "structural injustice" (McKeown 2015; Young 2011). This focus is inspired by the fact that many refugees and other conflict-affected individuals I have interviewed throughout my twenty-year research career are citizen-activists occupied with justice and civic virtue. This reality made me wonder about the links between their civil-political engagement and their life histories. What drives individuals to act not only in response to a calculation of their own good but also in terms of the responsibility they hold to others? Experiences of forced migration may catalyze new forms of organization, mobilization, protest, and claims making. As earlier research has shown, there can be a correlation between personally experiencing violent conflict and high degrees of political participation (Blattman 2009).

Uncertainty is a permanent condition in human lives, a fundamental experiential realm of human existence. The type of precariousness that conflict and displacement create reconfigures societies in abrupt, dramatic, and contradictory ways and thus drastically increases this uncertainty. The speed and unpredictability of unfolding events, the experience of violence, and the need to take risks in conflict situations delimits an experience of radical uncertainty (Horst and Grabska 2015). In contexts of conflict and violence, the need to act is often urgent, but action is difficult because of a dearth of information. Yet, exactly in the openness created by uncertainty, there is the potential for innovation and societal transformation as well. When faced with situations of uncertainty where taking action can save lives, individuals take great responsibility. And while the changing nature of things can lead to a desire to hold on to the familiar and a resistance to transformation for some, in the space for negotiation that it creates lie opportunities to push for change (Grabska and Fanjoy 2015).

The creative aspects of being in between—of being in a situation where "normality" and the status quo are questioned and challenged in radical ways—have been important in anthropological work on liminality (Turner 1967; Van Gennep 1960). In anthropology, liminality refers to the quality of ambiguity or disorientation that occurs in the middle stage of rituals, when participants no longer hold their pre-ritual status but have not yet begun the transition to the status they will hold when the ritual is complete. Use of the term has broadened to describe political and cultural change as well as rituals. During liminal periods of all kinds, social hierarchies may be reversed or temporarily dissolved, continuity of tradition may become uncertain, and future outcomes once taken for granted may be thrown into doubt (Horvath, Thomassen, and Wydra 2009). The liminal stage is both a stage of profound uncertainty and at the same time a period of unique potential for individual and collective transformation. Refugees have been described as liminals par excellence, with Liisa Malkki (1995b) pointing to their liminal position in the "national order of things." Their liminal position could also be explored from the perspective of being in between moral orders.

Several authors argue that we need a new perspective on war and displacement when it becomes the context for normal life rather than an exceptional event that disrupts it and creates liminality (Davis 1992; Horst 2006a; Lubkemann 2008a; Utas 2003; Vigh 2006, 2008). Research also shows the fluctuations in the levels of uncertainty visible in the lives of individuals over time, thus illustrating the importance of taking a biographical life-history approach. In my own research, I have worked with individuals who throughout their lives were faced with periods of radical uncertainty as violent conflict erupted around them and they made the decision to flee—alone or with their families (Horst 2006a; Horst and Grabska 2015). Capturing their life histories and exploring transformative moments in those stories as well as the impact of role models, I studied motivations for acts of civic engagement in the past and present as well as understandings of virtue and morality. This chapter is based on thirty in-depth and life-history interviews with refugees in Oslo, Norway, as well as ethnographic work since 1995 with refugees in a wide range of contexts (refugee camps, regional urban spaces, resettlement contexts, and upon return).[3] The concrete life-history data for this chapter was analyzed using qualitative data analysis software to explore themes such as civic engagement, transformative action, agency, responsibility, power, belonging and community, compassion, care, and sense of justice.

In this chapter, I introduce Bashar and Forough. Bashar is a Palestinian filmmaker in Scandinavia who tells us that growing up as a teenager under Occupation shaped his identity, current transnational political activism, and preoccupation with safety and freedom. Forough came from Iran with her family to Norway when she was a baby in the late 1980s. Her words remind us that refugee experiences do not end after flight for those who experienced traumatic events and for their families. These past stories can shape a family in many ways, and as Forough's experiences illustrate, living in exile can lead to new experiences of violence and exclusion that shape young children in life-changing ways. Both Bashar and Forough are engaged in a range of civil-political activities in their country of settlement—Bashar using his films to point to a range of local and transnational injustices, and Forough by fighting discrimination of various kinds through her job in Norway. By exploring the impact of defining moments in these two individuals' lives, the chapter connects the transformative action that refugees engage in after flight to their experiences of conflict and flight. Moving beyond earlier work on local and transnational coping in and after situations of radical uncertainty (Horst 2006a, 2006b), I argue that these refugees do not manage to engage locally, nationally, and globally as active citizens *despite* their experiences but *because of* those experiences.

Political Agency in Conflict: The Anthropology of the Good

Anthropologists and others have grappled with the issue of individual agency in situations of liminality and constraint. Much of this work takes place in conditions of extreme suffering and wrestles with questions of how people live together during and after war and displacement as well as what responsibility they hold toward the other. Henrik Vigh (2008) discusses this continuity of suffering as "chronicity" and asks how people navigate in conditions that are constantly in flux. In the ethnography of war, researchers thus investigate how the inhabitants of war zones live under trying new conditions and how culture and social relations are transformed as a result (Lubkemann 2008a). Others study how people navigate in stable yet impermanent conditions, or in conditions of severe dispossession or abuse (Brun 2015; Horst 2006a; Wilkinson and Kleinman 2016). Erin Baines (2015) discusses coping during violent conflict in relation to the agency of "complex victims"— persons who live in extremely violent contexts and are implicated in the same violence they endure. In all this work, researchers discuss the agency of people living in conditions of radical uncertainty as severely constrained agency focused on survival. This work explores mere coping in conditions of human suffering, while often paying little or no attention to acts that individuals engage in to counter injustice and human cruelty in their attempts to initiate a process of change.

The "anthropology of the good," introduced by Joel Robbins (2013), describes a shift toward an interest in exploring virtue, morality, empathy, care, gift-giving, and hope in situations of marginalization. In my view, the strength of the anthropology of the good is that it allows the field to theorize agency in new ways by exploring the moral inspirations of people's acts. Robbins's vision presents an anthropology that is deliberate and value-based, choosing to explore "the good" in an urgent need to understand human morality and not just human suffering or mere coping. Inspired by this trend, I am particularly interested in studying the drivers of individual deeds that stem from a willingness to act for the benefit of others in such contexts of suffering and constraint. When do individuals feel called to act in the face of suffering and abuse? For what reasons do some people act for the benefit of others even in situations where this involves great risks for themselves or their families? What are defining moments in people's life history where their political agency is "awakened?" Zahra, a Somali social activist in her fifties, explains the moment she decided to stay in Kismaayo during the war and set up camps for the displaced:

> My mother and relatives had already reached a decision to send all the young women in the family to Kenya right away as there were reports of widespread rape in the city. . . . As my half-sister and I got closer to the ship I saw to my right an older woman who seemed to have been sleeping and a child sleeping on top of her and a young girl who was to their side. The scene caught my attention, so I stopped and turned toward them. I discovered then that the woman was dead, and her child was also dead. The young girl, who was around 13 years old but who looked like an 8-year-old and was naked, seemed to be dying of hunger. I stood there over her and started to cry. I made a decision then that before that girl lost her life, I would feed her. . . . I told my mother that I had decided not to leave. My mother was furious. She was afraid I would get raped like other girls in the city. (Zahra, interview, July 2014, Mogadishu)

In such life-altering moments, individuals often go against the wishes of others and at times engage in radical or dangerous acts to help others or to challenge exclusionary trends. In every war, there are stories of everyday acts of resistance, and that resistance can help save many lives. Amina Abdi, who had to flee from Mogadishu through "enemy territory," recalls how she was able to survive with the help of others: "Those men came in, they were older men, and they said 'we know that you are not Hawiye, we know that you are Darood. But we are against these clan wars and we can save you. You will have to learn how we pronounce our words. And when they come, they will ask you who you are, which clan, and we can teach you that'" (Amina Abdi, interview, November 2014, Oslo).

Focusing on these moral acts of empathy, care, and protection to support fellow human beings in conditions of suffering, marginalization, and extreme human rights abuses provides a powerful counternarrative to common understandings of those caught up in conflict and displacement as "bare life" (Agamben 1998), passive subjectivities (Hyndman and Giles 2011), or self-interested calculated crooks (for a critique, see Horst 2006a). At the same time, it counters understandings of refugee political agency that focus solely on militarization and the image of "the refugee warrior" (Lebson 2013; Leenders 2009; Lischer 2007). What is lacking in accounts of human agency in conditions of conflict and displacement is a focus on the small but often heroic everyday acts of common people who attempt to resist or challenge dehumanizing trends of exclusion and abuse. Collecting these stories of political agency and moral action before, during, and after violent conflict provides an important counternarrative to images of vulnerability, survival, navigation, or warriorhood.

I argue that the small everyday acts of individuals are crucial to our understanding of societal transformations. By underestimating the importance of the civic acts of individuals and merely focusing on macropolitical and macroeconomic processes, we lose out on the opportunity to understand how individual resilience and strength connects to societal cohesion and rebuilding and what this allows us to say about agency in situations of liminality and constraint. One of the contributions of anthropology is that the discipline—through rich ethnographic empirical work—always studies the individual embedded in social, cultural, religious, political, and economic collectives. What is of interest is the mutual influence of collectives and their embedded individuals. I am inspired by earlier work that understands everyday resistance as subversive acts against domination, which shows the subtle political nature of the everyday (Abu-Lughod 1990; Scott 1985, 1990). Sherry Ortner (2006) conceptualizes power and agency in terms of thinking about the dynamics of local agency in the face of domination by others, what she calls the elementary structure of agency. Yet transformation is possible exactly because power dynamics within social entities lead to instability of practices as they entail an ever-present possibility of resistance.

The Relevance of Ethnographic and Biographic Methods

The life-history method is not just a great way to trace the in-depth stories of people's deeply personal lives; through these biographical narratives, it is also possible to understand wider societal and political patterns (Bornat 2008; Chamberlayne, Bornat, and Wengraf 2000; Rosenthal 2004). Throughout my work with refugees and others, I have used life-history methods to get insight in a range of individual choices and societal processes. Using bibliographical methods facilitates a more nuanced and grounded understanding of the ways in which certain events, practices, and ideas appear meaningful for those who take part in them. They foreground agency and subjectivity and hold transformative potential for producing knowledge critical of gendered and ethnocized power relations (Erel 2007). Biographical methods enable individual life experiences to be generated, analyzed, and drawn on to explain the social world, thus encouraging understanding and interpretation of experiences across common experiential divides (Bornat 2008).

The life histories of refugees often exhibit periods of radical uncertainty and major upheaval and illustrate the contrasts between the dehumanizing realities of parts of their lives and the strong civic virtues expressed and practiced. In these stories lies an important key to understanding their civic engagement, as Idil Abdilahi, a young Norwegian-Somali woman who came to Norway as a toddler and is actively engaged in her local neighborhood, confirms:

> I have a culture at home which is different from the culture that I have in my everyday outside home. And that has . . . helped me to be more active, because I know how important that is. What it contributes to society. [This is] because of my personal and my family's background. I believe my background as a refugee, and as a woman with a minority background outside and in Oslo, is a major reason for why I became the person I am today. (Idil Abdilahi, interview, March 2016, Oslo)

Another aspect that I find important in biographic methods is that they allow us to understand societal transformations as processes that happen through everyday acts of common people rather than necessarily (only) taking place on the macro level through decision makers in structures of power. In this way, traditional understandings of power and powerholders can be contested without necessarily overstating the agency of the actors involved (Lazar 2013). The encounter between the researcher and the person telling her life history matters in co-creating agency as well, just like the consequent production of knowledge does. As Eric Wolf (1994) reminds us, the ways in which academics re-create the world is not only influenced by social reality but also has an influence on public discourse within that reality and thus on actions. What we choose to focus on analytically and methodologically ultimately may influence ontological reality. Alima Husseini, who came to Norway as a child fleeing Afghanistan, expresses similar thoughts after reflecting on a range of experiences where immigrants and Muslims are "othered" in Norwegian society, directly impacting her own family. For example, her young daughter asks her why people do not like Muslims after hearing about a PEGIDA demonstration.[4] Alima argues,

> I believe we need to emphasize the importance of engaging and participating in society. You don't always have to say something or express your feelings, but to be present and aware of things that are happening is very important. Take me as an example: I know there are a lot of injustices in the world such as Islamophobia. I always think "is it about me? Does it affect me?" and then I say to myself no. It is not about me, it is about them. If a stranger insults me or looks at me differently while passing the street, I feel sorry for them. I feel sorry for those people that violate innocent people. I also feel sorry for the victim of course. I want people to

participate in civil society to reduce hate and prejudices. I think it would be more beneficial to focus on the good rather than the bad in order to change perspectives towards the foreign. (Alima Husseini, interview, May 2015, Oslo)

While the stories of the individuals I draw on for this chapter portray many differences, there are a few important similarities. First, they have left a country at war and they themselves or their close relatives and friends have experienced violent conflict. Second, they find themselves in Norway as refugees. Third, they each discuss in their own way what it means to be civically engaged and in what ways they are. I aim to show the connections between these understandings of civic engagement and the individual, family, and national histories of war, violent conflict, and flight. After presenting excerpts of the stories, I explore the importance of defining moments in people's life history. I then discuss how transformative action is understood by the refugees we spoke to and on what levels and in which arenas societal transformation takes place in these stories. Civic engagement is often understood in relation to a single nation but can take place on the local, national, transnational, or global level. To understand refugees' political participation, it is crucial to explore the importance of the local, national, or transnational—as well as the possible interconnections between these levels—empirically. Finally, I reflect on what the life histories presented here allow us to say about refugee political agency and refugees' role in resolution processes and peacebuilding more widely.

Bashar

I look at the first 14 years of my life and at growing up under occupation in Palestine. That was a very important part of my life and I developed a complete identity and found out that, "OK, I'm growing up here now, this is a place where I don't have freedom." You can't go out in the middle of the night in safety, you can suddenly be shot anonymously. Most likely by those occupying or soldiers or whatever, so that has shaped my personality to the largest extent. So I was very occupied with security and freedom while at the same time, when I was 15 years old, I was active politically, in many different activities or political parties in Palestine. . . .

. . . When I was 16 years old I went on a holiday across the borders. . . . I took a dangerous trip to the old Palestine which they call Israel and I went to Tel Aviv where I went to the sea. I was arrested there and put in prison and tortured and they asked me "What are you doing here?" So I said that I was a tourist and they said that a Palestinian can never be a tourist but is a terrorist. This has meant so much in my heart so I get upset. . . . The same year I got out of prison I lost several members of my family and . . . friends from my class, they were shot at school, on the streets on the way home, at different places. So this was a very important period in my life where I found that in this place there is no hope so either I get out or I do something bad . . . and give up. Or I just have to move out, and that was the best solution, just get out of there. . . .

. . . I like the art scene because they look at things from a completely different perspective, they can show things differently from others. . . . I made an art-political project myself, it was about "one state" for all. One state, many faces. . . . So I was taking part in this event together with a Jewish friend, we made this performance and started a one-state embassy. . . . She has not chosen to be born there, she has moved out because of the conflict. She does not want to be part of the conflict. She does not want to be part of the occupation. . . . Why should she move out when she is born there? . . . I see her as a person who is a victim of the conflict. . . . We showed pictures about borders and where violence can take us . . . to create higher borders and a more violent situation and more complications. . . . My films are always about minorities, about unjustified people. . . . If they did not have that human message I would never have cared to go through the long process of making a film. . . .

. . . The moment a person is born, two minutes later someone else has decided which religion they will have and which language and which values . . . and their whole life, after those two minutes, will revolve around fighting hard to get rid of those values they did not choose themselves. . . . I don't want my kids to have the same conflicts and move from the places they are. . . .

. . . There is something behind the photography. I do photography and film. But I started early as photographer when I was 16–17 years, I always took pictures when I was young. But not artistically. But when I was 16 years I saw the camera as a tool. The camera was like a weapon to me. I saw how powerful those who expressed solidarity with the Palestinian case were. I saw several episodes when I was young. I saw when Israeli snipers shot several friends of mine and many others I knew. They hunted them. They had no bad consciousness. They hunted them like animals, you see? But I saw the same soldier, when there were journalists with cameras, stand still and not do anything and wait ten minutes and go home. So I asked myself what's that about, why are those the same soldiers but they do not kill us? Is it because they are white? Blonde? Is it because they are protected from countries like Norway? But the next time, the next episode. . . . There were several occasions when solidarity was expressed and they were from Africa. So I understood it did not have anything to do with skin but maybe with the camera. Because they have a camera, they can send pictures to the whole world. So, then I simply knew that the camera can document crimes and Israel is not interested in showing its bad side out in the world and they are very scared.

[interviewer]: *Do you feel that you have an opportunity to have influence with these projects?*

I have to. If I do not have influence I need to find something else. There has been a lot of change because of the films I have made.

Forough

I was *less than a year* when I came to Norway via Turkey.[5] It was much easier to flee those days. That was *in the 1980s*. The first place we lived that I remember was *a small town* which had not seen brown people before. . . . We moved to Oslo when I was maybe four, five, six, I can't quite remember.

There are at least two identities that have shaped me to a great degree. Even if I do not remember the actual flight, it has affected my whole life and my family. And the first memories I have are of racism. Which . . . well, I cannot remember anything else than that I have been conscious of being different from the others. It was very white . . . and I . . . I was not. Not everyone welcomed us but there were some families and we are still in touch with them. I remember very well that I wanted to have freckles and blond hair . . . and that the racism I experienced already when I was so young was very violent, was very brutal. . . . The first memories I have are that dad was going to put me to bed when we lived in *this small town* and there was someone that broke our bedroom window or threw a stone. I don't remember quite whether it broke, but I remember and I have been told—I was of course very young so I don't remember quite what I have been told and what I remember myself—but that mom went around with a broom to scare them off, those who came to our house. And that she went around the schools in *this small town* to say that—she of course could not speak Norwegian—but she went around saying "mitt blod rødt, ditt blod rødt" (my blood red, your blood red) and she tried. And I grew up in a family that was very political and very revolutionary. Both my parents, so politics has always . . . we have always had political discussions at home . . . and class and racism have been themes that were very natural for us to discuss at home. . . . My siblings are probably more affected by the war because they remember; they were older when I was born. My youngest *sibling* did not talk before we moved to Norway and I think my oldest *sibling* was a bit scared of fireworks and such typical stuff that are reminders of war. But I have not had such direct, or primary trauma or whatever it is called. . . . In a way, [to be] refugee, that . . . shapes the whole family.

. . . And my dad was sick for a period, or long. Or . . . he was in prison in Iran and I have heard many of his stories about the torture he experienced in Iran as a political prisoner. So that was very present, this consciousness that we are a part of society and the importance of how society functions or does not function. [Laughs] And I have been . . . it has been very natural for me to engage politically, surely partly because of my upbringing but also because, I think the most important reason is that I experienced at an early age that I was treated differently because I looked different. So that has shaped me: I have always been conscious of the fact that my otherness is not appreciated and will make things a bit more challenging for me in life.

. . . So I grew up in an anti-racism organization. My mom was active and engaged, that organization unfortunately doesn't exist today. So I was part of that from a very young age, when mom organized meetings, and it was an organization I got engaged in and took part in for many years.

. . . For me this is about it being a survivor's strategy. . . . "We take part because we have to." After all I am very privileged, I have a job, I am married, I have a family . . . I have the money, I am very privileged. . . . For me, solidarity is what I learned most at home, that is maybe the most important from both my parents and especially a lot from my father. . . . When I get how things connect together then I just cannot not do something. So it is not necessarily because I think it is fun and it is not necessarily because I feel brave, because I do not. . . . I am very occupied with representation. I believe making people invisible and under-representation contributes to racism. It contributes to exoticizing, to producing stereotypes. . . . I act because I feel I have to.

Refugee Experiences: Shaping Political Actors

The life stories of Forough and Bashar are unique, and what I represent of their stories here is just a very small, consciously selected part of interviews that easily took two to three hours and in themselves reflected representations of what they wished to share from their young lives. Yet I present these very partial stories within the context of having collected approximately a hundred life histories and several hundreds of interviews with refugees as well as having done extensive participant observation over the last two decades.[6] Thus, I know that these stories reflect the experiences of many refugees. While most of my work has focused on Somali refugees in regional camps, the United States, and Europe, I have been surprised by the fact that a number of central aspects of Somali refugee experiences are recognizable in the life histories of other refugees as well. I will highlight those elements that are absent from public as well as academic debate, leading to what Mladjo Ivanovic (2016) terms "epistemological injustice," as representations do not reflect lived realities of many refugees very well.

First, many refugees who were among the first to flee a violent conflict and found protection beyond the region, through resettlement, come from the political or social elite of their country. They are among those who run the biggest risk of being persecuted, and they have the resources to leave (Horst 2013). This means that they and their families have often been political actors in formal politics, whether in government or opposition, or through civil society and social movements. These individuals may have taken part in political decision-making or had political influence through opposition movements, often risking their lives and putting their families in danger. They possess human, social, and financial capital, and after flight many continue to want to use those resources in order to have influence on political processes that matter to them, locally or transnationally. This is an important observation to remember when looking at the impact of experiencing violent conflict and persecution because, besides the transformative impact such experiences can have on motivations for political acts, there is a preexisting correlation between the two.

Second, almost all refugees have gone through deeply dehumanizing experiences and were confronted with the potential for cruelty that human beings expose, which is unfathomable. As devastating as the loss of loved ones and possessions can be, especially if it is combined with a total sense of disempowerment because of not being able to prevent the loss from happening, the risk of losing all trust in humanity might be as shattering. One of the most important strategies by which individuals "rehumanize" their everyday realities is by engaging in acts of empathy and care and by assisting others. Being able to help and protect others provides people with thin straws to claim their humanity again and to challenge the sense that humanity is fundamentally evil.

From the specific stories of Forough and Bashar, there are a few more points I would like to highlight. First, both of them are young individuals who can expect to have a long life after resettlement in a very different context from the one they or their parents grew up in. Bashar describes growing up under occupation as being formational, and the horrendous experiences he went through during his teenage years—experiencing violence and abuse, death of close friends, and torture—left a very stark impression on him.

Forough, on the other hand, describes a reality where she did not experience war herself but still feels that flight has shaped her family. Her father was heavily traumatized, leaving a deep imprint on the family, and her older siblings displayed signs of war-related anxiety. The kind of impact traumatic events have on individuals and families of course differs by age, just like the way people handle it will be affected by the age at which they escape violent conflict.

The family plays a central role, where parents not only impact their children with the traumas they carry but also function as crucial role models. Forough describes politically active parents who carried on their political activism after coming to Norway and instilled in their children many of the values they had fought for. To what extent refugee communities have such a formal political profile depends to a great extent on the political system and type of conflict in the countries they fled and on what room for opposition existed. Yet Forough's descriptions of her father's activism are far from exceptional and resemble, for example, Alima Husseini's family background. While I have not included this in Bashar's story, he describes a similarly politically engaged father who held a deep respect for individual freedoms and advocated a society on socialist principles, making the family an outlier in the Palestinian context. Bashar also discussed some of the fundamental virtues he feels his father and mother passed on to him, and he wishes to contribute to creating a society where his children do not have to undergo what he did.

A final theme I would like to bring forward here is the link between refugee life experiences and transformative action. Bashar describes a turning point in his life as follows: "I found that in this place there is no hope so either I get out or I do something bad . . . and give up. Or I just have to move out, and that was the best solution, just get out of there." Leaving gave him the opportunity not to give up, and in Norway he dedicates his life to working toward change. His political art allows him to do this through unconventional means, and to him it is vital to continue to make films in order to have influence. He represents an important voice on the Palestinian conflict through his art and at the same time also addresses injustices in Europe with his film projects. As I have argued above, these tools for societal transformation and political participation play central and fundamental roles in the sense-making needed to process the many dehumanizing experiences that become part of a refugee's life history.

Conclusion

Collecting life histories of refugees—and analyzing these individual stories within a framework of civic engagement in different societal contexts—provides an important counternarrative to images of refugee vulnerability, survival, navigation, or "warriorhood." These stories do not aim to negate those commonly discussed aspects of refugee experiences, which focus on deep human suffering and structural inequality and abuse. I am not suggesting that all refugees manage to transform their experiences into something positively transformative for themselves, their families, or societies, as that requires great levels of luck, courage, and persistence. What I am arguing is that there are many like Bashar, Forough, Alima, Zahra, and Idil, and we need to understand their lived experiences and the political agency they display in order to gain a fuller picture of what it means to be a refugee. Stories of refugee political agency and their role as change makers in a range of societies, despite earlier attempts (Essed, Frerks, and Schrijvers 2004), are still largely absent from academic and policy debates. Aiming to expose the injustices of global structures that govern refugees, influential authors like Michel Agier (2011) and Miriam Ticktin (2011) often still end up reproducing images of refugees as passive victims.

Now the question is how a life-history-based perspective can inform our understanding of the role of individuals in larger resolution processes, including peacebuilding. Where do their activities need to take place in order to be included as relevant for such processes? Does it need to be at the negotiation table, in which case none of the stories presented has any relevance? Or can it take place through political art projects like those Bashar engages in? And in our attempts to understand the "political agency" of refugees, are we interested in this agency only when it is directed at their countries of origin? Or can we also move our gaze to the ways in which those with a refugee background engage in their countries of settlement, for example, as Forough does through antidiscrimination work in Norway? As Megan Bradley and colleagues (in the introduction to this volume) highlight, displaced persons' roles in resolution processes are mediated by a range of historical and contextual factors, but commonly their participation in peacebuilding processes continues to be seen as only peripherally important. I have argued that the political acts of individuals are crucial in their own right because societal transformation rarely takes place through top-down peacebuilding processes. Thus, I question whether the main issue is guaranteeing political participation of displaced populations at the top level when the underlying aim is to create more inclusive societies and sustainable peace (Horst 2017). The latter can be created through everyday acts of individuals, including refugees.

Anthropology studies how individuals are embedded in cultural, religious, social, political, and economic collectives. While individual acts are *influenced* by this embeddedness, they are not *determined* by it. In this chapter I have explored what motivates courageous acts of resistance during and after violent conflict. I believe that the strength of the anthropology of the good is that it allows the discipline to theorize agency in or after conditions of extreme violence and marginality in new and interesting ways. With its focus on morality as enacted through relationships with others and envisioned in the future, the anthropology of the good allows us to explore moral acts in uncertain conditions of conflict and displacement. People engaging in such acts are inspired by their sense of morality, opposing "evil" or "indifference." That is why Forough says "I act because I have to" and Idil explains that she is active "because she knows how important that is, what it contributes to society." Their stories and those of Zahra, Bashar, and Alima provide a first glimpse into how refugee life histories are important tools in exploring what inspires individuals who have experienced violent conflict to stand up and act, embedded in and possibly inspiring larger collectives.

What is currently still lacking is an empirical and theoretical exploration of the transformative power of acts inspired by perceptions of the good. It is crucial to understand not just the *inspiration* but also the *impact* of such acts, and more work needs to be done there. Further research is needed to explore the links between individual action, collective agency, political influence, and societal transformation in new ways. In the meantime, as I show in this chapter, the life histories of refugees illustrate that moral action does not take place *despite* having experienced deeply dehumanizing experiences but *because* of those experiences.

Notes

1. This chapter is an output of the project Active Citizenship in Culturally and Religiously Diverse Societies (ACT), funded by the Research Council of Norway (RCN).

2. This theme also draws heavily on feminist insights.

3. The bulk of this data was collected for the ACT project. Furthermore, I draw on interviews collected for "Gender in Politics in Somalia: Access and Influence in a Post-Conflict State," funded by the RCN (https://www.prio.org/Projects/Project/?x=1632), and Diaspora Return: Implications for Somalia, funded by the Norwegian Ministry of Foreign Affairs (https://www.prio.org/Projects/Project/?x=1630). Data was collected by Ebba Tellander, Cindy Horst, and Maimuna Mohamud.

4. PEGIDA (Patriotic Europeans against the Islamization of the West) is a nationalist and anti-Islam movement founded in Germany with offshoots in various European countries, including Norway.

5. The text in cursive replaces more exact information that would compromise anonymity.

6. While I have conducted a considerable proportion of this work, in recent years I have led teams of researchers where I would always do some of the data collection, but the brunt of the work was done by junior scholars whom I mentored extensively.

3

Displacement Resolution and "Massively Shared Agency"

Blair Peruniak

This chapter examines a concept that is crucial to the goal of achieving durable solutions to displacement, the concept of shared action. The term "durable solutions" typically refers to the planned resolution of large-scale, protracted forms of displacement that require the participation and coordination of vast numbers of individuals, institutions, and agencies. Even small-scale efforts to resolve displacement, such as the resettlement of individual refugees, tend to rely on complex networks, hierarchical structures of power, and the work of many hands. I argue that the legal philosopher Scott Shapiro's (2014) novel account of shared agency—"massively" shared agency—is relevant to moral assessments of refugees' roles in displacement resolution processes in two ways. First, Shapiro's model can account for certain constraints that resolution processes impose on refugees as actors in nonideal circumstances that might otherwise disqualify those processes as morally or politically legitimate forms of action. Second, the theory of massively shared agency can supply us with important normative criteria for evaluating the success of joint ventures to resolve displacement as more or less legitimate.

Critics of durable solutions processes, particularly large-scale undertakings such as major return movements, often contend that these processes are incompatible with or inappropriately constrain refugees' status as significant agents of social change and as moral agents who are capable of entering into relations of mutual accountability and respect. At a time when refugee and forced migration scholars are making concerted efforts to align their descriptive methodological goals with refugees' interests, beliefs, and aspirations, highlighting and defending refugee agency has become a powerful means of

policing the discourse on displacement resolution. Proposals for durable solutions that fail to account for refugees as fully autonomous agents or those
that do not offer to place refugees in authoritative roles are often treated dis-
missively.[1] In this context, the language of agency is at risk of being co-opted
into a rhetorical form of criticism that unfairly rejects the plausibility of durable solutions as a conceptual framework for understanding morally legitimate
responses to displacement. The theory of shared agency offers proponents of
durable solutions a way of answering critics on their own terms in anticipation of future debates that must be prepared to examine the relative merits
of competing conceptions of what it means to be an agent or to have agency.

I begin the chapter by showing how efforts to conceptualize and resolve
displacement have led to worries about the status of refugees as significant
moral and political agents within durable solutions frameworks. I then consider two tasks that any account of agency must be able to perform if it is to
be adequate to the analysis and assessment of refugees as participants in durable solutions processes. First, the concept of agency must reflect the scale
of human action that characterizes modern responses to forced displacement. Second, it must account for the fact that in every large-scale effort to
achieve a durable solution, there will be at least some participants who do
not share—or may even oppose—the goals of the resolution process. To this
end, I introduce and explain Shapiro's model of "massively shared agency." I
argue that Shapiro's criteria of massively shared action can usefully explain
and accommodate both the scale and the alienating dimensions of displacement resolution processes. I demonstrate this by applying the criteria to two
historical cases of refugee settlement: post–World War II Soviet repatriation
and the settlement of refugees in rural areas of Greek Macedonia following
the 1923 Turkish and Greek population exchange. I then examine how Shapiro's model can lay the groundwork for evaluating refugees' roles as responsible agents whose capacity to be held accountable for their participation in
joint ventures to resolve their displacement makes them appropriate subjects
of praise and blame. In order to address unequal distributions of power and
authority in resolution processes, I propose a new criterion of shared agency
that can be appended to Shapiro's model. I conclude by suggesting additional
ways in which the model could be strengthened by incorporating insights
from critical studies on refugees and forced migration.

Durable Solutions and Refugee Agency

The search for durable solutions to displacement includes the search for
shared concepts that can foster agreement and social cooperation in resolving displacement while recognizing the moral and practical limitations of

human agency. The concepts that guide the design, implementation, and evaluation of efforts to resolve displacement should be broad enough to command wide assent and specific enough to be useful in certain circumstances (Bradley 2013a, 2013b). Unfortunately, refugee scholars remain divided on the merits of previous and ongoing attempts to implement durable solutions, such as voluntary return, local integration, or resettlement (Bradley 2013b; Chimni 2004).

Critics of durable solutions have long sought to expose the apparent incompatibility of state-led responses to displacement, on the one hand, and the recognition of refugees as full and equal moral persons, on the other (Harrell-Bond 1989). This is not surprising since early definitions of durable solutions privileged the authority and interests of states while excluding refugees as key actors (Skran 1995; Stein 1986). Recent proposals, including explicitly moral accounts (Carens 2013; Gibney 2015; Miller 2016), fare little better, prescribing limited or nonexistent roles for refugees as negotiators or planners in resolving their own conditions of displacement. Under these schemes, complex, long-term planning between democratic and nondemocratic states, institutions, and refugees in resolving displacement is either reduced to the maintenance of individual moral rights and responsibilities under rigid legal categories of displacement (Hayden 2006) or driven toward market-based solutions whose underlying norms are set by elite (state and corporate) interests (Betts and Collier 2017; Blocher and Gulati 2016; Schuck 1997).

In response, a growing number of forced migration scholars have sought to demonstrate that refugees are significant agents of social change as well as primary authors and rightful authorities in resolving their personal conditions of displacement (Landau, Sherwood, and Baines, chapter 8, this volume). Calls to revisit the norms and strategies of displacement resolution are further bolstered by the skepticism of those who maintain that states have proven to be virtually incapable of achieving justice for refugees (Chimni 2004, 72; Kukathas 2016, 264). At the same time, these claims raise serious doubts about whether it is actually possible (or even desirable) for refugees and state-led institutions to accept common principles and shared goals for resolving or improving conditions of exile. Some scholars have suggested ways to circumvent this impasse, for example, by encouraging states to adopt political reforms that reflect more democratic conceptions of agency that would highlight the essentially contested nature of displacement and durable solutions. This would allow for more radical deliberative practices that prevent elite or majoritarian interests from settling debates on fundamental procedures or normative standards (e.g., Bassel 2012). Others have argued that only an adversarial form of transformational politics in perpetual defiance of state authority can do justice to refugees' moral and political agency

(Soguk 1999; Nyers 2006a). These critics suggest that support for durable solutions (which inevitably relies on states and state-led institutions) is incompatible with a conception of refugees as equal moral and political agents and, thus, that the very idea of "durable solutions to displacement" is normatively incoherent. Unfortunately, this approach offers little in the way of constructive or practical advice for resolving large-scale displacement. It is all the more troubling in that forced migration scholars have rarely defined what they mean by the term "agency"; not only are claims about refugee agency seldom held to clear or common standards but it is also clear that refugee scholars have largely presupposed what it means for someone *to be* an agent. The next section introduces some important recent philosophical developments in the theory of action that can encourage new ways of thinking about agency in the context of durable solutions that may lead to a more productive exchange between proponents and detractors of the traditional durable solutions framework. On these accounts, it is important to distinguish not only between shared and more individuated forms of action but also between small- and large-scale agency.

Individual, Shared, and "Massively" Shared Agency

To understand the difference between individual and shared forms of agency, consider a pair of citizens fleeing from persecution. In choosing to leave their country for safer territory, each may decide to go it alone; alternatively, they may choose to cross the border together. What makes it the case that, though they may walk alongside one another, their doing so constitutes a *joint* activity? What makes it the case that when they cross the border, they cross it *together*?[2] On one popular account, they will cross the border together not as a matter of sheer luck or strategic calculation but only insofar as each has an intention that they cross together, intentions that are openly communicated and that set the conditions for planning and negotiating their movements during the course of their flight from persecution (Bratman 2014b; Roth 2017).[3] Roughly speaking, then, shared agency is distinguished from individuated forms of action by the presence of specialized psychological features of coparticipants, namely, shared intentions.[4] To understand what it means to share an intention to act together, it is useful to think in terms of the role of intentions in structuring cooperative, interpersonal relations. Shared intentions allow individuals to coordinate individual behavior, to coordinate planning, and to specify background conditions for bargaining in cases of conflict (Bratman 2014b, 9–12; Shapiro 2014, 258). This is easily done in the case of small-scale activities among two or three equally competent and equally committed participants. In such cases, participants can simply communicate their intention to follow their part of a plan (i.e., their subplan), and each can track the others' behaviors directly, adjusting their individual roles over time in the face of potential conflicts (Shapiro 2014, 263).

Accounts of shared agency are capable of addressing a wide range of ordinary group activities, specifically "the shared intentional activities of small, adult groups in the absence of asymmetric authority relations within those groups, and in which the individuals who are participants remain constant over time," such as baking a cake or singing a duet (Bratman 2014b, 7). In such cases, it is a working assumption that none of the participants has authority over the others and that each person shares a commitment to the success of the activity.[5] As a result, however, the theory of action has been at a loss to account for a wider range of everyday activities commonly associated with large-scale group activities involving bureaucracies or other hierarchical arrangements that entail inequalities among participants both in terms of their relative power and commitments to the goals that the bureaucracy aims to achieve. This lacuna is particularly significant for the study of durable solutions to displacement. It means that the models of shared agency currently on offer have almost nothing to say about large-scale efforts to resolve large-scale displacement.

The novelty of Shapiro's approach consists in showing how shared agency is possible in conditions of large-scale action where interpersonal forms of communication are difficult or likely to break down. These will be cases where the numbers of participants and complexity of the task make effective face-to-face interpersonal communication virtually impossible, such as in large-scale repatriation processes where individuals are unlikely to have direct personal knowledge of everyone's intentions to act together or to fulfill their roles in resolving displacement effectively. Shapiro's main innovation is to show that the functional or causal roles that are normally played by shared intentions (which, in small-scale activities, arise through direct communication or signaling between participants) can be "outsourced" to other social mechanisms of coordination, communication, and collective governance. In this sense, shared intentions are "multiply realizable" (Shapiro 2014, 276). This is important because in cases of large-scale activities "the source of the organization is not likely to be an intention shared by the participants. Instead, the complex social coordination is externally orchestrated by a managerial group" (Bratman 2014b, 10). (In the case of efforts to resolve displacement, such managerial groups might include the United Nations High Commissioner for Refugees, states, or formally organized groups of refugees.) What Shapiro wants to show, then, is how (physical) plans can function in place of shared intentions as a social mechanism for harnessing and coordinating actions on a large scale in a way that would allow us to understand such activities as genuine forms of "massively" shared agency. On this view, not everyone party to large-scale activities can author the plan or play an equal role in controlling its implementation. Authority structures therefore play a crucial role in the efficient implementation of shared intentions in the form of plans, as Shapiro (2014, 284) explains: "Authority . . . represents a major technological advance in social ordering. Rather than requiring befuddled or squabbling participants to waste their time and energy arguing or bargaining with each other, authorities can simply cut through the doubts and confusion and impose a solution. Mesh is thrust upon the participants from on high, rather than being stitched together by them at the grass roots." Although no authority structure will necessarily ensure the success of efforts to implement a durable solution such as voluntary repatriation, *some* form of centralized authority is likely to be necessary in coordinating the actions of thousands or hundreds of thousands of people toward common goals. Shapiro (2014, 258) notes, "Without some centralized control over behavior, the odds that many people will organize themselves toward the same objective and resolve their conflicts in a peaceful and efficient manner is apt to be low."[6] Plans can be formed through deliberative democratic processes rather than imposed from above by political elites or centralized institutions (Braithwaite et al. 2010, 119–20; Isaac and Franke 2002; Scott 1998, 5). But it is highly unlikely that plans or their initial stages will emerge in social contexts that do not involve or presuppose centralized forms of power. Nor would decentralized plans themselves be devoid of hierarchical arrangements such that every participant could be equally well informed or well placed to carry out the plan or to resolve disputes in cases of conflict (Cooke and Kothari 2001). A division of labor in large-scale activity requires differentiated roles and structures of authority that can prevent unnecessary forms of bargaining and conflict.

Elizabeth Dunn has argued that humanitarian assistance can "rob" displaced persons of their agency by failing to institute a "master plan or coordinating body" to minimize uncertainty and create opportunities for displaced persons to envision their future and participate in its creation (Dunn 2014, 302). Unfortunately, the greater the number of participants, the more likely it becomes that at least *some* participants will be alienated from the goals of the activity: "In any large-scale activity, there are bound to be participants that intentionally contribute to the group effort but are not committed to the success of the group venture" (Shapiro 2014, 272). In the next section I show how Shapiro accommodates these insights in developing a set of criteria of shared agency for large-scale forms of action. I then apply these criteria to contexts of refugee settlement as a way of showing how the theory can illuminate descriptive and normative features of durable solutions processes.

Durable Solutions and Massively Shared Agency

Shapiro's criteria of massively shared agency emerge through his detailed and critical reconstruction of Bratman's and others' work in the theory of action. I will not rehearse these arguments here, nor do I explain or defend this approach as a general theory.[7] Even if we accept that Shapiro's account is theoretically plausible, his approach may strike us as overly simplistic or intuitively unattractive in contexts of forced displacement. In anticipation of these sorts of reactions, then, I want to show how the criteria might be applied directly to specific cases of displacement resolution. According to Shapiro (2014, 277), a joint activity will count as an instance of massively shared agency if it meets the following criteria (where G stands for the members of the group engaged in the joint activity; J, the activity itself; and P, the plan):

1. There is a shared plan (P) for G to J;
     The conditions of a *shared* plan being met if and only if:
     (a) P was designed for members of G so that they may J by following it; and
     (b) Most participants of G accept P.
2. Each member of G intentionally follows her part of the shared plan;
3. Members of G resolve their conflicts about J-ing in a peaceful and open manner;
4. It is common knowledge that (1), (2), and (3); and
5. J takes place in virtue of (1) and (2).[8]

On this definition, the goals in view of which plans are created will not necessarily reflect the goals or interests of each individual participant or the values that feature in their conceptions of the good life. The sorts of plans Shapiro has in mind, then, are ones designed *for* participants, not necessarily *by* the participants. This raises an important problem for an account of refugee agency in the context of durable solutions. Any plan to implement a durable solution in a particular context of displacement must clearly state its goals, including the kind of solution it hopes to achieve. Now, it is possible that individuals who agree to participate in such activities may be committed to the success of the joint activity even though they are indifferent or even hostile to its intended goals (Shapiro 2014, 272). For example, many citizens are prepared to vote or campaign for a presidential candidate whose policies they oppose in order to avoid a "greater evil." However, Shapiro wants to show that there can be shared agency even in cases where some of the participants are not equally committed or are even opposed to the *success* of the joint venture (Shapiro 2014, 270–71). To follow one's part in a plan, one need not accept the goals of the plan, and one does not need to understand the plan at all times. The point is that one must follow one's own part and allow others to do the same (Shapiro 2014, 279). In cases of conflict over one's role in the overall plan or between members of the joint activity, individuals must take the authority's directives as final. This does not mean that authorities cannot be responsive to those under their authority. (I discuss this point further in the final section.) The requirement that there be common knowledge of the plan is similarly relaxed. It would be impossible for individuals to be briefed on and memorize plans for every aspect of large-scale operations, such as mass resettlements. These operations occur in radically complex settings over time. In such circumstances, plans may change and official updates can be intermittent. Shapiro claims, therefore, that the plan must merely be "publicly accessible" so that participants *could* know the overall plan, were they so inclined to find out (Shapiro 2014, 279). On this view, coordinated efforts to resolve displacement can be understood as forms of shared agency even if they include some (or, indeed, many) refugees who participate even though they are not equally committed (or are even opposed) to the success of the joint venture. As long as *most* of the participants in the durable solution intend for the operation to succeed, intentionally fulfill their role in the process, and commit to resolving their disputes peacefully and openly, where all of these intentions are effectively communicated in a likewise open and forthright manner, there will be shared, intentional activity (Shapiro 2014, 282).[9]

Of course, there may be reasons to refrain from participating in joint activities where authorities are clearly immoral or dangerously incompetent. For example, the Nazi resettlement plans of 1942 that "envisaged the resettlement of millions of Germans and other so-called Aryans west of the Urals and the consignment of most of the native population to slavery, deportation, or extermination" (Ahonen 2003, 22) were inherently immoral. Indeed, Shapiro claims that "many shared activities are morally noxious, and there can be no obligation to participate in morally noxious enterprises" (2014, 268). Yet, as Shapiro points out, even immoral plans can command rational assent: "Once someone has formed an intention to treat the authority's directives as trumps to their own planning, they have changed their normative situation and are rationally committed to follow through unless good reasons appear to force them to reconsider" (Shapiro 2014, 268). Unfortunately, reasons that might otherwise force one to reconsider their commitments may not always be available. They may be hidden or suppressed, or the reconsideration of one's commitments may impose costs that make assent to another's authority virtually automatic. It is important, then, to determine whether Shapiro's account will permit morally dubious cases of this sort.

Consider the repatriation of 5.2 million displaced persons under Joseph

Stalin's regime after World War II. This is a striking example of the coercive power of modern authority structures. It is also an important reminder of the degree to which it is possible to coordinate action on a vast scale by imposing a plan on a population, forcing individuals to accept their part of the plan, and ensuring conformity to their given roles over time through fear and intimidation. As Nick Baron (2009) points out, "every repatriate had to articulate his or her individual account of displacement and return, although the narrative was pre-scripted and sanctions for deviation were severe" (91). However, Baron also observes that this is consistent with the idea that, in many cases, returnees acted under coercion in a way that advanced their own goals: "That [Soviet repatriates] conformed to state expectations concerning mutual surveillance and denunciation does not exclude the possibility that they were also, probably in collaboration with one another, serving their own interests" (102). Baron's suggestion that Soviet refugees retained a semblance of agency under coercive conditions is an important reminder that where reasons for action are complex and motivations are mixed, common standards or notions of agency may be difficult to apply. Individuals often face difficult choices in contexts of displacement, and attempts to resolve those conditions (or simply to deal with them as they are) may jar our sense of what "counts" as agency (Baines, chapter 5, this volume). In some cases, we may be sufficiently compelled to revise our assumptions about agency; in other cases, we would do better to stick to our guns.

The case of Soviet repatriation thus serves as an important test case for Shapiro's account. On the one hand, if Soviet repatriation is a genuine instance of massively shared agency, then Shapiro's account is prima facie compatible with gross violations of human rights. On the other hand, if Shapiro's model is incompatible with durable solutions that emerge from human rights violations, this raises doubts about the broader relevance of the theory since efforts to resolve displacement often unfold in contexts brought about by various kinds of human rights abuses. (I return to this last point shortly.) The upshot is that Shapiro's theory is either unacceptably broad or unacceptably narrow.

Before we abandon the theory, however, let's return to the case at hand. Was the large-scale Soviet return process following World War II an instance of massively shared agency?[10] Soviet repatriation efforts were certainly planned and coordinated under a highly centralized form of authority designed, at least in part, for members of the group, G (i.e., Soviet returnees).[11] Returnees were subjected to a meticulously orchestrated screening system carried out at numerous "filtration" camps or checkpoints. Soviet repatriation was, in Baron's (2009) words, an "immense and time-consuming campaign of individual verification and registration" (90) using detailed methods of classification for the purposes of resettlement, deportation, or other more notorious forms of punitive relocation including imprisonment and banishment (92–93). Interrogation checkpoints served as internment camps, dividing returnees into groups for the purposes of forced labor, health screening, reeducation, and other propaganda programs. Many returnees were processed multiple times through different verification procedures and reverification processes, sometimes over the span of years through social monitoring and police surveillance techniques involving "extensive networks of informers and agents" (106). The process of filtration itself was the product of collusion between Soviet and Western state officials, whose own identification and worker-recruitment initiatives relied on the assistance of special committees and international humanitarian organizations (Baron 2009, 99; Skran 1995, 149–56).

It is plausible then that Soviet repatriation met the first and second criteria of massively shared agency: there was a shared plan for Soviet returnees (*G*) to repatriate (*J*), and each member of *G* intentionally followed their part of the plan. Yet, even if we assume that Soviet returnees gave rational assent to Soviet filtration procedures, the idea that the returnees resolved their conflicts about repatriation in "a peaceful and open manner" (3) and that all of this was "common knowledge" (4) is clearly absurd. Although there may be cases where the presence of coercion is not sufficient to rule out genuine shared activity (Bratman 2014b, 38, 101–2), Shapiro's third and fourth criteria rule out the possibility of shared activity under *purely* rational or coercive pressure, which, in the case of Soviet repatriation, was pervasive and overwhelming (Inkeles and Bauer 1961; Voisin 2007). We may conclude on these grounds that postwar Soviet repatriation fails as an instance of massively shared agency.

However, whether Shapiro's model can serve as a normative guide in contexts of displacement resolution depends less on its ability to deliver judgments that correspond with our intuitions in relatively uncontroversial cases than on the plausibility of the model's more basic epistemic and normative claims. The basic epistemic claim says that we can distinguish between cases where action writ large is constitutive of shared agency and cases where it is not. The normative claim says that the descriptive criteria of shared agency—the social norms through which we generate shared goals and shared intentions—can help us to identify morally legitimate forms of action (Bratman 2014b, 16–18; Gilbert 2014). Both must be plausible if an account of the characteristics of shared action (much like an account of individual agency) has the potential to serve as a basic normative framework for assessing durable solutions as morally legitimate forms of action, a framework within which legitimate actions may still be more or less legitimate. This raises the question of whether or to what extent Shapiro's model can offer guidance in more controversial cases.

A more challenging case concerns the Convention on Exchange of Populations (1923) and the Geneva Protocol signed in the aftermath of the Balkan Wars, which paved the way for the settlement of refugees in Greek Macedonia, one of the largest refugee settlement operations of the twentieth century. Between 1922 and 1930, over 1.5 million refugees were settled in rural and in urban areas in the relatively undeveloped nation of Greece, whose own population totaled some 5 million people. Here I will focus on the settlement of 800,000 Ottoman refugees under auspices of the Refugee Settlement Commission (RSC) in rural areas of Greek Macedonia, as described in Elisabeth Kontogiorgi's (2006) excellent case study. The case of Macedonia provides important insights into the inner workings and management by international organizations (notably, coordination between the League of Nations, the Greek government, the RSC, and refugees, both individually and under various forms of representation) in an attempt to stabilize the region during a violent period of nation-building and ethnic strife (Kontogiorgi 2006, 5–6). It also seems to call for an account of shared action, one that can make sense of the scale and centralized elements of planning characteristic of massively shared agency. As Kontogiorgi notes, "Because of the magnitude of the refugee population, the resettlement project had to be group-oriented and moulded to the development needs of the country" (2006, 79).

At the same time, Macedonian settlement was not accomplished without coercion and mishap. Many lives were lost in the compulsory population exchange, especially as a result of disease and malnourishment. Under the direction of the League of Nations, the RSC retained significant powers over the duly elected Greek government and thus over the population as a whole. Furthermore, many aspects of RSC policy were conspicuously unfair. For example, refugees were settled alongside native peasants but were deprived of similar rights of inheritance and made to repay loans for lands and equipment. However, unlike the plans of the Stalin regime, neither the goals nor the motivations under which the settlement policies were created and implemented could be described as "morally noxious." Decisions made in first years of settlement and integration were often based explicitly on achieving humanitarian goals and durable solutions for the displaced. The refugees were immediately naturalized, and donors and charitable organizations were continuously mobilized to support relief and temporary settlement efforts, while further funds and loans were arranged on the behalf of refugees for longer-term settlement goals (Kontogiorgi 2006, 74–76). Indeed, as Kontogiorgi (2006, 154) argues, "the settlement and integration of the refugees in Greek Society has been judged, as indeed it was, the greatest peaceful achievement of the modern Greek state and nation."[12]

Under the RSC's centralized authority, an official plan (1) was formed for the refugees (1a), most refugees accepted the plan (1b), and each followed their part in the joint activity (2). In addition, it seems fair to suggest, according to (5), that refugee settlement took place in virtue of (1) and (2). However, not all conflicts between native landowners and refugees were resolved peacefully or openly (3). Although the formalized processes of agricultural settlement and political and legal associations formed by refugees gave way to a significant amount of peaceful and open bargaining, the period of agricultural settlement saw much intermittent violence, amid "irregular" transactions, and to some extent the forceful redistribution of land (Kontogiorgi 2006, 169–84). This is important since the violation of (3) entails the violation of (4).

As in the previous example, we have applied Shapiro's criteria of shared agency in only a cursory fashion. However, it is reasonable to suggest based on the available data that the rural settlement of refugees in Macedonia offers a much more plausible instance of genuine massively shared agency. That it ultimately fails on a straightforward comparison with Shapiro's criteria is not a reason to doubt the appropriateness of the theory to these or similar contexts. Rather, it suggests that the criteria can help us to evaluate the roles and contributions of individual participants.

These examples help to show that agency is always a "moralized concept" (Bratman 2014b, 38). This is important since, in cases where the moral or legal justifications of plans for resolving displacement are controversial, where plans themselves are either opaque or hidden from public view, or where evaluating the results of implementing a plan raises new and equally controversial normative judgments (e.g., Bradley 2013a, 129n10), the concept of refugee agency may be valued not as a helpful guide but as a rhetorical device. The rhetorical value of the concept of "refugee agency"—for which it is liable to be abused—consists in its capacity to legitimize resolution processes that are morally and politically *il*legitimate and to delegitimize those that are morally sound. Given the interests at stake, the complexity of resolving displacement, and the lengthy periods over which such processes take place, there will be many opportunities to describe or redescribe acts and events along the way as negative or positive instantiations of moral agency. Hence, involuntary and forced resettlements may be touted as shining examples of autonomous choice, while evidence of a vibrant people's movement or political self-determination are reduced to acts of collective subservience or illicit agency (Sherwood, chapter 9, this volume).

These points raise more considerations than I can address here. However, one preliminary step to avoiding the rhetorical abuse of the concept of agency is to demand that descriptive and moral criteria of action be made explicit. Beyond this, the criteria of shared action must also allow us to evaluate individual participants in terms of their roles and the merits of their contributions in the light of the differences they make, or might make (Hornsby 2004), in bringing about a genuine durable solution. For unless we can hold individuals accountable for their actions, we will not be able to claim that they are *responsible* agents. Since few would allow that someone can be an agent but not be responsible for their actions, our account of agency must seek to show how basic attributions of responsibility are possible under the model of massively shared agency. In the remaining section I take up this challenge. My aim is to show that criteria of shared agency are also basic conditions of shared responsibility and that Shapiro's model can accommodate a conception of refugees as responsible agents and, thus, appropriate subjects of praise and blame.

Shared Agency and Shared Responsibility

So far, I have argued that the pursuit of durable solutions to displacement is underwritten by a specific conception of agency, massively shared agency. On this view, durable solutions entail complex plans and authority structures that make the pursuit of shared goals efficient. Plans save time by curtailing endless and costly forms of bargaining, allowing participants to direct their energy and attention to fulfilling their part of the plan (Shapiro 2014, 283). Since subplans identify individuals in specific roles, they also supply an important (epistemic) precondition for holding individuals accountable for succeeding or failing to carry out their part of the plan. However, this does not get us very far, because assigning persons roles in a plan is consistent with their being exempt from attributions of responsibility for those roles. For example, there is deep reluctance to attribute responsibility to persons whose displacement has come about through no fault of their own, or to those who may be ill suited to carry out, or justifiably defiant in carrying out, a task. To be held responsible for agreeing to participate in a joint activity that one has helped to plan is one thing. To be held responsible for following or failing to follow a plan that one did not design, for the sake of goals that one does not accept, is something else. Can refugees really be held *responsible* for the outcomes (successes or failures) of their part in the shared activity of displacement resolution? If so, *who* should hold them responsible? How should accountability work in such situations? I cannot do justice to these questions here. However, the answers will largely turn on whether Shapiro's model accommodates the kinds of norms and practices needed to track appropriate levels of responsibility and to prevent spurious or unjust ascriptions of blame. Misattributions or poor ascriptions of responsibility threaten to undermine support for shared plans and shared agency over time by eroding trust or creating untrusting dispositions that can exacerbate existing levels of participant inequality and alienation. Unfortunately, the conditions of authority that increase efficiency are also ideal for supporting abuses of power that can fuel resentment and attract resistance from the very participants whose cooperation is necessary to ensure the success of the joint project.

One way to limit these problems is to make responsibility attributions specifiable in terms appropriate to the level and complexity of roles in displacement resolution processes. Assigning individuals to roles in a plan requires careful deliberation about whether a person's character or capabilities are compatible with carrying out the tasks required by their role (Pettit 2001, 15). This suggests that certain aspects of responsibility attribution will need to be negotiated and disclosed ahead of time (Williams 2013), including agreements about associated norms or standards for attributing responsibility. To show how participants of joint action are to be held responsible for the foreseeable consequences of their actions as contributors to shared activity requires appropriate norms that track relations of power and commitment among large numbers of people in complex settings over long periods of time. Such are the demands of large-scale joint activities. Where plans fail to live up to such standards, or where they are inherently immoral, their only use may be in determining the degree of moral culpability for the harms that result from imposing the plan and for articulating specific claims of redress (de Greiff 2008).

Another way to mitigate the negative effects of the centralized distribution of authority is to look for opportunities within the model of shared agency to challenge, redefine, or otherwise contest one's role. It is worth noting here that Shapiro's model does not preclude limited or less costly forms of bargaining that do not directly conflict with the central plan. Indeed, for any given plan there will often be opportunities to use one's role to renegotiate the terms of embedded subplans among similarly situated participants. At this level, relations between participants are less authoritative and thus more or less negotiable. Unfortunately, while these opportunities may expand the autonomy of refugees or other participants under authority structures, they do little to impose restrictions on how that authority may be used at higher levels of planning.

A different way of attending to worries about abuses of authority is to build in a criterion that directly addresses the distribution of authority and aims to devolve significant planning roles to individuals or members or sub-groups who may otherwise be excluded from positions of authority. My proposal here is to append a subclause to Shapiro's initial criterion of shared action—that is, within the very definition of shared planning (condition 1, above). On this approach, the conditions of a shared plan will be met if and only if, in addition to designing a plan for a relevant constituency (1a) where most participants accept the plan (1b), the majority of participants must also accept the planned distribution of authority: (1c) where the distribution of authority in *P* should be devolved to the lowest level of political representation consistent with the effective administration of roles and subplans.[13] On this view, the distribution of authority is itself a constitutive feature of shared agency. Authority distribution concerns basic norms. It also underwrites the planning structures without which there may be reasons for most individuals to reject the overall plan, scuttling attempts at genuine forms of shared action. By the distribution of authority, I mean the distribution of power within positions of administration, delegation, and enforcement. These roles are typically held by state representatives as well as economic and political elites. By devolving authority to the lowest levels of political representation, I mean to challenge the democratic accountability deficit inherent to Shapiro's model of agency that presupposes an elitist structure of authority distribution by consent of a simple majority. A worry here is that the distribution of authority can itself be a reason for persons to reject proposed plans for shared activity insofar as they violate basic social norms of cooperative association that bear on attributions of responsibility that are partially determinative of moral agency. Elite distributions of authority dramatically increase the likelihood that one will be treated "as if" they are responsible, where attributing responsibility is a strategy for ensuring compliance with some directed role or imperative rather than a reactive attitude to persons who have sufficiently robust control over their activities (Pettit 2001, 16). By contrast, pluralist and devolved distributions respond to the need for a (nonideal) criterion of shared agency that can better approximate conditions conducive to interpersonal relations of mutual cooperation and control in shared planning (Pettit 2001). While different forms of distribution may be consistent with shared forms of agency, shared action can always be more or less "shared," plans can command wider or narrower consent, and they can be more or less stable over time. The distribution of authority within shared plans thus determines to a large extent the quality and durability of shared forms of action that in turn depend on political representation within specific contexts of shared planning. The devolution of authority means that participation in plans will be less easily decoupled from political projects and less antithetical to democratic forms of representation that are increasingly correlated to successful forms of participatory development strategies (Hirst 1994; Hickey and Mohan 2005). Such are the aspirations of durable solutions as a form of massively shared agency. The main point, however, is that the criteria of shared agency can be seen as basic conditions of shared responsibility. These criteria determine what it means to say that one is responsible for participating in a plan and for carrying out their part in corresponding shared activities. The norms of responsibility in turn coordinate individual behavior, the logistics of intermeshing subplans, and the basic conditions for bargaining in cases of conflict.

In this way, Shapiro's model not only offers a more plausible conception of agency within the sorts of contexts that durable solutions typically operate. It also supplies parameters within which more demanding and particularist criteria of moral agency can be developed, and, on the basis of which, claims about the moral and political legitimacy of responses to displacement can be made explicit. To be sure, Shapiro's theory does not offer a full account of the norms that govern processes of displacement resolution. Shapiro's model offers necessary (not sufficient) conditions of shared action within which more specialized questions about responsibility and authority can be understood and addressed. Using this framework, we can appeal to supplementary principles or concepts identified in normative, policy-oriented accounts of displacement resolution. For example, Shapiro's model could be usefully supplemented by Megan Bradley's (2013a) conditions for just return movements, or Pablo de Greiff's (2008) framework for "massive" reparations programs as they relate to refugees. These works offer important insights into the practical contexts of displacement settings and the potential for developing and sustaining bargaining structures that can generate stronger, more egalitarian forms of massively shared agency than are initially allowed for in Shapiro's account (Bratman 2014a, 332–35).

Conclusion

I started with the thought that the pursuit of durable solutions to displacement entails large-scale forms of action and that this fact imposes parameters on our understanding of refugees' roles within resolution processes. These facts also place constraints on our understanding of the concept of agency, which, I argue, must be capable of reflecting both the scale of durable solutions operations as well as the idea that refugees can, in principle, be held accountable for their actions as participants in efforts to resolve their own conditions of displacement. If we wish to take refugees seriously as agents, we cannot rely on unrealistic conditions of equality, shared goals, or shared intentions among similarly situated participants. Furthermore, to insist that processes for resolving large-scale displacement should emerge from conditions of equality and shared commitment is to deny the significance of nonideal forms of action and deliberation that can create opportunities for more legitimate ventures. Thus, although critics of durable solutions offer important insights into the challenges of resolving displacement by legitimate means, not all concerns about how displaced persons are treated as agents will be equally valid or worrisome in this regard. Indeed, on the view defended here, certain restrictions on individual agency will be permissible, if not morally required, for the sake of other ends.

It is possible that some attempts to resolve displacement will count as genuine instances of massively shared agency and yet fail to be morally or politically legitimate according to more particularistic standards of individual agency. Moreover, Shapiro's model does not provide an exhaustive set of evaluative criteria for displacement resolution processes, and it cannot substitute for a robust account of morally legitimate displacement resolution. Nonetheless, the fact that many cases of large-scale displacement resolution will fail to count as genuine instances of shared agency under Shapiro's model suggests that it can do important normative work. My own view is that shared agency is a kind of achievement and that where large-scale responses to displacement exhibit shared agency in Shapiro's terms, they will also be, *to that extent*, morally legitimate. Ultimately, however, durable solutions to displacement call for robust forms of shared agency "in which the participants themselves are the source of the social organization" (Bratman 2014a, 335). This means that the criteria of massively shared action must eventually give way to more robust and explicitly moral norms that track refugees' agency within durable solutions processes over time. They must also track relations of equality that all long-term resolutions must have as their final goal. The plans that structure, and that are partially constitutive of, shared action derive their value from securing conditions that allow displaced persons to live their lives according to autonomous, self-authored plans (Gibney 2015, 460). However, given the scale of modern refugee movements, the conditions necessary for the development of these forms of social organization are unlikely to be immediately available. In such contexts, problems of authority and alienation are sure to arise. Some tenable conception of agency is needed to show how we can move toward more ideal conditions of action and accountability in long-term responses to displacement (Horst, chapter 2, this volume). This is not to criticize those standards of individual agency regularly invoked by critics of durable solutions. The point is that many refugee scholars have assumed what it means to act or to be an agent in responding to large-scale displacement. As a result, many critics of durable solutions appeal to a conception of agency that offers little room to account for action-explanation under the moral and practical constraints of participation in nonideal conditions. I have argued that, for these sorts of cases, we need an altogether different account of agency. Of course, we need not accept Shapiro's version of his own theory. But any moral account of large-scale displacement resolution must be able to show not only how it is possible for vast numbers of people to resolve displacement. They must also be able show how it is possible for individuals to do so by acting *together*. Indeed, the possibility of a moral or justice-based theory of displacement resolution that is fit to scale seems to presuppose that there is some morally legitimate way of constituting such a group. If this is right, then the theory of massively shared agency may yet offer a way of bridging the gap between critics and proponents of durable solutions. This would be a marked improvement over the current situation. For, at present, the concepts of (refugee) agency currently on offer and the theoretical commitments they entail have done more to divide than to unite scholars with common interests. Left unchallenged, they will continue to function more as practical and conceptual impasses than as routes to a more robust and normatively satisfying account of displacement resolution.

Notes

I would like to express my thanks to all the participants at the contributors' workshop and to Megan Bradley, James Souter, and Dom Taylor for especially helpful comments and suggestions on earlier versions of this chapter.

1. Nevzat Soguk (1999, 8, 9) has claimed that "the prevailing discourse on displacement . . . affords no place for the refugee and the refugee's voice" and that "the voicelessness of the refugee . . . is the *effect* of the refugee discourse." Similarly, Peter Nyers (2006a, xiv) writes that "the prevailing attitude in conventional analyses of refugee movements is one that provides no place for refugees to articulate their experiences and struggles or to assert their (often collectively conceived) political agency."

2. Here I adapt Gilbert's well-known example (2014), although I do not follow her approach. On the differences between Gilbert's and Bratman's approaches to shared action, see Gilbert (2014, chap. 5) and Bratman (2014b, 114–17).

3. Bratman does not subscribe to the view that there are metaphysical group agents or "group minds." Shared agency is instead a form of "augmented individualism" (Bratman 2014b, 11; Shapiro 2014, 260). For an account of shared agency that seeks to combine individualism and collectivist approaches, see Pettit (2001, 114ff).

4. A more detailed account would be necessary if I were hoping to defend either the planning theory or the way it features and sustains massively shared agency. My goal here, however, is to simply offer enough of the theory to show its relevance to issues of durable solutions to displacement.

5. Shapiro acknowledges that small-scale activities can involve differences in au-

thority and commitment between participants (Shapiro 2014, 257). Unlike Bratman, however, Shapiro's model is meant to apply to both large- and small-scale activities. For the purposes of this chapter, I focus only on cases of large-scale displacement where relations of authority and differences in levels of commitment are central.

6. What counts as "centralized control" is a matter of controversy. The important point is that whatever form centralized control takes, it will be indicative of hierarchical power relations and, thus, unequal distributions of power among at least *some* participants.

7. For a good survey of the literature with an up-to-date bibliography, see Roth (2017).

8. Specifications 1(a) and 1(b), which appear later in the text (Shapiro 2014, 283), are added here to explain 1. In the next section, I add a further condition, 1(c), to account for the distribution of authority within a given plan.

9. As I discuss below, this is not to suggest all participants' roles will be scripted in detail or set in stone. Shapiro notes that other accounts of shared agency are less demanding than Bratman's. For example, Christopher Kutz's (2000, 90) "minimalist conception" of acting together suggests that shared agency requires only that each participant's idea about what goal they are contributing to as a group "overlaps" in sufficient and appropriate ways. Similarly, Bratman's account might be amended to accommodate the fact that individuals can have different motivations for participating in a joint activity (Shapiro 2014, 264–70). However, as Shapiro points out, none of these theories accommodates participants who are opposed to the success of the joint activity.

10. The question is of some important since, if the theory of massively shared agency is compatible with events or processes that are morally outrageous or repugnant, this would constitute a major strike against the theory. Since I argue that massively shared agency offers important conceptual and normative resources for evaluating durable solutions and refugees' roles within them, it is important to determine whether Shapiro's criteria are sufficient to avoid this sort of worry. It is important to keep in mind, however, that the notion of durable solutions is not necessarily incompatible with coercion. For instance, Skran (1995, 146, my emphasis) speaks of the "uncoerced return of refugees back to their country of origin as the *most desirable* durable solution" though not the only kind.

11. Two qualifications are in order here. First, G specifies the class of members specifically intended to fulfill the plan. It includes Soviet refugees, but it also includes members of the Stalin regime, among others. I highlight the returnees since they are the focal point for the discussion and because, in this case, the majority of participants were returnees. Second, that the plan was made in part "for" Soviet returnees does not mean "in the interests of," where "interest" specifies the returnees' actual preferences. For a related discussion, see Shapiro (2014, 281–83, 283n40). My thanks to Dom Taylor for pressing me to clarify these points.

12. This is not to downplay or to overlook the period prior to the resettlement, which was characterized by extreme violence, persecution, and hostility between Greece and Turkey (Mourelos 1985, 391; Kontogiorgi 2006, chaps. 1 and 2; Barut-

ciski 2008: 27). The 1923 Greek-Turkish exchange was itself a compulsory exchange (Mourelos 1985, 410) that initially generated great hostility between new arrivals and native inhabitants (Kontogiorgi 2006, 167). On the history of the concept of population transfer as well as the influence of the Treaty of Lausanne on British European and Middle Eastern minority policy before World War II, see Frank (2008, chap. 1).

13. I owe this formulation to a principle of organization central to associational democracy articulated in Hirst (1994, 20).

4

Transformative Justice and Legal Conscientization

Refugee Participation in Peace Processes, Repatriation, and Reconciliation

Anna Purkey

This chapter is based on research I conducted on the nature of participation of refugee communities from Myanmar in the cease-fire, peace, and repatriation negotiations occurring within Myanmar. Although there is reason for cautious hope, the transition to peace and democracy is marred by a legacy of human rights violations, distrust, and decades of conflict under military dictatorship. One shortcoming of the current peace and reconciliation mechanisms that has the potential to obstruct the sustainable resolution of conflict is the failure of the Myanmar government, ethnic armed groups, and international actors to engage in a meaningful way with the refugee populations in neighboring countries. This is not merely an oversight in an extremely complex multiparty situation; the failure to include refugees in the resolution of conflict or to fully consider their interests is endemic.

Accordingly, this chapter offers a normative analysis of a complex problem that is reproduced in conflict situations around the world. I propose that the resolution of both conflict and displacement require the full and meaningful participation of refugee communities in a process of transformative justice. Without such engagement, voluntary return, reconciliation, and lasting peace are unlikely. Indeed, it is well-acknowledged now that the resolution of conflict and displacement are two parts of the same process (UNSG 2011; Deschamp and Lohse 2013). To achieve this resolution, the focus should not be simply on the mechanics of participation but also on the development of capabilities, capacities, resources, and human capital, which are vital to ensuring effective refugee engagement. In short, the emphasis needs to be on the empowerment of refugees and refugee communities, a process and outcome that is intimately linked to an individual's agency and dignity and to her ability to act as an agent of her own destiny, to take action and achieve desired ends (see Narayan 2002, vi; Alsop, Bertelsen, and Holland 2006, 1; Sengupta 2008, 31–32).

Peace negotiations and the associated discussions of transitional justice frequently focus on the product: What will a final peace look like? How will power be divided between different groups? Which transitional justice mechanisms will be implemented? While these questions must eventually be answered, an emphasis on outcome may overshadow an equally important discussion of process. The nature of the state that emerges from conflict is defined both by the terms of peace agreements and by the process by which those terms were decided on. While the participation of refugees is no guarantee of a successful peace, an inclusive peace cannot be achieved unless the process of defining and building that peace is also inclusive, and the frequent exclusion of refugees from the process of peacemaking severely decreases the likelihood that the outcome of a peace process will adequately address the needs or consider the interests of displaced populations.

The purpose of this chapter, then, is to critically analyze the need for, and conditions under which, active refugee engagement in the resolution of conflict and displacement can be successful through the examination of three concepts: transformative justice, participation, and legal conscientization and empowerment. Using examples from Myanmar and other post-conflict situations, I argue that a sustainable resolution to displacement and conflict might best be achieved by espousing a transformative justice paradigm in which transformative justice is understood as a process of challenging and transforming the structures, institutions, and power relationships that caused conflict through engagement with the legal, political, economic, and psychosocial dimensions of justice (Lambourne 2009, 28; Haider 2014, 207). Adopting a transformative, rather than transitional, justice approach more fully acknowledges that peace, repatriation, and reconciliation are dependent on a fundamental transformation of relationships that addresses both overt physical violence as well as the structural violence at the root of conflict. Following a brief discussion of methodology, I explore the importance of refugee participation both in terms of the outcomes of the peace process and in terms of redefining the relationship between returning populations and the state. I then examine the role of legal conscientization, the process through which individuals develop a critical legal consciousness and learn to perceive and take actions against their own structural conditions of oppression (see Freire 1970, 17) as an initial stage of the empowerment process and a precondition to ensuring effective participation in transformative justice during peace negotiations, returns, and reconciliation.[1]

Methodology

This chapter's argument is not so much empirical assertions as proposals based on a review of current scholarship and supported by examples from different conflict situations. One of the challenges in attempting to draw normative conclusions regarding a wide range of cases is that while situations may share certain general characteristics, each situation is unique. My aim, therefore, is not to identify concrete solutions that are applicable in all situations but to reveal the critical questions that must be asked and answered in each situation and to construct a conceptual framework that can inform specific instances of conflict and displacement.

Why focus on refugees? Other groups, including internally displaced persons, have also suffered greatly and may need the type of reconciliation, conscientization, and legal empowerment discussed below. The emphasis on refugees is not intended to deny the harm suffered by other groups but to recognize refugees' unique situation. Having lived in exile for years, refugees have suffered perhaps the most complete break with the state of origin, so the process of reintegration and reconciliation is at its most complex. At the same time, refugee communities offer a unique entry point for the type of institutional change that is proposed in this discussion. Exile is frequently highly disempowering; nevertheless, refugee situations present possibilities for innovation and development. Refugee communities are often communities in a state of flux in which hierarchies, values, and traditions, including gender roles, are tested and challenged. Marginalized groups may find themselves with access to positions of power within community governance. Training and capacity-building initiatives instigated by aid providers may open doors to further education and alternative vocations as well as foster the acquisition of new skills and knowledge that can be employed in exile and during the negotiations and process of return and reintegration. In short, despite its incredible hardships, displacement also has the potential to create a space for innovation and a unique entry point for refugees to act as agents of change.

Background

At the core of this discussion lie several hard truths. First, over 40 percent of postconflict societies return to conflict within five years of the initial resolution; this underscores the challenge of achieving a sustainable peace despite interventions intended to consolidate peace (see Lundy and McGovern 2008b). Second, displacement levels are at their highest since World War II (UNHCR 2016b, 5). Third, despite the critical links between displacement and conflict, displaced persons have had little involvement in peace negotiations or transitional justice initiatives. Similarly, transitional justice mechanisms and peace processes have not traditionally engaged in depth with refugees' concerns (see Campbell 2012, 65–67). The absence of refugee engagement in transitional justice and conflict resolution runs counter to the view that the inherent dignity of the individual requires that each person be able to make and realize choices regarding her own life. It is also in opposition to the view of the UN secretary-general's office on the importance of public and victim participation in transitional justice (UNSCOR 2004).

The absence of the rule of law and the absence of civic trust (see UNSCOR 2004) stand out as recurring obstacles to democratic reform and sustainable peace, including reconciliation and the resolution of displacement. According to the UN secretary-general, the rule of law refers to "a principle of governance in which all persons, institutions and entities, public and private, including the State itself, are accountable to laws that are publicly promulgated, equally enforced and independently adjudicated, and which are consistent with international human rights norms and standards" (UNSCOR 2004, 4). The absence of the rule of law entails not merely the lack of an independent, functioning judicial system but the breakdown of legal institutions of the state and of the law itself and the entrenchment of impunity. Reform of these structures is a key component of peace agreements and reconciliation, while the reestablishment of the rule of law is "regarded as a prerequisite for the emergence of stable and peaceful societies" (Lundy and McGovern 2008b, 266). Reestablishing the rule of law and using the law to restore social norms is of heightened importance in postconflict contexts because the law is often used to subvert the orderly functioning of society and to initiate and perpetuate conflict and atrocities (Fletcher and Weinstein 2002).

Civic trust pertains to the expectation of certain patterns of behavior based on shared normative commitments between members and different segments of a society and between the civilian population and the state and its institutions (de Greiff 2013, 18). A collapse of civic trust involves a breakdown of the constitutive norms of a society or institution and affects not only direct interaction with the state or an institution but also society as a whole by undermining the very threads that bind a community together. Understandably, then, one of the primary objectives of transitional justice is to foster civic trust through strategies such as acknowledgment of the injustices suffered, recognition of individuals as rights bearers, creating a shared narrative, and ensuring accountability (de Greiff 2013).

While conflict generally results in a fracturing of civic trust, refugees arguably suffer a particularly grievous breach in this regard. Civic trust must begin to be rebuilt in order to facilitate refugees rejoining the political community of the state and re-availing themselves of the protection of the state and their rights as citizens (Duthie 2012a, 37). In the case of refugees from Myanmar, the absence of civic trust between the people and the state is a deeply rooted legacy of decades of conflict, bred by discriminatory and abusive legislation, government implementation of divide-and-conquer strategies, human rights violations, and lack of transparency and accountability. In the context of the resolution of a conflict, trust can be further eroded by the failure of power holders to adequately engage and consult with their constituencies, including refugees (Hargrave 2015, 95). In Myanmar, this lack of engagement has been of particular concern for refugee communities that have not only been excluded from the peace process but have largely been excluded from discussions of their own repatriation and reintegration as well (Burma Partnership and Burma Link 2015). While distrust of the state and its institutions may be a rational response in many postconflict situations, without some degree of trust and some level of consensus on shared normative commitments, there is no stable foundation on which to build peace and effect meaningful change (Hargrave 2014; 2015, 95).

Transformative Justice

Too often peace is understood as an end point, reduced to a simple absence of direct physical violence. This oversimplification may lead to an incomplete peace that in turn increases the likelihood of a return to violence. A peace that is truly sustainable must be a positive peace that goes beyond the absence of physical violence and eliminates structural violence and other forms of injustice. For this reason, it is critical to understand the resolution of displacement as an integral part of any peace process. The various dimensions of conflict resolution may be discussed in different forums but need to be understood as part of a single process. Thus, when discussing refugee participation in the following sections, I am concerned with refugee participation not only in resolving displacement but also in resolving the root causes of conflict.

Although discussions of transitional justice have frequently advocated a comprehensive, empowering, and flexible approach, transitional justice has been historically associated with a hegemonic liberal democratic paradigm that views negative peace and Western-style liberal market democracy as the desired end point (Lundy and McGovern 2008a, 99; Gready and Robins 2014, 339). Transitional justice initiatives have tended to be state-centric and dominated by elite international experts and donors and have often adopted a relatively orthodox and narrow approach to justice and the rule of law, emphasizing the role and reform of formal legal institutions over alternative, grassroots forms of justice (Gready and Robins 2014, 339). Under this formal conception, transitional justice initiatives often overlook the reality that liberal democratization on its own will not necessarily result in conditions that are conducive to lasting peace or reconciliation and the repatriation and reintegration of displaced populations (Sharp 2011–12, 780). Moreover, transitional justice is predominantly backward looking, seeking to remedy specific violations, provide accountability, and address institutional shortcomings. Although necessary, this form of reactive justice only addresses part of the problem; what is needed is a more forward-looking, proactive approach.

In contrast, a transformative justice approach is better able to conceptualize and address the root causes of protracted conflict by acknowledging the relationship between structural violence and the direct or physical violence that is often a concrete manifestation of social inequalities (Gready et al. 2010). Whereas transitional justice can be seen as a means to an end, transformative justice is an ongoing, forward-looking, long-term process that seeks to establish conditions under which justice and positive peace can be achieved and sustained (Lambourne 2009, 28). To achieve this transformation, this approach emphasizes local agency and empowerment and requires that the multiple justice needs of populations be recognized and addressed through mechanisms that are informed by local contexts and that coexist alongside the dominant Western worldview (Lambourne 2009, 28; Gready and Robins 2014, 339).

The choice of a transformative justice framework is not intended to deny the potential utility of formal transitional justice mechanisms such as truth commissions or criminal prosecutions. Instead this choice highlights that a sustainable peace that permits the return and reintegration of refugee communities requires radical transformation of relationships and power dynamics and is far more than simply a transition from one system of governance to another. In practice, many transitional justice initiatives do have a strong transformative component; thus, some transitional justice scholars and practitioners might contest this distinction. Indeed, in many cases what has long been referred to as transitional justice may in fact possess all the characteristics of transformative justice-making, thus blurring the distinction between transitional and transformative justice (see Haider 2014; Lambourne 2009). Nevertheless, by choosing to speak of transformative as opposed to transitional justice, I seek to shift focus, broaden the scope of inquiry, and recognize the weaknesses of a traditional understanding of transitional justice without dismissing the lessons that can be learned from initiatives that took place within that framework. Above all, this distinction underscores both the need for transformation in the postconflict context as well as the transformative potential of justice and justice mechanisms understood broadly.

By prioritizing the local and acknowledging the indivisibility of human rights (civil and political as well as economic and social), transformative justice is better suited than formal transitional justice to address the dominant concerns of refugees. In studies of refugee populations, several issues have repeatedly emerged as obstacles to a voluntary and just return (Burma Partnership and Burma Link 2015; Duthie 2012a, 41). First and foremost is the fear of insecurity and the lack of confidence among refugees in the ability (or will) of the state to guarantee their basic security and rights. Tied to this lack of confidence is concern regarding the absence of accountability or acknowledgment of past abuses, the violation of rights, and the violence and harm suffered, which in turn fosters a lack of trust in the government and the peace process itself. Another major concern pertains to socioeconomic security and includes the limited availability of livelihood opportunities, land tenure insecurity, and the absence or lack of access to social and other services (see, e.g., Kurze, Lamont, and Robins 2015, 260; Bradley 2012, 189; McCallin 2012).

At the heart of these legitimate concerns are two clear themes: the ongoing socioeconomic impacts of structural violence and the caustic relationship between refugee communities and the government. Indeed, as socioeconomic violence is often used as a deliberate strategy against civilian populations during conflict, the process of establishing peace and achieving justice needs to be able to directly address this type of violence in a way that formal or traditional transitional justice mechanisms are ill equipped to do. Similarly, perhaps more than any other group, refugees have suffered a dramatic break in their relationship with the state and a particularly profound violation of civic trust. Not only did the state fail to protect and ensure the rights of these citizens but, in perhaps the ultimate breach of civic trust, it also may have been directly responsible for the violations that forced them to flee. The relationship between the state and the refugee population may be further undermined by the fact that many refugees have a fractured legal relationship with the state. It is largely unthinkable, then, that there will be any real peace, not to mention any widespread voluntary refugee return, until the socioeconomic concerns of refugees have been at least partly addressed. What a transformative justice approach calls for is not a return to the preconflict reality but a fundamental transformation of relationships and institutional structures that enables confrontation of the dominant narratives of the past and can establish the conditions for a sustainable peace.

Refugee Participation in Peace and Repatriation Negotiations

In seeking to achieve lasting peace, an integrated approach to the resolution of conflict is necessary, specifically one that addresses the resolution of displacement as being inseparable from issues of security, economic reform, reestablishment of the rule of law, and so on. Consequently, it is critical that individuals who have been subject to displacement have standing to assert their rights, voice their claims, and pursue their interests within this process. Universal principles of human rights affirm that individuals should have a degree of control over the decisions that affect their lives; this is the essence of human dignity (Lundy and McGovern 2008a, 99). This broad engagement is not only a moral or ethical requirement; it may also be a means of achieving a better and more sustainable peace by helping to identify and address local needs and interests and to more fully take advantage of local capacities.

As discussed above, despite acknowledgment and optimism that increased participation and engagement of all stakeholders, including refugees, is likely to yield more positive outcomes in terms of peace and justice, refugee participation in peace processes has been very limited, and the concerns of displaced populations remain sidelined. Take once again the ongoing peace process in Myanmar. Even though displacement of civilian populations was a deliberate strategy used by the military, there has been virtually no effort made by the government to ensure the participation of refugees in the peace process generally or in discussions concerning repatriation. With few exceptions, conflict-affected communities have been largely excluded from participating in the cease-fire negotiations (see, e.g., Burma Partnership and Burma Link 2015; South and Jolliffe 2015; KCBO 2012). While most refugees are members of ethnic groups that are represented by ethnic armed groups at the peace negotiations, refugees have different experiences of conflict, capacities, interests, and needs, and it cannot be assumed that representatives of the ethnic minorities represent the specific interests of the refugee populations (Petrie and South 2013).

The failure to facilitate the meaningful participation of refugee communities in the discussion of repatriation is especially problematic. What little participation there has been has largely been limited to the presence of representatives from the refugee camp governing committees at some meetings as well as some nominal consultation, including through a survey of refugee opinions concerning repatriation that was conducted by the United Nations High Commissioner for Refugees (UNHCR) and the Mae Fah Luang Foundation in the refugee camps along the Thai border (UNHCR and MFLF 2014). Despite these few initiatives, the general perception in the refugee community is that their voices and perspectives have been largely absent from the official processes and that there are few opportunities for participation (Burma Partnership and Burma Link 2015; Petrie and South 2013). In this vein, it is interesting to note that a group of community-based organizations from the Karen ethnic group in Myanmar released a statement in 2012 specifically explaining that they were choosing to use the word "return" as opposed to "repatriation" because when translated into the Karen language, "repatriation" is a very passive term that implies a lack of participation, while "return" refers to a process that includes "full participation in the decision-making process at all stages of the return process, through [their] own decisions and willingness" (KCBO 2012, 1).

Although the exact dynamics of each situation are determined by the individual circumstances in play, the exclusion of the Burmese refugees is not exceptional. Even when refugee participation is solicited, it is usually through very "thin" forms of engagement limited to the provision of information to refugee communities and the gathering of their opinions, without any indication of the extent to which these will guide decision-making. For instance, refugee views were specifically sought by transitional justice mechanisms in situations such as Afghanistan, Guatemala, and Sierra Leone (see Duthie 2012a, 10; AIHRC 2005, 50). By imposing a veneer of legitimacy, this type of token participation risks turning refugees into mere instruments in the state's consolidation of power (Taylor 2014).

The exclusion of refugees from peace and repatriation negotiations or the adoption of these nominal forms of participation is symptomatic of a general ambivalence toward meaningful refugee and civil society engagement on the part of states (McConnachie 2014, 161). The language of participation, self-sufficiency, and voluntariness is used in formal policies and public statements concerning refugees, but the true content of these concepts is rarely fully embraced in practice, to the great frustration of refugee stakeholders. This raises substantial concerns about the extent to which peace and repatriation negotiations are actually able to respond to the needs and interests of refugees and thus foster a durable end to displacement.

Transformative Participation

Where transitional justice mechanisms have been criticized for being elite-driven and adopting only nominal forms of participation, substantive engagement of all stakeholders is at the very core of transformative justice (Gready and Robins 2014; Lambourne 2009). Indeed, "peacebuilding and transitional justice [only] become transformative when they emphasise the principles of local participation and empowerment" and when they take into consideration the context as well as the needs, expectations, and experiences of all parties (Lambourne 2009, 28). As Paul Gready and Simon Robins note, "transformative justice requires a radical rethinking of participation in transitional justice interventions" (2014, 358). Transformative participation ultimately seeks not only better outcomes from the transitional justice and peace processes but also transformation of the individuals involved in the process, their situation (whether through the development of skills, the expansion of their views and understanding of conflict, organization around issues of concern, or the adoption of strategies to address socioeconomic injustice), and ultimately the relationships and conditions that act to instigate and enable conflict (Gready and Robins 2014). This process of transformation is ultimately a process of empowerment that supports the agency of individuals in challenging existing power structures and reveals and defines new roles for civil society members, individuals, and external actors. Transformative justice is not merely intended to reach a specific end point in the form of a signed peace treaty or a certain number of criminal prosecutions but to "unleash transformative dynamics" that will have a long-lasting effect on the society being rebuilt and to contribute to establishing conditions that will sustain peace over time (Gready and Robins 2014, 359).

At a concrete level, participation in transformative justice needs to be broad, deep, and comprehensive. Broad participation includes all important stakeholders and is not limited to certain elite actors. In the refugee context, this would mean that participation in peace processes and the negotiation of return and reintegration should not be restricted to the elite but should include representation from refugee communities, women, religious minorities, youth, victims' groups, and other civil society or community-based organizations. Deep participation is more than just nominal or passive participation; it is participation that is linked to substantive decision-making that enables stakeholders to have a degree of control over their lives and the decisions that affect them.[2] This does not mean that lesser forms of participation such as the provision of information to refugee communities or the implementation of opinion surveys cannot also be valuable tools, but these lesser forms of participation have little transformative impact on participants in terms of their agency, empowerment, or value and identity formation (Drydyk 2005, 260). In this context, transformative participation supports or enables individuals and groups to exercise their agency to challenge existing and oppressive power relations (Gready and Robins 2014). Transformative participation enables individuals to develop what Gready and Robins refer to as "civic competence," or the ability to advocate for justice and to contest marginalization (2014, 359). Finally, comprehensive participation is inclusive and transparent about whose voices are being heard and involves engagement at all stages of the justice "project cycle," including in the choice, design, implementation, and evaluation of transformative justice strategies (Gready and Robins 2014, 358; see also Carmona and Donald 2015; Lundy and McGovern 2008b). While justice processes that involve this level of participation are far more challenging than the top-down justice that occurs in most situations, the result is a more durable and just peace.

Transformative Participation and Trust Building

Participation in a transformative justice approach to the resolution of conflict and displacement has the potential to help address many obstacles to peace, reconciliation, and repatriation, including the absence of civic trust and rule of law. To start, transformative participation is itself a process of trust building. Civic trust and respect are forms of social capital that can be fostered through interaction and voluntary cooperation in transformative justice processes. Positive interactions that occur through participation in a transformative justice approach can help to provide a basis for future trust in the government, the community of citizens, and the peace process itself, which in turn is necessary for real justice, peace, and reconciliation. In the words of Daniel Posner, "Trust and norms of reciprocity are formed as a positive externality of collective activities undertaken for other purposes" (2004, 242). Thus, the very process of refugee participation in peace and repatriation negotiations has the potential to have a positive impact on the relationship between refugees and the state of origin.

Laurel Fletcher and Harvey Weinstein (2002) note that one of the principal effects of widespread violence and conflict is the powerlessness experienced by communities. Engaging individuals and groups in the process of rebuilding the state and the community may help to promote the agency of those groups, strengthen the community, and restore some degree of the trust that was undermined by conflict.

Conversely, the failure to allow refugee participation in the peacebuilding and repatriation processes has the potential to reinforce distrust and feelings of powerlessness and may even raise fundamental questions about the legitimacy of the processes (Burma Partnership and Burma Link 2015; Lundy and McGovern 2008b). Likewise, limiting participation in resolution processes to certain individuals, groups, or types of individuals may reinforce and strengthen existing divisions within society, including those that contribute to the outbreak and continuation of conflict. The failure to engage refugee communities meaningfully in the peace processes may leave these communities with the impression that peace initiatives are not being carried out in good faith, thus undermining the objective of rebuilding civic trust and creating the potential for either a lack of cooperation in repatriation and reconciliation initiatives or even a backlash against them.[3]

Refugee participation in transformative justice also has the potential to change the very structures and institutions of governance. As noted above, transformative change of individuals, relationships, and social structures is at the very heart of transformative justice. Transformative justice approaches are compelling specifically because lasting peace requires sweeping changes in the conditions that initiated and perpetuated conflict. Effective participation in transformative justice is critical because it has the potential to be emancipatory; through participation in transformative justice, marginalized groups become able to "challenge, access and shape institutions and structures from which they were previously excluded" (Gready and Robins 2014, 358). The collaborative potential, reciprocity, and civic or political trust that results from meaningful participation in transformative justice can fundamentally change the relationships between stakeholders and the patterns of local governance. Transformative justice is a process of bottom–up social and political transition and conflict resolution. It is through this type of change that the principle of the rule of law can begin to take root and find support.

Legal Conscientization and Empowerment

Séverine Deneulin (2009, 202) writes, "Full political participation entails not only including everyone in a discussion but ensuring that every person included is equipped with an adequate level of political functioning and adequate cognitive and communications skills to advance her claims." If refugees have a right to meaningful participation in transformative justice, which may positively affect conflict resolution processes and outcomes, concerted efforts need to be made to facilitate that engagement. Transformative justice seeks to transform inequitable power relationships and the participants themselves by adopting a much more expansive understanding of the justice requirements of lasting peace than what is typically associated with transitional justice. As such, a transformative justice approach is intrinsically linked to the ideas and processes of legal conscientization and legal empowerment. On the one hand, participation in transformative justice is a key means through which empowerment, generally, and legal empowerment, specifically, can be achieved. On the other hand, the ability of individuals and groups, including refugees, to engage in transformative justice depends on their capabilities and resources, their agency, and the opportunity structure. These capacities and opportunities can be achieved through legal conscientization and empowerment.

The starting point of effective participation is knowledge, both of transformative justice processes and of the power dynamics and realities within refugee and host communities and the state of origin (Bradley 2012, 189). Within Myanmar, a strong willingness and desire to participate in the peace process is being undermined by an inability of many individuals to envision how that participation could occur as well as a lack of understanding of what the process of reconciliation might even entail (see Jones 2014; HURFOM 2014; ICTJ 2014). Absent human rights education and training, information sharing, and even the experience of living under a functioning justice system, it is unsurprising that ensuring the active engagement of marginalized communities within the state of origin may be challenging.

By contrast, refugees may have greater potential than those who remain within the state of origin to act as agents of change, as exile may offer an important opportunity or entry point for capacity building, which could facilitate participation in transformative justice. In turn, the participation of refugee communities, enhanced by training and education received in exile, can potentially act as a precipitating factor for more widespread change within domestic civil society and governance institutions. In Sierra Leone, for example, UNHCR notes that it "has, in fact, been repeatedly observed that education, training and capacity building programmes administered in refugee camps can play a crucial role in preparing the ground for successful reintegration and community empowerment after repatriation" (Sperl and DeVriese 2005, 48). UNHCR found that the most successful committees involved in community empowerment projects are staffed by individuals who have received training or worked with nongovernmental organizations in refugee camps (Sperl and DeVriese 2005, 47). This potential was also noted by the Burma Lawyers' Council, which suggests that if refugee communities become accustomed to living in a society based on the rule of law in exile, their return to Myanmar would potentially help to promote human rights and foster peace and stability in their country of origin (Burma Lawyers' Council 2007, 40). Indeed, the International Center for Transitional Justice has stated that "even in a sustained culture of impunity, important preparations can be undertaken so that when the opportunity for justice arrives the necessary records are available to appropriately recognize victims and their families, and to hold those most responsible accountable" (ICTJ 2009).

The desire to participate in transformative justice initiatives and in the process of negotiating peace, repatriation, and reconciliation necessitate some degree of critical consciousness even before concrete skill development and training. This is where the concepts of legal conscientization and legal empowerment enter into play.

The way in which power is manifested, exercised, and possessed is not always obvious (see Rowlands 1997). In exile, refugees are subject to numerous sources of direct or overt power, including the host state, the state of origin, UNHCR, aid organizations, and camp authorities. But more subtle and insidious forms of power also exert considerable control over refugees. As Steven Lukes asserts, "The most effective and insidious use of power is to prevent . . . conflict arising in the first place . . . by shaping [people's] perceptions, cognitions and preferences in such a way that they accept their role in the existing order of things, either because they can see or imagine no alternative to it, or because they see it as natural and unchangeable" (1974, 23).

This more subversive exercise of power can be seen in situations where individuals have consistently been denied access to power and influence in society. In many such cases, individuals internalize the messages they receive from powerful actors about what their interests are and what they are meant to be and do, either out of habit or as a survival mechanism (Rowlands 1997). Referred to as "internalized oppression," this dynamic can be found in refugee camps and communities (Harrell-Bond 2002). Portraying refugees as helpless, vulnerable victims with little agency of their own, as is often done, can have a very negative impact on their self-perception as well as their capabilities. If the "good" refugee, the one that will receive assistance, is passive and vulnerable, individuals may adopt this role in order to ingratiate themselves to the authorities and facilitate their survival or may actually internalize this perception of themselves (Harrell-Bond 2002, 58; see also Hyndman 1996).

Faced with the hardships associated with displacement, the need for empowerment-based strategies is evident. Although there is no single satisfactory definition of empowerment, it may be understood as both a process and an outcome that is intimately linked to an individual's agency and dignity. The process of empowerment involves expanding the knowledge and capabilities of individuals to make purposive choices and transform those choices into desired actions and outcomes (see Narayan 2002, vi; Alsop, Bertelsen, and Holland 2006, 1; Sengupta 2008, 32). Albert Breton and Margot Breton describe the passage from disempowerment to empowerment as involving three essential steps: (1) changing one's views of self and the world, (2) taking action to change one's situation, and (3) provoking a political response that ensures the desired change in the situation (1997, 176). The first stage is the one that is most closely associated with the idea of conscientization.

The concept of conscientization was developed by Paulo Freire as an approach to pedagogy and refers to "learning to perceive social, political, and economic contradictions, and to take action against the oppressive elements of reality" (1970, 17). In other words, conscientization is "a critical state of consciousness rooted in popular experience and people's knowledge of their own structural conditions of oppression" (Lundy and McGovern 2008a, 108). At its core, it is a transformative process of reflective reevaluation of knowledge and experience through which individuals are awakened to the realities of their own oppression and spurred to action. Initially, marginalized or oppressed individuals, including some refugees, may not identify themselves as disempowered or be aware of how social and political structures affect not only their individual situation but also that of broader groups (Breton and Breton 1997; Hur 2006). It is through a process of conscientization that individuals begin to create a new identity for themselves and recognize, in dialogue with others, the interconnectedness of their personal situations and the broader patterns of oppression instigated or sustained by the socioeconomic, political, cultural, and legal conditions of society (Breton and Breton 1997; Hur 2006). For conscientization to live up to its full potential and to be consistent with Freire's belief that the liberation of human beings is a praxis that involves both reflection and action, this new self-perception and collective consciousness must not be understood merely as a process of "cognitive restructuring" but as the foundation and the trigger for politicized action (Rozario 1997, 45; Walker 2009). It is only at that stage that the development of capabilities, training, skills, and the concerted organization recognized as empowerment truly begins.

There is no question that refugees possess important knowledge about the causes of conflict, the violations that occurred, and their own needs and interests in the context of repatriation and reconciliation; through conscientization this knowledge and information is brought to the fore, and then, by increasing refugees' capacity to access and use the law and legal mechanisms, legal empowerment strategies can help refugees express and translate that knowledge into action—in other words, act as self-determining agents. To this end, in refugee contexts, conscientization seeks to combat internalized oppression by fostering an awareness of oneself as an agent capable of effecting change and a member of a community with legitimate needs and interests. For refugee communities, conscientization also involves developing and articulating a more comprehensive understanding of both the proximate and ultimate causes of oppression and displacement. For many refugees, the proximate cause of their own displacement may be conflict and impoverishment. The ultimate causes of displacement and oppression, however, are much more complex and may pertain to factors including historical prejudices and discrimination, abusive government laws and policies, global political and economic factors, and the absence of accountability mechanisms. Today, with few exceptions, refugees are not persecuted individuals but members of afflicted groups; thus, the resolution of displacement requires broader understanding of where each individual stands in relation to others and understanding that oppression is rarely suffered individually but is instead part of established patterns of human interaction.

Legal conscientization is a subset of conscientization that focuses on the law and legal mechanisms and institutions understood broadly.[4] It is a process of coming to know how the law affects one's life and the role that law and legal institutions play as mechanisms of oppression as well as potential tools for change. The development of this deeper form of legal awareness is a critical step to effectively participating in transformative justice. For refugees, legal conscientization means developing or sharpening an awareness of themselves as legal subjects and actors capable of effecting change as well as an understanding of the role that the absence of the rule of law has played in instigating and perpetuating conflict, the abusive nature of many laws and policies, and the way these laws and policies contributed to the socioeconomic and political conditions that sustained conflict and resulted in forced displacement. Legal conscientization can also include the process through which refugees become able to conceptualize and understand some of their problems and the hardships they face as legal issues, for instance, as a violation of legal rights (UNDP 2005). In the postconflict stage, the legal conscientization of refugees also means developing an understanding of the mechanisms and potential outcomes, both legal and otherwise, of transformative justice and the rights and freedoms to which they, as refugees and citizens, are entitled. Equally important, just as Freire's definition of conscientization includes the process of learning "to take action against the oppressive elements of reality" (1970, 17), the legal conscientization of refugees involves developing strategies to use the law and legal mechanisms and institutions to effect substantive change and resist the structural oppression to which they are subject.

How might legal conscientization occur in refugee contexts? Freire rejects the "banking" concept of education whereby students are viewed simply as empty, ignorant receptacles to be filled with information by those considered to be more knowledgeable. This is largely what happens when external or foreign legal experts drop into a refugee community in order to impose legal reform, train leaders, and provide education to the community. While these initiatives may succeed in imposing a veneer of change, one must question to what extent the information and the values and judgments that underpin that information are internalized by the refugee community. However well-intentioned, aid providers and external experts are part of the hierarchies of power and may contribute to the structures of (potential) oppression and disempowerment to which refugees are subject. Thus, according to Freire's theory, liberation or humanization cannot come through them (see Meyer 2006), or at least not through them alone.

Conscientization is largely an internal process that comes from within the individual and the community through active dialogue and direct engagement with the realities of one's own life (Walker 2009). It is through narrating their own stories and listening to others that individuals discover or hone their voices and the claims they wish to raise; they begin to "name the world" (Freire 1970, 88; see also Breton and Breton 1997, 183). Nevertheless, it is not realistic to assume that the process of conscientization and legal conscientization will occur without any external engagement. The law, even at its most informal, does involve a specialized body of knowledge that members of oppressed groups may or may not possess on their own. Thus, there is a role for legal experts and educators to play in the conscientization of refugee communities. The key, however, is that the entire process must still be driven from within the community, not imposed externally. External actors may act as resources, as repositories of knowledge, and potentially even as facilitators who can help refugees navigate the legal world, but conscientization itself occurs only through the direct engagement of individuals in a critical, dialogical praxis through which they begin to reimagine their own identities and reconstruct their perception of the world.

Legal conscientization is an ongoing process that continues so long as reflection and dialogue persist and new information is acquired and revealed. Nevertheless, the praxis that is a key component of conscientization almost inevitably leads to a broader process of legal empowerment involving activities such as organizing group action and capacity building. Legal empowerment can be defined as "the process through which refugees and refugee populations become able to use the law and legal mechanisms and services understood broadly to protect and advance all of their rights and to acquire greater control over their lives, as well as the actual achievement of that increased control" (Purkey 2015, 134). On a concrete level, legal empowerment is a bottom-up approach focusing on the needs of marginalized groups, rather than elite actors, that adopt and adapt predominantly (but not exclusively) legal tools including legal literacy initiatives, legal services provision, alternative dispute resolution strategies, and law and institutional reform initiatives (Waldorf 2013).[5] In short, legal empowerment seeks to realize legal conscientization by developing the agency, knowledge, skills, and capacities to enable individuals and groups to act and, thus, to effectively participate in transformative justice.

In the case of refugees from Myanmar in Thailand, it is possible to identify several domains in which legal conscientization and empowerment are necessary but lacking as well as several strategies that have been implemented. Although not couched in the language of legal empowerment, the most substantial initiative has been the Legal Assistance Centre (LAC) established in the camps by the International Rescue Committee. While they have been largely focused on life in the camps, these centers have provided both information and skills that are critical to the development of an empowered community. In particular, the Legal Assistance Centre has run an assortment of public legal education meetings to inform the refugee community of their rights under Thai law and under international refugee law and to familiarize them with the justice mechanisms at their disposal. The Legal Assistance Centre has also been involved in training decision makers and community leaders and in educating members of the refugee community to act as paralegals, community educators, and monitors of the justice system.[6] The justice-related activities of the many civil society organizations in the refugee camps and along (and over) the border also have a legal conscientization effect and may have an impact in terms of the potential for reconciliation and return. For instance, several civil society organizations, including the Karen Human Rights Group and the Network for Human Rights Documentation–Burma, have engaged in documentation processes in order to create a detailed record of the abuses committed by the government during the civil wars. In contrast, the International Center for Transitional Justice has found that decades of military dictatorship and repression have meant that within Myanmar "a rights-based discourse requiring accountability for systematic abuse is not fully formed in Burmese civil society" (ICTJ 2014, 15). As a final example, understanding that their decision to return to Myanmar must be truly voluntary—in other words, free and informed—has helped refugees resist pressure imposed by the Thai government, the Burmese government, and ethnic armed groups and to protest certain moves (like the selection of return locations without consultation) by the international aid providers (see Jolliffe 2012). Similarly, refugees could make more informed decisions and increase their understanding of the political and legal realities of transition by gaining an understanding of the existence and nature of immunity provisions, land tenure laws, human rights guarantees, and the presence or lack of accountability mechanisms through community legal education and information campaigns.

While a full analysis of legal empowerment in the refugee context is beyond the scope of this chapter, the purpose here is to draw attention to the initial stage of legal conscientization, which is often overlooked. Conscientization provides the foundation for transformative change and for empowerment to take root and develop organically, fundamentally changing or seeking to change perceptions, values, and power structures. Without that solid base, legal empowerment initiatives risk being merely another set of externally imposed activities that serve to occupy time and bring about superficial changes without any real transformation.

Conclusion

Does this focus on legal conscientization and legal empowerment place too great an emphasis on the law or ask too much of the law? Just as economists are inclined to seek solutions in economics and the free market, lawyers are often inclined to view the law as one of the highest forms of social ordering; yet anyone who has interacted with a legal system will understand that there is a definite distinction between the law (even loosely defined) and justice. In fact, it is for this very reason that the law and, thus, legal conscientization and legal empowerment are so important. Understanding the law and one's interactions with it is critical because the law is one of the most legitimate forms of ordering power within society today and because the law can so easily switch from being an instrument of empowerment to one of oppression. Legal conscientization and legal empowerment contain an inherent normative assumption that the law *can* be empowering even if it isn't necessarily so in a certain situation. It is true that legal strategies have historically tended to serve the interests of the elite and often employ specialized or technical discourse that is inaccessible to many, including the disempowered; therefore, law has the potential to reinforce power structures within a society that place elites and experts in positions of authority (Kurze, Lamont, and Robins 2015). Nevertheless, adopting a broad understanding of the law, of the growing field of study pertaining to legal empowerment and the grassroots use of the law, and of the concept of legal conscientization that is inherent in these movements has helped to identify strategies and mechanisms through which individuals and groups can counter this imbalance and usurp the power of the law.

That is not to say that success is easy or always ensured. One has only to look at the situation of refugees from Myanmar, where—despite having developed a strong, organized, and knowledgeable community with a vibrant and active civil society—refugees in Thailand have remained excluded from the official process of negotiating peace and repatriation. Nevertheless, the very fact that some of the community-based organizations in the refugee camps have contested this lack of engagement suggests that there is a critical awareness of their right to be agents of their own destiny (see Burma Partnership 2012). If supported through further processes of capacity building and legal empowerment, Burmese refugees might have the opportunity to become change makers in the peace process, to reestablish themselves as citizens within the state, and to transform what has long been a toxic situation of distrust and violence. Thus, while legal conscientization is not necessarily a solution, it can be a starting point.

Law is ubiquitous in everyday life and particularly in the context of conflict resolution, peace negotiations, repatriation, and reconciliation. These periods of transition provide opportunities for challenging existing power structures and for legal mobilization (Waldorf 2013). If the reestablishment of the rule of law is now regarded as "a prerequisite for the emergence of stable and peaceful societies" (Lundy and McGovern 2008a, 99), then the law needs to be an important feature of the transformative justice process.[7]

The idea that individuals should be able to participate and have control over the decisions that affect their most vital rights and interests is a core premise of respect for human dignity and is all the more important in protracted refugee situations in light of the profound indignities refugees have endured. Nevertheless, refugee communities frequently demonstrate an astounding level of resilience and initiative. To ignore these strengths is to undermine refugees' agency and to deprive the world of a valuable resource. Legal conscientization of refugees may be recognized, then, as a fundamentally transformative process on the way to reestablishing the civic trust and rule of law that is critical to a successful and sustainable resolution to displacement and conflict.

Notes

1. It is important to note that return and repatriation are not the only ways in which displacement can be resolved; both resettlement to a third country and local integration in a country of asylum have, under certain circumstances, offered displaced groups the opportunity to begin their lives anew. Nevertheless, for most displaced persons, those alternatives are not feasible options, hence the decision to focus on reconciliation and repatriation.

2. For different typologies of participation, see Drydyk (2005, 260); Pretty (1994, 41).

3. See, for example, the case of Myanmar in Jones (2014).

4. This includes legislation, customary law, religious law, regulation, alternative dispute resolution, formal court procedures, law enforcement, enforceable social norms, treaty law, international law, and their related and supporting institutions.

5. Specific examples of legal empowerment strategies include the use of paralegals, community legal education, public interest litigation, law reform advocacy, legal training, and alternative dispute resolution, but it can also include strategies such as literacy programs, leadership training, and support for civil society organizations.

6. For a description of the International Rescue Committee's Legal Assistance Centre project, see Harding and Varadan (2010).

7. This is obviously not to the exclusion of other factors such as the political, economic, and social conditions.

Part 2

Pursuing Peace and Social Reconstruction

Displaced Persons' Roles

5

Complex Victimhood and Social Reconstruction after War and Displacement

Erin Baines

In the past few years, nearly one million persons have left displacement camps created during the more than two-decade war in northern Uganda and have finally returned to their villages. There, they are in the process of rebuilding their villages, digging new gardens, and resuming the rhythms of daily life: cooking, fetching water and firewood, and tending to children. The war and displacement had placed a tremendous strain on civilians—so much so that Chris Dolan came to call these camps spaces of social torture (Dolan 2013). Subject to constant harassment, violence, and attack by the Lord's Resistance Army (LRA) and the Ugandan People's Defence Forum (UPDF) and deprived of basic life-giving services and needs, the displaced population was humiliated, debilitated, and exhausted. Tens of thousands of children were abducted by the LRA and forced to kill, maim, and harm civilians; an unknown number joined militias and the UPDF to "protect" the camps.

Like most displacement situations, the camps rarely afforded protection and were raided regularly by the rebels. People slept *alup*—going temporarily to shelters in different locations for the night—and up to forty thousand children walked to town centers every evening, where they would sleep at bus stops and stadiums to avoid abduction. Without parental protection or guidance, many children and youths were vulnerable to sexual exploitation and violence, disease, cold, and hunger. Others were abducted on their way to seek shelter, their parents learning of their disappearance only when they did not come home in the morning. While many parents defended their families the best they could, others faced the decision of saving their children any way they could—by begging the rebels to leave them at least one child and take another, or by helping the rebels to identify homes of other children in the neighborhood and exposing where some children slept. Those who perished (at a rate of one thousand persons a week) were hastily buried in the confines of the camps, others buried in mass graves, and still others left where they were murdered. The dead wreaked social havoc on the Acholi people. Spiritual haunting, known as *cen*, resulted in grave misfortune and suffering (Baines 2007).

In the context of frayed social relationships, resuming quotidian life and work in the villages became a site of reconstituting social relations and responsibilities. Communal labor and interaction brought youths back "into culture" as they relearned the relationships between land and culture (Rosenoff-Gauvin 2013). Others began to resume the rights and passages that reweave the social fabric, including courtship and marriage practices, funeral rites, birthing ceremonies, and ancestor veneration, which were denied or difficult in camp settings. Within this space of lively social reconstruction, I draw attention to the children who returned from the LRA following their escape, release, or capture by the UPDF. Some were victims who had been abducted as children and spent up to a decade or more with the rebels, were forced to fight and, for some, were forced to marry and have children. Returning as adults, they no longer recognized their home or family, despite a longing for both and holding on to the hope and desire to return while "in captivity" (Schulz 2015).

In this chapter, I consider how displacement is both physical and social. Resolutions involve not only holding the most responsible to account but also reweaving the social fabric. Women abducted as girls who were able to return home remained "out of place." Moral judgments of persons accused of collaboration often result in social exile and shape their capacity to participate in and influence formal institutions, policies, or processes. Such judgments also affect the possibilities of persons who stand accused to recreate a new social life and to find a place of belonging. In other words, one's social displacement is measured within affected communities not only in terms of loss but also in terms of what one was perceived to have done, or not to have done, during the war. The agency and accountability of those who were abducted are interconnected in the minds of communities affected by the war, who assume an abducted person survived as a result of what they did. One might return in a physical sense, but, socially, what is home after the social fragmentation that is war? Northern Uganda is not unique. In all war zones and sites of insecurity, there are varying degrees of collaboration with fighting forces, and of the emergence of black markets, sex rackets, and other profits of war (Nordstrom 1997); the conditions of camps, moreover, lead to raised levels of domestic violence, theft, and labor exploitation (Okello and Hovil

2007). It is therefore not only the externally imposed violence of war and displacement that shapes the process of reconstructing the social but also the more intimate violence people do to one another.

To illustrate, I draw on an example of a young woman, Sara, who grew up in northern Uganda and experienced multiple forms of violence, resulting social exclusions. Between 2008 and 2014 I worked with a group of some thirty women who had spent between seven and seventeen years in the LRA, returning with their children between 2004 and 2005 to document their life stories. This research project considered women's political agency within the LRA and presently in northern Uganda, where they strive to make a new life for themselves and their children (Baines 2017). Sara's life story was one of many told during this research period in storytelling circles held at a location of the participants' choosing. These storytelling circles were designed to minimize interruption by the researcher and encourage women to speak about the experiences that each had within the homestead they were confined to. The circles assumed an Acholi storytelling method, which allows each person to speak for as long as they desire before moving on to the next speaker. Each storytelling circle lasted between two and three hours, depending on the topic. We first asked women to share their stories with others in the group. Each woman could draw her life story on a piece of paper, identifying significant events (birth, family, school, abduction, and so forth) with a picture or symbol, and then narrate these to each other. Researchers transcribed the women's accounts, and each woman, including Sara, then met one-on-one with a researcher to review her story and to add anything she might want.

Through this project, women described their social dislocation from their families and the ways they experience daily forms of stigma, rejection, and social exclusion for their perceived complicity with rebels. Tensions and relations of power based on accusations and assignments of guilt are important to consider when we speak of agency, displacements, and resolutions. Moral judgments of persons accused of collaboration often result in social exile, shaping their capacity to participate in and influence formal institutions, policies, or processes. Such judgments also affect the possibilities of persons who stand accused to recreate a new social life and to find a place of belonging. Sara's life story highlights how she navigates various forms of violence and social and physical displacement as well as the ways she contests her exclusion from social life. In this chapter, I first develop the concept of complex victimhood and agency before turning to Sara's life stories, which demonstrate her active negotiation and contestation of her worth as a human being. I conclude with reflections on why this is important for thinking about responsibility and social repair after violence and displacement, recasting the concept of "resolution" in displacement studies as located in the sociohis-torical processes of seeking to belong once more in the context of complex victimhood.

Complex Victimhood and Social Repair

After displacement, how will people live together again, and what responsi-bility does each hold toward the other? These questions bring together the fields of forced migration and transitional justice (Bradley 2008). Both fields employ human rights–based frameworks, documenting harms done to peo-ple and categories of victims in need of redress. Often victim categories are constructed around discrete forms of violations and social positions, each requiring specific sets of programmatic interventions and policies for "child soldiers," "forced wives," "persons with disabilities," and the "displaced," al-though a person can be all of these at once, and more. In other words, the fields reiterate victims as encountering discrete—rather than interrelated—forms of harm and as requiring different interventions. In effect, victims are understood as persons without agency and in need of rescue; perpetrators are understood as persons with too much agency and in need of control (Mibenge 2013).

The victim-perpetrator binary defines the scope of the field of transitional justice and possible political outcomes. Bronwyn Leebaw (2011) adroitly demonstrates how human rights frameworks that undergird most approaches to transitional justice mask the complexity of victimhood, individualizing responsibility. Mechanisms such as truth commissions and trials, she argues, depoliticize and dehistoricize violent events, limiting them to individual acts and experiences of harm and obfuscating attention to wider systems that give violence its shape and momentum. Official narrative accounts (such as testimonials during trials or truth commissions) focus on what is done to victims by perpetrators; this reduces the process of violence to a set of events in which the victim is in need of justice and the perpetrator is in need of punishment. Leebaw recognizes the limitations of human rights frame-works to usher in a deliberation of the political after violence—including the need to rethink questions of responsibility that move beyond static victim-perpetrator narratives to consider questions of complicity among bystanders.

I am interested in unpacking the ways some victims are implicated in the very structures of power that govern their lives. I draw on the concept of complex victims, persons implicated in the same violence to which they are also subject (Baines 2017). As Sherry Ortner reminds us, "the dominant of-ten have something to offer, and sometimes a great deal" (1995, 175), reveal-ing internal political struggles within a subordinate group. No subordinate group is homogenous; it is often internally divided by age, gender, kinship, or any number of social and political factors (Clark-Kazak and Thomson, chapter 11, this volume). Recognizing the internal tensions and fissures provides a greater insight into both the infrapolitics of a certain group and the operation of relations of power. Acts of resistance are often contradictory, conflated, and effectively ambivalent, in large part owing to these internal complexities. Engaging stories of complex victimhood reveals the possibilities of repairing the social and renegotiating the social contract after violence. I do not wish to suggest that complex victims are a "type" of victim group that should be identified and added to the remit of the field of transitional justice and forced migration. Rather, I work toward a conceptualization of justice that unsettles categories and makes possible the praxis of judgment, one that involves the polity in deliberation over what it means to be a human being in the face of violence, what it means to exist in relation to one another, and what responsibilities each hold toward one another and for the future (Bikundo 2012).

I am concerned with the aspect of "resolution" that focuses on the social and political governance of communities. Bradley, Milner, and Peruniak (2015, 3) argue that we should understand "the term 'refugee' broadly to refer not only to an individual who has 'lost the protection of her basic rights,' but who has in important ways been 'deprived of her social world'." Citing Gibney, they explain that "to be a refugee is 'to be someone who has been displaced from the communities, associations, relationships and cultural context that have shaped one's identity and around which one's life plan has hitherto been organized'" (2015, 13). This is an important extension of the definition for thinking about agency, for it highlights the interconnections between displacement from land, rights, and social worlds and the capacity to "make and pursue life plans, whether individual, communal or even inter-generational" (Bradley, Milner, and Peruniak 2015, 3). It also offers the possibility of thinking about displacement and agency as place-based, rooted within the sociocultural worlds that give agency meaning.

Various anthropological studies of violence have begun to examine the processes through which persons affected by mass violence live with and work through violence. These emphasize the uses of memory to cope with violence, such as mastering the past through artful acts of forgetting and re-remembering (Shaw 2002). Others demonstrate how people draw on sociocultural and spiritual resources to identify harms done and seek public redress through ritual and ceremony (Finnström 2008). Still others focus on the uses of storytelling to reclaim violence through meaning making and mastering violence. Finally, there is a growing body of work that examines how people "descend" into the everyday, resuming the flow and flux of daily life to repair the social (Das 2007). All focus on the agentive ways the war-affected and the displaced cope with, resist, and push back against violence in their lives. This chapter seeks to contribute to this literature, focusing on the concept of complex victimhood and the challenges posed to social reconstruction after displacement and war by the figure of child-soldier, forced wife, and children born of war.

Political Agency of Complex Victims

When people are forced to act in ways that transgress their moral understanding of good and evil in settings of coercion, they become complex victims. Various studies document the tactical agency of women, men, and children within settings of open conflict, documenting the "choiceless decisions" (Coulter 2008, 61) people make to navigate difficult realities (Nordstrom 1997; Utas 2003, 2005; Vigh 2006). Yet I believe it is important to think of them as exercising choices not only to survive, and to live another day.

This conceptualization of political agency is located in the quotidian and daily interactions of oppressor and subjugated. It insists that the subject (in this case, the victim of violence) is never closed or fixed but rather exists in relation to others with whom they are in continuous negotiation over the meaning and value of a life. Such negotiations may be verbal or nonverbal (gestures, performances) and enter the realm of the political when we find evidence of the victim "recognizing and asserting themselves as particular subjects, in relation to others, to the structures in which they are situated, and to subject positions that may be imposed on them" (Elwood and Mitchell 2012, 4).[1]

As with James Scott, I understand that public protest, demonstrations, and actions are unavailable to those who occupy the space of deprivation, but this is what forces us to turn to the intimate and daily interactions that give and take away from a person's being (Scott 1990). Scott and others focus on the myriad acts of protest, refusal, foot dragging, and subtexts—often unbeknownst to the oppressor—that frustrate the powerful and render life more livable for the oppressed (Scott 1990; Thomson 2013). While these are rich in political import, I want to focus more specifically on those precise moments that the very meaning of being human is contested and life itself is reclaimed in the very "space of devastation" (Das 2007, 74).

For instance, while examining the everyday politics over rights among Palestinian refugees, Ilana Feldman (2012b) employs the term the "politics of living" to refer to the "contestations over fixed values of life . . . [that] illuminates and structures a range of contestations over precisely these questions" (169). The political involves contestation of one's marginalization in relationship to others or the exclusion from enjoying the rights of a person; political agency is relational in that it involves an exchange between two or more people that seek to renegotiate an inequity, or at the very least make it known that the inequality (and harms that stem from it) is unjust. The form of that contestation is rich in context. Again, it is helpful to turn to Häkli and Kallio (2014, 183), who argue that "political agency is promoted when matters of importance are challenged or called into question, because . . . those involved have something at stake in them." Further, the political is found in "the social world that the embodied individual encounters in multiple different subject positions, averting, accepting and altering them through individual and concerted action" (Häkli and Kallio 2014, 191).

I am interested not only in forms of political life that make life more sustainable or frustrating to those in positions of power (as in resistance studies) but also in a form of politics practiced by persons in settings of coercion, which might be understood as the negotiation over the value of a human life. These expressions and contestations are always relational and historically and contextually grounded; they are defined intersubjectively at moments in which a person's value as a human being is in doubt or degraded. In the context of northern Uganda, we might turn to the work of Acholi intellectual Okot p'Bitek (1931–82), who argues, "The question of 'Who am I?' cannot be answered in any meaningful way, unless the relationship in question is known." Personhood is realized in the everyday lived sociality of the Acholi: "in the meaningful practices of people's daily activities, or in life as it is actually lived" (Rosenoff-Gauvin 2013, 36). Thus, we might look to the relationships in question and the social action that gives them meaning to understand the question "Who am I?" To consider the political, we might look at social action and the negotiation of relationships to answer the question "Who is a person?"

In his insightful study of the sociocultural coping mechanisms of Acholi child-inducted soldiers in northern Uganda, Opiyo Oloya (2013) demonstrates the ways abducted children retain a sense of self in the face of brute violence designed to turn them into hardened combatants, and he follows their return and social exclusion based on the perception that they are "of the bush." He introduces the reader to the Acholi concept of *dano adana*, or what it means to be "a human person," which was frequently evoked by his research participants who sought to reclaim social value within Acholi: those children who escaped were not *olum* ("of the bush" referring to their wild, animalistic character), as their communities argued, but were *dano adana*.[2] Throughout his study of children in the northern war, he draws on the concept of *dano adana* to describe the essence of being human, "a core identity endowed on each individual which determined how that individual viewed him / herself and was treated by others within the community" (Oloya 2013, 17).

I am also interested in forms of the political that insist upon the person in relation to another. In this conceptualization, political agency is understood as that which brings into conversation what it means to be a human being within the realm of social action. The political in this sense is always a process of contestation over the meaning of who is human and who is not. This stands in contrast to, and displaces the privileging of, concepts of the power as "the capacity to define who matters and who does not, who is disposable and who is not" (Mbembé and Meintjes 2003, 27). If we understand that a person's subject position is never fixed but relational, and that social action defines a person, we must think of persons as always *in the process* of becoming. Intersubjective exchanges shape, and are shaped by, who we are and how we are defined. This has material consequence for how we live as individuals and as a collective; some lives are deemed of less value, less worthy. This conceptualization of the political recognizes that the subject is implicated within relations of continuously negotiated power, meaning one's vulnerability in one relationship does not define the person as always and only vulnerable. Social action, furthermore, actively and continuously redefines the boundaries of the lives that are of value and those that are not. It is not that every social action is determinative of a human being; it is that cumulatively they are. It is the contestation and negotiation of acts that exclude one from being human that interests me. Political agency is from this perspective defined by one's ability to improvise social action to remake the self in relation to others, to push back against violent acts, and to "reconfigure new life" (Bayat 2009, 5).

If we understand the subject as unfixed and relational, we must also understand the powerful as such. Therefore, the political emerges not only in grand gestures to claim the rights of a person (protests, human rights campaigns, and movements) but in the myriad exchanges between persons (which constitute the meaning of sociality) and, when this exchange turns to the meaning of personhood, in the meaning of politics itself. If the powerful is also relational in terms of who has the capacity to define who matters and who does not, then there are infinite encounters of the political. This leads us away from the political as a grand project of mass transformation and into sites of constant change, in the realm of the everyday and of matters that give life meaning.

I turn now to consideration of Sara's life story, focusing on specific moments in which she is treated as a nonperson and how she responds to this by challenging those who would harm and negate her as a person. I then conclude by reflecting on why this is important to the themes of this volume.

Sara's Story

Sara begins her life story with a warning. She tells us that her life has "revolved around nothing but misfortunes. I have never experienced what is called peace in my life or learned to laugh and enjoy life. All I know is anger and sadness." In this, she foreshadows the connections between her past, present, and future and underscores the continuities between violence experienced as a child and now as an adult. Her anger and sadness become, as I will elaborate, political contests of her dehumanization. Her "truth" is testimony to the unjust conditions of the life of a child and woman in northern Uganda who is afforded neither the protection nor respect she justly deserves as a human being. If in Acholi a person is a human being only in relation to another and in the exercise of responsibility for the well-being for other people, we will learn that Sara is rendered nonhuman. "The truth is," Sara states, "I have nothing except death, if it is there."

Today, I want to speak out the truth

Sara was born in a village in northern Uganda in 1980, the second of three children. When Sara was around five years old, her mother left an abusive husband; although she attempted to take the children with her, Sara's father insisted the children belonged to him, and they remained with him in his paternal village. Both grandparents were deceased, so Sara's aunt assumed the role of caregiver until her own premature death. Sara describes her father as "an ill-tempered, cruel and violent man," which rendered him a social pariah throughout the area who "did not have a single friend." A thief and a drunkard, no one intervened when he beat and tortured his children. Sara explains, "People feared him, all they could do was say 'if he wants to kill his own children, let him do it.'"

Eventually, Sara's father brought a new wife into his home. The new wife resented the children and denied them food. "My brothers and I began to steal cassava from the garden and eat it raw while hiding. We would then drink water afterwards." Sara's father would punish the children by placing iron sheets in the sun and once hot, force the children to lie on them while placing another sheet on top of them. He would then step on the children and cane them. Sara told us she began to "study" her situation and conclude that her future would only repeat itself unless some action was taken: "The mistreatment entered my brothers and my hearts. . . . I started to analyze my life. If all men were like my father, then I would end up married to someone like him when I grew up. If I, at such a tender age, was subjected to his wrath, what worse things would I experience when I grew up?" Sara and her brothers decided to confront their father. "One day my brothers and I made a resolution. We realized that my father and stepmother would eventually kill us. . . . We could see no future for ourselves in this world, so it was useless to prolong our suffering. . . . So, prepared to die, we decided to speak out next time they mistreated us." Following a disagreement between her father and his new wife sometime later in which the children were about to be punished, Sara indeed confronted her father and urged him to kill them, but not before she alerted him to the harm he had caused:

> Today I want to speak out the truth. Though you are our biological father, your wife is not our mother! She tells you many lies about us because she wants you to kill us. What I therefore want to say is that my brothers and I have agreed to let today be our last day to live on earth. Kill all of us so that we can find peace but before you do that, I will tell you the truth. Every day we keep quiet but today I will tell you about our suffering to your face—it is up to you to kill me if you want. I am tired. I have been suffering from the time I was very young.
>
> After I said this, my father sat down and said, "Tell me all that you have in your heart." Then I said: Okay, this is what I am going to tell you. From the time you took us away from our mother until now, we have never experienced any peace, only pain and sadness. Even as I speak now, I am angry—you are still inflicting more pain on us now and who knows how much more is yet to come? We are very young and not capable of hiring out our labour. But this woman keeps telling us daily to tell you that we eat. But the reality is that we do not eat from this home. . . . With all this, why do you again inflict more pain on us by beating us when you come back home? Because of all this, it is better if we cease to live. This woman of yours always warns us that should we dare tell you that we have not eaten, she will cane and kill us. Now that she vows to kill us and you also want to kill us, it is better if both of you kill us so we can rest.

Following this confrontation, Sara's father stops drinking, asks his new wife to leave, and takes responsibility for his children until his own death. After his death, Sara and her brothers went to a town center to live with an aunt and her children.

I will die before I let you see my teeth

After relocating to her aunt's home in the town center, Sara and her brothers, aunt, and cousins traveled back to the village for the harvest. When the rebels appeared in the gardens, they demanded her aunt choose two chil-

dren to go with them. Her aunt hesitated, unable to make the terrible decision, and the rebels abducted Sara, her brothers, and her cousins. Her cousins
were killed within the same week during a military attack, but Sara and her
brothers joined the march to Sudan, where the rebel bases were located at
the time. Sara was given to an older commander "with spotty grey hair on
his head." Immediately he called her to sleep with him in his house. Sara was
confused by the words and actions of the old commander, who told her to
go and lay in his bed for him in the hut, indicating that they would sleep together in the same place. Sara knew that men and girls do not sleep in the
same hut and that this was a serious infraction of morality. She asked other
women in the compound about the old man's intentions, but they told her
to just do as he asks.

> In the evening the commander sent someone to tell me to go to his bed.
> I went. He said, "Come and sleep." I asked him, "Do women share beds
> with men here?" He said, "Are you speaking back to me? Just come and
> lie on this bed." I told him no and that "back home we girls slept in a dif-
> ferent hut from the boys. We didn't even sleep in the same hut with our
> father when he was still alive. You are even older than my father so how
> can I sleep with you on the same bed?" He said, "Come here immediately
> or I will cane you." I answered him, "You're lying to me. At our home we
> don't sleep with men in the same house."
>
> He immediately called the boys and they came and beat me up se-
> verely. I did not know the reason why I was being caned. I thought they
> were caning me for having gone to sleep at his place. After they beat me
> they grabbed and took me back to his place forcefully. [The commander]
> started this man and woman thing with me, at the time I had no idea what
> he was doing. First he told me to turn to face him. I asked him, "Why
> should I turn? Don't you see that I am already sleeping?" I picked a bed
> sheet to cover myself with but he said, "We are going to use one bed sheet
> only." Immediately he started his act and I started crying out aloud. I did
> not make a mild cry, I cried out aloud. I said, "Have you started casting
> spells on young children? You start your abomination on young children?"
>
> He started beating me while saying that he would do all he wanted to
> do with me. He kept having sex with me as I cried out aloud. He kept
> on like that until he was done.

As the sexual abuse continued, Sara began to question God's intentions
for her, asking him why he continued "to avert the very death that should
come my way and instead let it kill someone else." Whenever she was alone,
she cried, something the commander became aware of and seized upon as an

act to be brought under his control; he began to discipline her not by force but, perhaps more cruelly, by trying to make her laugh. His attempt to nullify her only expression of dissent becomes the site of everyday violence and resistance. He continuously attempted to tease and tickle her, to which Sara vowed to him that "it was better to die than to laugh with him":

> The man said he would keep having sex with me until I could freely laugh and chat with him, until I began to love and play with him. I would retort, "For the rest of the time that I spend here in the bush, I will die before I let you see my teeth. The only opportunity that you will have to get a glimpse of my teeth is when I am crying. I won't laugh with you because no one else in my life has ever done to me what you did."

The abuse continued until one day when the commander was injured in a battle. He returned to the compound to be nursed and accused Sara of having placed a curse on him because "she never loved him."

Do me a favor and kill me first

When Sara was sent on standby to raid a village in Uganda, she escaped. She stayed for a short period at a rehabilitation center for "child soldiers" before the staff tracked down her village and reunited her with the aunt who had originally taken her and her brothers in, and whose children had been abducted with them. Sara's aunt took away the goods she was given by the rehabilitation center but told Sara she would never take care of her. She even cooked and ate in front of Sara but failed to share food (considered an abomination in Acholi culture). Sara realized her aunt was unable to forgive herself or forgive Sara for the abduction and for the deaths of her children, so Sara decided to leave to find herself a man, reasoning that "even if I risk catching AIDS I will get to eat if I find a man." Sara approached a childhood friend and asked to join his home. He already had four wives and accepted that Sara might live with him as a wife, but on the condition that she must harvest from the garden. The presence of rebels made this a dangerous task but one he told her she was well equipped to do, given her experience and knowledge of life in the bush. Sara gave birth during this time, but the man refused responsibility for the child, stating it looked "typical of a bush child."

One day, as Sara walked with her cowives along the path to the gardens and with her child tied to her back, they were ambushed. A group of young LRA soldiers ordered the women to stop where they were and not to flee. All but Sara fled. The rebels recognized Sara from Sudan and accused her of betrayal for having escaped. The punishment for this was typically death.

The soldiers took her to an abandoned homestead and proceeded to torture Sara, heating a panga (machete) and then beating her with it and with canes, stepping on her, and cutting her with a knife. They tormented her by making unreasonable demands, telling her to produce a goat, a cow, and a sum of money.

At each stage of the interrogation, Sara felt she had nothing to live for and permitted the young men to kill her, but first, she told them, "I must tell everything that is in my heart. I will speak freely before you kill me." She pointed out the lack of logic in their actions: Why kill her when she had been the only person to obey their order not run away? Why demand such ridiculous items, when it was clear she has nothing? The rebels grew angry and told her she would die a painful death. They beat her and would pause to ask, "Are you dead yet?" to which she would respond, "Not yet." Frustrated that they were unable to kill her, Sara reminded them that God is the only one to decide her fate, not the boys; if God does not permit it, their efforts would be in vain. Further, she warned, "What you do before God is a sin, God cautioned us not to judge anyone." And then she uttered the challenge, "It is okay, you kill me."

Sara's words began to destabilize the boys, who considered chopping her in half. They grew concerned she was a witch, but she defended herself, "I am not a witch!" Finally, the officer in charge became perplexed. He claimed, "This isn't right. This girl is speaking for nothing, she is just a dead body." The rebels turned their attention to her baby. Sara again spoke "freely": "People, even Kony [the LRA spiritual leader] used to say that this kingdom shall be for children. You are the very people who fathered this child and now even if I am taking care of him, he remains yours. A time will come when you should come and take him away to grow with you.[3] So why kill this innocent child? If I escaped, then kill me but spare the life of my child." Then, as they prepared to put her child in a polythene bag to suffocate him, Sara made this request: "Before you kill my child, do me a favor and kill me first. Then kill the child after, when I cannot see. So that my child will not think it was my fault that he died since he would have seen all that you have done to me. Even God in heaven will know that you are the ones who did it but not me." In killing her, the rebels would strike no victory against their enemy but would bring harm to themselves and their own future; they had made her pregnant and forced her to raise a child alone, a child they were now prepared to kill. It was as if to suggest that this potential act of filicide is what would ultimately defeat them—not the Ugandan military or the civilians the rebels assume betray them. Through her words and actions, Sara called on the young rebels to consider what they were about to do and cast doubt on their actions. They retreated, leaving Sara and the child barely alive.

They are my eyes

> The way things are, there is no one supporting me. In case of any sickness, the very
> children I have are the ones who help me. They are my eyes, my helpers, there is no
> relative to go to except the children that I have.

Sara was beaten unconscious and found by a hunter who carried her to a
nearby village where she was transported to hospital. She recovered slowly
from a brain injury: "When I tried to speak, I was only opening my mouth;
no sound was coming out of it. . . . I felt as though sand was packed into my
head, which felt like a child's play ball with no life in it at all." Sara returned
to her husband with her baby, but he told her she was no longer of any use to
him as she could not work; "You are just useless," he stated, calling her child
"just a rebel child." Sara left his home with her baby and went to the town
center to search for her mother, begging and living in abandoned huts. She
eventually located her mother, who agreed to take her and her child in, but
her mother's new husband refused: "Impossible! . . . Do you want her [Sara]
to kill and finish off all our children? A person who stayed in the bush? [A
person who has] killed and committed all sorts of atrocities? Impossible!"
Sara then found refuge in a hut overrun by ants, where the landowners let
her stay for a minimal rent. She continued to beg for food until she was reunited with her brother's two children (both born in the LRA as the result
of forced marriage), who had been captured by the Ugandan military. She
learned that her brother had been killed in battle, and Sara assumed responsibility for their care.

Sara then decided to "find a husband" to help care for the children. She
revealed her past to him, and he accepted her into his home. She soon gave
birth once more. However, shortly after the baby's birth, her new husband
accused Sara of having participated in a massacre in his village. Neighbors,
too, began to agree that she resembled "the person who carried out the massacre." One night, after listening to his abuse, Sara confronted her husband:
"It is true that I was in the bush and I can accept that I killed [soldiers] at
the battlefield, but outside that [context], I haven't killed anyone [any civil-
ians]. In fact, I was the one whom they [the rebels] committed violence on.
I did not kill anybody, but if you have now started seeing me as your enemy
then let me leave . . . it is better than having to live with your enemy and feel
hurt." Sara's new husband continued to accuse her of being a "mad woman,"
so she left to again live in borrowed huts and beg for food.[4] Sara then fell
sick, and her baby with her last husband died. She returned to the village of
the child's father to bury her son, but the father accused her of killing the
baby as an act of revenge against him: "He said I was a serial killer." Sara's in-

laws and her own mother intervened, calling a family meeting to resolve the dispute. Sara discovered she was pregnant. She lived with her husband once more but refused to sleep with him. He in turn refused to give her food. She asked him, "How can a human being live without food? Even prisoners who are on death row are still given food until they are hanged"; she decided to leave for good.

Sara stated she would rather care for her remaining children on her own, even if she had to resort to prostitution. She recognized that although her children were all she had, no husband would ever accept them. "It is like when our stay in the bush becomes known to people, it cannot be erased." "My former husband (the first one) hated my child when I had only one. Now that I have four children, how will a man react?" She reflected on the fact she had nowhere to go, no village to return to, no relatives to lean on. She has only her children now, and she devotes herself to their care "while I work hard. That is my only hope."

Political Agency and Social Reconstructions

Victims are any persons who have suffered a harm. In human rights–based approaches to justice, a harm (such as rape or physical injury) often defines a person (a rape victim, a war disabled) and thus gives grounds for recourse. Victimhood, moreover, is socially constructed by and shaped by ongoing interpretations of harms that are contested within the specific historical moment in which they unfold and over time. Victimhood does not define a person or determine their ability to act; nor does it overwrite other aspects of one's life experience, fixing them in time. I have offered a conceptualization of victimhood that moves beyond static and essentialist categories of victims as persons without agency. This has rested on the assumption that violence is more than singular acts (attributable to one person or group of persons to be held accountable), but it is rendered possible through a matrix of actions and nonactions of persons in relation to one another (thereby recasting responsibility as socially held, thus requiring a political judgment).

Sara's life story exposes the limitations of victim categories when they fail to recognize intersecting forms and continuities of violence as socially diffuse. Her suffering as a victim did not begin with the moment of her displacement or abduction. Throughout her childhood and following her escape, she endured poverty, disease, marginalization, abuse, and neglect. The intimate familial relations that should have protected Sara either failed her or deliberately harmed her as a daughter, a wife, and a mother. No neighbor intervened to help her and her siblings from her father's abuse ("If he wants to kill his own children, let him do it"). Her stepmother overworked, abused, and starved her. Later, her aunt refused her shelter and food. Her husband and his cowives used her only for labor and rejected her firstborn child. Her new husband and his neighbors came to view her only as a killer, and while her in-laws attempted to save her marriage, they ultimately understood her as mad. In all these moments of violent abuse and neglect, Sara was seen as less than human.

Sara's life demonstrates the interconnection of systems of violence (the intimate, structural, and overt) and exposes relations of power that relegate Sara to the status of a nonperson and that fuel her ongoing contestation of those relations and subordinate social position. Where postconflict Acholi grapple with the process of social reconstruction in the wake of social dislocation and violence, Sara demonstrates the fraught nature of such relationships before, during, and after the war. This is not to suggest that such acts place those implicated on the same or even a relative scale of those most responsible for violence during and after conflict. Rather, I aim to illuminate the ways in which victims are pulled into the reproduction of the workings of power and to highlight the complicity of different parties involved in the commissioning of harm. It is also to point to the responsibility each party then holds following periods of transition, both individually and in relation to one another.

Sara exercised political agency in contesting those relationships that would harm her or fail her as a person. First, she confronts her father and "speaks out the truth," inviting him to kill her and her brothers as it is no longer tolerable to live as less than human, as something to torture rather than someone to nurture. Second, Sara recognizes the immorality and wrongfulness of being forced into a marriage to an old man and tells him so; although she cannot stop him from violently raping her and forcing her to assume domestic work, she exerts her resistance in the refusal of a smile. Third, Sara complies with each of the rebel soldiers' orders, refusing to allow them to place any blame on her for what they are about to do. In her words and actions, Sara contests the way the rebels reduce her to "just a dead body." Finally, Sara attempts to make new familial relations after her recovery, seeking first to rebuild a relationship with her mother and then later a new husband and his family. She is rejected repeatedly and treated poorly, and she decides to leave, an action interpreted here as an assertion that she once more refuses to live as someone without recognition as a person. Instead, she invests her future in the only relationships that remain—her children, her "eyes and helpers"—and in this act she once more asserts that she is a human being worthy of living. In effect, Sara is a political agent in the sense that she asserts her personhood in relation to others who would treat her otherwise, contesting their actions and forcing them to recognize their own complicity and responsibility.

While the conception of the political articulated here takes on significance in Acholi cosmological understandings of what it means to be human, it is applicable to other settings and situations that define one's humanness in relationship to and with others, the essence, I submit, of politics—Who am I? Who are we in relation to each other? How do we want to live with one another? All of these are questions posed not only in formal mechanisms for drawing up the social contract but also as lived in the quotidian interactions that constitute the complex web of human relations (Arendt 2013). If we understand politics as relational, we understand the possibilities of acting in even the most debilitating circumstances to contest and assert one's self in relation to others and, likewise, to offer a political judgment of those who are complicit in the suffering of others and enjoin them in a critical reflection of how violence is rendered thinkable and, as such, becomes possible. Political judgment, in this sense, is not based on predefined sets of rules ascribed in law (although such rules and judgments exist) but in the active and ongoing contestation of how we do, or ought, to live together, including what responsibilities we hold to one another.

To summarize, recognizing the agency of complex victims in the study of "resolutions" has several implications for thinking about responsibility and reconstruction after mass displacement. First, it moves us beyond human rights categories that limit how we might conceptualize victimhood and that risk rendering refugees as ahistorical and apolitical persons. It also moves beyond the singular categories (as in child soldier, forced wife, displaced person) and frameworks policy makers and researchers have developed to understand the impact of violence on a person's capacity to act, and moves toward the intersecting ways people's experiences of violence and their responses to it overlap. This resonates with Bradley, Milner, and Peruniak's (2015) assertion that the displaced have "intersecting experiences and identities" that must be acknowledged and considered for their import in working toward resolutions.

Second, it raises larger and important questions regarding political responsibility after violence and works toward a praxis of justice. Fundamentally, Sara's life stories are about profound political questions concerning responsibility and judgment after violence. Her stories ask how the Acholi will live together again, what they owe each other, and how they will sort through these questions by challenging the displacement of responsibility onto children taken from them in the night and forced to labor and fight in the name of someone else's war.

Finally, it suggests that any study of social reconstruction after displacement must reckon with those who are considered no longer worthy of membership to the collective (for example, those whose identities may include being a prostitute, an AIDS patient, a widow, a returning soldier) and who, by virtue of their low social status and contextual vulnerability, have little capacity to act to change their life circumstances or seek a life worth living. These are often perceived to be persons who brought about their own suffering or who cause the suffering of others, persons who generate tensions and fissures within communities seeking to repair their social world after violence. Such groups challenge historically determined moral orders and render visible the inability of sociocultural systems and values to always remain inclusive, prompting the reinvigoration of past moral schemes and thresholds of social acceptability.

Notes

This chapter draws from Sara's life story considered in Baines (2015) and the conceptualization of the political in Baines (2017). The interviews with Sara are reproduced with permission from Baines (2015).

1. Sarah Elwood and Katharyne Mitchell address the perception that children are unable to exercise political agency within the boundaries of narrowly defined, adult-centric Western political scripts of adulthood. If one understands that all persons are in a state of (political) becoming in relation to others, and this is not something granted by state or citizenship at a particular age, then the delineation of "child" and "adult" are arbitrary in any event. While the contexts are radically different of each author's study, the conceptualization of the political for persons deemed outside of political life is relevant and useful here. See also Nakata (2015).

2. *Olum* in English means "the bush" or "wilderness," a place in Acholi culture that is considered a realm beyond humanity.

3. This refers to the Acholi cultural practice of *koko* in which the paternal clan pays a fine to the maternal clan, after which the child is their responsibility.

4. She is suspected of having *cen*, the phenomena of being haunted by persons who died a wrongful death, because a manifestation of *cen* is to become mad.

6

Refugees, Peacebuilding, and Paternalism

Lessons from Mozambique

James Milner

A growing body of research and examples from practice have outlined the various ways that refugees in neighboring countries can contribute to peacebuilding in their country of origin.[1] In areas as diverse as safety and security (Obura 2002), political processes (Grace and Mooney 2009; Johansson 2009), basic services (Chimni 2002), core government functions (Lumpp and Stromberg 2004), and economic revitalization,[2] refugees have the demonstrated ability to contribute to peacebuilding—either while in exile or upon return—if asylum and peacebuilding policies create conditions conducive to their involvement. The ability of refugees to contribute to national peacebuilding programs is frequently determined by conditions created by the asylum policies of host states and the willingness for peacebuilding actors to overcome a myopic, country-specific approach to peacebuilding and engage with actors *outside* the country who can contribute to peacebuilding priorities. As argued elsewhere (Milner 2015), the contribution of refugees to a formal peacebuilding program can be more fully realized if the policy and practice of peacebuilding is expanded in scope to include nontraditional peacebuilding actors, in space to engage with actors located outside the country emerging from conflict, and in time to incorporate peacebuilding activities before the formal cessation of hostilities. More generally, recent literature on "bottom-up" and community-based approaches to peacebuilding highlight the importance of peacebuilding efforts that are not recognized or prioritized by formal, "top-down," externally driven peacebuilding processes, including those by refugees in exile and upon return to their country of origin.[3]

Given these lessons and our evolving understanding of peacebuilding, it is beneficial to now revisit historical case studies to consider the role of refugees in the peacebuilding process, their contributions within and beyond national peacebuilding programs, and the factors that either enhanced or inhibited their active inclusion in the national peacebuilding process. In response, the chapter draws on the case of Mozambique as an opportunity to revisit the factors that explain the role of refugees in the peacebuilding process, especially their relationship to the internationally supported national process. The chapter argues that the various contributions of refugees to the peacebuilding process were initiated at the local level and that opportunities were missed by formal institutional actors, especially UN actors, to engage more fully and systematically with the actual and potential peacebuilding contributions of repatriated refugees. A more detailed understanding of the factors contributing to their approach holds important lessons for future peacebuilding initiatives.

The selection of Mozambique was motivated by several factors. First, "the Mozambican peace and repatriation operations are regarded almost unanimously in humanitarian circles as unlikely but undoubted successes, if success is understood in the traditional terms of the creation of a relatively stable democracy and prompt, durable return" (Bradley 2013a, 156).[4] On October 4, 1992, the General Peace Agreement (GPA) was signed in Rome between the Mozambique Liberation Front (or Frelimo) and the Mozambican National Resistance (or Renamo), ending fifteen years of conflict. To support the implementation of the GPA, the UN Security Council established the United Nations Operation in Mozambique (ONUMOZ). Between the signing of the GPA and the declaration of election results on November 19, 1994, more than 1.7 million refugees returned to Mozambique from six neighboring countries. While many of these refugees repatriated spontaneously in time to register to vote in the elections and to plant their crops according to the agricultural seasons, the United Nations High Commissioner for Refugees (UNHCR) claims credit for the success of the return and reintegration program. As noted by UNHCR: "The Mozambican repatriation and reintegration programme is one of the largest ever undertaken by UNHCR, involving 1.7 million returnees and costing some $145 million to implement, over $100 million of which was devoted to activities within Mozambique. Given the enormous devastation and displacement generated by the armed conflict in Mozambique, the reintegration process has encountered remarkably few problems" (UNHCR 1997a, 24).

A preliminary reading of documents held in the archives of ONUMOZ, however, suggests that this narrative of UNHCR's unproblematic successes is in fact contested and that competing narratives may be found to explain how refugees were able to return and successfully reintegrate in Mozambique before the start of UNHCR's official program in early 1994,[5] in addition to concerns relating to UNHCR's role in the national peacebuilding program in Mozambique. More specifically, the archives contain frequent suggestions that UNHCR's priorities in the return and reintegration program were not informed primarily by the needs and interests of refugees, and that several opportunities were missed to ensure that the contributions and capacities of refugees were more fully incorporated into the peacebuilding program. This may in turn contribute to our understanding that, while peacebuilding in Mozambique may be understood to be a "success" when measured against the absence of violence post-1992, a closer reading would suggest that much remains to be accomplished for Mozambique to achieve a "positive" peace, where the roots of the conflict, dating back to the colonial and precolonial era, are more fully addressed (see Costy 2004).

Mozambique was also selected as a case study as it was one of the first UN postconflict operations to be initiated following the 1992 report by the UN secretary-general, *An Agenda for Peace*, which identifies peacebuilding as an important area of UN activity, along with preventive diplomacy, peacemaking, and peacekeeping (see UNSG 1992). Mozambique consequently became a case against which future peacebuilding operations, especially in Africa, are understood. Given the twenty-year limit under which UN archives are opened to external readers, Mozambique is also the first case available in the archives. A more comprehensive and critical reading of these archival records could usefully be followed by a reexamination of other cases, such as Rwanda, Burundi, Sierra Leone, and Liberia. In terms of policy and archival research, the case of Mozambique consequently serves as a potential template for future comparative research.

In this light, this chapter considers the role of refugees in the planning and implementation of the peacebuilding program in Mozambique between the signing of the GPA in October 1992 and the holding of postconflict elections in November 1994. Specifically, the chapter asks: What factors explain UNHCR's articulation of a passive relationship between refugees and peacebuilding, despite the level of agency demonstrated by refugees through their mass return to Mozambique and their early abilities to reintegrate before the launch of UNHCR's official program in 1994? In response, this chapter employs the notion of "international humanitarian paternalism," most recently articulated by Michael Barnett.[6] Barnett notes that "paternalism," understood as "the interference with a person's liberty on the grounds that it is in his or her best interests," is central to understanding the fusing of "care and control" in humanitarianism (2011b, 107). Drawing on the example of UNHCR's repatriation policies, Barnett explains that "the underlying assumption . . . is that UNHCR knows what is in the best interest of refugees—a population that is often assumed to be too uninformed to know what is in its best interests or too weak to act on them" (Barnett 2011b, 107). In such circumstances, Barnett outlines how UNHCR draws on expert authority ("when an actor's voice is given credibility because of his or her specialized training, knowledge, or experience") and moral authority ("when an actor is perceived to be speaking and acting on behalf of the community's values and interests and defending the lives of the weak and vulnerable") to exert dominance over refugees and other actors. In this way, UNHCR employs "productive power," defined as the "production of subjects through diffuse social relations" (Barnett and Duvall 2005, 20), to create realities and categories that serves its interests, even at the expense of the interests of others and the needs of refugees.

As suggested by an early reading of the ONUMOZ archives, UNHCR exhibited paternalism through its characterization of the capacities and actions of refugees, its relations with other actors, and the priorities that informed the styling and timing of its return and reintegration program in Mozambique. UNHCR's paternalism may in turn be seen to have limited the extent to which the actions of refugees were reflected in the national peacebuilding process, specifically the ability of refugees to contribute to the provision of basic services and political processes in postconflict Mozambique. While this argument is not intended to diminish what the UNHCR was able to accomplish, closer examination of the case of Mozambique points to the various ways that the capacities and contributions of refugees can be more fully understood, along with the institutional factors that may inhibit the active inclusion of refugees in the national peacebuilding process. Just as Bradley argues "the fact that the resolution of land claims and the redress of survivors' grievances took place largely outside the structure of formal state institutions does not mean that they are not significant contributions to creating conditions of just return" (Bradley 2013a, 152), it is equally important to consider how these efforts also contributed to peacebuilding at the local level. While Mozambique arguably remains a success story, especially in terms of the number of refugees who were able to return and reintegrate following the signing of the GPA, the counternarrative found in the ONUMOZ archives suggests that opportunities may have been lost to more fully incorporate these efforts into an understanding of national peacebuilding efforts and that important lessons remain to be learned from this historical case.

Refugees and Peacebuilding

The past fifteen years have witnessed several developments in the theory and practice of peacebuilding, especially within the UN system.[7] To the recommendations of a 2004 UN High-Level Panel and the UN secretary-general (UN High-Level Panel 2004; UNSG 2005), the UN General Assembly established a UN peacebuilding commission in December 2005. Since its inception, the commission has concentrated its work on six countries: Burundi, Central African Republic, Guinea, Guinea-Bissau, Sierra Leone, and Liberia. The work of the commission, along with other UN peacebuilding programs, has largely concentrated on the five priority areas outlined in the 2009 *Report of the Secretary-General on Peacebuilding in the Immediate Aftermath of Conflict*, namely support to basic safety and security; political processes; provision of basic services; restoring core government functions; and supporting economic revitalization (UN 2009, para. 17). These areas of activity serve as both the expected elements of national peacebuilding programs supported by the UN and a useful analytical framework for disaggregating the various dimensions of national peacebuilding programs.

Although these activities now form the core of national peacebuilding initiatives *within* the country in question, there has been some recognition of the need to engage with dynamics *outside* the state's borders that may affect peacebuilding in positive and negative ways. For example, the prolonged presence of refugee populations in neighboring countries is a significant cross-border issue that has been raised by international peacebuilding planners. As noted by former UN secretary-general Kofi Annan (2005), "the return of refugees and internally displaced persons is a major part of any post-conflict scenario. . . . Indeed it is often a critical factor in sustaining a peace process and in revitalizing economic activity."

In fact, there is growing evidence to suggest the various ways that refugees in neighboring states can contribute to the five priority areas for national peacebuilding programs identified by the United Nations. In support of basic safety and security within the country of origin, efforts in cases as diverse as the Democratic Republic of Congo, Eritrea, Ethiopia, Kenya, Uganda, Liberia, Guinea, Sierra Leone, and Côte d'Ivoire illustrate how peace education programs can enhance refugees' conflict resolution and mediation skills (see Obura 2002). Likewise, a more systematic engagement with youth within refugee populations can also contribute to peacebuilding. Livelihood and vocational training targeting youth leaving secondary school could help address the tendency for unemployed youth, especially males, to be susceptible to recruitment by armed groups and to engage in activities that are either illegal or undermine peace, while community-level reconciliation efforts can make important contributions to the prevention of conflict.

A strong link also exists between refugees and support to the political process in the country of origin, which includes planning and holding elections, developing conflict management mechanisms, promoting inclusive dialogue, and facilitating the broader process of national reconciliation. In fact, refugees in exile often remain engaged in the political process in their country of origin. A range of cases demonstrate that allowing refugees to be directly involved in the peace process and in planning the subsequent peacebuilding program can enhance the legitimacy of the outcomes of negotiations, incorporate the capacities and resources of refugees in the process, and ensure that refugees are committed to supporting the subsequent peacebuilding process.

One of the most recognized links between refugees and peacebuilding relates to the opportunities to provide training to refugees in exile to help provide basic services in their country of origin, including health and primary education. For example, teacher-training programs in the Kakuma refugee camp in Kenya have been found to help address the significant shortage of teachers in South Sudan. Likewise, Liberian refugees repatriating from Ghana have been able to return with a range of skills acquired in exile that can contribute to a range of public services in Liberia. More generally, however, the return and reintegration of refugees remains a significant challenge and a potential strain on the ability of a country emerging from conflict to provide basic services for its citizens. The scale of this challenge is magnified in situations of prolonged conflict and prolonged exile. In response, there is growing recognition of the benefits associated with engaging with refugees while in exile to ensure that the skills and capacities they possess may be more fully taken into account during the process of return and reintegration.

Another area of engagement relates to support for core government functions. Many countries emerging from prolonged conflict face significant challenges relating to basic public administration and public finance. In addition to training refugees in exile to help address these functions upon return, several activities may be undertaken in neighboring countries to ease the demands on core government functions as refugees return. These activities include the adjudication of land claims and the issuance of key government documents, including birth certificates, citizenship papers, and other documents that establish identity and credentials. Such activities are especially important in instances of prolonged exile, where restitution and resolution of property disputes can make an important contribution to peacebuilding at local and national levels.

Finally, engagement with refugees while in exile can make a significant contribution to economic revitalization in the country of origin. As UNHCR has noted,

> People who have benefited from education, skills training and livelihood opportunities during their time as refugees, and who have been able to attain a degree of self-reliance while living in a country of asylum, retain

their hope in the future and are better placed to create and take advantage of new economic opportunities after their return. While living in exile, long-term refugees also have an ideal opportunity to acquire valuable skills in areas such as leadership, advocacy, mediation and conflict resolution, which will again enable them to contribute to the rebuilding of their communities once return becomes possible.[8]

The potential for refugees to make these kinds of contributions to economic revitalization in their country of origin will be enhanced considerably by conditions in the country of asylum that allow refugees to be self-reliant and unhindered in their pursuit of livelihood opportunities.

UNHCR and International Humanitarian Paternalism

The contributions that refugees can make to peacebuilding are often enhanced as a result of open asylum policies in host states, the active inclusion of refugees in the planning and implementation of peacebuilding programs, the development of repatriation programs that are informed by the needs and capacities of refugees, and a recognition of the complementary role of local and national peacebuilding initiatives.[9] Despite these benefits, the experience of the past twenty-five years suggests that UNHCR is more frequently associated with the implementation of restrictive asylum policies in host states and repatriation programs that are increasingly involuntary (see Slaughter and Crisp 2008; Chimni 1999). How can this apparent tension be understood?

Barnett suggests that tensions such as these may be more fully understood through the lens of international humanitarian paternalism. Drawing on earlier literature, Barnett defines paternalism as "the interference with a person's liberty of action justified by reasons referring exclusively to the welfare, good, happiness, needs, interests or values of the person being coerced" (2012, 487). While there may be "defensible reasons for paternalism" (Barnett 2011b, 107), and while paternalism has "not received the attention it deserves . . . partly because of its radioactive nature" (2012, 489), it is "quite common and present wherever global compassion has become institutionalized" (2012, 487). In particular, Barnett outlines the many instances when international humanitarian actors interfere with the lives of beneficiaries, "without their consent, on the grounds that it helps the person or group being intervened upon" (2011b, 114). Crucially, he explains how paternalism is often buttressed by claims of expertise, as experts "almost always claim to know more than anyone else especially those who appear to be illiterate, poor and backwards" (Barnett 2011b, 115).

Barnett draws on the example of UNHCR to illustrate both the functioning and implications of paternalism. He argues that UNHCR employs productive power to create realities and "draws our attention to what 'counts' as a problem" (Barnett 2011b, 109). In this way, UNHCR has expanded "its protection and assistance activities to more populations around the world over the decades" while also "confer[ing] on it the role of spokesperson for and guardian of refugees" (Barnett 2011b, 107). To do this, UNHCR has drawn on two forms of authority. First, UNHCR has drawn on its "expert" authority, claiming credibility because of its "specialized training, knowledge, or experience" (Barnett 2011b, 110). Second, UNHCR has drawn on its "moral" authority, claiming to be able to speak and act "on behalf of the community's values and interests and defending the lives of the weak and vulnerable" (Barnett 2011b, 110). Barnett explains how UNHCR combines these two forms of authority to exercise a certain form of paternalism in the context of involuntary repatriation: "While UNHCR does not possess the physical means to violently force refugees to repatriate against their will, it has manipulated information so that the refugee will 'consent' to return home; the agency defends such actions on the grounds that while the conditions at home might not have radically improved, the refugees' long-term interests is getting out of camps and returning to their villages as quickly as possible" (2012, 507).

Many of these tendencies were present in UNHCR's return and reintegration program in Mozambique. As suggested below, paternalism provides a useful lens through which UNHCR's actions in Mozambique can be more fully understood, especially in terms of UNHCR's relations with refugees; its relations with other UN actors, especially the UN Office for Humanitarian Assistance Coordination (UNOHAC); and the inclusion of community-based peacebuilding efforts in national peacebuilding programming (see Synge 1997). At the same time, the case of Mozambique provides an opportunity for potentially expanding our understanding of the role of paternalism in explaining UNHCR's actions. Barnett's treatment of UNHCR largely relates to UNHCR's increased use of involuntary repatriation and the understanding that "refugee assessment of the situation or consent to repatriation was no longer necessary" (2011b, 124). In contrast, Mozambique represents a case in which the vast majority of refugees repatriate spontaneously and prior to the launch of UNHCR's return and reintegration program. This is not to suggest that UNHCR did not exhibit paternalistic tendencies in response. On the contrary, UNHCR sought to problematize the spontaneous return of refugees and construct the substance and timing of the reintegration program in terms that furthered its own institutional interests, arguably in opposition to needs of refugees. In the case of Mozambique, however, Barnett's understanding of paternalism helps explain why local peacebuilding efforts following repatriation were not recognized more fully by UNHCR and integrated more systematically into a broader understanding of Mozambique's national peacebuilding program.

Case of Return to Mozambique

On October 4, 1992, the government of Mozambique and Renamo signed the GPA in Rome, bringing to a close fifteen years of war. On October 13 the UN Security Council passed Resolution 782 (1992), approving the appointment of Aldo Ajello as the special representative of the secretary-general to oversee UN activities in Mozambique. Then, on December 16, 1992, the UN Security Council passed Resolution 797 (1992), which created ONUMOZ. Its mandate specifically addressed the need for a "fully integrated approach" to peacebuilding in Mozambique, with emphasis on the relationship between the political, military, electoral, and humanitarian challenges. ONUMOZ was tasked with supporting a process leading to elections, monitoring the cease-fire and the demobilization of one hundred thousand soldiers, overseeing the impartial delivery of humanitarian assistance throughout the country, and coordinating the activities of UN agencies and nongovernmental organizations involved in humanitarian assistance.

The repatriation of refugees was but one of the many overlapping challenges faced by Mozambique. In October 1992 there were an estimated 1.7 million refugees in six neighboring countries, with 1 million in Malawi alone (see Bradley 2013a; Juergensen 2000). In the weeks following the GPA, border areas of Sofala, Tete, and other provinces began to experience several "scouting visits" by refugees who had spent many years in exile in Malawi (Sumba and Wilson 1993).[10] This began a process of large-scale, spontaneous return, with refugees themselves determining that conditions were appropriate for them to return. In fact, this was seen as a continuation of a longer-term strategy by many refugees to move back and forth between Mozambique and Malawi to spread risk, to maintain contact with their land in Mozambique, and to be prepared to return and resume cultivation according to the agricultural seasons and in response to a close reading of the local security situation (see Juergensen 2000). It was estimated that some two hundred thousand refugees returned from Malawi alone in the year following the GPA and that "not a single one of these refugees had returned under the auspices of a Tripartite Agreement and the elaborate assistance framework of UNHCR" (Sumba and Wilson 1993, 12). Moreover, it was noted that "recent field studies in Malawi have indicated that a major factor influencing refugee decision-making is information. These studies demonstrate that refugees make considerable effort to obtain good quality information about the issues that they consider important to them. In field work conducted in July 1993 in a number of sites in Malawi . . . it was discovered that most refugees had either visited their home areas themselves, or had close relatives or associates who had done so" (Sumba and Wilson 1993, 15). It is important to note that early planning in support of refugee repatriation recognized the diversity of refugee experiences and the efforts refugees were investing in making informed decisions about the timing of their own repatriation (see Koser 1997). As UNOHAC noted in June 1993, "The most important rule of the repatriation operation is that the refugees themselves are in control. The majority will go home at a time of their own choosing and either walk or take transport which they themselves have organized. The humanitarian assistance effort is adapting to this, helping refugees to organize their own repatriation and pick their own time, thus channeling and facilitating return migration rather than attempting to control it" (ONUMOZ 1993, 7).

This view stands in stark contrast to UNHCR's characterization of the ability of refugees to make informed decisions about their repatriation and of the range of skills returning refugees would bring to Mozambique. On March 16, 1993, UNHCR signed a memorandum of understanding with the government of Mozambique, which in turn provided the legal framework for the negotiation of tripartite agreements with six neighboring states. In May 1993 UNHCR launched a $200 million appeal to support a three-year program to support the return and reintegration of 1.5 million refugees from six neighboring states. This was soon followed by a mission to the region by Douglas Stafford, UNHCR's deputy high commissioner, from June 6 to 12, 1993. His mission report illustrates the contradictions in UNHCR's thinking at the time on the capacity of refugees to be responsible for the styling of their own solution and the need for UNHCR to also impose solutions on refugees. He reports that "the cease-fire had an immediate impact. Refugees and internally displaced are returning at a very fast pace. Over 260,000 have returned from Malawi into Tete province. . . . The results are dramatic. In overflying the border between Tete and Malawi and driving through the province, we were shown, in Malawi, whole refugee camps, empty and dismantled, the roofs taken from the building, and in Mozambique, new villages everywhere, surrounded by well-planted and tilled crops."[11] He goes on, however, to argue:

> I would recommend that we break the iron rice bowl and encourage . . . return in the manner outlined below. This is of course predicated on the continuation of peace and security and on the voluntariness of return. Steps: 1. Enhance food security in Mozambique; 2. phased closure of camps, to be completed by the end of the next harvest (April 1994);

3. A plan should be developed and implemented immediately to begin shifting resources—human and material—from the asylum countries to Mozambique.[12]

To this should be added the way UNHCR characterized the refugee population in its 1993–95 country operations plan for Mozambique, which emphasized that "the majority" of the 797,000 refugees who had spontaneously returned to Mozambique "are of rural background, illiterate and have a relatively large number of female-headed households."[13] This characterization clearly echoes Barnett's explanation for the justification of paternalism by organizations like UNHCR.

In fact, neither the country operation plan nor the 1993 repatriation and reintegration plan includes any mention of the decision-making of refugees, the skills with which they were returning, or the contribution they could make to the massive task of postconflict reconstruction in Mozambique. This stands in stark contrast to understandings of the economic activity of refugees while in exile, especially in Malawi (see Ager, Ager, and Long 1995; Callamard 1994a, 1994b), and UNHCR's own assessment of the skills possessed by returning refugees. For example, Agnes Callamard (1994b, 59) notes that both refugees and local communities in Malawi "found a trading system and generate incomes within an economic space limited, on one side by refugee status, refugee policy and refugee assistance, on the other by the structural economic conditions of the area of settlement." Likewise, UNHCR's own surveys illustrated the range of skills with which refugees were repatriating. Among refugees returning from Tanzania, UNHCR found that there were 80 carpenters, 39 masons, 21 teachers, 23 blacksmiths, 85 drivers, 3 doctors and 12 mechanics.[14] Likewise, UNHCR found that among heads of families of Mozambican refugees in Zambia there were 113 carpenters, 5 mechanics, 16 drivers, 18 agricultural instructors, 50 teachers, 44 bricklayers, and 1 geologist.[15] All of these skills could have been directed to support the 1,500 Quick Impact Projects supported by UNHCR between 1993 and 1996 (see UNHCR 1997a, 26), yet there is no evidence in either UNHCR or UNOHAC documents to suggest that there was an effort to match these capacities to peacebuilding and reconstruction efforts.

While UNHCR later noted that its program planning could have done more to involve "UNHCR offices in the refugees' country of asylum" (see UNHCR 1997a, 25), suggesting that a lack of coordination may explain the outcome, documents from March 1994 offer a different explanation. Sadako Ogata, the UN high commissioner for refugees, arrived in Mozambique on March 2, 1994, as part of a visit to the region relating to the implementation of the repatriation program.[16] Following her visit to Mozambique, Ogata convened a meeting of UNHCR's representatives in Southern Africa. In preparation for that meeting, UNHCR prepared the document "Mozambique Repatriation Operation, 1994: Policy Objectives, Country Plan and Issues to Be Monitored." This document stated that UNHCR's primary objective in 1994 was

> to ensure that as many refugees as possible (up to 650,000), currently in countries of asylum, return to Mozambique in 1994. UNHCR needs to accelerate the repatriation operation as soon as possible because:
> * The best time to return is during the dry season starting in April
> * The next planting season starts in September
> * The elections are due to be held latest in 1994
> * Some countries of asylum may be growing weary of hosting so many refugees for an extended period
> * The operation must be implemented rapidly in order to maintain donor interest
> * New emerging problems elsewhere may compete for attention and resources (UNHCR 1994)

It is significant to note that UNHCR's motivations with the repatriation of Mozambican refugees only partially related to the well-being of refugees, as understood in relation to the timing of repatriation. More generally, UNHCR appears to have been motived by its relations with states, its image as a result-delivering organization, and an assessment of the availability of donor support. These motivations are in keeping with the organization's global preoccupations at the time (Loescher 2001). In fact, there are several mentions in the document about the need to develop a "media-friendly" approach, and several action points on engaging the media to "raise the profile of the programme." The consequence of this decision, however, meant that refugees lost control over repatriation decisions. Bradley notes, "as the return operation progressed, its voluntary nature was compromised by UNHCR's decision to accelerate repatriation from Malawi, where the vast majority of refugees were sheltered, by halting food distribution in the camps" (2013a, 157).

A preliminary reading of documents in the archives also suggests that UNHCR's desire to remain a prominent actor in the eyes of donors also affected its willingness to cooperate with other humanitarian actors in Mozambique, despite UNOHAC's mandate of coordinating humanitarian activities. This, in turn, was found to have undermined the role of refugees in the national peacebuilding program, specifically the ability of refugees remaining in exile to be registered to vote in the 1994 elections. While documents from 1993 suggest that UNHCR actively contributed to the coordinated approach of UNOHAC in Mozambique, it may be suggested that this collaboration waned as UNHCR's presence in Mozambique grew. UNHCR reported that its staff presence in Mozambique had grown from 36 in early 1993 to 257 by early 1994.[17] At roughly the same time, the archival record suggests there was an increase in tension between UNHCR and UNOHAC, relating largely to UNHCR's relations with other humanitarian partners. Communications between UNOHAC staff included statements such as "I feel that UNHCR should be more transparent. . . . UNHCR should be prepared to defend its programme and its implementing partners."[18] It was increasingly noted that UNHCR did not participate in UNOHAC assessment and planning missions.[19] Likewise, concerns were increasingly raised about elements of UNHCR's budget. In July 1994, for example, a procurement office with UNOHAC sent a message to the director of UNOHAC (himself a former UNHCR employee). The message reviewed the costs of the Quick Impact Projects proposed by UNHCR and found that they were "to put it mildly, somewhat disproportionate," with the example of a project for thirty-one latrines being budgeted for $61,840—or about $2,000 per latrine as opposed to the expected $5. The message concludes by asking the director to "take up this matter with UNHCR to see if anything can be done, if only as a form of damage control."[20]

Much more work is required with the archival documents to more fully trace the evolution of the relationship between UNHCR and UNOHAC and the implications of this relationship on UNHCR's own activities and its ability to represent the needs of refugees within the national peacebuilding program in Mozambique. Preliminary results, however, suggest that UNHCR's limited engagement with the integrated UN mission in Mozambique may have resulted in its marginalization from decisions on matters that affected refugees remaining in neighboring countries—specifically their ability to vote in the general elections, widely held to be the UN's marquee accomplishment in Mozambique (Synge 1997, 115–44). On November 26, 1993, the ONUMOZ brokered an agreement with the two main political parties on a number of outstanding election issues, including voting rights for expatriate Mozambicans, including refugees. Voter registration was initially scheduled between April and June 1994. In this context, UNHCR argued that it was working to complete repatriation by June 1994 so that refugees could be home to register for elections. In April 1994, the ONUMOZ operations meeting discussed the issue. The officer in charge of the electoral division noted that he had met with UNHCR on April 20 to discuss arrangements for the 350,000 eligible voters who were estimated to be among the 800,000 refugees remaining in neighboring states. While the meeting heard that UNHCR was "making great efforts to repatriate as many as possible" in time for voter registration, UNHCR had been advised that "for those of whom timely repatriation is not possible, various options are being considered."[21] The matter was not raised again in the operations meetings until July 21, 1994, when it was reported that the National Elections Commission "had decided that Mozambican emigrants abroad [i.e., refugees] will not be permitted to vote in the elections."[22]

More generally, it is important to highlight how the archives reflect a narrow understanding of the potential contribution of refugees to the peacebuilding process. UNHCR's approach to repatriation emphasizes the programmatic and logistical challenges of facilitating the return of such large numbers of people from neighboring states. UNHCR's own review of the reintegration process notes that it had "encountered remarkably few problems" but does not reflect on the initiatives taken at the local level to facilitate this process (UNHCR 1997a, 24). This is especially true in the resolution of land disputes, where "many Mozambicans marshalled cultural practices and worked with traditional authorities to help themselves resolve their claims and grievances" (Bradley 2013a, 159).

While such issues had the potential to compromise national peacebuilding priorities, these local efforts were neither recognized or incorporated into national peacebuilding planning nor reflected in UNHCR's repatriation programming. As a result of these local efforts, "most returnees were able to access some land for building a shelter and planting crops, which relieved immediate pressure on the government and international actors to tackle the problem" (Bradley 2013a, 161). While Bradley notes that this "melding [of] top-down and bottom-up approaches" made a significant contribution to the ascribed success of the repatriation to Mozambique, it is important to note that this melding was often outside of formal efforts by institutional actors, especially UNHCR. In this way, the case of Mozambique provides an important illustration of the important contributions of local peacebuilding initiatives, often including or initiated by returned refugees and how these initiatives may be apart from formal, internationally supported national peacebuilding programs. While this underscores the importance of developing the intersection between top-down and bottom-up approaches to peacebuilding, it further underscores the need to more fully identify and understand the many contributions to peacebuilding initiated by refugees that are not part of national peacebuilding programs.

Conclusion: Lessons from Mozambique

A recurring refrain of UN Secretary-General Boutros Boutros-Ghali during his visit to Mozambique in October 1993 was "the future of Mozambique lays in the hands of its people and their leaders." Indeed, it can be argued that the people of Mozambique seized that opportunity and engaged enthusiastically and diligently in the peacebuilding process. The elections of late October 1994 were peaceful, found to be "free and fair," and saw the participation of more than 90 percent of eligible voters. Moreover, the two years between the GPA and the elections witnessed the return of some 1.5 million Mozambicans, of whom only 375,000 "were provided with transport and reception facilities by UNHCR" (UNHCR 1997a, 26). Some twenty-five years later, the ability of Mozambique to emerge from such a protracted and devastating conflict and accomplish what it did in a relatively short period of time sustains the understanding that Mozambique can be regarded as a "success."

A preliminary reading of the recently opened archives of ONUMOZ, however, suggests that there are nuances of this success that need to be more fully understood. Specifically, the documents raise important questions about the actual and potential role of refugees in the peacebuilding process and about the possibility of missed opportunities. In contrast with UNHCR's official account of its program, the archives also contain possible counternarratives that suggest UNHCR played a paternalistic role, which may have constrained, not enabled, the role of refugees themselves as decision makers and agents in the national peacebuilding process while overlooking the significant contribution of peacebuilding efforts at the local level. These preliminary conclusions suggest that a more complete reading of the Mozambique case reveals that while the return of 1.5 million refugees may have been a success in that they returned and have largely remained in Mozambique, there were several opportunities to actively engage them in the planning and implementation of the national peacebuilding process, especially in relation to the political process, the restoration of core government functions, and economic revitalization, while their contributions to the resolution of disputes at local levels have been undervalued in the official record of peacebuilding accomplishments. Instead, a preliminary assessment suggests that UNHCR asserted its expert and moral authority in pursuit of its own institutional interests. In this way, the case of Mozambique illustrates the utility of Barnett's treatment of paternalism to explain UNHCR's position on refugee repatriation, even in instances where refugees were repatriating *ahead* of UNHCR's program. Likewise, the case of Mozambique suggests the need for additional research to revisit a wider range of historical and contemporary cases to understand how notions of paternalism may provide a methodological context in which the ability or inability of refugees to engage in political process may be more fully explained.

Even this preliminary revisiting the case of Mozambique holds important lessons for the relationship between refugees and peacebuilding. First, it confirms that the ability of refugees to contribute to core peacebuilding priorities can be constrained by the policy choices of states and international organizations like UNHCR. Second, it highlights the potential benefits of incorporating the role and contributions of refugees more fully into integrated national peacebuilding programs—rather than treating refugees as a stand-alone, postconflict priority. Finally, it suggests that the thematic, temporal, and geographic scope of peacebuilding can usefully be expanded to more fully incorporate the contributions that can be made by refugees in neighboring states prior to their repatriation, along with a more comprehensive understanding of the significant contribution of local peacebuilding initiatives.

Notes

Research for this chapter was supported by a Standard Research Grant from the Social Sciences and Humanities Research Council and the Office of the Vice President (Research and International), Carleton University. The author is grateful for the invaluable contributions of Martha Chertkow and Katherine Kenney, two research assistants on the project "Refugees and the Regional Dimensions of Peacebuilding." The author would also like to acknowledge the help (and great patience) of the United Nations Archives and Records Management Section, New York, during research in the UN Archives in February 2015.

1. For an overview of this research and examples, see Milner (2011, 2015).

2. "Protracted Refugee Situations," discussion paper prepared for the High Commissioner's Dialogue on Protection Challenges, Geneva, December 2008, UNHCR /DPC/2008/Doc. 02, 20 November 2008, http://www.unhcr.org/492ad3782.pdf.

3. See, for example, Autesserre (2010); Maphosa, DeLuca, and Keasley (2014); Porter (2003).

4. While Megan Bradley notes this characterization of the repatriation process within humanitarian circles, it is important to note that her treatment of the case problematizes this characterization as arguably superficial.

5. According to the monthly report of the United Nations Office for Humanitarian Assistance Coordination, dated February 22, 1994, the first meeting of the "working group on repatriation and resettlement issues" was held in February 1994. UN Archives S-0295-0032-0006, accessed February 2015.

6. See Barnett (2012, 485–521; 2011a; 2011b, 105–32; 2017).

7. This section draws from Milner (2011, 2015).

8. "Protracted Refugee Situations," UNHCR/DPC/2008/Doc. 02, November 20, 2008.

9. As noted by Christopher Mitchell (2012, 2), however, "the relationship between local and national peace processes is more complicated than was first assumed."

10. It is interesting to note that the document in the archives includes the handwritten note "Catherine—this is the doc Sam mentioned before this morning's

meeting—perhaps you'd enjoy reading it—John, 24 February 1994," in reference to a UNOHAC meeting in Maputo, Mozambique, that day, suggesting that these details were known prior to the launch of UNHCR's reintegration program.

11. "Visit of Douglas Stafford, Deputy High Commissioner—Mission report—6–12 June 1993," UN Archives S-0382-0010-0005, 1.

12. "Visit of Douglas Stafford," 3–4.

13. UNHCR, "Country Operation Plan for Mozambique: 1993–1995," n.d., UN Archives S-0382-0004-0001.

14. UNHCR, "Survey of Mozambican Refugees in Tanzania," n.d. (likely 1993), UN Archives S-0382-0004-0005.

15. UNHCR, "Mozambican Refugees in Zambia: Classification by Occupation," n.d. (likely 1993), UN Archives S-0382-0004-0006.

16. Full details of Ogata's visit were shared with ONUMOZ only on March 1, 1994 (Letter from Alfredo del Rio Court, UNHCR Representative to Mozambique, to Behrooz Sadry, Deputy Special Representative of the Secretary-General to Mozambique, UN Archives S-0295-0062-0008). It is interesting to note that the briefing package included a one-page biography of the high commissioner and a one-page list of honors she had received, such as honorary degrees.

17. UNHCR, "Country Operation Plan for Mozambique: 1993–1995," n.d., UN Archives S-0382-0004-0001.

18. "Fax from Alistair Hallam, UNOHAC Tete to Catherine Huck, UNOHAC Maputo: Subject: Visit to Tete Province," March 25, 1994, UN Archives S-0382-0003-0003.

19. "Report from Sam Barnes, Chief of the Assessment and Planning Unit of UNOHAC following a mission to Northern Niassa and Cabo Delgado—7 and 8 April 1994," April 19, 1994, UN Archives S-0295-0020-0003.

20. "Note for the file from Trevor Hockley, A&P Officer UNOHAC to Felix Downes-Thomas, Director UNOHAC," July 12, 1994, UN Archives S-0382-0005-0006.

21. Report of Mr. R. Dreyer, OIC, Electoral Division, in "Draft Minutes of 21 April 1994 Operations Meeting," April 21, 1994, UN Archives S-0295-0025-0003.

22. Report of Mr. Albert Djemba, Deputy Director, Electoral Division, in "Final Minutes of 21 July 2014 Operations Meeting," July 27, 1994, UN Archives S-0295-0025-0002.

7

Displaced Persons as Symbols of Grievance

Collective Identity, Individual Rights, and Durable Solutions

Patrik Johansson

During fieldwork in Azerbaijan 2008, I was told by the head of an international organization working on displacement that one of the reasons internal displacement has been so difficult to address is that "the IDPs are the physical indicator of Azerbaijan's claim to Nagorno-Karabakh" (Johansson 2010). The message was that Azerbaijan is reluctant to integrate the internally displaced persons (IDPs) locally because they have come to symbolize something beyond their own displacement—namely, the territorial struggle for Nagorno-Karabakh—and, consequently, a solution to their displacement in the absence of a resolution of the conflict would undermine the legitimacy of Azerbaijan's position in the territorial conflict. And Azerbaijan is not the only case where displacement is being prolonged by government preferences on settlement options. The Internal Displacement Monitoring Centre (IDMC) argues that this is the case in a fifth of all situations examined in its 2015 global overview of internal displacement (IDMC 2015).[1]

This symbolic role of IDPs, which can of course also befall refugees, has attracted limited attention in previous research. In this chapter I conduct an exploratory analysis of two such cases: the internal displacement of some six hundred thousand Azerbaijanis since the war over Nagorno-Karabakh in the first half of the 1990s, and the Palestinian refugee problem, which has been one of the most intractable aspects of the Israeli-Palestinian conflict since the late 1940s and today involves more than 5 million refugees. The aim of this chapter is to analyze how certain displaced populations come to assume this symbolic role and what consequences it might have for conflict resolution processes and the search for durable solutions to displacement. The questions I explore include: How have the Azerbaijani IDPs and the Palestinian refugees taken on the symbolic roles they have today? Do displaced persons assume this role voluntarily, is it forced on them, or do elements of both co-ercion and choice shape this process? How do symbolic aspects of a conflict relate to material aspects, and how can they be combined into a single analysis? How does this symbolic significance affect resolution processes and the search for durable solutions, and how does this play out at different levels of analysis?

In both cases, physical remnants of where displaced persons used to live have been largely destroyed. Walid Khalidi (1992) catalogs 418 Palestinian villages depopulated during the war of 1948, most of them destroyed and made uninhabitable soon thereafter. Large-scale destruction also characterizes the war over Nagorno-Karabakh, such as the destruction of several towns in the occupied districts, including the removal of electrical wiring, pipes, and other infrastructure (ICG 2005a). The displaced persons themselves, however, are a constant, tangible reminder of the loss sustained by Palestinians and Azerbaijanis, a loss greater than the sum of displaced persons' individual losses. In this way, they have come to manifest injustices in need of rectification.

I lay the foundation for my analysis through a brief discussion of previous research on how displacement is related to issues of conflict and peace. I then discuss what I mean by symbolism and how I approach it analytically. Next, I analyze the symbolic significance of displacement in the cases of Nagorno-Karabakh and Palestine and how it affects conflict resolution and the search for durable solutions to displacement. While there are important differences between the cases—not least that one is mainly about IDPs and the other about refugees—they are both large, protracted displacement situations in which the displaced populations have become symbols of grievance, and this makes them useful for comparison. The chapter's exploratory approach is also facilitated by that symbolism being more pronounced in these cases than in many others. I argue that, in these cases, the symbolism of displacement serves to prevent change rather than to promote it; I comment on this symbolism at different levels of analysis; and I discuss alternatives to the traditional durable solutions to displacement.

Exploring Displacement, Conflict, and Peace

The broader struggles that displaced persons may become symbols of are often (though not necessarily) related to territory. The political bond between population and territory is highlighted by the 1933 Montevideo Convention on the Rights and Duty of States, which, in its first article, sets out the criteria for statehood: (a) a permanent population, (b) a defined territory,

(c) government, and (d) capacity to enter into relations with other states. Further, conquest and colonization have often gone hand in hand, with the movement of people being used to establish territorial control or justify territorial claims. Researchers (such as Bookman 1997; McGarry 1998; Morland 2014) use the term "demographic engineering" to describe strategies aimed at increasing the demographic strength of certain ethnic groups, often in terms of both perceived legitimacy and control. Demographic engineering is intentional, it can be the result of political decision-making or social pressure, and the actual strategies used can involve everything from genocide via the physical movement of people and discriminatory policies to changing the basis of group identity.

Whether or not demographic engineering has taken place, armed groups will often manipulate displacement to their advantage. Stephen Stedman (2003) argues that by controlling access to refugees, armed groups can force other actors such as international organizations to work with them, thus increasing their legitimacy; by controlling various forms of aid, armed groups can strengthen their control over refugees; and by using refugee camps for sanctuaries and to recruit new soldiers, armed groups may boost their fighting capability. Positioning displaced populations as symbols of a national struggle may, alongside these strategies, be an additional way in which armed groups manipulate forced migration to their advantage.

Kelly Greenhill (2008, 7), instead of looking at the decisions or manipulation of those already displaced, analyzes "strategic engineered migration," which refers to "those in- or out-migrations that are deliberately induced or manipulated by state or non-state actors, in ways designed to augment, reduce, or change the composition of the population residing within a particular territory, for political or military ends." Previous research has also addressed the relationship between durable solutions to displacement and the resolution of conflict. Part of this research has addressed the development of return as the default solution to displacement since the 1980s (Barnett and Finnemore 2004; Chimni 2004).

The perception of repatriation as a necessary condition for peace after armed conflict has been established as "the conventional wisdom of most refugee experts" (Adelman 2002, 273), but later analyses of this claim have found that reality is more complex. Howard Adelman (2002) analyzes the intrinsic logic of the assumed importance of repatriation and finds that there is no singular relationship between refugee repatriation and peace: in some cases repatriation makes a positive contribution to peace, but in other cases it is irrelevant or even negative. Patrik Johansson (2010) refers to the assumption that the return of displaced persons is a necessary condition for peace as "the peace-by-repatriation thesis" and sets out to test whether it holds across several cases. He finds that repatriation is not necessary for peace after armed conflict, either by itself or in combination with other factors such as territorial partition or ethnic fractionalization. Ending displacement turns out to be positively related to peace—but as far as the quality or sustainability of peace is concerned, repatriation is not better than any other durable solution.

While the dynamics surrounding return and peacebuilding vary, return is central to the positioning of displaced populations as symbols of grievance, in that even if the uprooted are able to access a different durable solution such as local integration or resettlement, the injustice of their displacement may not be perceived to have been addressed unless they can return to and reclaim their homes. In the conclusion I discuss the limits of the traditional durable solutions and suggest alternatives that may be useful in cases where displacement has taken on symbolic significance.

Studying the Symbolism of Displacement

For the purposes of this study, a displacement situation takes on a symbolic significance when the importance of that situation goes beyond the immediate question of the rights and well-being of the displaced population. This is related to—but not the same thing as—the need to consider displacement as not just a humanitarian but a political problem requiring political solutions (for example, Gil Loescher and James Milner [2005, 2008] make this argument in relation to protracted refugee situations). In cases where displaced persons become symbols of grievance or of a broader political struggle, there is also a need to address the resolution of conflict and durable solutions to displacement in concert—and not just for pragmatic reasons but because different solutions have different implications in terms of rights or rectification of losses. To be clear, most conflict-induced displacement can be seen to symbolize the conflict that caused it; continued displacement can be seen as a sign that a conflict remains unresolved, but once the conflict is resolved, displacement loses this symbolic quality and becomes an essentially humanitarian issue. In some cases, however, displacement takes on a symbolic value in its own right, constraining resolution processes and the search for durable solutions—indeed, the symbolism of displacement can make both resolving the conflict and improving the situation of the displaced more difficult to accomplish. This latter kind of symbolism is what I address in this chapter.

Regarding the case studies below, Palestine is well researched, and I rely completely on secondary sources. In the case of Nagorno-Karabakh, I draw on my findings from field research conducted in 2008, complemented by more recent secondary sources. The case studies contribute to understanding how the different forces and perspectives around displacement, conflict resolution, and durable solutions relate to and interact with one another. The case studies attempt to answer the following questions: How is the symbolism of displacement manifested in the respective cases? How does this symbolism affect conflict resolution and the search for durable solutions to displacement? And how does it affect displaced persons' roles in shaping solutions to conflict and displacement?

The Azerbaijani IDPs

Nagorno-Karabakh has been an issue of contention between Armenians and Azerbaijanis since the 1920s, when the Armenian-dominated enclave was made part of the Azerbaijan Soviet Socialist Republic (SSR) rather than the Armenian SSR. Through most of the Soviet era the dispute was suppressed, but as the political climate began to open up in the late 1980s, tensions grew and in 1988 Nagorno-Karabakh officially demanded to be transferred to Armenia. Initially, the Soviet Union attempted to prevent the changes called for by Nagorno-Karabakh and Armenia, but with its dissolution in 1991, the conflict developed into civil war between the government of the newly independent Azerbaijan and its secessionist enclave Nagorno-Karabakh, backed by Armenia. The war ended in 1994 with the Bishkek Protocol brokered by Russia, establishing a cease-fire along the "line of contact" with Nagorno-Karabakh and most of seven adjacent districts under de facto Nagorno-Karabakh/Armenian control (ICG 2005b).

Large-scale displacement began during the late 1980s, as ethnic Azerbaijanis left the Armenian SSR for the Azerbaijan SSR and ethnic Armenians went the other way. When the cease-fire was agreed, there were around 290,000 ethnic Armenian refugees from Azerbaijan in Armenia and another 100,000 in Russia, and around 185,000 ethnic Azerbaijani refugees from Armenia in Azerbaijan. These refugees have since generally integrated in their respective host societies. Similarly, most of the 70,000 internally displaced Armenians have either been able to return or to integrate in host communities. However, some 600,000 internally displaced ethnic Azerbaijanis (40,000 from Nagorno-Karabakh proper, and 560,000 from the surrounding occupied districts) are still in need of durable solutions. Gradually, these IDPs have become symbols of the struggle for Nagorno-Karabakh. This symbolism is one reason why the IDPs remain displaced more than two decades after the cease-fire—more specifically, the failure to resolve the conflict over Nagorno-Karabakh is the main reason the IDPs have not been able to return, but the symbolic significance of displacement is one reason their displacement has not been ended through local integration.

For a long time, most of the IDPs lived in precarious conditions, unable to meet their basic needs. Coming from a rural background, many IDPs have had problems finding employment in urban areas. The IDMC concluded in 2005, ten years after the cease-fire, that "the national agenda has been focused on return rather than local integration" (IDMC 2005), and more recently they argued that IDPs "have become an inherent part of a national narrative around occupation" (IDMC 2014a, 3). This emphasis on return resulted in a failure to provide permanent shelters for IDPs, instead forcing many to stay for years in "camps, trains, half-constructed buildings, makeshift houses, and on roadsides" often lacking insulation, water, and sanitation facilities. By 2014 the general situation for IDPs had improved, not least in terms of housing (IDMC 2014a), but the government's continued insistence that displacement is temporary has important consequences. For example, many IDPs are offered new housing, but because it is temporary, they are not allowed to rent or sell property or to mortgage it.

The IDPs need not be poor. If that was ever a deliberate policy on the part of the government, it does not seem to be today. However, the basis for all assistance efforts is the desire to maintain the social cohesion of the IDPs in order to make an eventual return smoother—often with negative consequences for the IDPs until that return becomes possible. New housing for the IDPs tends to be separated from existing communities, and this undermines their ability to integrate and become less reliant on assistance. Schooling is also segregated, with more than half of all displaced children being schooled separately from their nondisplaced peers. While many IDPs value this, it contributes to stigmatization and hampers integration, thereby undermining their social prospects even further. The political participation of IDPs is severely limited as they can vote and run for office only in their places of origin, administrative structures that are maintained in anticipation of return. Their inability to vote or run for office in their place of refuge for all practical purposes denies them influence on local issues where they live.

Peace negotiations have been conducted under the auspices of the "Minsk Group" of the Organization for Security and Cooperation in Europe since 1992. The Minsk Group is chaired by France, Russia, and the United States, and the local parties involved are Armenia and Azerbaijan; the self-proclaimed Nagorno-Karabakh Republic (NKR) is not officially party to the negotiations, but it has close political ties with Armenia. The negotiations conducted in the Minsk Group are typically highly confidential (de Waal 2009). However, in 2006, the cochairs released several basic principles for a settlement. They did this to counter the hard-line narratives presented by both governments at home and let the public know what was being discussed. The principles involved, inter alia, the withdrawal of Armenian forces from the occupied territories, deployment of international peacekeepers, demining and reconstruction, return of IDPs to the occupied territories and Nagorno-Karabakh,[2] and the final status of Nagorno-Karabakh to be determined by popular referendum (ICG 2007; OSCE 2006).

The most contentious issue is the status of Nagorno-Karabakh, with both sides being adamant that sovereignty must lie with them. So far the international community considers Nagorno-Karabakh and the surrounding districts as de jure Azerbaijani territory, and no state including Armenia has recognized the NKR. Similarly, there is broad international support for the right of return for the Azerbaijani IDPs, but practical efforts to assist them tend to be geared toward local integration.

During field research in 2008, I was told by the head of an international organization in Baku that "the IDPs are the physical indicator of Azerbaijan's claim to Nagorno-Karabakh" (Johansson 2010). The displaced persons serve as a constant reminder that the territorial conflict is not resolved. More importantly, in the Azerbaijani narrative, the displaced persons' need for a durable solution is framed exclusively as a need for return, which presupposes Azerbaijan's regaining control of its lost territory. While the NKR would accept the return of Azerbaijanis to certain areas under its control, IDPs would be unwilling to return to territory controlled by Armenia/NKR.

In terms of identity and narrative, the IDPs nourish their Karabakh identity and their roots in Nagorno-Karabakh and the surrounding territories, rather than emphasizing their identity as displaced persons per se. There is a strong sense of the need to preserve their Karabakh identity, both on the part of the displaced persons themselves and on the part of the government. This is part of the explanation for the difficulty of finding durable solutions for the displaced persons. Neither the IDPs themselves nor the national and international organizations that work with the IDPs believe that the Azerbaijani government is keeping them displaced for propaganda purposes (Johansson 2010).

The active role of displaced persons in shaping solutions to conflict and displacement in Azerbaijan is negligible. This is not because the government or any other party prevents them from participating but because there seems to be a broad consensus that the responsibility for resolving the political conflict with Armenia and the self-proclaimed NKR rests solely with the government. This consensus also encompasses the view that return is the only acceptable (and workable) durable solution to displacement, which for practical reasons will be possible only once the political conflict is resolved. In the meantime, any efforts at improving the situation for the IDPs are determinedly temporary.

During my interviews, both civil society representatives and IDPs expressed very little knowledge about what the government is doing in terms of trying to resolve the conflict or address displacement, other than that it is party to the highly confidential Minsk Group talks. The same is true in Armenia. Even a high-level official at a government ministry in Yerevan refrained from answering questions about the peace process, arguing that "only the minister of the exterior is authorized to deal with these issues" (Johansson 2010). Importantly, this was taken for granted by interviewees, officials, and IDPs and was generally not perceived as a problem. Whether negotiations are open or not is of limited consequence to civil society; the problem with the Minsk Group process is that it has not produced any results.

Several interviewees stressed return as the only acceptable durable solution to displacement. Because the armed conflict caused the displacement and, by implication, the various problems associated with displacement, peace will bring about return and put an end to these problems. Nostalgia plays a part in this understanding of how to resolve problems associated with displacement. As in other cases of displacement (Kabachnik, Regulska, and Mitchnek 2010), IDPs compare the poor living conditions of displacement with what their life was like in places of origin, discounting the fact that the place of origin is no longer the same. A displaced person from Aghdam explained, "There is no alternative, no alternative to returning to Nagorno-Karabakh, because the conditions here are bad, but conditions were okay in Karabakh" (Johansson 2010). At the same time, because any possibility of return depends on a solution to the political conflict, durable solutions to displacement are by default put on hold in anticipation of conflict resolution. Many IDPs have de facto integrated into communities in their places of refuge, but the government—as well as most IDPs—would not consider this a durable solution. However, the government has cooperated with several international organizations in developing what is referred to as the "Great Return Plan," which, inter alia, outlines the conditions for voluntary return once there is a peace agreement. Within the Great Return framework, many IDPs have also been relocated to government resettlement communities near Nagorno-Karabakh (ICG 2005b; NRC 2008). In terms of symbolic significance, these resettlement communities reaffirm the government's commitment to the IDPs to work for their return, and IDPs in other areas have expressed envy toward those who are close to home (ICG 2012).

None of this means that IDPs and civil society are unable or unwilling to engage in the political conflict and the problems of displacement, but it narrows the scope of that engagement. Civil society organizations, Armenian as well as Azerbaijani, stress the failure of their respective governments to talk to their populations about compromise, reconciliation, and coexistence. Despite being involved in negotiations through the Minsk Group, both governments have consistently presented hard-line positions to their constituencies.

This is where civil society organizations see a role for themselves: to work for reconciliation, to undermine stereotypes, and to prepare the public for the coexistence that would be the result of a future resolution of the conflict.

Interviewees made a clear distinction between, on the one hand, the problem of displacement per se, which is symbolically important, and, on the other hand, the various problems that the displaced persons face during (and as a consequence of) displacement, which are not symbolically important. The former is intimately related to a resolution to the conflict and is left to the government to deal with. Conversely, the latter are the kinds of problems highlighted by, among others, the IDMC, such as "inadequate housing, precarious livelihoods, gender-based violence, segregated education, discrimination against children of the displaced and IDPs' limited participation in decisions that affect them" (IDMC 2014a). Civil society organizations, including IDP organizations, are working to address these issues, sometimes with the explicit aim of strengthening the displaced persons' capacity to address their own situation. This is being done both in and around Baku and in the government resettlement communities closer to Nagorno-Karabakh. By the same token, the IDPs (at least the older generation) are generally happy to play the symbolic role bestowed on them, though this does not prevent them from wanting to improve their living conditions during displacement.

The Azerbaijani IDPs are at the same time symbolically significant and practically marginalized, a situation that is less paradoxical because of the distinction between the problem of displacement and the problems of the displaced. One IDP representative noted that because of the symbolic significance of the internal displacement, the government does not want to be seen as ignoring or neglecting the IDPs. This, he said, does not mean that the IDPs are able to use this as leverage against the government on their own initiative, but it means that the government extends certain privileges to the IDPs, or sometimes turns a blind eye to IDPs taking advantage of their position. Further, while the IDP community may well be described as politically weak in Azerbaijan, it is not necessarily weaker than the rest of the population in this authoritarian society.

There are different understandings of the IDP situation in Azerbaijan. Some representatives of international organizations clearly believed that an important reason for the government's rejection of local integration was that continued displacement was essential to its territorial claims to Nagorno-Karabakh. Conversely, local nongovernmental organizations and IDPs themselves emphasized the government's efforts to preserve the social coherence of the IDP community in anticipation of return, ambitions that they largely sympathized with.

The Palestinian Refugees

Conquest and foreign rule had characterized the Middle East for centuries when modern forms of nationalism began to gain traction during the late nineteenth century. After the Second World War, the newly established United Nations proposed to resolve the tensions between Jews and Arabs through a partition of the territory of British Mandate Palestine, as laid out in General Assembly Resolution 181. The partition plan awarded 55 percent of the former British Mandate to the Zionists, who responded favorably to it and in the spring of 1948 declared the establishment of Israel at the eve of the termination of the British Mandate, which had been established by the League of Nations during the interwar period. The Arabs, however, rejected the partition plan and attacked Israel. The ensuing war forced more than 700,000 Palestinian Arabs to flee their homes in what was to become Israel. During the June War of 1967 another 250,000–300,000 Palestinians were driven from the territories that ended up under Israeli occupation.

In the late 1940s, the United Nations set up two separate agencies to protect and assist the refugees and to provide durable solutions. First, General Assembly Resolution 194 (III) of December 11, 1948, established the UN Conciliation Commission for Palestine (UNCCP) to, among other things, "facilitate the return or resettlement, restitution, and compensation of the refugees based on their individual choices." Second, General Assembly Resolution 302 (IV) of December 8, 1949, established the United Nations Relief and Works Agency for Palestine Refugees in the Near East (UNRWA) to assist the refugees through, for example, maintaining refugee camps and providing education (Dumper 2007, 37). Since 1966, however, the UNCCP has existed on paper only, and UNRWA has gradually taken on a protection role as well, a move that has been recognized and commended by the General Assembly (Dumper 2007).

UNRWA's definition of who is a Palestinian refugee was originally intended for establishing assistance procedures, not for determining legal status of refugees (Dumper 2007, 40). Accordingly, UNRWA assists "persons whose normal place of residence was Palestine during the period 1 June 1946 to 15 May 1948, and who lost both home and means of livelihood as a result of the 1948 conflict" and who are registered with the agency. The descendants of Palestinian refugee males are also eligible for registration, and today around 5 million Palestinian refugees are registered with UNRWA.[3] The largest community is the 2 million Palestinian refugees in Jordan. Many have become Jordanian citizens, and even more have (restricted) Jordanian passports. Until the civil war in Syria, 560,000 Palestinian refugees lived there, some 300,000 of whom have been newly displaced by the war. Syria is probably where the Palestinian refugees were most integrated in practice. The Syrian government tried to support their situation for humanitarian reasons while remaining committed to eventual repatriation. Lebanon, which hosts 450,000 Palestinian refugees, is the most hostile Arab host state to the refugee population. The Lebanese government actively aims to prevent the integration of Palestinian refugees. This has led policymakers and negotiators to recognize that "the refugees in Lebanon should be prioritized in any resettlement or repatriation scheme" (Dumper 2007, 88–89). There are also nearly 2 million refugees in the Occupied Palestinian Territories—1.2 million in Gaza and 750,000 in the West Bank.

The situation for Palestinian refugees varies both between and within countries, and it is not possible to do justice to all the relevant facets in a single book chapter. As hosts of most Palestinian refugees, the Arab states have adopted very different approaches to their respective refugee populations, but they have continually supported the right of return, which, in the Palestinian case, is understood in a range of ways but typically involves the repossession of lost homes and lands.

The Palestinian refugee problem has always been intimately linked to the wider Israeli-Palestinian conflict and a major Palestinian concern in any negotiations. Indeed, when the contemporary Palestinian national movement first emerged in the 1950s and 1960s, it made no distinction between the national agenda and refugee rights; implementing the right of return *was* the national agenda (ICG 2014, 3).

Immediately after the war in 1948, the United Nations encouraged social and economic development for the refugees in Arab countries, including for employment and self-sufficiency. However, such "efforts at alleviating the situation were rejected by the refugees because they feared the efforts were designed to deprive them of their right to return to their homes in Palestine" (Dumper 2007, 87). The leaders of Arab states initially were willing to accept resettlement, but because their publics were vehemently against it, they instead ended up as the defenders of the right of return until the emergence of a national Palestinian leadership. In this role they politicized humanitarian assistance, ensuring a strong linkage between UNRWA's mandate and General Assembly Resolution 194 (III) (Al Husseini 2007). That resolution, in addition to establishing the UNCCP, resolved "that the refugees wishing to return to their homes and live at peace with their neighbours should be permitted to do so at the earliest practical date, and that compensation should be paid for the property of those choosing not to return" (UNGA 1948). This resolution has since constituted one of the cornerstones of the Palestinian refugees' right of return.

The most concerted effort to resolve the conflict and find a solution to the refugee problem was the Oslo peace process, which engaged Israel and the Palestine Liberation Organization (PLO) for most of the 1990s, the most substantive result of which remains the establishment of the Palestinian National Authority. One of the final status issues to be negotiated during an interim period of Palestinian self-governance was that of refugees. However, the refugee problem turned out to be one of the most difficult issues to resolve, in close competition with Jerusalem, not least because of the symbolic implications of any solution in terms of responsibility for the creation of the problem. Because of the central role of the refugees in the Palestinian national narrative, a resolution of the conflict that did not satisfactorily address the refugee problem could not be accepted by the Palestinian negotiators, but throughout the process concrete commitments remained elusive. Robert Malley, who was on the American negotiating team at Camp David in 2000, concludes, "As for the future of refugees—for many Palestinians, the heart of the matter—the ideas put forward at Camp David spoke vaguely of a 'satisfactory solution,' leading Mr. Arafat to fear that he would be asked to swallow an unacceptable last-minute proposal" (Malley 2001). At the same time, "refugees have felt that their rights were being traded away in favor of obtaining the basic territorial components of a Palestinian state in the [Occupied Palestinian Territories]" resulting in the establishment of several refugee rights groups (Dumper 2007, 33–34).

The Palestinian refugee problem is a highly material problem, involving a refugee population that over the years has grown to more than 5 million people. At the same time, the refugee problem is very symbolically significant. Their claims are an important part of the individual identity of most refugees as well as of the Palestinian national identity, not limited to those who are actually displaced. Being a refugee means being living proof of the injustice done to the Palestinian people, an injustice that needs to be remedied. As in the case of the Azerbaijani IDPs discussed above, maintaining a distinct identity is closely linked to the preservation of political claims. In the Palestinian case, this has led many refugees to try to maintain a distinct identity as camp residents. This is true also for refugees in the Occupied Palestinian Territories, who have been politically marginalized by their own leadership, including by camp leaders. "To an extent, this was to serve a political goal: maintaining the camps' exceptional status to ensure that they do not lose their identity as symbols of the demand for return" (ICG 2014, 24). This tension between naturalization and upholding the right of return has two important consequences. First, as indicated, for the refugees themselves, remaining displaced becomes an issue of loyalty to the cause. Accepting resettlement, for example, is seen by some Palestinians as tantamount to treason. Second, and more controversial, it singles out the fact of having been displaced as the cause of the refugees' contemporary suffering, thereby overlooking the influence of restrictive host state policies in entrenching the refugees' marginalization and impoverishment. As Diana Allan notes in her study of Palestinian refugees in Lebanon, the assumption that the refugees need to remain displaced in order to retain the right of return has been interpreted by the Lebanese government as "sanctioning the abandonment of integrative policies in favor of temporary solutions oriented toward ultimate repatriation" (Allan 2014, 12). In other words, the Lebanese government deliberately prevents the integration of Palestinian refugees into Lebanese society; this is in part to protect the delicate confessional system of power distribution in Lebanon but also to protect their right of return. For example, until 2005 Palestinians were prohibited from working in some sixty professions, and even after most of these opened up, the necessary working permits have been few and hard to come by (Dumper 2007).

As both refugees and several host countries, particularly Lebanon, uphold the incompatibility of naturalization and the right of return, "any form of assimilation is taboo, because it is seen as forsaking nationalist aspirations and legitimizing historical dispossession. In the discourses of both nationalism and international diplomacy, refugees have been reduced to symbols of a historical and political grievance awaiting redress, and their political and legal claims are almost always discussed with reference exclusively to Israel" (Allan 2014, 3). In spite of this taboo, naturalization does happen, but is less organized and less transparent than in many other places. According to Michael Dumper, "local integration has not taken place as part of a deliberate policy option but incrementally, in most cases unwillingly, and certainly by default. Thus, the preparation, investment, monitoring, and evaluation all envisaged by the formal UNHCR [United Nations High Commissioner for Refugees] process set out in the [Resettlement Handbook] is sadly absent in the Palestinian case" (Dumper 2007, 88). Importantly, not only the displacement and the displaced persons take on symbolic significance, but so do durable solutions, which, more than anything, is why the symbolism of displacement has implications for conflict resolution. This is most evident in relation to the Palestinian refugee problem, where the symbolism of durable solutions is strongly related to responsibility for the creation of the problem in the first place. Any solution other than return is perceived by the Palestinians as absolving Israel of guilt for the creation of the refugee situation. For its part, the government of Israel has long viewed accepting the right of return as incompatible with the existence of Israel as a Jewish state and as inappropriate because it sees the Arab states as bearing primary responsibility for the refugee situation because (from the Israeli perspective) the Arab states started the war in 1948 and subsequently prevented the refugees' full local integration in exile. This means that, in the words of Michael Molloy and colleagues (2015, 301), "the capacity to effectively address material aspects of the refugee issue depends on appropriate responses to the intangible issues."

Most serious formulas for a resolution of the conflict suggest that Israel admit at least partial guilt for the creation of the refugee problem (which does not undermine its right to exist within secure and recognized borders) in exchange for a Palestinian recognition that a right of return will actually be exercised only by a small minority of the refugees. The problem on the Israeli side is that those who could legitimately make the decision to admit guilt are unwilling to do so. The problem on the Palestinian side is that those who are willing to recognize the need for far-reaching limitations to the right of return are unable to do so legitimately.

Analysis and Conclusions

The symbolic significance of displacement in the cases of Nagorno-Karabakh and Palestine is something different than the manipulation of displacement or displaced persons highlighted in previous research, such as Stedman's research on refugee manipulation or Greenhill's on strategic engineered migration. Instead, the symbolism of displacement in these cases is related to legitimizing the persistence of claims for justice and rights, directly related to displacement and indirectly related to territory. By serving as a justification for an unwillingness to compromise on certain issues, they are symbolic of broader struggles in ways that preclude certain resolutions to conflict or displacement.

The same kind of symbolism can be observed in other cases as well, including the internal displacement situation in Serbia and the Western Saharan refugee problem.[4] In Serbia, some 250,000 people were displaced from Kosovo during the NATO bombing campaign of 1999 (carried out to counter a Serbian offensive in Kosovo, which had displaced more than 800,000). Fifteen years later, very few of those displaced during the bombing campaign have returned, and Serbian authorities have been unwilling not only to integrate the IDPs but also to carry out reregistration. It has been argued that Serbia fears that a decrease in the official IDP figure might undermine its position regarding Kosovo's status (Global IDP Project 2005). Western Sahara, like Palestine, is a question of unfinished decolonization, with displacement going back as far as to the late 1950s. UNHCR currently assists around 115,000 refugees and people in refugee-like conditions from Western Sahara, though in rhetoric, the figure of 165,000 Western Saharan refugees has been used for several decades. In addition to the symbolic significance of displacement in the Western Saharan conflict, there is a decidedly practical aspect to the situation as well, with the organization of the refugee camps in Algeria serving "as a political and ideological strategy for progressively establishing the basis of a future Sahrawi state" (San Martin 2005).

Greenhill (2008) argues that strategic engineered migration is usually generated by the weaker group in order to elicit sympathy and support. In the cases discussed in this chapter, however, displacement was not caused in order to foster symbolism. Instead, the displaced persons have become symbols after displacement, and today they contribute to the exercise of "asymmetric leverage," the use of nontraditional means by weaker actors to put pressure on stronger actors.

To be clear, the failure to advance peace in the Middle East and the Caucasus does not mean that the situation is static. What we see in these conflicts is not the preservation of the status quo in anticipation of a solution. Instead, in the absence of successful negotiations, Israel and, to a lesser extent, the NKR are advancing and consolidating their positions. Interestingly, this is done perhaps most importantly through demographic engineering, at least in the Israeli case. The Jewish settlements in the Occupied Palestinian Territories are of both symbolic and material significance in the consolidation of Israeli territorial control and the legitimation of it, a role many of the settlers are happy to play. Likewise, in Western Sahara, it is estimated that Moroccan settlers currently outnumber the Sahrawi population by two to one (Shefte 2015), the result of a policy of demographic engineering initiated with announcement of the Green March in 1975 (Zunes and Mundy 2010).

This way displaced persons become symbolically very important not in terms of generating change but in terms of resisting it—or at least in terms of resisting the approval of that change, for example, by reaffirming their commitment to a Palestinian or a Sahrawi identity. Just as return can be a sign that peace is in place, continued displacement is a reminder that conflict is not resolved, that grievances remain unaddressed. Azerbaijan has by and large integrated the refugees from Armenia, to which it makes no territorial claims, but is unwilling do so with the IDPs from Nagorno-Karabakh and the occupied territories, where the conflict remains unresolved. Similarly, Rhodri Williams (2011) notes that Serbia has renounced any territorial claims to other constituent republics of the former Yugoslavia and has integrated refugees from Croatia. However, it has not renounced its claims to Kosovo and is very reluctant to integrate displaced persons from there.

The symbolism of displacement may cause tensions between different levels of analysis, most importantly between the individual displaced persons and the displaced population as a collective. More research is needed on this as well as on the importance of temporality for understanding the symbolism of displacement, and I will mention these themes only briefly here. In terms of symbolic significance, the collective level is arguably the most important both during displacement and when the problem is being resolved. Legal rights, however, such as the right to return to one's country, typically pertain to individuals. With a few exceptions, even group rights are in practice most often rights of individuals belonging to certain groups (Jovanović 2005). In the Israeli–Palestinian conflict, both Israel and the PLO prefer to treat the problem at the collective level—the PLO because it elicits sympathy for the national cause and Israel because it wants a settlement of the refugee problem to be the end of the story, to preclude any future claims. At the same time, "for the [individual] Palestinian refugee the fact of displacement remains a personal wound that is not eased by palliatives of compromise and compensation. What comes across as intransigence is in fact a very personal need for completeness" (Dumper 2007, 5). Further, the notion of ending future claims by individual refugees through agreement at the collective level illustrates that a temporal dimension needs to be added to the vertical levels of analysis. If accepting/finding a durable solution means giving up future claims related to displacement, this is a sensitive issue for an individual. For a leader, it becomes even more crucial if that acceptance is done on behalf of a collective of hundreds of thousands of displaced persons as well as their descendants. Compensation to descendants of victims of slavery and reparations to descendants of Jews whose valuables were stolen during World War II show that these types of grievances do not necessarily become invalid just because the immediate victim is no longer alive, but they can pass from generation to generation. However, once compensation (or any other resolution) is accepted, that is the end of the story. This makes the issue one of great intergenerational responsibility, an aspect that cannot be taken lightly.

Durable solutions can also take on symbolic significance, and not only to displaced persons but to the international community. Above all, return is of symbolic significance as a sign that peace is in place and that the causes of displacement have been at least partially remedied (Adelman 2002; UNHCR 1997b; Wallensteen 2015) as well as a signal to future ethnic cleansers that they will not succeed. In Bosnia-Herzegovina, the international community worked hard to achieve both refugee return to the country and so-called minority return within the country, arguing that the return and remixing of displaced persons was necessary for sustainable peace. Indeed, the International Crisis Group (ICG 2000) concluded that "the key to [Dayton Peace Agreement] implementation is refugee return, which is guaranteed in Annex 7 of the DPA and the Bosnian Constitution. All other DPA annexes either depend on refugee return, or were created to assist in implementing refugee return." The return of displaced persons has been a priority of many post–Cold War peace agreements and peacebuilding operations, occasionally against the wishes of the displaced and contrary to the advice of humanitarian organizations. Somewhat paradoxically, however, in the cases discussed in this chapter, where return is the preferred solution among the displaced, the international community has rather promoted other durable solutions.

How should displacement situations that have taken on this kind of symbolic significance be addressed? In conflict resolution theory a distinction is made between interests and positions, where interests represent a party's needs and positions represent what the party believes is the best (or only) way to satisfy those needs (Ramsbotham, Woodhouse, and Miall 2016). A mediator needs to ask not only "What do they want?" but also "Why do they want it?" For example, territorial control might be one way to ensure access to holy places, but there are others; being stronger than your opponent might be one way to protect an ethnic group from discrimination, but there are others. The idea is that the same interest can usually be satisfied by more than one position, and by focusing on interests it might be possible to move beyond incompatible positions and find an acceptable agreement.

Curiously, the three durable solutions to displacement are positions rather than interests, which is likely to be an important reason for their insufficiency, with only a minority of displaced persons finding durable solutions every year and the average time in displacement continually growing. Strictly speaking, the durable solutions are exhaustive since there is no alternative to (a) the country of origin, (b) the host country, or (c) somewhere else (Johansson 2016; Long 2014). However, they are exhaustive because they are formulated as if the problem were geographic location (a position indeed) rather than protection (the underlying interest). Put differently, even though most migration is voluntary (refugees constitute less than 10 percent of all international migrants) and even though "migration can be a positive force for development [and is becoming] a priority for the international community" (UN Population Division 2016), durable solutions to involuntary migration are typically geared toward ending migration rather than toward ending involuntariness, with solutions regularly forced on the displaced persons.

Alternative ways to address forced migration include transnational return as well as more clearly defined interim solutions. Criticizing the traditional understanding of return as "permanent and place-bound," Marita Eastmond (2006), among others, suggests that return is better conceptualized as an open-ended process, including the possibility of short-term or seasonal return. The situation in the country of origin is often uncertain, and citizenship or permanent residency in the host country can provide the backup plan necessary for displaced persons to make a tentative return. Relatedly, Williams (2011) calls for a clearer distinction between interim integration and the durable solution of "local integration." He argues that the former is about sustainably ending humanitarian crises and the latter about ending displacement in a manner compatible with the rights of the displaced. As long as these two ambitions are confused, however, humanitarian crises are likely to persist until durable solutions can be found. This will be particularly pronounced in cases where prolonged displacement has taken on symbolic significance that feeds into the conflict. A clearer distinction between interim and durable solutions might also lessen the responsibility for embodying the cause placed on many refugees and IDPs (as well as their leaders), which most of them could probably do without, even though they take pride in their identity as displaced.

Notes

1. The countries are Azerbaijan, Burundi, Laos, Myanmar, Palestine, Russia, South Sudan, Sudan, Syria, Thailand, Turkmenistan, and Uzbekistan (personal communication with IDMC analyst).

2. The Organization for Security and Cooperation in Europe press release I refer to uses the term "resettlement" rather than "return," but it is meant to indicate the return of IDPs to the areas they came from, not the durable solution of resettlement in a third country or place.

3. "Palestine Refugees," United Nations Relief and Works Agency, http://www.unrwa.org.

4. With Kosovo now recognized by more than one hundred countries, it could be argued that people displaced from Kosovo to Serbia should be referred to as refugees (just like many Armenians and Azerbaijanis who fled before 1991 were reclassified when the Union of Soviet Socialist Republics was dissolved). However, Serbia still claims Kosovo and therefore considers Kosovars to be internally displaced, and this is part and parcel of the symbolism of displacement in the Serbian case.

Part 3

Seeking "Solutions" to Displacement within and beyond Traditional Frameworks

8

Shunning Solidarity

Durable Solutions in a Fluid Era

Loren B. Landau

Forced migration scholarship often imagines displacements as socioeconomically disruptive events fragmenting, if not shattering, people's socioeconomic foundations. As this volume's introduction notes, refugees are understood as those who have "lost the protection of [their] basic rights," not only in a legal sense but more broadly as those deprived of their social worlds (Gibney 2015, 13). Such framing establishes a problematic in which "solutions" restore, replicate, or at least approximate the status quo ante through the provision of legal rights and the reconstruction of place-bound socialities. While often elusive, the global humanitarian apparatus and much humanitarian scholarship draw lines beneath the displacement period when the displaced, alone or with assistance, achieve such goals (see Long 2014; Black and Koser 1999). Even while recognizing that displacement, like other movements, catalyzes irreversible change (see Lubkemann 2010), discussions of durable solutions nonetheless evoke a sense of permanent resolution: a return to predictability, solidity, and solidarity.[1] This is not the kind of global solidarity the United Nations or others call for in addressing mass crises or social movements. Rather, the discussion here is over the forms of place-based social cohesion informing Durkheimian sociology.

The pursuit of solidarity is evident in both definitions of "durability" and humanitarian efforts to "restore" and achieve sustainable solutions. The emphasis on reunification, a return to families' mechanical solidarity whether in sites of origins, sanctuary, or elsewhere, is perhaps the most visible illustration of this (see UNHCR 1983). Beyond households, resettlement, return, or local integration offer complementary endpoints rooted in place-bound, organic solidarity premised on exchange, labor markets, and generalized interdependence. Such solidarities will be differentiated and unequal, with disparities persisting for generations (see Portes and Zhou 1993). Nonetheless, the understandings of durability embedded in the 1951 Geneva Convention Relating to the Status of Refugees evoke metaphors of relatively stable, almost organic formations in which the various parts interact along systems of shared rules and mutual recognition (see Malkki 1995a). In almost all cases these are evoked as spatially delimited at the settlement or national scale. Debates on the nature of family and the specific mechanisms and meaning of integration continue, yet most scholarship—and almost all policy interventions—still conceives of displacement as a temporally defined arc beginning with tragedy and ending with durable forms of geographically bound solidarity.

This chapter questions solidary durability by recognizing how, in precarious urban spaces in which refugees increasingly seek protection, "solutions" may be premised on actively and selectively evading certain forms of connections and solidarities. It accepts that solidarity remains a strong normative guide for many displaced people and humanitarians and that the rejection of membership at one scale by no means precludes it at others. Indeed, the structures of global capitalism and urbanization mean that displacement to or within Southern cities shifts the basis on which people chart life courses, not only for the displaced but also for other full- or part-time urban residents. For some, at least, there can be little sense of site-specific durability but rather a future imagined as continual mobility accompanied by tactical connections and disengagements. In an era in which finding economic security increasingly means spreading family and individual risk across multiple spaces, displacement may create new opportunities and demands within existing and emerging translocal relationships and diasporas. Moreover, given the challenges of rebuilding "sending" communities, access to external resources and remittances may become central to individual and familial economic security. In some instances, individual survival or success are dependent on shunning solidarity and going at it alone for abbreviated or extended periods. Under such conditions, the most durable solution may well be the opportunity to continue moving within or across borders unencumbered by social responsibilities. If so, what first appears as the (self-)preservation of social marginalization and vulnerability in the form of alienation from family, kin, and community represents tactical agency: a quest for protection and durability amid the structural uncertainty of contemporary urbanism.

Drawing my definition from this volume's introduction, agency is observed when "displaced individuals (and, in some cases, communities) make and enact choices that potentially affect outcomes, particularly of resolution processes, recognizing that the extent to which displaced persons can exercise agency generally and in particular circumstances will depend on complex, shifting constellations of political, socioeconomic, cultural, historical, and institutional factors." In this chapter, agency appears in precisely the social acts often coded as vulnerability: disconnection and continued mobility. While such behaviors may well be tactical—a response of the generally disempowered to structurally oppressive conditions—they nonetheless represent an effort to build lives (see de Certeau 1984). But in this case, long-term welfare is premised on the ability to avoid what we typically understand as "durable solutions." That is, relative long-term security comes from keeping things unsettled.

This chapter proceeds through four primary sections. The first comments on my approach and the empirical inquiries underlying my analysis. The second embeds questions of urban humanitarianism within broader sets of "urban questions." It draws attention to the precarious nature of African urban life and how stability and fixity can work against residents' ability to accumulate the social and material capital necessary to thrive or survive. The third section illustrates means by which refugees and other migrants (the two are often legally and sociologically indistinguishable; see Landau and Duponchel 2011) forge socialities that allow them to negotiate the urban condition while avoiding precisely the kind of solidarities typically presumed to shape durable solutions. The last section—more schematic than substantive—points to a range of practical, ethical, and epistemological concerns stemming from the empirical discussion. Apart from problematizing teleologies of solidarity embedded in international refugee law, it speaks to how knowledge is constructed within "refugee and forced migration studies."

Methods and Approach

This chapter fundamentally explores the meanings of durability and agency amid urban precarity and fluidity. In doing do so, it makes no claims to represent the totality of people's diverse intentions, aims, or experiences but instead points to avenues for further exploration and the possibility that disconnection and social alienation—shunning solidarity—may be critical to achieving lasting welfare and de facto protection. This perspective may be uncomfortable for those wed to teleologies of displacement, social cohesion, and the elimination of socioeconomic marginalization. Perhaps more importantly, it unsettles the philosophical and political foundations typically informing debates over the ethics and practices of hospitality, integration, and citizenship. It is instead premised on a belief that only by first understanding the nature and necessities of urban life and the agency of the displaced can we then consider their potential practical and ethical implications.[2]

Although this is largely a conceptual inquiry, I draw on an ecumenical set of data in support of my position. The data also enable me to shift from more generalized assessments to individualized stories and accounts. Most of the information used here stems from migration-related research in Southern and Eastern Africa—beginning with Johannesburg and expanding to Nairobi, Maputo, and Lubumbashi—undertaken between 2002 and 2015. The cities included in these studies are destinations and transit points for domestic and international migration including significant numbers of displaced persons. Together they represent a range of social, economic, and political characteristics that allows for modest generalizations about trends and possibilities about African cities and, potentially, the rapidly expanding metropolises of the Global South.

The survey data used intermittently throughout stem from interviews with 2,211 people in three of the cities: Johannesburg, Maputo, and Nairobi. These data do not fully represent either the migrant or host populations in any of the sites, let alone the experience of migration and displacement elsewhere on the continent.[3] Rather, data collection targeted groups of foreigners categorized by nationality. Except for Mozambicans included in the Johannesburg survey, data were collected on selected groups—Somalis, Rwandans, Sudanese, and Congolese—that straddle the line between economic migrants and those who might be considered (in substance, if not in law) forced migrants or displaced persons. Such sampling does not cover the cities' full geographic footprints, as doing so would have generated too thin a sample. Instead, sampling concentrated on gateway areas and "estuarial zones" of high traffic and diversity (see Saunders 2011; Singer, Hardwick, and Brettell 2008; Landau 2014). Although statistics do not feature prominently in this chapter, they inform prior works (cited throughout) that inform it. Instead the text relies more heavily on illustrations from secondary sources and qualitative fieldwork conducted in collaboration with doctoral students in Johannesburg and Nairobi, two African cities attracting significant numbers of displaced persons (see Campbell, Crisp, and Kiragu 2011; Krause-Vilmar and Chaffin 2011).

The Emergence of Urban Humanitarianism

It is for good reason that urban refugees have received a great deal of attention of late.[4] As UNHCR notes on its "urban refugees" web page, "only one-third of the world's 10.5 million refugees now live in camps."[5] While any figure will soon be dated and inaccurate, as of December 1, 2015, there were approximately 2.2 million Syrian refugees in Turkey. Of them, just over 10 percent were being housed in purpose-built camps or settlements. Similar proportions almost certainly hold for countries throughout the region. Across Africa, there is a growing awareness that most refugees and other displaced people—in some places the vast majority of them—live and seek protection in what are often deeply impoverished, unequal, and undercapacitated but increasingly global urban centers (see UN-Habitat 2014).

Whether in Kabul, Khartoum, or a dozen other cities proximate to seemingly interminable conflicts, refugees and the internally displaced significantly contribute to urban population growth and position in regional and global flows of information and material (Beall and Esser 2005, 6; Segbers, Raiser, and Volkmann 2007; Gow 2005). One need only glance at the cities of Jordan and Lebanon to know that displacement from Syria's civil war has reshaped their internal composition and global position (see World Bank 2015). Even where the displaced are proportionately fewer, their presence can rapidly reconfigure social and economic life. Elsewhere, the displaced move almost invisibly into cities, disappearing among longer-term residents who may share class, language, religion, or other commonalities. Given that the alternatives to urban settlement include decades in camps, administrative detention, or another "protracted refugee situation," it is hardly surprising that the displaced increasingly find their ways to population centers (see Kamal 2016). Although the urban displaced may not find golden-paved streets, cities nonetheless offer at least faint promises of upward economic mobility and physical freedom.

Although it is unclear if refugees' presence in global cities is as novel as many suggest—authors have flagged urban refugees' presence for decades (see Malkki 1995a; Cooper 1992; Rogge and Akol 1989)—strong normative, political, and financial motivations have recently fixed the humanitarian gaze on what the eye had previously "refused to see" (Kibreab 1996). Rather than crediting a rise in urban numbers, the emergence of "urban refugees" as an object of study extends from broader efforts to "visibilize displacement": to identify and expose the vulnerability of varied groups and define them in terms that make them suitable objects of humanitarian action (see Lubkemann 2010; Polzer and Hammond 2008). Even if driven by a valuable humanitarian impulse, the result is a certain kind of analytical blindness that leaves presumptions unchallenged. In particular, a continued focus on vulnerabilities associated with displacement—an orientation due to researchers' close connection to humanitarian action and organizations—often limits the field's engagement with broader questions of urbanism, precarity, and resilience. That characterizing social realities in rapidly transforming urban centers is difficult without the added challenge of hunting down new arrivals who may seek invisibility (Jacobsen and Furst 2011) only exacerbates this isolation. If nothing else, this chapter suggests there are compelling normative and intellectual reasons for sustained attention to both cities and the people seeking protection within them. However, such inquiries' potential will be achieved only through a substantial redefinition of the modes through which we "see" and understand displacement and humanitarian intervention.

As noted in the chapter's introductory paragraphs, the focus here is on what the presence of displaced people in cities—particularly those in the Global South—means for understanding displacement and, particularly, durable solutions. It also hints at the inverse of the equation by asking what displacement may mean for studies of global urbanism. Doing so contributes to a better understanding of an increasingly diversifying pool of cities proximate to conflicts and other sources of displacement. It also asks us to reconsider the forms of protection displaced persons seek, the means through which protection should be achieved, and the meaning of durable solutions. At the heart of this discussion is an account of how the nature of the South's conflicts and global cities—precarity crossed with potential; fluidity and resistance—creates forms of almost perpetual displacement and mobility. In an era in which finding economic security increasingly means spreading family and individual risk across multiple spaces (Halliday 2006), displacement may create new opportunities within existing and emerging translocal relationships and diasporas. Moreover, given the challenges of rebuilding "sending" communities, access to external resources and remittances may become central to families' economic security (see Deshingkar and Farrington 2009). Without discounting the possibility or desirability of return, local integration, or third-country resettlement, the chapter argues that durable solutions may well be premised on shunning the solidarity and stability often underlying the language of "durable solutions." While the focus here is explicitly on the highly informal and infrastructurally frail cities of Southern and Eastern Africa, there are lessons in this analysis for displaced people in politically marginal but deeply networked urban spaces worldwide.

Protection in Flux

Understanding the meaning of solutions forged within urban spaces demands moving beyond immediate efforts to improve service delivery and protection in urban spaces. We must instead delve more deeply—empirically and philosophically—into the nature of contemporary urban life. Doing so reveals extraordinarily high levels of economic and physical precarity associated with living in Africa's urban centers and residents' tactical and strategic responses to these conditions. (For the most part, such risks face all poor urban residents, but they can be potentially exacerbated by a history of displacement.[6])

This is not the place for a thorough review of Africa's "urban condition," let alone cities across the Global South. Indeed, a piece of this length cannot accurately reflect the diversity of opportunities and obstacles present within even a single city (for such approaches, see De Boeck and Plissart 2004; Myers 2011). Rather, it summarizes a condition perhaps best characterized as "possibility amid precarity."[7] The precarity of Southern city life is a familiar strain in the Malthusian narratives underlying much academic and policy work. Many of these accounts note the tremendous growth rates (UNDESA 2014; UN-Habitat 2014) and note that, as cities swell, new arrivals (and long-term residents) find few new jobs. Others note that, rather than embracing their population while planning for future growth, urban governance systems are instead captured by narrow interests or crumbling from lack of financial support, technical capacity, and de facto political centralization. With a forthcoming "youth bulge," cities will again host growing numbers with little concomitant growth in formal economic opportunities (UN-Habitat 2014).

Apart from those profiting from the poor, the elite—political and economic—are largely disengaged from the cities' majority, often physically separating themselves in gated communities or new cities (Kermeliotis 2013). When possible, they are retreating to physically removed, purpose-built urban sites. In Caroline Wanjiku Kihato and S. Muyeba's words, "the dominant images that Africa's cities conjure are ones where the landscapes are rolling shantytowns, where toilets 'fly' and rivulets of sewerage snake through cobbled-together homes. Africa's cities it seems, tell a story of failure—the failure of modernization, capitalism and the African state" (2015, 3).

Yet, for all of their evident shortcomings and risks, Africa's globalizing cities and their counterparts elsewhere are nonetheless alluring with their often-elusive potential for profit, protection, or passage elsewhere. Ideal by almost no imaginable developmental metric, these sites nonetheless offer relative access to varied opportunities and possibilities, and urbanization is correlated with increased human development indices, a better quality of life, access to services, and the possibility to earn (UNDESA 2014). Even slum dwellers often live longer and healthier lives than similar folks living beyond the city. Indeed, the potential for investment and work in rapidly expanding urban markets offers comparative advantage in terms of trade and economies of scale when compared to Africa's relatively sparsely populated rural hinterlands.[8]

For present purposes, the question is what people—migrants, internally displaced people, refugees, and even long-term residents—do to capitalize on cities' opportunities while avoiding the pitfalls of economic and physical precarity. With few possibilities for return to communities of origin or organized resettlement to a wealthy Western country, de facto durable solutions for millions of displaced persons will be forged in these urban sites. In the absence of elaborate states or humanitarian interventions, these solutions, whatever their form, will be designed and realized by urban residents working alone, together, or with connections living beyond the urban edge. This is a form of tactical agency that is often overlooked or dismissed as "survivalism" in terms that analytically disconnect it from residents' potential longer-term objectives.

In describing the necessities of urban life, AbdouMaliq Simone (2010) suggests that across much of the Global South, daily existence is a process of constant breaking down and recomposition. People living in the city constantly contend with current conditions while also imagining and preparing for a different future. And as movement comes to characterize the city, the possibility of fixing people in place becomes more difficult. So even as authorities seek to create a stable and ordered mode of living—an impulse that James Scott (1998) ascribes to the genetics of stateness—people's everyday necessities and imaginations help to undermine the very possibility of doing so.

Going further, Simone argues that through their knowledge and relationships, people are cities' most significant infrastructure. Due to the fluid nature of employment combined with perennial material precarity, urban success demands people regularly reconfigure and, if possible, upgrade the infrastructure to which they are connected. "Where people are the important infrastructure, the value of an individual existence rests less in the elaboration of a 'meaningful' life or a coherent story about a person's character. What is important is individuals' ability to be 'hooked in' to different daily scenarios, dramas, networks, and affiliations that provide a constant set of alternatives for how to put bread on the table or how to become a person that can be taken seriously" (Simone 2010, 126). In an earlier work (2006, 358), he similarly posits, "Cities everywhere exert pulls on each other in a force field in which the maintenance of localized coherence becomes increasingly problematic." Part of this desire for constant restructuring and ongoing motion is rooted in the need to maintain an ever expanding or diversifying set of "weak ties" (Granovetter 1973). This may be accomplished from a fixed point or it may demand movement within cities or between them.

Reciprocal obligations along with the economic precarity of the postindustrial (or, perhaps more accurately, the neoliberal, nonindustrial) era further encourage an impulse to decouple from local and distant social relations and the corollary connections to space. Take, for example, Eric Worby's (2010) discussion of Zimbabwean refugees/migrants living in Johannesburg. In his account, the desire for disconnection is rooted less in the nature of the city, per se, although he recognizes the risks from police, employers, and others typically associated with urban life. Rather, the need for consistent connection and reconnection stems from the elaborate and occasionally oppressive social networks extending among vulnerable populations migrant and otherwise. These take the form of demands from family and sending communities to send money, food, durable goods, and clothing to their places of origin (see Dzingirai, Mutopu, Landau 2014; Kihato 2013; Madsen 2004). Perhaps more immediately, these demands may also manifest in requests to physically host and support relatives and friends—a flexible, often expansive category of people—in continual succession or even simultaneously. The result is a kind of dependency pyramid in which a refugee pioneer ends up hosting close relatives followed by ever-more-distant connections, frequently under cramped and unsustainable conditions: self-built houses, storage rooms, sublet and subdivided apartments, or even occupied offices.

Rather than offering comfort or social security, such relationships introduce not only material obligations and inconvenience but also an additional source of uncertainty. In Worby's (2010, 417) words, "The open-ended condition of displacement brought about by violence, insecurity and the present political impasse within Zimbabwe lends itself to a particularly vexing moral economy for Zimbabweans abroad—one in which the temporal horizon for reconciling credits and debts, present capacities and future dependencies, is unknowable." For people living in the fluid, economically marginal neighborhoods of Southern cities, denying others support when even marginally more resource endowed is almost unimaginable. Those with the courage to do so risk acute costs: shaming oneself and even one's parents who may be accused of raising a disrespectful child. For migrants, betraying expectations not only means exiting from potential reciprocal support at some indeterminate date but also may elicit explicit countermeasures ranging from reputational costs to curses, theft, or physical threats. In these cases, the strong social networks and sets of overlapping reciprocal obligations—social formations scholars and practitioners often celebrate for providing protection and resilience (see Landau and Duponchel 2011; Deshingkar and Farrington 2009; World Bank 2005; Aguilera and Massey 2003; Kanaiapuni et al. 2005; Munshi 2003)—become burdensome and counterproductive. The failure to maintain those relationships during periods of crisis can lead to what Peter Kankonde (2010) terms "social death": one's indefinite social exclusion and stigmatization.

Confronted with the likely failure to meet social obligations or the sometimes onerous costs of doing so—not only short-term material costs but also comfort and capital accumulation possibilities—refugees hoping to make their lives in fluid, global cities often seek forms of social invisibility. For many, desiring disconnection and invisibility stems from the seemingly shameful activities one undertakes to make it in a new place (see Kankonde 2010; Kihato 2013; Malauene 2004). For those involved in sex work or other criminalized behaviors, the source of stigma is perhaps obvious even if many take pride in supporting their families (see Oliveira and Vearey 2015). For others the downgrading of skills—from accountant to taxi driver; from teacher to day laborer—may be what they hope to shroud. Even where the work is "honorable," maintaining local and translocal connections comes with costs. While many rely on local and translocal contacts to negotiate obstacles and gather resources, these potentially valuable networks also transmit damaging information about profession activities, relationships, and behavior that can damage individual and families' reputation and status.

Even if desires for disconnection are not universal, they nonetheless capture an important aspect of contemporary life in global cities of the South. Economic precarity, predatory policy and states, and reciprocal obligations are giving rise to a desire for fluidity and ethics of disconnection that furthers what is perhaps a generic condition of city life. In one of sociology's foundational works, *The Metropolis and Mental Life*, Georg Simmel (2004, 16) remarks on a tendency to social distance among metropolitans, a reserve that shades "not only into indifference, but, more often than we are aware . . . a slight aversion, a mutual strangeness and repulsion." Going further, Jane Jacobs (1964, 403) speaks of cities as places in which one finds freedom about "countless numbers of people," a freedom in part that comes from the ability to be disengaged from those physically closest to you. As Fran Tonkiss (2003, 298) notes, "While a language of community has been important for articulating various politics of difference, I suggest that forms of indifference also afford certain rights to and freedoms in the city." Indeed, the ability to be anonymous and unknown allows for a freedom—for differences to be undisciplined by the bonds of solidarity and one's social connections to be regularly (if not infinitely) reconfigured (see Wirth 1995, 70).

Durable Solutions amid Mobility and Disconnection

In cities where rooting is either undesirable or effectively impossible, residents—including the displaced—treat the sites in which they may live for decades as sites in which to gather the resources needed to further onward movement or build status and security beyond the city's boundaries (Geschiere 2009). Doing so often means directly countering community and the forms of place-based solidarity—organic or mechanical—evoked by talk of "durable solutions." Proximate and translocal rooting may be important, but so too are regular shifts between rural (or peri-urban) and urban areas, within urban areas, or between cities. For many, urban sites are "places of flows" (Castells 2002) or "nowherevilles" (Bauman 1998) where rooting and local representation is not the goal and the burdens and binding that connections and political participation offer are often something to be avoided (Kankonde 2010; Madsen 2004). Given the insecurity of land tenure, the possibility of violence, and ongoing economic deprivation, a durable solution means actively maintaining feet in multiple sites without firmly rooting in any (Freemantle 2010). As such, migrants—including refugees and other displaced persons—are turning cities (or parts of them) into stations rather than destinations. This helps generate a kind of permanent temporariness in which tactical agency is visible in actively resisting incorporation (Kihato 2013; Landau 2014; Malauene 2004).

In such environments, formal citizenship and stability may have value for some, but with only limited enforcement capacity and a minimal reliance on state-provided services—schools, clinics, jobs—it is safe to say that documentation and legal status often do little. At the most practical level they are poor predictors of people's welfare (Landau and Duponchel 2011). Even in South Africa, arguably the continent's "strongest" state, these processes are negotiated on the ground through a panoply of rationalities and calculations, sometimes involving laws and state actors but not always in predictable ways (Hansen and Stepputat 2010). In such environments, finding space and resources within a city involves an ongoing process of forming and abandoning horizontal and vertical connections and of constant, often constrained, calculations.

The forms of belonging and solidarity that matter for people increasingly are themselves fluid, syncretic, and translocal. Even churches—often seen as instruments of local integration, community formation, or stable transnational mobilization (see Cadge and Ecklund 2007)—are now sites for "tactical cosmopolitanism" and other forms of fluidity and liminality (see Landau and Freemantle 2010, 2016; Garbin 2012; Schiller, Çaglar, and Guldbrandsen 2006). Within them and similar bodies, people find ways of maintaining the levels of social engagement and recognition necessary to negotiate everyday life, but without the kind of place-based fixity often associated with durable solutions. The forms of solidarity forged through these bodies are often inherently transient, translocal, post-territorial, and, in the case of millenarian religious configurations, potentially post-terrestrial. Not only do people frequently shift liturgical allegiances but the churches themselves also foster a kind of disconnection from those beyond the ever-more-fragmented congregations (Kankonde 2017).

Conclusions: Ethical and Epistemological Reflections

By using such strategies of partial inclusion and rights claiming, international migrants' illegality and continued mobility can prevent capture by the state or communities—local or diasporic—enabling a kind of invisibility that, though precarious, allows them to elude obligations and occasionally exploit the city for resources to which they are not legally or socially entitled. Instead of transplantation and legibility to the society and political systems under which they ostensibly live, urban refugees may well be striving for a kind of "usufruct" rights—a form of exclusion that is at least partially compatible with social and political marginalization. Rather than integrating or assimilating, they exploit their position as the permanent outsiders in ways that "[distance] him or her from all connections and commitments" (Said 2001, 183). They may use a variety of tactics to claim rights in their sites of residence, but we must not presume this reflects a desire for the forms of solidarity that typically inform externally designated durable solutions. These kind of slippery connections and disconnections are, in themselves, a kind of norm making and recognition—a form of solidarity—but one forged around a sense of distance and disengagement (see Ye 2015).

Their behaviors raise several important questions. Perhaps most obviously, they question what a durable solution might mean within the highly fluid and fragmented spaces that characterize global cities. In African cities—as elsewhere—inclusion is something more than claiming a "right to the city" or becoming part of a stable, urban community. We must avoid assuming the existence of such communities but also recognize that for many domestic and (especially) international migrants and the displaced among them, moving to a city, whatever the reason, is also a step into a global "imaginary" and spaces beyond bounded place. For such migrants, a durable solution may mean a continued effort to find not only a place to stay, work, or find physical protection but also entrée into global culture, new universal urban lifestyles (however understood), or, more concretely, opportunities for onward journeys. They may never realize these ambitions, but the city is nevertheless a space of possibility with access to trading and travel opportunities unavailable in villages or camps. Where integration or inclusion into a city of residence is either impossible or undesirable, membership into these decentered, socially regulated, globalized networks may represent a far more significant form of belonging and source of rights and recognition. Alternatively, they may pursue almost total alienation or loose, easily reformed networks that provide information and guidance without observation and obligation.

Urban refugees' potential desire for continued instability raises important ethical and policy issues that we can grapple with only by better understanding the Southern "urban condition" that they are helping to create. The rapid expansion of urban populations—and the concentration of migration and urban growth in certain urban gateway neighborhoods—forces us to question the use of the terms "local" or "host" to talk about the destination areas (see Landau 2014). It also raises concerns over what integration or a durable solution might look like in practical terms or the ethics of engagement. As long as a durable solution requires stability and solidarity, at what point has the displacement crisis merely given way to the ongoing crisis-like modes of everyday urban life? What, under such conditions, would humanitarian benchmarking look like? The humanitarian sector's Sphere standards may help provide guidance on material conditions, but within contemporary urban life in much of the Global South almost no one—refugee or "local"—lives at such standards. Moving forward may require first evaluating the extent to which displaced people (or formerly displaced people) continue to be relatively constrained by the experiences of displacement (assuming they were) or are merely having their lives shaped by the more generalized socioeconomic and political circumstances in which they operate. In all cases, effective interventions may best be understood as expanding agency that may afford opportunities for both fixed settlement and ongoing mobility and disconnection.

Apart from fundamental questions of policy intervention, the trends outlined above raise epistemological questions for scholars seeking to understand displaced persons' agency under constrained circumstances. Arguing that striving for ongoing flux and mobility is part of a durable solution and a demonstration of agency raises significant methodological challenges to the observer. It is, after all, difficult to know if someone is in constant movement because they are unable to settle or because they have read the environment in which they operate and are actively choosing to remain unrooted and potentially in motion—what I have termed "tactical agency." To be sure, the fact that churning is part of what contemporary urban life requires suggests a degree of vulnerability and structural constraints that all residents experience—particularly those who are relatively poor. But this is no more so than for those who remain trapped in place, limiting their ability to capitalize on the potential benefits of migration (which, after all, may include basic physical security and the ability to maintain even bare life; see Lubkemann 2008a). In a world where economic precarity can be thrust on individuals by local policies, global structures, and even one's family and kin, the desire to move and the ability to do so is of enormous tactical importance. In this regard we must take the lead from critiques of the human trafficking, sex work, and humanitarianism itself, which ask us to problematize questions of victimization (Ticktin 2011; Gould 2011; Fassin 2011; Hallgrimsdottir, Phillips, and

Benoit 2006; White 1990). In such cases, empathy effectively empowers humanitarians to intervene while both the discursive framing and subsequent interventions potentially undermine ostensibly vulnerable people's tactical agency. Yet we must also recognize, as do Amartya Sen (1993) and others, choice under highly constrained situations is itself a problematic concept, and people's desires are often shaped as much by perceived possibilities as by objective or consistent moral principles and commitments.

In closing, it is worth noting that whether one's primary interests are scholarly or practical, there are benefits of recalibrating the nature of "refugee and forced migration studies": there is much to gain from embedding our approaches to displacement within a broader scholarship on the places and processes in which refugees participate. In this case, an explicit engagement with both urban studies and African urbanism helps reframe the meaning of durability and its potential desirability in the ways it has typically been understood. It also helps us recode actions that may in part appear to represent signs of constraint to ones of empowerment or, more mildly, agency. Beyond thematic broadening, there are further gains from following Jean Comaroff and John Comaroff's (2012) suggestion to begin more substantially theorizing from the South.

As Raewyn Connell (2007) notes in describing the sociology of globalization, we tend to look toward the South as a source of data to flesh out models formed in the backyards of the more powerful knowledge producers. Several urbanists have begun this process (see Parnell and Robinson 2012; Watson 2009; Mbembé and Nuttall 2004), and there is much to learn from them. However, given that the humanitarian enterprise and the headquarters of most global humanitarian agencies are rooted primarily in "the North" and operate through knowledge forged there (see Fassin 2011; Malkki 1995a, 1996), it is often difficult for "refugee studies" to shift fundamental frames. Indeed, if we take seriously the question of agency, we must then also take seriously the question of how we theorize about the agency of refugees. Beginning from a position that "solutions" are compatible with state objectives and looking at how refugees and displaced people might ultimately be accommodated within them still grants an unnecessarily privileged position to global and national regulatory frameworks. If instead we start from the perspective of what is required (or what is perceived to be so) among refugees, our understanding of "solutions"—durable or otherwise—begins to look substantially different. As scholars. we must not allow our desire for relevance and policy influence to foreclose the possibilities and critiques emerging from authors generating insights from a wide range of geographic and intellectual sites and traditions.

Notes

A special thanks to Cara Mazetti Claassen for her valuable research assistance in preparing this chapter.

1. On the quest for stability and solidarity, see various contributions to Black and Koser (1999) and Allen and Morsink (1994); for Durkheimian solidarity, see Lukes (1973).

2. This responds to calls by Skrbis, Kendall, and Woodward (2004, 132) and Beck (2009).

3. For more details on the survey data employed here, see Madhavan and Landau (2011).

4. See, for example, *Forced Migration Review*'s 2010 issue dedicated to urban refugees along with a range of other studies conducted in Africa, Asia, the Middle East, and Latin America by or on behalf of humanitarian organizations (Zetter and Deikun 2010) and a series of studies by such high-profile organizations as the Women's Refugee Commission (Krause-Vilmar and Chaffin 2011) and the International Rescue Committee (Lyytinen and Kullenberg 2013).

5. "Urban Refugees," n.d., UNHCR, http://www.unhcr.org/pages/4b0e4cba6.html.

6. Earlier research indicates that people who claim to have moved because of persecution and conflict were on aggregate no more vulnerable than those who moved for other reasons (see Landau and Duponchel 2011). However, in situations where cities are proximate to active conflicts—Gulu in northern Uganda, for example—or under situations of mass and rapid displacement, there may be close correlations between people's reasons for movement and their socioeconomic position.

7. While my use of "precarity" is influenced by the work of Standing (2011) and others, I am not speaking of the economic uncertainty associated with declining industrial production, the weakening welfare state, or crumbling unionization. These processes are largely foreign to Africa outside the more industrialized Southern cone. Instead, precarity refers to a generalized condition of economic uncertainty and unpredictability.

8. For more on the socioeconomics of African urban development, see UN-Habitat (2014;) Myers (2011); and Potts (2010).

9

"Grabbing" Solutions

Internal Displacement and Postdisaster Land Occupations in Haiti

Angela Sherwood

In Latin America, people squat. Then they organize. Then they ask the municipality. So first they take, and then they settle. But in Haiti—there is no plan. People react to opportunity or instability. You go there and you take it and then you hope someone will recognize you. But they never do.

—Interview with international urban planner, Port-au-Prince, Haiti, May 2014

This chapter explores the meaning of durable solutions to displacement in urban, postdisaster Haiti. On January 12, 2010, an earthquake registering 7.3 on the Richter scale hit Haiti's capital city, Port-au-Prince. By conservative estimates, over 200,000 lives were lost because of the earthquake, as well as 105,000 homes (Sherwood et al. 2014). The earthquake also prompted unprecedented levels of mass displacement as people took refuge in different spaces in the city and left in large numbers for the countryside. At the height of the crisis, international aid agencies recorded 1.5 million internally displaced persons (IDPs) living in 1,500 camps and spontaneous settlements across the earthquake-affected area (IOM and ACTED 2011). Countless organizational reports have detailed both the magnitude of Haiti's earthquake displacement and the complexities of urban reconstruction. Most often these reports present the impossibility of providing durable housing solutions for each displaced person given acute levels of urban poverty, informal settlements, and the absence of strong governing institutions (Davis 2012).

Rather than review the administrative and political constraints to finding solutions for Haiti's displaced, the objective here is to assess settlement processes through a framework of urban power relations. Over the past seven years, a series of class-based struggles over land have taken place across the severely altered metropolitan area, overlapping with an influx of humanitarian aid and capital-intensive reconstruction. In urban Haiti, it is particularly important to grasp the economic determinants of mass displacement and thereby come to terms with the material processes that are mediated through political-legal interventions and discursive representations of people and places. Approaching the question of solutions this way reveals how international aid practices, in the name of aiding displaced people, have the potential to advance systems of elite privilege and accumulation. Noting the transformative power of disasters and reconstruction over urban spaces (Schuller 2016), this chapter demonstrates how Haiti's urban landless—many of whom were labeled "IDPs" when they moved to camps in the aftermath of the earthquake—have exercised agency and resistance in their mobility decisions and methods of extra-legal land occupation. Because of the risks involved, agents do not always directly confront structures of power through open public discourse or organized social movements (Scott 1985). Instead, dominated social groups may resort to furtive tactics to contest power according to their means by foot dragging, sabotage, desertion, clandestine squatting, and other methods of resistance that nibble away at exclusion or work the system to one's advantage (Scott 1985, xvi). In Haiti, humanitarian return programs sought to enable camp closures by "returning" IDPs to their former housing status, if not to their pre-earthquake dwellings. For the thousands who were renters, this involved the distribution of cash grants intended to subsidize the rental of a new residence; in practice, however, many recipients used these grants in other ways that they determined to be a better long-term investment, such as to finance movements to new, informal settlements. These actions altered social and legal landscapes, even if the state and humanitarian bureaucrats viewed resistance as irrational or criminal and dismissed certain outcomes as overly complex and disorderly (Rajagopal 2003).

This chapter has two main aims in applying these insights to the structural relationship between humanitarian-administered IDP return programs and the spontaneous emergence of informal settlements in postdisaster Haiti. First, it explores IDP regimes of truth and their role in the hierarchical reconstruction of Haiti. In this regard, this chapter pays special attention to the contact points between international norms on IDPs and international humanitarian practices, especially in terms of backstopping legal claims to property ownership and controlling population movements according to rigid ideas of where people "belong" (Keenan 2014). Second, the chapter explores the discourses of resistance in Haiti's camps and informal settlements. It draws out local justifications for, as well as the strategies and effects of, land occupations in terms of evading the past and coping with the present. Although the state and international community have downplayed the number of people who are pursuing their own "solutions" by illegally purchasing land and refusing return to overcrowded and unaffordable slum areas, Haiti's mass squatter movements have opened land access for hundreds of thousands of people. Poor Haitians' resistance has mitigated their exclusion from the city and has forced international and state actors to recognize some degree of local agency in reconstruction efforts to resolve their displacement. Even so, Haitians' everyday power struggles, long-term "property making," and attempts to access land are hindered by material processes and lack of control over the discourses and conditions of reconstruction and urban development.

Methodology

The chapter draws on 225 in-depth, qualitative interviews I conducted in Port-au-Prince between October 2013 and August 2014. One hundred individuals were selected based on their level of involvement and decision-making responsibilities in camp governance and the reconstruction of Port-au-Prince. These individuals represent a wide spectrum of roles in Haiti's humanitarian relief and reconstruction efforts and provide insight on official discourses as well as interventions by state and quasi-state actors. When interviewing humanitarian actors, I occupied a semi-"insider" position based on my prior practical involvement in international humanitarian interventions and my ability to speak the same bureaucratic "language." This helped me gain greater access and achieve a high level of trust with my interlocutors which, in turn, enabled me to reach a fuller understanding of the interpretive frames surrounding displacement and durable solutions. I also benefited from introductions by international humanitarian counterparts when meeting government officials, which increased their willingness to share information.

I conducted another one hundred in-depth interviews in four purposefully selected case study sites with Haitians who had been directly affected by the earthquake. Most of these individuals had been labeled as IDPs at some point in the relief and reconstruction process because of their presence on plots of land that were identified as camps and were included in the internationally led, camp management and coordination cluster system. At the time of the research, two of these sites were "open" IDP camps (not yet subjected to camp closure), and two represented new informal settlements on the northern periphery of Port-au-Prince. These individuals were interviewed with a local interpreter for approximately one to two hours each. Several individuals were interviewed more than once to allow them space and freedom to express their views on their displacement and housing situation. In building up case studies of these four sites and interrogating their spatial and social characteristics, I also conducted other interviews with members of self-declared land committees, land sellers, grassroots organizations, police, and other government and quasi-government officials visiting the areas. In addition to these four areas, another twenty-five IDPs were interviewed from a variety of camps and spontaneous settlements. Other methods included participant observations, often of land settlement and mediation processes, and document analysis.

IDP Recognition and Labeling Practices

In the early 1980s, human rights experts and humanitarian practitioners successfully lobbied for the recognition and protection of IDPs on the grounds that people uprooted within their own countries as a result of conflicts or natural disasters constituted an empirically distinguishable group with specific needs that were different from people who were not displaced (Cohen and Deng 1998, 28; Kälin 2014, 166). Scholars have since pondered the political meaning of IDP recognition as well as the risk for social misrepresentation and preferential treatment of IDPs vis-à-vis victims of other human rights abuses (Hathaway 2007; Dubernet 2001). Regardless of these concerns, international IDP advocates successfully pushed for the recognition of IDPs as a specific group with distinct rights through an influential series of normative and operational guidelines (Hathaway 2007; Cohen 2007). Most important are the UN Guiding Principles on Internal Displacement, which establish the normative basis for IDP protection, conceptualize IDPs as a category of concern, and clarify their rights under international law (Orchard 2014). Today's global IDP regime consists of international and domestic laws, institutional mandates to protect and assist IDPs, established humanitarian practices, and even distinct displacement tracking technologies (Orchard 2010). This ensemble of law, policy, and practice is meant to enhance the protection of displaced persons, resolve displacement, and address displacement-related human rights violations (Brookings Institution 2015). While research and practice on internal displacement tends to focus predominantly on IDPs in conflict situations, IDP norms have also been applied in situations of natural disasters (Kälin 2014; Cohen and Bradley 2010; Ferris 2011).

Scholars have examined the meaning and implications of international processes that construct, differentiate, and govern people because their movements are perceived to be out of place (Bloch, Nando, and Zetter 2014; Zetter 2007; Andersson 2013; Mezzadra and Neilson 2013). Critics of these processes argue that they tend to obscure local realities and enhance social control over "the other" (Zetter 2007). Similarly, processes of labeling encourage the dismissal of alternative identities and claims that challenge accepted ideas and stereotypical experiences, especially in terms of what constitutes harm and suffering, order and justice (Rajagopal 2003). For instance, homelessness has become discursively normalized in the public sphere, while the closely related notion of internal displacement has achieved international recognition and concern. Some scholars point out how identity constructions help to naturalize the roles of law and international bureaucracy in the creation of solutions for specific problems of governance, including displacement (Duffield 2008). Such critiques highlight the repressive or disciplinary aspects of governance that are veiled through simplified pictures of law's neutrality, international good will, and capacity to protect people against human rights violations (see Mattei and Nader 2008).

A full interrogation of the concept of internal displacement and related notions such as durable solutions is beyond the scope of this chapter. Briefly, however, critical analyses point out the omission of capitalist dynamics and political-economic decisions in common understandings of displacement and its resolution (Nail 2015; Green 2005). Internal displacement is regularly framed as a social and political phenomenon that disrupts an otherwise normal pattern of daily life, thus creating new needs and vulnerabilities (Polzer and Hammond 2008). It is not uncommon to read that internal displacement is the "first step" of a long journey of mobility (Brookings Institution 2015)—a viewpoint that silences much longer histories of exclusion, mobility, and dispossession. In this sense, IDPs are characterized as dispossessed citizens (having once possessed something) and victims of state failure and broken social relationships (Cohen and Deng 1998; Morel 2014). Displacement is commonly understood to entail a variety of losses including home, property, social networks, community, material goods, and citizenship (Lubkemann 2008b). Stemming from this picture of the past, the triad of durable solutions (in the case of IDPs, voluntary return, local integration, or relocation elsewhere in the country) offer to "re-root" the displaced person and reinforce their social bonds and political citizenship (Malkki 1995b; Agier 2011; see also the introduction and Landau, chapter 8, this volume). Normative discussions on durable solutions for IDPs emphasize the importance of law and protection of private property rights in advancing solutions—in other words, determining who belongs where—after situations of mass displacement (Smit 2012). As the following section demonstrates, attempts to apply the notions of internal displacement and durable solutions in postearthquake Port-au-Prince were particularly fraught, further revealing the tensions inherent in these concepts and the ways in which they are products of and, in turn, produce complex power relations.

Conceptualizing Displacement Inside Haiti's Urban Crisis

Haiti's 2010 displacement crisis has significantly overlapped with conditions of urban marginality and structural violence. Since the 1980s, economic liberalization and state neglect have brought growing numbers of impoverished rural people to Port-au-Prince as a matter of economic necessity (Lundahl 2002). Haitians have also migrated en masse to countries such as the Dominican Republic and the United States, to the extent that 24 percent of Haiti's gross domestic product is composed of remittances.[1] Haiti is further marked by extreme inequalities. An estimated 1 percent of its population controls 50 percent of the nation's wealth, while the bottom 20 percent collectively share only 2 percent of Haiti's national income (Bailey 2014). Haiti's predatory state does not provide social welfare or govern beyond the preservation of elite interests; rather, the state is visible to most of its citizens only in forms of social control, taxation, and violence during political and social struggles (Lundahl 2002; Fatton 2002). Under these conditions people often do not want to live in the city but feel compelled to migrate given lack of food security and income in rural areas (Leader 2013). Indeed, there are few benefits to living in a city such as Port-au-Prince, which was built for 250,000 but now claims over 2.7 million residents (Gros 2011). Most of these residents are landless and do not have permanent homes, instead occupying land and renting where they can afford to do so (Schuller 2016, 38). This has resulted in a highly mobile urban population, who move in response to pressures and opportunities.

Against this background, Haiti's earthquake laid bare several intertwined crises, especially around housing, mobility, and employment. Even before the earthquake, 70 percent of the city's population was concentrated in slum areas, where living conditions often fell below the humanitarian community's Sphere Standards (Beunza and Eresta 2011). Population pressures and lack of housing had also generated acute levels of tenure insecurity and homelessness. In fact, conservative estimates placed Haiti's housing deficit prior to the earthquake at 100,000–300,000 housing units; using this estimate, only 25–50 percent of the city's postdisaster housing deficit was the direct result of earthquake destruction (Levine et al. 2012). Nevertheless, the destruction of approximately 105,000 homes greatly exacerbated the existing crisis, leading to mass displacement.

At the onset of the humanitarian response to Haiti's earthquake, Humanitarian agencies and development-focused organizations disagreed on the importance and potential implications of distinguishing "earthquake-induced displacement" from the broader housing crisis in Port-au-Prince. While humanitarians familiar with norms on IDPs and camp-based response systems favored focusing on IDPs, some housing specialists voiced their disdain for an IDP-specific approach given the number of urban citizens who already lacked access to land and housing prior to the earthquake.[2] From their perspective, focusing on "re-rooting" IDPs displaced in the earthquake would neither lead to progress in the equitable distribution of aid resources nor help to produce a more accessible and affordable housing market. Furthermore, because of Haiti's fragile economic situation, the "ultra-poor" risked being squeezed out of an overheated rental market if assistance was tailored to people classified as "earthquake displaced."

Despite these ethical and practical considerations, housing and reconstruction policies proceeded in line with a humanitarian interpretation of the normative framework on internal displacement. While the humanitarian community in Haiti focused significantly on IDPs as a primary population of concern, their interpretation of international norms on internal displacement differed in some significant ways from the approach laid out in influential standards such as the Guiding Principles on Internal Displacement. Most importantly, IDPs were understood to be those residing in camps, effectively excluding the displaced who sought shelter elsewhere, such as with friends or family. From this perspective, resolving displacement was first and foremost a matter of closing camps. This in turn entailed a primary and almost exclusive focus on identifying alternative housing options for camp residents, notwithstanding the view in international normative frameworks on internal displacement that durable solutions for IDPs require the achievement of a much broader range of rights-based criteria pertaining to issues including livelihoods and participation in decision-making. Ending displacement became highly politicized because the persistence of massive, squalid camps in public squares and parks, near the airport, and across a variety of other open spaces was too visible and disruptive from the perspective of the state and much of the humanitarian community, a constant reminder of the failures of the relief and reconstruction process.

Monthly reports from humanitarian actors strung together a narrative on Haiti's earthquake displacement that emphasized the assistance needs of camp-based populations, site-specific eviction threats, movement dynamics, and the provision of housing and settlement solutions. As routine data collection on the camps continued, it became clear by 2011 that the composition of the IDP population had shifted, revealing both the broader political-economic causes of mobility and the conceptual inadequacy of humanitarian discourses on IDPs. At this point, 85 percent of people living in camps were identified by IDP registration as former renters, squatters, homeless individuals, and migrants from the countryside (IOM and ACTED 2011). Their difficulty in accessing housing after the earthquake, in other words, was not entirely earthquake related. Various organizations began to report that in some camps at least 25 percent of the camp population had not sheltered there immediately after the earthquake.[3] Population surveys suggest that the primary reason people continued to seek shelter in spaces registered as camps was lack of income (IOM and ACTED 2011). This data quickly eroded sympathy for people in camps who did not fit the stereotype of the displaced victim.

Though the IDP label was widely applied to anyone living in a camp, the reality was that camps hosted many people whose predicaments were only partially attributable to the earthquake's effects. "Seeing" Port-au-Prince through the lens of IDPs essentially meant that IDP spaces (camps) were coded with terminology that did not accurately reflect the way that Haitians were actually living on city land (see Scott 1998). For some, camps had become among the cheapest rental spaces in the postdisaster housing market, with former camp residents renting their shelters to newer arrivals. In some instances, camps represented potential places for permanent construction. During my camp-based interviews, Haitians narrated their journeys "looking for land" immediately after the earthquake, describing how they ended up in spaces later labeled IDP camps. In these stories, the earthquake presented tremendous opportunities by removing certain barriers to land. For example, it destroyed fences and gates and revealed what was actually available for the people. These conversations made little mention of what was legal or illegal but focused on what was necessary, fair, and legitimate given the dispossessed's lack of income and fear of returning to former slums that had "fallen on top" of them during the earthquake and the responsibility of the state to provide housing. Although not every camp presented these dynamics, it is important to understand that in some camp contexts, the opportunity to access land and affordable housing was created through the earthquake itself.

Addressing Housing Needs through IDP-Specific Approaches

At the time of writing, few camps remain in Port-au-Prince. According to the Haitian government and humanitarian agencies, Haiti's earthquake population has been assisted to return to their pre-earthquake "normal lives," and their housing situation now depends on future economic development. However, considering that there have been no structural changes in Haiti in terms of exploitative economic practices and the use of the state to secure elite privilege and property rights, there is little reason to believe that access to housing for the urban poor will improve under Haiti's model of neoliberal development.

The measures taken to "end displacement" have been mediated through bureaucratic interpretations of displacement experiences and rights-based entitlements of IDPs. In this respect, the clearest priorities for state and international actors have been to identify and track displaced populations, meet immediate humanitarian needs, achieve IDP camp closures, and restore IDPs living in camps back to their original position prior to the earthquake. Humanitarian agencies carefully articulated that their only responsibility was to meet IDPs' "displacement-specific" needs. Drawn from the guidelines of the Camp Coordination and Camp Management Cluster Returns group, IDP-specific support for housing was meant to "close the cycle of displacement and help families back into living conditions comparable to those in which they were living before the earthquake" (Fitzgerald 2012). In practice, this has meant that an IDP's former land tenure status was used as the main reference point for determining access to different housing packages and land settlement options. Through this method, more permanent housing reconstruction was made available to property owners and people with access to land, while those who remained landless were resigned to the provision of cash grants intended to subsidize one year of rental housing within a costly and overheated rental market.

There are obvious objections to housing interventions that have virtually ignored prevailing conditions of landlessness, insecure tenure, and lack of access to adequate housing. It is particularly interesting to see how property concepts linked to IDP rights have legitimized hierarchies in solutions and housing assistance. In monetary terms, property owners have received significantly more support than renters and other landless individuals. For example, a transitional shelter for a former home owner could cost up to $7,000, ten times the amount of rental cash grants given to former renters, squatters, and other landless people (who received on average $650) (Davis 2012). This disparity reflects the fact that IDP return and restitution programs generally disregarded the complexity of the relationship between prior land tenure status and exposure to mobility and displacement in the aftermath of the earthquake. Instead, losing a physical, privately owned home was seen as a legitimate claim for IDP status and displacement-related assistance, but the inability to secure a home because of a lack of economic means constituted a far weaker claim.

To maintain their claims to neutrality, lower transaction costs, and minimize organizational risk, the international community turned to legal strategies that brought together Haitian law and international law and standards. By connecting IDP property-related norms with private property protections in Haitian law, international actors have played a key role in determining the legitimacy of land claims and reinforcing property exclusion. Operationally speaking, humanitarian legal strategies have included researching and mapping legal histories, creating easy-to-use manuals on Haitian law, providing property enumeration exercises, and addressing legal barriers to land tenure. In applying these legal strategies to activities such as camp closures, eviction responses, and land tenure regularization, the effect has often been to empower Haitian landlords to claim land and property rights (even when using forged documents to backstop their claims). To a lesser extent, these international efforts have resulted in assisting squatters and landless populations to justify their land claims, especially if they were made after or in response to the earthquake. This disparity is especially clear since the Haitian legal system grants far stronger legal protection for private property rights than for the rights of renters and squatters. Given that 70–80 percent of the urban population falls into the latter categories, the property rights approach to resolving displacement and providing housing solutions has helped reproduce and exacerbate existing inequalities (IFRC 2014). One human rights lawyer described what she perceived to be discriminatory impacts of legal discourse and the fixation on property status as a reference for providing housing packages and resolving urban land conflicts:

> So suddenly the authorities are aware that people are living here who aren't "supposed" to—but where should they live, and how should we organize this? This talk of regularity and irregularity only came after the people [IDPs] were already there. Which means that, in terms of what is fair, people become irregular before even knowing they are irregular. Blaming a person for living in a place that is not regular is not the way to say it . . . you give a negative connotation. . . . Land in Haiti is not regularly parceled, the land is not regularly defined, so the people are not irregular. They are not illegal. They are people that have the right to live there or somewhere else. You have crowded cities where people have nowhere to live and the places to live are very expensive. . . . If we focus on regular and irregular, we are motivating for social exclusion.[4]

Finally, IDP return-focused programs and assistance have failed to grapple with the predatory nature of Haiti's property system and the historical role of Haitian law in protecting class privilege (Fatton 2002). During conflicts over land, the humanitarian community appealed to the legal system in ways that assumed that Haitian law was independent of political and economic interests, not predominantly shaped by them (Kennedy 2005). Humanitarian actions such as selecting camps for closure based on demands from state officials and property owners have further helped to legitimize a property system highly tainted by histories of violence, theft, and exclusion (Dubois 2012).

Beyond controversial involvement in camp closure programs, humanitarian agencies have failed to support claims for other housing-related rights in situations where people were resisting eviction.[5] According to Article 22 of the Haitian Constitution, Haitian citizens have the right to housing, although the scope and content of this right is vague and not in line with international standards (Amnesty International 2013). When asked about their roles in protecting the right to housing and using it in political strategies to help local people resist evictions, humanitarian agencies were skeptical of the feasibility, validity, and justiciability of this right. Altogether, helping Haitians to progressively fulfill housing rights seemed both illogical and counterproductive to humanitarian interests in producing immediate solutions to end displacement by closing camps.

Informal Settlements and Discourses of Resistance

The previous sections discussed the analytical limitations of IDP concepts and their disempowering effects in terms of reinforcing urban social hierarchies and restoring former property relations. This section presents broader discourses of resistance identified during my fieldwork. These discourses emerge, first, out of local perceptions of socioeconomic injustice and, second, through visions of the earthquake as a rare opportunity to pursue freedom and dignity through land occupation. These discourses serve an important role in explaining why many Haitians, many of whom were labeled IDPs, have rejected return to their former land tenure position as a purported solution and turned to informal land markets to seek a better life. Indeed, the proliferation of illegal land sales and informal settlements challenge the assumed desirability of bureaucratically organized, legally recognized solutions to displacement. These discourses and dynamics also highlight how long-term struggles against landlessness can overlap with postdisaster mobility decisions and have the potential to reshape wider processes of reconstruction and urbanization.

The following discussion of resistance and informal settlements focuses on the settlement of Canaan, which went from an empty piece of land north of Port-au-Prince to Haiti's third largest "city," in terms of population, after the 2010 earthquake. This northern periphery is broken up into several neighborhoods and smaller settlements, housing more than two hundred thousand people. The land was officially expropriated by the government, although under Haitian law the legalities of the expropriation process were never completed and the land was not meant for spontaneous settlement. Rather, the expropriation was undertaken under major international pressure to release land for temporary relocation of IDPs from hazardous areas in the city. However, the expropriation of a new tract of land for "earthquake victims" provided an opportunity that was seized upon by a much larger group, who, through various forms of squatting, immediately took it over for settlement construction. From a legal perspective, the squatters' land-ownership goals are difficult to achieve through the existing body of Haitian law, and for political and economic reasons, the state has little motivation to recognize land claims. Haitians' efforts to "grab" a durable solution in these informal communities must be understood as a response to these overarching constraints.

While discussing the effects of the earthquake, Haitians generally interpreted their condition of mobility through broader understandings of urban exclusion and structural violence. The most obvious illustration of this was heavy emphasis on suffering experienced as a result of lack of land and tenure insecurity. Far more than the experience of displacement, Haitians could speak at length about the experiences as renters and landless persons. The lack of land was the source of multiple urban vulnerabilities including crime, insecurity, hunger, lack of space, and consistent exploitation. In the words of one interviewee, "In Port-au-Prince, the price of rent is always high, and the landlords always raise the price. And you are living in a dangerous zone. No one wants to live in a bad zone, and you are always looking for a quieter zone according to your means. People come from everywhere and live here."[6] Inside a city with few jobs, poorly serviced neighborhoods, high crime rates, and a mass shortage of housing units, renters were always moving (see Fass 1987). It is easy to see why Haitians believed, then, that it was cruel to be labeled a renter during IDP registrations—as if this was their natural position within the property order.

Within informal settlements, Haitians made no attempt to distinguish IDPs from non-IDPs in terms of earthquake experiences. Importantly, Haitians also never referred to their IDP identity (or lack thereof) in discussions of their victimization, rights violations, or entitlements. Furthermore, the rights of IDPs did not factor into the way that they discussed or legitimized their land claims. Instead, the focus of their contention was on the historical predatory behavior of large landowners and the failure of the state to protect them from such behavior through the provision of livelihoods, land, and affordable housing. For example, in a focus group discussion of earthquake displacement and victimization, participants implicitly problematized the relationship between victimization and earthquake-induced displacement:

FG respondent #1 (former IDP camp resident): "When the state doesn't address the needs of people, then the people are victims. It's not just about January 12 [2010]. The state owes you housing, health and security. If you have these then you are not a victim. But when you don't have anything at all, then you are a victim."

FG respondent #2 (non-IDP): "The majority of people in Haiti are victims."

FG respondent #3 (non-IDP): "Some people came out here [to the informal settlement] because of the stress of the earthquake. They are victims too."

FG respondent #4 (former IDP camp resident): "We have a state that is late. That is our greatest problem. And that we are uneducated and not mobilized. This is why we are victims."

Within the informal settlements and camps, people provided a wide variety of reasons for why they rejected state and international solutions that would force them to return to slums and insecure land tenure situations. Unsurprisingly, the lack of affordable housing and the availability of cheap land were the main drivers of movement to the informal settlements within the sample of interviewees in informal settlements. The clear majority of people interviewed in IDP camps and in informal settlements articulated that, prior to the earthquake, they moved between every six months to two years because of issues of housing affordability and lack of income. Each movement was painful and traumatic because it required the family to face worse living conditions and greater insecurity. This cycle of urban displacement was a form of unmitigated stress on families, putting them in dire economic circumstances, contributing to family splitting, and creating extreme uncertainty surrounding where one could live. In the words of one urban resident: "What is not good about renting house is that you don't have the money. You are always waiting until the six-month deadline, your heart is always beating."[7]

Interviews with renters and landless people also captured the relationship between land, personhood, and dignity—an extremely important theme within the ex-slave colony of Haiti. One interviewee explained that unless a person has a home, he or she could not be considered a full person.[8] This motivated him to resist return to the rental market and to subversively take his rental subsidy cash grant and buy land on the informal land market. In a similar case, a former IDP camp resident rationalized his land occupation in the following manner:

We had been renting houses for fifteen years. We are so happy now that we are not moving now. You cannot have a home in Port-au-Prince. Landowners do not respect you. When the [rent] deadline comes you cannot pay, and he won't put up with you in terms of patience, he will just evict you immediately. He will break the door when you are in it, disrespect you, and evict you. The landowners will just raise the rent on you [without warning].[9]

Grievances against the state and landed class also factored into explanations for postdisaster movements to seize and occupy land. Different explanations were given for why and how the state was the source of their suffering. While some interviews discussed the importance of a stronger state, others described the problem of state power and capture by the landed elite (in which the "building capacity" of the state would only increase its abilities as a repressive apparatus). Interviewees' own class-based analyses of land and housing exclusion led to the generalized perspective that "rich people in Haiti wanted all the land."[10] The Haitian state, therefore, placed no limits on what the landed elite could take, and this directly impacted settlement options for the impoverished urban majority. Those living in informal settlements referenced a series of eviction attempts in new informal settlements to illustrate the insatiable appetite for land by the Haitian elite, at the direct expense of the poor.[11] It was therefore problematic that "the state had been filled by the *grandon*," a term used for Haiti's landowning class.[12]

These insights show how extra-legal claims for land, often depicted as "land grabbing," were understood as methods of local protection against more insidious forms of land grabbing by Haiti's landowning class. A twenty-year-old university student helped to distinguish the difference between the social and material value of Haiti's land: "You see, there is a difference between rich and poor. The rich people are using their land for investment and profit. Those people have no intention to live on the land. But there are people in poverty who are trying to run away from the city to this safer place [new informal settlements on the city's periphery]. But the state didn't say anything about it."[13] Again, these grievances aired in new informal settlements illuminate the perceived collusion between the Haitian state and landowning elite. These discourses reached across different areas of informal settlements and buttressed confidence in the legitimacy of extra-legal land occupation given that "everyone knows that the state owes the people."[14] In summary, land occupations were significant in everyday lives because they promised greater urban inclusion, security, choice, personhood, and justice— goods that could not be achieved through the "solutions" promoted by humanitarian actors in cooperation with the Haitian state.

Turning Access into Property: The Struggle to Defend Land Gains and Informal Settlements

As agents seeking solutions to the injustices of impoverished urban life in Port-au-Prince (and not merely to displacement caused by the earthquake), those who have moved to the informal settlements have had to navigate different structures of power and authority, first, to access and secure land and, second, to turn this access into recognized property. Access to land was ultimately determined by one's individual means and the price of land plots upon arrival to the settlement; land prices were responsive to the limited availability of housing and the closure of IDP camps in Port-au-Prince. There is ample evidence to suggest that pressures relating to Haiti's prior housing crisis and humanitarian camp closure programs (and evictions) all affected the affordability and availability of rental housing inside the city, fueling the development of informal land and housing markets. The provision of rental subsidy cash grants further stoked housing demands given that people had new purchasing power. Interviews with urban experts monitoring informal settlements as well as with people living in them confirm that the rental subsidy cash grants were used to purchase cheap land on the outskirts of Port-au-Prince—a limited, one-time offer for many people.[15]

Perhaps like smugglers who facilitate the crossing of tightly controlled borders and hold a degree of power over their clients, land sellers have been some of the main facilitators of access to land for landless Haitians and former renters. In the very early stages of land occupation, some individual squatters marked out plots and built fences to demonstrate their ownership claims, but for later arrivals (who are also suspected to be poorer), land access has been facilitated by sellers who first occupied large areas, divided it, and sold it for a price determined by the market. In the beginning land was cheap and risk of eviction was high. But like any land market, the price of illegally purchased land has fluctuated according to demand and risk. While land may have been cheap in 2010, it had nearly doubled in price by 2014, also influenced by start-up businesses and construction. This point is important to understanding that time and market changes influenced access, plot choice, and long-term security on the land. A local community organizer helpfully explained some of the key difficulties in land settlement for the poorest:

> The tough people are the ones who first got it. Even if the land was public, you had to have money to buy the land—it wasn't for free. If you have no money to buy, you could be in trouble with the mafias. The second thing is even when people bought land, they might have to sell it to be able to find some money to live. Then they would have to go back to the same vulnerable place that they had been before. Or they might have a piece of land in a normal zone [in the informal settlement], but because they had no money for food they would have to sell it to buy a cheaper one in a risky zone, in the mountains or in the ravine, that could cause their death later.[16]

Field observations also suggest that the spatial form of informal settlements, over time, began to mirror that of the city. In other words, permanent access to land was short lived for poor households, who were continually pushed to the margins of the settlement because of poverty and were exposed to increasingly high risk of eviction.

By no means were all the land sellers the same in their dealings with people pursuing a safer and more permanent living situation. Land sellers were occasionally accused of selling the same plot to multiple people, causing disputes and requiring different forms of local mediation. On the public radio or in interviews with state officials and humanitarian agencies, land sellers were commonly portrayed as criminals who had grabbed land and perpetuated lawlessness. However, land sellers were also sometimes characterized by settlement residents as heroes and necessary facilitators in creating access to land. In this sense, their role and image were more positive than that of the state and humanitarian institutions, who were seen as policing the land behaviors of the poor and granting the claims of the landed elite. In some cases, land sellers became governing committees and assumed responsibilities for negotiating with government officers over eviction threats.

People living in informal settlements have faced enormous difficulty in achieving recognition of their claims. For several years now, the residents of Haiti's new informal settlements have been denied any information or clarity on the status of their landholdings. While significant resources have been poured into clarifying property rights in Haiti, only limited measures have been taken to define the rights of squatters, particularly in the new informal settlements. This lack of clarity and the political sensitivity of these settlements barred international organizations from recognizing people moving to them and from providing more permanent types of housing assistance there. Without clarity, informal settlers pursued different channels, such as paying local brokers to approach local authorities and secure some form of documentation, in attempts to legalize their property (although many explained that they lacked the "means" to do so). This led to multiple types of exploitation of new landholders. Several profit-seeking groups and quasi-government entities (with strongly rumored links to formal government offices) demanded "taxes" or duped people by claiming they could help people register and legalize their properties. (This despite the fact that Haiti's existing legal framework does not permit the easy transfer of state expropriated land to private parties.) Perhaps owing to the lack of legitimacy and recognition of squatters, rampant fraud and extortion was not framed as a significant "protection issue" in discourses on new settlements. Rather, it was left up to squatters to defend themselves against such abuses—sometimes by emblazing strong messages such as "Go Away, Thief!" on the sides of fences and in the entrance of settlements.

Finally, land claims have been delegitimized through the discursive representation of informal settlements. Informal construction violates international and aesthetic principles for safe housing and modern development. The unplanned and extra-legal character of settlements has held humanitarian agencies back from considering these sites as places in which Haitians may reasonably pursue the progressive realization of solutions or housing rights. Observations of international working groups on return and housing also reveal an understanding that humanitarian agencies deliberately avoided research (or research questions) that would illustrate a relationship between the provision of rental subsidy cash grants and their use to purchase land in informal markets.[17] Arguably, a series of deliberate efforts to maintain a narrow, dominant discourse around internal displacement and settlement has direct implications on the legitimacy of alternative claims to land and property in the reconstruction period. A more open community of urban and housing experts working in Port-au-Prince has helped jar the discourse by reframing the narrative of settlements as new opportunities and sites of major investment. This has, however, opened the door for other neoliberal discourses to be applied to the informal settlements, such as discourses on the market-based value of self-construction and the "resilience" of Haitians who have succeeded in pursuing solutions without external help (overlooking recipients' redeployment of rental subsidy cash grants to finance purchases in informal settlements). Poor Haitians' own discourses on land redistribution and social justice have not been seriously considered or integrated into discourse at the national or international levels on the informal settlements.

Conclusion

In this chapter I have argued that rather than advance the postdisaster land claims of Haiti's urban marginalized and landless, international principles, labels, and rights-based claims related to internal displacement have helped to protect elite property claims and reproduce urban spatial divisions. This is partially explained by the limitations of IDP discourse in conceptualizing urban displacement and solutions to it and in understanding diverse and ongoing patterns of mobility across an informal urban landscape. The humanitarian community's reliance on international frameworks and practices on internal displacement to analyze and categorize experiences in post-earthquake Haiti is largely at odds with earthquake victims' own interpretations of their problems and has significantly underplayed the wide variety of ways urban people live without the protection of housing, land, and property rights.

Urban discourses and acts of resistance show how poor Haitians are dealing with the effects of uneven development and urban exclusion by pushing the boundaries of land access and redistribution. As discussed, nonnormative methods of land occupation and self-construction either have been targeted and restricted by state and humanitarian actions or have been co-opted and relabeled as "resilience" in order to demonstrate that people can live without a strong, responsive state. Many see their land-claiming efforts as a legitimate response to their long-standing grievances surrounding historical cycles of displacement and inequitable land and resource distribution, but this perspective has been silenced in national and international conversations on the emergence and evolution of new informal settlements after the earthquake. Integrating these perspectives into evolving discourses on the right to housing, reconstruction, and urban development in Haiti is essential in order to achieve a clearer picture of how the purported beneficiaries of humanitarian efforts to promote solutions to displacement actually understand and participate in the pursuit of solutions.

Finally, I have problematized the critical assemblage of Haitian law, IDP norms, and state-humanitarian practices that together determine a very narrow set of "durable housing solutions." Poor citizens in Port-au-Prince who have tried to claim urban land after the earthquake have often seen their status shift from a recognized, registered IDP to an unrecognized/criminalized squatter because of the way their movements and efforts to find a solution to their predicament have been framed by state and international actors. The deployment of legalistic and property-centric concepts related to displacement, aiming to "root" IDPs through a set of sanctioned solutions, have instead created new patterns of mobility and have led to the development of new squatter identities. While some gains have been made in terms of land access, legal restrictions still apply to squatters that starkly limit their recognition and protection and, in turn, the durability of the solutions that they seek.

Notes

1. World Bank, "Personal Remittances % of GDP, 1970–2017," http://data.world bank.org/indicator/BX.TRF.PWKR.DT.GD.ZS.

2. Repeated interviews were conducted with six international housing experts providing technical support to the government between January 2014 and August 2014.

3. Interview with American nongovernmental organization worker in Port-au-Prince, Haiti, in May 2014.

4. Interview with an international human rights lawyer, May 2014.

5. Haitian law on adverse possession is exceptionally biased toward landowners—and it has been argued by some legal commentators that an imbalance in the rights between squatters and property owners is the underlying basis of Haiti's class division (Calhan 2014). According to the Haitian Civil Code, to become the owner

of the land, a squatter must reside on a property continuously, peacefully, publicly, and in the capacity of owner for twenty years or more (IFRC 2014). In addition to this, a squatter must file for ownership with a local court—and bear legal costs, which are far outside the means of such people.

6. Interview A, Port-au-Prince, June 2014.

7. Interview B, St. Cristophe Informal Settlement, July 2014.

8. Interview C, St. Cristophe Informal Settlement, June 2014.

9. Interview D, St. Cristophe Informal Settlement, June 2014.

10. Interview E, Canaan 3 Informal Settlement, July 2014.

11. This eviction has been documented; see the documentary *Mozayik*, directed by Jon Bougher (SnagFilms, 2013), http://www.snagfilms.com/films/title/mozayik.

12. Interview F, St. Cristophe Informal Settlement, June 2014.

13. Interview G, Canaan 3 Informal Settlement, August 2014.

14. This was a common assertion in several interviews in both informal settlements and camps.

15. Interview, housing expert, June 2014.

16. Interview, local community leader, Canaan Informal Settlement, August 2014.

17. This was directly observed in meetings in June 2014 and further raised with the author in four interviews that took place in May–July 2014.

10

From IDPs to Victims in Colombia

Reflections on Durable Solutions in the Postconflict Setting

Julieta Lemaitre and Kristin Bergtora Sandvik

From 2012 to 2016, the Colombian government and FARC (Fuerzas Arma-das Revolucionarias de Colombia, or the Revolutionary Armed Forces of Colombia) negotiated a peace agreement intended to end fifty years of civil war; this agreement was ratified in 2016, and demobilization formally began in 2017.[1] The peace agreement signals a new phase for Colombia. Years of peace talks have raised enormous hopes, both in the country and abroad. The slow shift in the pattern of violence has been preceded by different government measures meant to address the accumulated harms of the war, including durable solutions for internally displaced persons (IDPs), who are the majority of the more than 8 million Colombians officially registered as victims of the armed conflict as of June 2016.

Government responses to the harms of war on rural populations and, hence, its definition of durable solutions for displaced populations have evolved in the last two decades. In public policy until the mid-1990s, forced migrants were framed as masses of rural poor joining the already large numbers of the urban poor and as needing measures to ensure they would benefit from slow but relentless economic development. By the late 1990s, however, the spike in forcible migration as well as changing international norms produced a new frame: the same populations were now considered internally displaced and protagonists of a humanitarian crisis. The decade between 1996 and 2006 saw rapid growth in humanitarian assistance and government efforts to integrate victims of war in existing poverty alleviation schemes, under the oversight since 2004 of the Colombian Constitutional Court. Between 2005 and 2007 Colombia engaged in a controversial program of transitional justice with paramilitaries, resulting in a relatively successful disarmament, demobilization, and reintegration (DDR) program and a less successful attempt to provide judicial reparations to victims. Spurred by the Constitutional Court, the government (under President Álvaro Uribe Vélez, 2002–10) started a program combining poverty alleviation and humanitarian aid, known as Acción Social. Under the following government of President Juan Manuel Santos Calderón (2010–18), this program grew massively and provided administrative reparations for civilian victims of the armed conflict under Law 1448 of 2011, known as the Victims' Law.

The process of administrative reparations and land restitution for IDPs pursuant to the Victims' Law is slowly advancing. Humanitarian aid remains an IDP entitlement administered by the agency that absorbed Acción Social, the Victims' Unit. These measures are defined as a legal right for IDPs "until such a time when the manifest condition of vulnerability ceases."[2] The conditions of this cessation and its relationship to durable solutions have been the subject of much debate. Starting in 2015 the Victims' Unit has been charged to use surveys to determine whether IDPs have overcome manifest vulnerability and are ready to accept a one-time reparation that would also contribute to durable solutions.[3]

This is a considerable challenge, for Colombia has one of the highest rates of internal displacement in the world; IDPs account for more than 12.5 percent of Colombia's 48 million inhabitants (IDMC 2014b). Most are rural residents forced to move to poor urban areas, giving up their land and livelihoods. They frequently encounter discrimination based on their rural (and often racial) origins as well as their political identities, and many Colombians imagine IDPs to be guerrilla collaborators, paramilitary informants, or participants in the drug trade (Lemaitre and Sandvik 2015).

One of the most striking features of the displacement situation in Colombia is the influence enjoyed by a loose alliance of internally displaced persons' organizations (IDPOs) and human rights nongovernmental organizations (NGOs) in national policies. At a local level, IDPOs have also been agents in policy transformations in ways that remain mostly undocumented. Some IDPO leaders even advocated for the Victims' Law, going to Congress after the peace process for the paramilitary and demanding benefits similar to those received by former irregular soldiers through DDR programs (see Cristo 2012). IDPOs have also organized protests, demanding a better government response to their plight and, as part of a vibrant civil society, have spoken out in innumerable participatory spaces.

IDPs, most of whom have been displaced for over a decade, have also been working intensely at grassroots reconstruction (Lemaitre and Sandvik 2016). Grassroots reconstruction is an ongoing process shaped by decades of civil war as well as rural–urban economic migrations and is related to the effects of the war as much as to economic processes and cultural and demographic changes and differences among IDP populations. It reflects both individual efforts to recover moral agency lost to the war and community efforts to build the shared physical and political space for their new lives.[4]

With the slowing of the war, the improvement in general standards of living, and the (sometimes meager) successes of DDR, humanitarian aid, and reparations, the country is slowly approaching durable solutions for its millions of IDPs. However, the Colombian experience raises questions about the relationship between peace, development, transitional justice, and durable solutions as well as questions about the impact of differences in experiences and identities on the construction of these solutions and the causes and effects of changes in institutional responses and frames.

According to the United Nations, durable solutions are achieved when IDPs "no longer have any specific assistance and protection needs that are linked to their displacement, and can enjoy their human rights without discrimination on account of their displacement" (IASC 2010). What does this mean in a dramatically unequal country like Colombia, where differences between rural and urban populations are particularly stark? Do durable solutions mean Colombian IDPs are at the same level of poverty as the urban populations in the slums where they resettle? Or at the level of poverty they experienced before displacement? Or at a level of poverty they would have had if they had not been displaced? Given the evident complications of defining durable solutions in this context, Colombia adopted an approach to durable solutions that strives to end IDPs' manifest vulnerability, combining general poverty alleviation efforts with special measures to benefit IDPs, including humanitarian assistance, land restitution, and other forms of reparation.

All IDPs are supposed to benefit from these measures equally, yet IDPs have different needs and aspirations depending on their experiences, identities, location, and capacity. This chapter explores some of these differences to reflect on the following questions: What kind of durable resolutions to the IDP predicament are on offer in the Colombian postconflict setting? How do different populations approach durable solutions, and how do the changing legal frames impact these approaches?

We make three arguments: First, the ways IDPOs conceptualize peace and strategies to achieve it are not static but rather respond to legal and institutional changes as well as to varying experiences of reconstruction. Second, institutional changes affect the identity of IDPOs as well as their security, the structure of their claims, and their participatory spaces; these changes impact IDPOs in significantly different ways depending on intersections between displacement and other identities. This differential impact also shapes views of peace and durable solutions, which vary according to gender and ethnic differences. Last, durable solutions themselves are shaped by the intersections and tensions between changes in legal and policy frameworks, IDPO adaptation to these changes, and the intersection between displacement and other identities. That is, while legal and policy frameworks may suggest a static set of options and processes to resolve displacement, what actually constitutes a durable solution in a particular context will be different from durable solutions in another context, as perceived by IDPs.

Methods, Data, and Summary of Findings

The 1997 IDP law and 2004 Constitutional Court structural litigation (T-025) provided significant visibility to the IDP issue and contributed to the rise of a large number of grassroots, IDP civil society actors, especially with respect to women's groups but also to indigenous mobilization. From 2010 to 2015, we studied the political organization of poor displaced women and an uprooted indigenous group, the Kankuamo of the Sierra Nevada, paying special attention to legal mobilization. This period witnessed major shifts in political and legal frames, from a humanitarian crisis frame to a transitional justice frame to the present peace process. In the context of continued large-scale displacement, we saw the women's and indigenous organizations that we worked with actively participate in the transitional justice process engendered by the 2011 Victims' Law as the political and legal currency of the IDP frame and of the Constitutional Court was fading. Our methods included observations and field visits, extended interviews, and ethnographic readings of documents. Participants were selected based on professional connections and snowball sampling. Trust was built through previous personal relationships with IDP leaders. In 2012 and 2013, the authors, together with the Kankuamo organization's lawyer and a group of law students from Universidad de Los Andes, documented the Kankuamo experience with legal protection measures from the Inter-American human rights system and the Constitutional Court. We benefited from unique access to the archive of the Organización Indígena Kankuamo and from the generous support of the Kankuamo leadership. Between 2009 and 2013 we also collaborated on a project studying legal mobilization by internally displaced women. The research team followed internally displaced women's organizations as they demanded government assistance and protection. We maintained updated reviews of the literature and press coverage of internal displacement in Colombia and mapped internally displaced women's organizations. By 2013 we had identified sixty-six organizations in twenty-six of Colombia's thirty-two provinces and interviewed sixty-three of their leaders; we also recorded their public appearances in various forums and collected media coverage of their appearances. We spent between six months and a year with three women's IDP organizations and three NGOs working closely with displaced women, producing extended case studies. In this chapter, we focus on one women's IDPO, the Liga de Mujeres Desplazadas (Displaced Women's League, "the Liga").

Comparing and combining the data from these projects demonstrates that women's and indigenous IDPOs reframed their claims and identity markers as "victims," embracing new types of discourses and to a certain extent new types of claims and conceptualizations of peace. This underscores the need to make sense of the material and symbolic ways in which national legal and policies shift when thinking about durable solutions to internal displacement in a postconflict setting, given that institutional changes affect the identity of IDPOs as well as the structure of their claims. Our data also indicate that poor, rural displaced women generally perceive sustainable local integration as the solution to their current predicament of insecurity and deprivation after displacement and that it is toward this objective that they organize and articulate their visions of peace. In contrast, for the Kankuamo, a return to their ancestral territories is perceived as the only solution that allows for collective survival. Return is a requirement for compliance with their ancestral *ley de origen*; compliance with this obligation is understood as necessary to generate cosmic balance (i.e., peace) both within and beyond indigenous territories. Hence, we concluded the intersection of displacement and other important aspects of certain IDPs' identities mean that laws and policies impact IDPOs' conceptions of durable solutions in significantly different ways, depending on the relationship between displacement and other identities. The following sections first describe the shifting legal and policy frames and explore our findings in relation to them.

Displacement through Shifting Policy Frames

The mass migrations from Colombia's rural to urban areas that occurred in the 1960s and onward have often been described as the result of a postwar population explosion, implying that the migrations were not political events (Schultz 1971). By the early 1990s, however, Colombian activists began to claim that the migrations had been triggered by political violence and to refer to them as "internal displacements," signaling the onset of the "humanitarian crisis" frame that was consolidated in Colombia in the late 1990s. The consolidation of this frame was advanced both by Colombia's remarkably active civil society and by the fact that, paradoxically, the country's armed conflict and pervasive inequalities coexist alongside a progressive legal system.

The Emergence of the Humanitarian Crisis Frame

Forced displacement has been in the spotlight in Colombia for several decades, but it arose as a major public concern in the 1990s, when the National Bishops' Conference (Conferencia Episcopal Colombiana 1995) began to collect and publish its own data on forced migration. Also in the early 1990s, the organization today known as CODHES (Consultoría para los Derechos Humanos y el Desplazamiento—Consultants on Human Rights and Displacement) also began groundbreaking reporting on growing forced internal displacement. In 1992, when the United Nations sent Francis Deng, its first representative of the secretary-general on IDPs, to Colombia, Colombian civil society, especially CODHES and the Bishops' Conference, was already advocating for government recognition of displacement as a human rights problem. Two years later, following extensive consultations with Colombian civil society, Deng issued a report and a series of recommendations on the growing IDP crisis (Deng 1994). This report was highly influential in the ensuing changes in domestic law and institutions.

Almost immediately, the government began to address displacement in budgeting and policy making. In practice, however, it was not until 1997 that the Ministry of the Interior's Human Rights Division received funding to execute the government's IDP policy. That same year Colombia adopted Law 387, landmark legislation that required the government to prevent and address internal displacement, enshrined IDPs' rights to protection from discrimination, recognized all civil and political rights previously recognized in international law, and provided immediate humanitarian aid for a three-month period as well as assistance with economic stability and return and resettlement. However, no agency was created to implement this law; instead, responsibility for execution was distributed among a host of local and national institutions, which received no additional funding to meet their responsibilities. In 1999 Deng visited Colombia again, on the invitation of local NGOs pushing for the implementation of Law 387. The resulting report noted that although Law 387 had proposed sound policy, it had not been implemented. That same year, the Inter-American Commission on Human Rights' special rapporteur on displacement for the first time described the Colombian situation as a "humanitarian crisis," and UNHCR began its official presence in the country (IACHR 1999). In 2003 the UN Office for the Coordination of Humanitarian Affairs opened an office in Colombia, and in

2004 it declared that Colombia had "the biggest humanitarian crisis in the Western Hemisphere" (UN News 2004).

Despite Law 387 and the ascendancy of internal displacement on the international agenda, the escalating rates of displacement in the early 2000s were met with little practical governmental response. IDPs were generally funneled into existing poverty alleviation programs, and humanitarian assistance was scarce. The severity of the situation was reflected in the increasing number of *tutelas* (writ for the immediate protection of constitutional rights) submitted by IDPs. In the course of reviewing IDP *tutelas*, the Constitutional Court began to shape the nature of the rights in question.[5]

A State of Unconstitutional Affairs

Over the rest of the decade, the displacement of millions within Colombia's borders created a protracted humanitarian crisis and led to impoverishment and rights deprivation. By 2004 the number of IDP cases demanding implementation of Law 387 had increased exponentially. That year the Constitutional Court combined 180 *tutelas*—affecting over five thousand IDPs—into a rare structural litigation process. In T-025, the court declared an "unconstitutional state of affairs" in relation to internal displacement, issued general orders for institutional reform and policy adoption, and set up a specialized office to oversee compliance. The court also required periodic reports from the government and NGOs on the IDP situation, called for public hearings, and issued follow-up orders (*autos*).

The subsequent litigation before the Constitutional Court has been enormously complex, generating multiple spaces for advocacy from organizations that represent the interests of IDPs. In combination, T-025 and its follow-up awards (*autos*) have judicialized humanitarian policies and delivered a unique remedy—known as the "differential approach"—that is sensitive to gender, ethnicity, age, and capacity. For the IDPOs in our projects, two follow-up *autos* are central: Auto 092 of 2008 and Auto 004 of 2009. In Auto 092 of 2008, the Constitutional Court found that the government's failure to address the disparate impact of displacement on women violated both the Constitution and Colombia's international human rights obligations. To provide a comprehensive structural remedy, the court ordered the creation of thirteen specific programs for displaced women and granted individual orders of protection to six hundred women across the country, giving them the right to be included in certain programs and to receive emergency humanitarian aid. By allowing feminist and grassroots women's organizations unprecedented access to the Constitutional Court—through the submission of documents and participation in public hearings—Auto 092 has shaped both the self-perceptions of displaced women and their relationship with feminist NGOs. In Auto 004 of 2009, the Constitutional Court assessed the impact of internal displacement on indigenous peoples who were in danger of being physically or culturally exterminated by internal armed conflict and who had suffered severe violations of their individual and collective human rights as well as of international humanitarian law. Auto 004 ordered the government to adopt a general plan for the survival of indigenous peoples as well as thirty-four specific plans for those peoples who are most endangered by armed conflict and, hence, are more vulnerable, including the Kankuamo.

Under Law 387, IDPs had the right to emergency humanitarian aid, including the provision of food, emergency transport, housing, and physical and mental health care, as well as inclusion in general poverty relief programs. However, despite the progressive legal framework, IDPs were for the most part directed to already existing, overstretched general poverty alleviation programs; humanitarian assistance remained scarce and vastly insufficient. The direness of the situation was reflected in the increasing number of petitions submitted by IDPs under the constitutionally mandated direct petition procedure (*tutela*). The court's intervention forced the government to create specific indicators of effective enjoyment of rights, which it monitored in follow-up *autos*; these indicators were wide ranging and included specific ways to measure the provision of the rights included in Law 387. The national government, through Acción Social, was charged with the immediate response to internal displacement and with integrating IDPs into existing poverty relief programs. Local governments were charged with specific responsibilities as well, especially contingency plans and the inclusion of IDPs in local education facilities and local health insurance benefits. The court also asked civil society representatives to provide information for following up on government implementation of its orders.

In T-025, the Constitutional Court signaled as a flaw of the public policies on IDPs the "absence of participation of IDPs in the formulation and execution of the institutional response."[6] Following this mandate, in 2008 the government adopted a complex participatory system that included electing IDP leaders to local IDP committees that would in turn participate in planning and monitoring public policies for IDPs. However, this structure had many problems and was not adequately implemented. Furthermore, the spaces for participation created by these rulings have been criticized for the poor quality of participation that they promote (Lemaitre 2013). The court insisted again on IDP participation in local development plans and budgets through Auto 383 of 2010, but once more these orders were never fully implemented. At the same time, the legal and institutional framework was undergoing a major legal transformation through the adoption of two major transitional justice laws in 2007 and 2011.[7] These laws generated incentives for IDPs to recast themselves into the new frames the laws presented.

Moving toward Transitional Justice: The Justice and Peace Law, and the Victims' Law

Efforts to use legal channels to identify and advance IDPs' rights cannot be separated from the peace process with the paramilitaries, which also impacted the framing of aid to IDPs. In 2005 Colombia adopted the Justice and Peace Law (Law 575), designed to regulate the peace process with right-wing paramilitaries—principally, the Autodefensas Unidas de Colombia (AUC)—started in 2002 under the administration of President Uribe. The Justice and Peace Law was the subject of widespread international and national criticism for neglecting victims' rights and for having been customized to meet requests made by the leaders of the AUC. Nevertheless, in contrast to previous demobilization efforts, the law did not promise blanket amnesty in exchange for peace but insisted on some form of punishment for perpetrators, compensation for victims, and information about war crimes (IACHR 2007). And although the law initially had little to say on the topic of victims' rights, it was later amended by the Constitutional Court (decision C-360 of 2006) and by Congress (Law 1592 of 2012) to add more stringent demands for truth, justice, and reparations. However, the implementation of the Justice and Peace Law faced a number of problems, including logistical barriers and security issues that often prevented claimants from fulfilling registration and reporting requirements.

In 2011 Colombia adopted the Victims' Law, which was the first law to include an explicit recognition of the existence of armed conflict in the country. This law transformed the problematic small-scale reparation mechanisms embodied in the Justice and Peace Law into a large-scale transitional justice process (despite the ongoing violence) designed to repair past harms suffered by victims of armed conflict through both land restitution and monetary awards granted by the government.

The new law established a set of judicial, administrative, social, and economic measures for the benefit of persons—including IDPs—who had suffered damages caused by violations of international humanitarian law or international human rights law that (1) had occurred after 1985 and (2) had been consequences of the internal armed conflict. In many ways, the Victims' Law was the state's response to civil society organizations, including many IDP organizations, which had objected to the fact that the Justice and Peace Law awarded benefits to demobilized paramilitaries but not to the victims of armed conflict.

In effect, the Victims' Law orders the establishment of an institutional system that responds to victims not only through the provision of humanitarian aid or through poverty relief programs but also through one-time reparation for past harms granted by the government and the restitution of land lost due to armed conflict. It replaced the preexisting framework, absorbing Acción Social and its local offices in charge of distributing humanitarian aid. Efforts to implement the Victims' Law largely replaced the term "internal displacement" with "victims of internal displacement" and included among the beneficiaries those victims of war who were not IDPs. The Victims' Law also sidestepped the issue of whether the government had a special obligation to guarantee IDPs social and economic rights, an endeavor that was referred to in the previous legal regime (Law 387) as "socioeconomic stabilization" but that became an ancillary concern to the disbursement of one-time reparations under the Victims' Law. It established a deadline for the inclusion of IDPs on the registry of victims entitled to reparation. The initial deadline of June 11, 2013, was subsequently extended to June 11, 2015. The Victims' Law also addressed return as a measure of reparation and included in return victims' rights to conditions of sustainability, security, and dignity (art. 69 and 70).

The establishment in 2012 of the new bureaucracy in charge of implementing the law focused on reparations, especially of the government agency known as the Unidad de Víctimas (the Victims' Unit, replacing Acción Social) and of a smaller but also important Unidad de Restitución de Tierras (Land Restitution Unit or Land Unit) changed the court's response to internal displacement. During 2013 and 2014 the court continued to oversee government compliance with T-025, but it also considered partially or completely lifting the declaration of an unconstitutional state of affairs, and it relinquished its previous activist role, losing much of its support and legitimacy among IDP and civil society.

This legitimacy was in part gained by the Victims' Unit but also by the Land Restitution Unit. The Victims' Unit implements and articulates other agencies' and local governments' response to victims of internal armed conflict and is charged with administering the national registry of victims, built on Acción Social's old IDP registry. Once victims appear in the system, they have the right to humanitarian assistance. The Victims' Unit provides this aid according to an initial assessment done at the time of registration, which is periodically updated. The Victims' Unit also administers the reparations program. Once victims declare they no longer need humanitarian aid, they are eligible for a one-time reparation for past harms, which may include remedies such as financial compensation, property restitution, and an apology from the government. In 2017 the government announced that between 2009 and 2016 "it has paid reparations payments to 580,415 victims" (Zulver 2018).

The Victims' Unit is charged with verifying returns and with implementing the mechanisms for the effective participation of victims in local development plans and budgets. However, like the previous system, the Victim's Law system has severe implementation problems, particularly in rural and conflict-ridden areas.

Shifting Legal Frames: The Promise of Postconflict Transformations

The peace process with FARC promises important framing and institutional changes in the future. The general agreement for the termination of the conflict and the construction of a stable and durable peace negotiated by the government and FARC addresses six issues: (1) agrarian reform, (2) the opening of spaces for political participation, (3) the concrete process to end the armed conflict, (4) ending drug trafficking, (5) the rights of victims, and (6) the democratic legitimation of the agreement. After a slim majority of Colombians rejected the peace agreement with a no vote on October 2, 2016, a new round of negotiations included the leaders of the no vote against a background of massive citizen mobilization supporting the continuation of the peace talks. This process produced a slightly modified agreement, ratified by Congress on November 30, 2016, a move accepted by the Constitutional Court.

At the same time, and despite the slowly growing peace, violence and internal displacement persist. In 2015, 128,482 persons became victims of armed conflict, according to the Victims' Unit.[8] Many were victims of new nonstate armed actors profiting from illicit drugs. UNHCR indicated that while it celebrated the establishment of a definitive cease-fire between FARC and the government, it still urged both parties to diminish the persistent impact of the armed conflict on civilians, including IDPs, and encouraged the inclusion of victims in the peace talks (UNHCR 2016a). National and international NGOs have stressed that despite hopes raised by the current peace process, Colombia still faces a humanitarian emergency.

We consider these constantly shifting legal frames to be a consequence of the persistent violence and, in a different text, theorize their impact on legal mobilization (Lemaitre and Sandvik 2015). The various laws and decisions affect and frame internal displacement differently, determining the kinds of reparations IDP can ask for and their options in terms of the resolution of displacement. It could be argued that legal frames, at least for certain contentious issues (e.g., minority rights), constantly shift across a wide range of contexts. Shifting legal frames are germane to the migration of political contestation to legal arenas, and the shifts in laws reflect the instability of the political coalitions that attempt to enshrine contested views in laws (e.g., women's rights generally). The changes often reflect which coalition is able to press its views forward in a given moment and may in turn be upended by the triumph of an opposing group.

In contexts of violence and insecurity, however, we agree with Mauricio García (1993, 2014) that shifting legal frames also reflect the persistent need for the renewal of state legitimacy through the symbolic power of the law.[9] In this sense, changing laws may be a direct effect of violent contexts. When a government is unable to guarantee its legitimate monopoly on violence, maintaining government power seems to demand the repeated renewal of other forms of legitimacy. As García (1993, 2014) argues, the adoption of new rules and regulations is one means of achieving legitimacy, at least temporarily, in Colombia—hence their proliferation. This legitimating effect, however, lasts only for a short period since violence and the incapacity to guarantee rights on the ground soon shatters the symbolic effect of the new laws. Notwithstanding their volatility, these shifting legal frames can have important consequences for individuals and groups affected by conflict, including IDPs, shaping their opportunities, advocacy strategies, and even self-identification. The shifts in legal frames, however, do not affect all groups of IDP equally. The following section details the differential impact of shifting frames on the IDP organizations we studied.

The Differential Impact of Transitional Justice on IDPOs: Security, Identity, and Claims

Given these major shifts in legal frames and policies, it is not surprising that IDPOs had to make significant changes to adapt to institutional developments. This involved changes in identity that were more obviously reflected in terminology ("victims"—of internal displacement—rather than "IDPs") but also in structures and forms of participation and ultimately in the content and premises of their claims. Legal and policy changes, we argue, entailed the legal and political re-inscription of displaced individuals as either IDPs or victims. These changes went beyond affecting available government institutions: they also affected the security climate in which IDPs made claims and organized themselves in IDPOs.

Comparing the findings of our projects, the first issue we observe is that the initiation of the paramilitary peace process from 2002 impacted IDP women and the Kankuamo IDPOs in significantly different manners, especially in terms of security. For the Liga de Mujeres, the demobilization of the paramilitary under the 2005 Peace and Justice Law created a new situation of insecurity, although lethal violence remained rare. Previously, its members had been subjected to the precarious conditions of violence in the slums caused by irregular armies and drug gangs. With the demobilization of large numbers of former paramilitary soldiers, insecurity took new forms as demobilized former paramilitary members settled in poor neighborhoods and started controlling local businesses. Some seemed to have ties to criminals who branched out into social and political control of the small municipality where they resettled. Conversely, from 2005 there was a dramatic decrease in selective murders of Kankuamo, and forced displacement slowly subsided, a decline that coincides with paramilitary demobilization under the 2005 Justice and Peace Law. This example highlights how steps toward peace that benefit some IDPs can create conditions of insecurity for others.

With respect to land restitution under the Victims' Law, displaced women who claim land individually face different security threats than indigenous groups claiming return of land or expansion of their collective territory. Part of the reason pertains to the nature of indigenous titles: collective and inalienable, they create different and generally less acute conflicts over land tenure than those of individual claimants who claim to have been dispossessed of land for which they do not have the title, especially when the land is now in the possession of other individuals.

The second issue relates to how the shift from the humanitarian to the transitional justice frame corresponded with a shift in how IDPs perceived—and presented—their identity before government agencies and the various NGOs that approached them. Access to the Victims' Law identity categories requires effort and resources (Sandvik 2012). For the IDP women we worked with, self-identification as internally displaced was the norm in 2009 and 2010, but this had often involved a shift from previous rural identities as peasants and homesteaders—which, in a sense, implied giving up a part of one's history. When asked about their lives, displaced women we interviewed identified first and foremost as *campesinas* or *gente del campo* (peasants or rural people). The loss of rural identities also entailed a loss of the political identities that had emerged from historical demands for land reform as well as from more recent involvement in coca cultivation.

With passage of the Victims' Law, restitution became the principal response to displacement-related human rights violations. While the IDP and transitional justice regimes formally exist in parallel, as the national discourse shifted from humanitarian crisis to transitional justice, IDP organizations began to change their names, their discourse, and their claims to fit the new framework—and thereby access new resources.

When seeking government protection, they also had to adapt to a complex

and shifting institutional structure. Of the IDP women leaders we interviewed, many were actively preparing themselves and their organizations to
be able to continue to pursue their demands for poverty alleviation under
the new transitional justice frame. It was clear that this was not the first time
they had adapted to shifting frames and institutional structures: many were
displaced because they were *already* leaders in their communities, organizing
under the headings of the peasant movement, the *cocalero* movement (movement of coca leaf growers), the indigenous movement or Afro-Colombian
land claimants. While a needs-based politics born out of poverty, exclusion,
and insecurity remained at the heart of their agenda, the framing of their
claims shifted over time, incorporating discourses of peasant movements,
human rights violations, humanitarian crisis, and then transitional justice.
On one level, this most recent shift to the transitional justice frame could
be handled by adding, as many IDP organizations did, the word "victim" to
the name of an organization and adding demands for reparations to previous demands. For instance, one organization that previously went by the ac-
ronym APROCOB (Asociación de Proyectos en Construcción de Vida en
Barrancabermeja, or Association for Life-Building Projects in Barrancabermeja) added "women victims" to their name and now goes by AVIPROCOB
(Asociación de Mujeres Víctimas Proyectos de Construcción de Vida en Barrancabermeja, or Association of Women Victims for Life-Building Projects
in Barrancabermeja). Explaining this change, their leader stated, "We are no
longer displaced, we are victims of displacement." Similarly, the Liga began
to solicit funding under the "victim of internal conflict" frame.

For the Kankuamo, as for indigenous groups generally, a subtle process
of identity claiming and making appeared to be at play. The Victim's Law
adopts the Constitutional Court's differential approach, recognizing that certain parts of the population have concerns owing to their age, sex, sexual orientation, and disability and thus require special guarantees and protections.
The challenge for the Kankuamo is to construct the "indigenous victim" of
armed conflict: the Kankuamo must settle on a new identity for differentiated rights, in a sense combining the essentialism of the victim with that of an
indigenous people. In their own words, "The Kankuamo people continue to
work for the legal ordering of their territory, for their autonomy and mostly,
so that they can live in peace" (Ministerio de Interior 2015). They characterize themselves as indigenous peoples who are essentially peace-loving: "Set
in dark times, peace emerges as a characteristic of the identity of first peoples
(*pueblos originarios*). It is a state of equilibrium with other natural beings and
within the people itself. This is why for indigenous people their own body
is evidence of their own territory, and this is not ignorance or backwardness,
but the fact that both are organisms that need to function without altera-

tions: to be is to be in peace" (ONIC 2015). Thus inspired, the Kankuamo have been participating in the peace process and seeking redress under the 2011 Victims' Law as well as testifying at the Victims' table in Havana, Cuba, in 2014 (Lopez 2014). For Kankuamo, peace is linked to the original indigenous claim for land rights: peace is self-government on their own (expanded) territory (see Ministerio de Interior 2015).

The third issue pertains to the contents of claims and strategies. Changes in designation seem for the most part to be strategic choices, as the "victim" identity appears to offer access to new alliances, venues (newly created agencies and participatory spaces), and resources (compensation, land restitution, and new "projects" for victims). The victim identity became the key to accessing government help on two fronts, both through humanitarian assistance and, eventually, through reparations that may help address extreme poverty. Many of the displaced women we interviewed claimed that the government's change in policy was a way of curtailing both the mobilization of IDPs and their emerging political identities by placing them in the same group with victims who had different origins and circumstances. Under previous legislation, IDPs were awarded special rights in light of their *ongoing* destitution. The Victims' Law, on the other hand, uses a transitional justice framework to grant the right to truth, justice, and reparations, in accordance with *past* victimization. This is not explicit in the law: humanitarian aid is ordered by the law for IDPs until such a time when "the manifest situation of vulnerability ceases." In practice, however, this manifest situation can be hard to distinguish from that of the 20 percent of Colombians who live in poverty or the 8 percent who live in extreme poverty (El Tiempo 2016). In any case, deliveries of humanitarian aid are reported by all the IDPs we spoke with to be few and far between. Yet by early 2015 the Victims' Unit reported that fewer IDPs were living in extreme poverty: only 33 percent, still a notably higher number than the national average (Unidad de Víctimas 2015). It is not surprising then that a significant number, including many of the IDP women we interviewed, were still potential beneficiaries of humanitarian aid.

This is not the situation with the Kankuamo, particularly those who returned after security improved and those who were liberated from confinement: within their territory their basic needs are provided for not by humanitarian aid but by the land and their community. Furthermore, claims of socioeconomic stabilization are not tied to the new victims' regime or to the situation of manifest vulnerability. The victims' humanitarian aid regime generally contemplates individualized victims. Instead, the Kankuamo are banking on two separate possibilities of ethnic specificity to access resources meant to guarantee their social and economic plans. The first is the government's adoption of an "ethnic safeguard plan" following structural litigation (Auto 004 orders).[10] The plan was formally presented to the Colombian government at the end of 2013, and by 2015 implementation was under way, informed by a previous consultation that included the sizable number of Kankuamo IDPs in Bogota (Reporteros Asociados del Mundo 2015). In addition to the plan, the Kankuamo are entitled to collective reparations based on their ethnic identity. Following the decree that functions as the Victims' Law for indigenous peoples, collective reparations must be agreed on with the Kankuamo (roughly fifteen thousand to twenty thousand individuals) through a process of consultation.[11] The ethnic safeguard plan will probably be part of the discussion since it was the result of a previous consultation process.

To conclude, the different situation of IDP rural women in slums, on the one hand, and the Kankuamo, on the other, illustrates the different effects of shifting legal regimes for differently situated IDPs. For the women, some of the shifts, especially the demobilization of paramilitary armies and the difficulties in the implementation of the vast Victims' bureaucracy, created negative impacts in their security and well-being. The changes also incentivized the adoption of new identities (victims rather than IDPs) and shifted aspirations to reparations rather than continued humanitarian assistance. For the Kankuamo, the shifts created opportunities, first because of improved security and well-being linked both to paramilitary demobilization and to the IAHR system's protection orders and later linked to the safeguard plan and collective reparations. Throughout the process, ethnic identity, linked first to victimization and then to peace, serves as a constant that allows the leadership to negotiate with the government. The next section further explores these differences in relation to different views of peace and, hence, of durable solutions.

Intersecting Identities and Different Views of Durable Solutions

The intersection between displacement and other identities has important effects for IDPs on the ground. In a very real sense the IDP identity in Colombia is a legal identity, a category of beneficiary of assorted welfare schemes designed to respond to a crisis that by definition is meant to be transitory. The different schemes are grounded on the urgency of the IDPs' present destitution and are oriented toward a future when the destitution that arose from displacement will be remedied—that is, toward durable solutions. In the transitional justice regime (the Victims' Law), present destitution is less of a concern, and the promise of reparations is oriented toward a remedy of past harms that also represents a durable solution to the problem. Implicitly, the resolution of displacement is understood to be a matter of justice. However, in intersection with other identities, different ideas of peace (and, implicitly, justice) also emerge. In this section we examine the case of a women's IDPO and the Kankuamo to show how their different aspirations (material survival in the slums versus cultural survival) also reflect different views on durable solutions (local integration versus return to ancestral territories).

Organizing for Material Survival: The Liga de Mujeres Desplazadas and Local Integration

Despite many successful examples of community organizing, poverty and insecurity continued to shape IDP women's everyday lives: the most important challenge faced by women activists was the poverty arising from displacement and their continuing inability to cover their basic needs (see Lemaitre and Sandvik 2016). While some leaders and some key organizations were inspired by the need to remember the dead and to reclaim their bodies and dignity, for most grassroots IDP women, the key objective of their community organizing and rights claims was to overcome poverty. For most, their politics was a concrete, needs-based politics of poor women in slum settings.[12]

The main case study in our project on women's IDPOs was the Liga de Mujeres Desplazadas, an IDPO well known for its many successes, particularly the construction of almost one hundred houses in the town of Turbaco, a settlement known as Ciudad de Mujeres, the City of Women (Sandvik and Lemaitre 2013; Lemaitre and Sandvik 2015, 2016). At the time of study, its membership included close to 160 impoverished women, most of whom were displaced in the early 2000s to the northern city of Cartagena and the nearby towns. The Liga's strategy combined legal claims made through courts and actions to achieve political visibility before donors and international humanitarian actors with obtaining financial support from donors for projects that directly funneled benefits to members. The day-to-day work of these different strategies involved both supportive professionals and grassroots leaders who learned on the go how to present *tutela* claims, petition local government, fill out surveys and forms, and recover evidence and testimony. Our studies suggest that, for Liga members, durable solutions to displacement—whether approached through the transitional justice or previous humanitarian frame—are inextricably linked to the poverty alleviation.

The importance of the pursuit of direct, material benefits for Liga members was evident when the Liga, together with other feminist organizations, successfully lobbied the court for a special auto for women. In 2008 the court adopted Auto 092, in which it ordered the government to specifically adopt thirteen programs for internally displaced women. Of the 600 women included in Auto 092, 150 were Liga members. Each received a cash transfer in the form of humanitarian assistance of around COP$1 million (approximately US$500), which many Liga members remembered as "the only thing the government has ever given them."

A second example of this centrality of material relief is present in the women's perception of security measures. From 2007 onward, under Award 200 of 2007, some Liga members had benefited from inclusion in the Ministry of the Interior's special protection program, given the numerous death threats they received and the destruction of their community center by arson. This program included a transport subsidy, a contact person, and a satellite cell phone. Later, the subsidy was changed to include an armored vehicle and bodyguards. As protection measures, these steps were generally perceived by the women as ineffective. All the women we interviewed who mentioned the issue implied that the local police and armed forces were complicit in threats, murders, and disappearances, and it therefore made no sense for them to be identified as providers of security. Instead, protection resources appeared to be understood as a form of monetary compensation, alleviating the costs of transport and cell phones.

A third example is when the Inter-American Commission issued precautionary measures for members of the Liga in 2009, 2010, and 2011, the content of which was to be negotiated with the government. In several rounds of negotiations, the Liga insisted on "integral" protection encompassing a host of constitutionally mandated guarantees, including the provision of socioeconomic support through an extension of humanitarian aid until they definitively overcame extreme poverty. In contrast to the Kankuamo case, the government representatives adamantly refused, arguing that precautionary measures were narrowly intended to protect life and physical integrity, and instead directed the Liga women to government poverty alleviation programs and welfare schemes.

In 2010 we conducted a household survey of the socioeconomic situation of Liga women using the indicators then used by the court to assess the effective protection of rights. We found that, despite improvement in some areas, the women still had extremely low incomes, a fact that severely impacted other indicators, such as health and access to food. The survey showed most, if not all, Liga members lived below the national poverty line. Only the wealthiest 3 percent of Liga households received the monthly minimum wage (COP$515,000 for 2010—approximately US$260). The poorest 27 percent received less than COP$128,750 per month per household (approximately US$65).

By 2016 the Liga was in the process of negotiating with the Victims' Unit for its own collective reparation measures and was at the stage of a diagnostic of past harms. Its demands will likely remain constant: its members seek local integration in the town of Turbaco, and integration means finding stable sources of income that would allow them to overcome extreme poverty, not just melting into the extremely poor communities of the cities and towns that harbored them. For Liga members, durable solutions and peace are inextricably linked to overcoming extreme poverty and hunger, resulting in complicated ways from displacement as well as from broader patterns of wealth distribution.

Cultural Survival as the Road to Peace and Durable Return: The Kankuamo of Sierra Nevada

The Kankuamo people live in the Sierra Nevada mountain range in northern Colombia. Long thought to be integrated into mainstream society, the Kankuamo kept specific cultural traits, and during the ethnic resurgence of the late 1980s and early 1990s the Kankuamo struggled to recover their status as an ethnic minority. The increased legal and cultural status of indigenous people after the adoption of Colombia's 1991 Constitution facilitated a "re-ethnization" of the Kankuamo.[13] The first Kankuamo congress was held in 1993 in the settlement of Atánquez, out of which gradually emerged the Organización Indígena Kankuamo, the umbrella organization for the Kankuamo political leadership. In 1999 the Colombian government recognized the Kankuamo as an indigenous group; in 2003 the government granted them collective ownership of their ancestral land.

However, closely interwoven with the collective process of "becoming Kankuamo" was an escalation in violence and persecution in the context of the civil war in the Sierra Nevada Mountains. Sierra Nevada, with its proximity to the Caribbean coast and the Venezuelan border, has been a haven for guerrillas, drug traffickers, and more recently paramilitary armies. From the late eighties FARC guerrillas dominated the southern slopes of the Sierra Nevada, where the Kankuamo live, and used it as a base to kidnap and extort wealthy Colombians in the lowlands. In response, in the late 1980s and early 1990s, landowners and other wealthy individuals formed paramilitary groups in the lowlands around Valledupar with the support of the Colombian Army. These groups joined the AUC, which identified Kankuamo territory as a FARC stronghold and the Kankuamo people as guerrilla sympathizers, even as they suffered from FARC rule. In the 1990s, with the support of the Colombian Army, the AUC began to target the Kankuamo for selective murders. Some were confined in their territory with limited access to food and medicine; others experienced massive displacement to Valledupar and other cities. Caught between clashing forces in the civil war, Kankuamo families suffered increased loss of their cultural heritage, and young men and women were recruited into the various armies.

For the Kankuamo, the large-scale displacement they suffered in the late 1990s and early 2000s constituted a double threat: both in terms of the sudden increase in targeted killings and as a collective threat to the survival of the Kankuamo people. In response the Kankuamo turned to the legal strategies that at the time were also helping them to gain recognition as a traditional people with a specific ancestral territory. Colombian scholars have argued the judicialization of ethnic claims has become so profound that legal mobilization is now a defining strategy of the indigenous movement (Lemaitre 2009; Rodríguez 2011; Mora et al. 2010). Indigenous identity allows them to establish relations with the state as legal recognition of collective identity or ethnicity has become essential to the ongoing construction of indigenous movements to fight for their interests in national and international arenas (Ulloa 2011). From around 2000 Kankuamo leaders developed an alliance with an association of academics working with indigenous people in the Sierra Nevada and the human rights NGO Colectivo José Alviar Restrepo, which was litigating indigenous rights cases before the Inter-American system. Over time, this alliance resulted in collective precautionary measures from the Inter-American Commission (OAS 2003) and binding collective protection measures from the Inter-American Court (2004).

Like the Liga, in their negotiations with the Colombian government over the content of protection measures, the Kankuamo demanded a host of socioeconomic measures to improve the everyday life of the tribe members. Significantly, they also demanded collective protection as a spiritual community with territorial claims. Important to the Kankuamo view of peace and protection are actions pertaining to cosmic rebalancing, which may be understood as a religious or spiritual dimension of security. According to Kankuamo cosmology, the Kankuamo are guided by the "*ley de origen*," which they regard as being the traditional ancestral science of wisdom and knowledge that governs all that is material and spiritual. The *ley de origen* designates the tribes of the Sierra to be the spiritual guardians of the world with the responsibility to protect all forms of life. The proper type of behavior and offerings in specific sacred sites ensures harmony between humans and nature and among humans. Acculturation of the Kankuamo and their absorption by the larger society is seen as a cause of violence. Violence among humans is directly linked to lack of respect for the territory of the Sierra. Hence, peace for the Kankuamo is articulated as compliance with *ley de origen* through cosmic balancing, which can be achieved only on ancestral land. Only through this type of peace can the Kankuamo experience both an expansion of their ancestral territory and a permanent return to this territory.

Reflecting these values, in their negotiations with the government the Kankuamo asked for measures that included the protection of the environment from harmful development programs. Beyond the negative impact of development projects on their everyday life, this request was based on the spiritual belief of the people of the Sierra Nevada that environmental disruptions (e.g., dams, roads, and logging) are directly responsible for increases in violence because they alter a delicate cosmic balance (Resguardo Indígena Kankuamo 2006b). Hence, cosmic imbalance threatens not only individual Kankuamo and their collective survival as a group but also, because they are the guardians, the rest of the world (Resguardo Indígena Kankuamo 2006b).

The Kankuamo also demanded that the government help counter the notion of Kankuamo partisanship and identification of Kankuamo with the guerrillas, a demand that needs to be understood in relation to appeals to neutrality that are commonly made by civilians targeted by armed actors. The literature on Colombian peace communities describes how practicing peace and rejecting relations with armed groups is a self-protective measure that raises the visibility of the communities' neutrality and status as noncombatants (see, e.g., Sanford 2003). In line with the neutrality claim, Kankuamo leadership vocally demanded the expulsion of armed actors from Kankuamo territory. They shared this demand with other indigenous groups who also demand that *all* armed actors, including the Colombian Army, guerrillas, and paramilitary forces, leave their territory. The strategy of using international protection mechanisms as a mode of enforcing both the creation of a territory and a return to this territory was complemented with the adoption of a self-protection program that had the goal of curtailing the civil war dynamics that led to selective murders of supposed guerrilla collaborators through "active neutrality," which entails reliance on indigenous authorities, noncollaboration with armed actors, and insistence on a right to civilian neutrality (Resguardo Indígena Kankuamo 2006a).

Hence, the Kankuamo claim neutrality and demand respect for the rules of international humanitarian law from all actors, including armed actors that are part of the Colombian state (see Resguardo Indígena Kankuamo [2006a]). Further claims were meant to improve both the quality of life within ancestral land and the capacity for ethnic differentiation and self-government. These claims are integrated into their ethnic safeguard plan and will probably also appear in the future plan for collective reparations as they are all integral to their vision of a life in peace within ancestral territory. In the meantime, an undocumented number of Kankuamo families have returned, and others travel constantly between their ancestral territory and the cities and towns close by, staying with relatives in varying family accommodations that make it difficult to precisely identify the extent of return. New youth organizations are especially keen on combining access to traditional knowledge with new forms of ethnic organizing (such as the indigenous guard, an unarmed civil defense group) while still frequently spending the school year in cities and towns. This flexibility of living arrangements and the changes and adaptations in Kankuamo identity over time reveal the wide variety of durable solutions and the difficulty of pinpointing them outside of their specific contexts.

Conclusion

We began this chapter by asking: What kind of durable resolutions to the IDP predicament are on offer in the Colombian postconflict setting? How do different populations approach durable solutions, and how do the changing legal frames impact these approaches? What do durable solutions mean in a dramatically unequal country like Colombia?

We conclude that, first, clearly displaced people's ideas about peace and, hence, about durable solutions in a postconflict setting are not static and are shaped by a matrix of shifting identities and claims, linked to shifting legal regimes, norms, and vocabularies. Moreover, accessing the benefits linked to these identities is not automatic but is the effect of negotiation and leadership: benefits and protection guarantees do not flow automatically either for individual IDPs or for IDPOs but require energy, personal efforts, and collective mobilization. Durable solutions for the IDP predicament are intimately linked to the available identities and benefits and to legal frames that are constantly shifting in a violent context. Durable solutions are also tied to the success of individual IDPs and of IDPOs in performing these identities and accessing these benefits.

Second, we argue that durable solutions are shaped by the intersection and tensions between changes in legal and policy frameworks, IDPO adaptation to these changes, and the intersection between displacement and other identities. Different groups are impacted differently by the shifting legal regimes that emerge from the violent context. This differential impact also shapes views of peace and durable solutions, which vary in light of factors such as gender and ethnic identities.

Last, our fieldwork raises more questions than answers about what durable solutions may mean in the context of Colombia's stark inequalities. A first concern is for the redistributive role of the different institutions created by the legal regime: how should the cessation of the situation of manifest vulnerability be interpreted? Can durable solutions for IDPs simply entail their absorption into the slums and into existing groups of people living in extreme poverty? There are clear institutional limits to the response to the extreme poverty of IDPs: the Constitutional Court is limited by its own institutional design and lacks the in-depth knowledge, institutional competence, and personnel to enforce its own remedies. These limitations also affect government agencies, and even the ambitious reparations and land restitution programs have already met with structural limitations owing to a lack of resources and a lack of territorial control by the Colombian Armed Forces. Furthermore, the post–peace agreement phase is likely to see a different security landscape with the emergence of new threats as well as new shifts in the legal regimes. Moreover, the type of structural violence and deprivation faced by IDP women is relatively impervious to legal action, while at the same time, for the Kankuamo, legal strategies have been a way to ensure both individual and collective survival.

It is necessary to make sense of the material and symbolic ways in which national legal and policy shifts matter when thinking about durable solutions to internal displacement in a postconflict setting. Clearly, institutional changes affect the identity of IDPOs as well as the structure of their claims and participatory spaces, and the intersection of displacement and other important aspects of IDPs' identities impacted IDPOs in significantly different manners. These changes, however, exist against a backdrop of poverty and inequality that affects all Colombians, internally displaced or not, and the very definition of peace and durable solutions.

Notes

1. There is still no agreement with the guerrilla group ELN (Ejército de Liberación Nacional, or the National Liberation Army). Organized crime continues to engender massive violence, and threats against civil society actors are increasing.

2. This phrase is repeated both in the Victims' Law (art. 67, para. 2) and in the Constitutional Court's Decision T-560 of 2008, among other decisions where the phrase is repeated verbatim. While the law does not specifically define manifest vulnerability (or the manifest condition of vulnerability), the court ties it to its interpretation of an existential minimum (*mínimo vital*), meaning access to basic shelter, food, education, and health care.

3. The compensation is approximately equal to seventeen months of minimum wage. It is capped at around COP$11,500,000 for 2016 (US$3,500). The unit also has programs to support IDPs to invest the money.

4. Forced migrants' agency is complex and contested. See Sandvik (2010a, 2010b, 2011).

5. In decision SU-1150 of 2000, the court unified precedent to officially declare

that IDPs had a human right to humanitarian aid; this decision rendered the provision of such aid immediately enforceable through *tutela* actions.

6. The court also underscored this flaw in other awards, such as Auto 178 of 2004.

7. For an overview of this transformation and its impact on IDPs, see Sandvik and Lemaitre (2015).

8. Registro Único de Víctimas (RUV), available at https://www.unidadvictimas.gov.co/es/registro-unico-de-victimas-ruv/37394.

9. For a discussion of refugees' engagement in such processes of renewal through legal empowerment and conscientization, see chapter 4 by Anna Purkey in this volume.

10. See "Plan de Salvaguarda étnico del pueblo Kankuamo" (Ministerio de Interior 2013, 5–8). The 2013 plan describes the principles of Kankuamo life based on the achievement of balance and harmony with nature according to original law, and the proper way to administer ancestral territory, self-government, and traditional culture to seek a good life for all. The second part of the plan describes the people's organization and social and economic situation, including a detailed description of the impact of forced displacement, and makes claims regarding three issues: territory, welfare, and human rights.

11. According to their safeguard plan, the Kankuamo had 18,268 persons in 2013 (Ministerio de Interior 2013).

12. For specific discussions, see Lemaitre, Sandvik, and Vargas (2014).

13. On the Kankuamo loss of identity, see Reichel-Dolmatoff and Reichel-Dolmatoff (1971). On the Kankuamo re-ethnization process, see Pumarejo and Morales (2003). For indigenous legal mobilization and its link to violence, see Lemaitre (2009).

11

Refugees' Roles in Resettlement from Uganda and Tanzania
Agency, Intersectionality, and Relationships

Christina Clark-Kazak and
Marnie Jane Thomson

Resettlement is the least used of UNHCR's three "durable solutions" but has recently gained more attention. At the 2016 Annual Tripartite Consultations on Resettlement in Geneva on June 15, 2016, forty-two participating nongovernmental organizations made an urgent call on all parties to support the UN secretary-general's goal, articulated in his April 2016 report, for states to provide resettlement spaces for at least 10 percent of the global refugee population annually (ECRE 2016). The proposed 10 percent goal contrasts with current resettlement rates: in 2015, 107,100 refugees were admitted for resettlement, only 0.5 percent of the total population of 21.3 million refugees globally (UNHCR 2016b, 2, 26) and less than 10 percent of the approximately 1.2 million refugees that UNHCR has identified as "in need of" resettlement (UNHCR 2016c). A much bolder—and unrealistic—proposal by US real estate developer Jason Buzi is to resettle all of the world's refugees into a new state, their own "refugee nation."[1]

In the context of the large-scale movement of Syrians, resettlement has also regained international attention. Canada's decision to resettle more than thirty-two thousand Syrians in less than twelve months (Government of Canada 2016a, 2016b) using a combination of government assistance and private sponsorship was lauded as an example to the world. In the margins of the UN General Assembly high-level meeting in New York in September 2016, the government of Canada, in collaboration with UNHCR and the Soros Foundation, announced plans to "export" its private sponsorship resettlement model to other countries (Raj 2016). At the conclusion of the high-level meetings, the UN General Assembly passed a resolution in which it stated, "We urge States that have not yet established resettlement programmes to consider doing so at the earliest opportunity. Those which have already done so are encouraged to consider increasing the size of their programmes. It is our aim to provide resettlement places and other legal pathways for admission on a scale that would enable the annual resettlement needs identified by the Office of the United Nations High Commissioner for Refugees to be met" (UN General Assembly 2016, para. 78).

In most of these policy discussions and in much of the academic literature on resettlement, very little attention is paid to refugees themselves.[2] Rather, the focus is on intergovernmental and state processes to identify, evaluate, and process refugees for resettlement. Indeed, Jennifer Hyndman and Wenona Giles argue that the very language of resettlement as a "solution" reinforces a "rescue narrative" in which the resettlement country is "cast as the saviour of helpless and hapless refugees who have no other options" (2016, 97). The framing of the conversation in New York in September 2016 as "responsibility-sharing" underscores this state-centric approach (UN General Assembly 2016, para. 11). In such discussions, refugees themselves are consulted and mentioned as an afterthought, if at all. For example, at the UN summit, a last-minute meeting between high-level UN officials and refugees was hastily arranged just a few days before the summit. Discursively, the low prioritization of refugees' involvement in resettlement is also apparent in the UN General Assembly Resolution A/71/L.1:

> We believe that a comprehensive refugee response should be developed and initiated by the Office of the United Nations High Commissioner for Refugees, in close coordination with relevant States, including host countries, and involving other relevant United Nations entities, for each situation involving large movements of refugees. This should involve a multi-stakeholder approach that includes national and local authorities, international organizations, international financial institutions, civil society partners (including faith-based organizations, diaspora organizations and academia), the private sector, the media and refugees themselves. (UN General Assembly 2016, para. 69)

While we contend that refugees are important actors in resettlement, they are mentioned last—after the media—while the roles of UNHCR and states are foregrounded.

In contrast, this chapter shifts the analysis to refugees' roles in these resettlement processes. We are interested in exploring how refugees use resettlement as a "protection *strategy*" (Hyndman and Giles 2016, 97; emphasis in the original) and engage in the work of resettlement (Sévigny 2012) in countries of first asylum to position themselves in relation to resettlement categories and processes identified in the *UNHCR Resettlement Handbook* (2011; hereafter referred to as *Handbook*). Using Ruth Lister's (2004) typology of agency and Leslie McCall's (2005) theory of intersectionality as intercategorical complexity, this chapter first presents a discourse analysis of the *Handbook* to determine how refugees' roles and positions in resettlement are framed in this key reference document. We then compare and contrast the *Handbook*'s approach with the ways in which Congolese refugees in two different contexts—Uganda and Tanzania—position themselves within these resettlement processes. The juxtaposition of a widely used policy document with the narratives and experiences of refugees themselves highlights insufficient attention to refugees' proactive roles, work (Sévigny 2012), and strategies (Hyndman and Giles 2016) in resettlement. It also reveals problematic assumptions underlying static resettlement categories articulated in the *Handbook*, which do not take into account the complexity of power relations in refugees' lived experiences. We conclude with some recommendations for ways forward.

Theoretical Framework: Agency and Intersectionality

In this chapter, we adopt Ruth Lister's broad conceptualization of agency as the capacity to act. As Lister notes, "Survival in the face of oppression and deprivation is helped by a belief in the ability to exercise some measure of control over one's own life, however limited" (2004, 126). Lister's framework was originally developed, and has since been widely applied, in contexts of poverty. The two case studies described here—Uganda and Tanzania—are environments of both poverty and displacement. As argued elsewhere (Clark-Kazak 2014), Lister's taxonomy of agency can be productively applied to analyzing people's actions in these impoverished refugee contexts as a way of problematizing the "forced" versus "voluntary" migration binary, which obscures decision-making within contexts of constrained choices. Lister's framework distinguishes among short- and long-term perspectives in both everyday and strategic decision-making. She graphically represents this as two intersecting axes: one as a "personal-collective" spectrum and the other as "everyday" to "strategic." The intersecting axes make quadrants that can be used to analytically categorize the complexity of agency. This conceptualization is imperfect in that both axes are intended to be spectrums, and not all actions can be neatly confined to quadrants.

Lister's framework is useful to the extent that it highlights the complexity of agency and allows for a systematic recognition of the many ways in which people—individually and collectively and in both positive and negative ways—exercise agency. This provides an important counterweight to problematic binary assumptions of "active" or "passive" refugees'"resettlement style" (Colic-Peisker and Tilbury 2003). Christina Clark-Kazak (2014) has previously summarized and applied Lister's taxonomy to impoverished refugee contexts in Uganda. This chapter builds on this previous application of Lister's work.[3] The "everyday-personal" part of Lister's taxonomy refers to "getting by"—micro level, banal actions that may go unnoticed but are important to refugee's individual and collective expressions of agency in contexts of constrained choices. Together these daily, routinized activities "represent important patterns of behaviour that can interact with larger economic, social, and political structures and relationships" (Clark-Kazak 2014, n.p.). At the other end of this spectrum, everyday-political/citizenship are "getting back at" expressions of agency. Here Lister (2004, 140) categorizes small-scale, quotidian forms of resistance that can include "destructive forms of agency against themselves, their families or neighbourhoods, or the wider society," like substance abuse or crime, or James Scott's (1985, 29) "weapons of the weak": "foot dragging, dissimulation, false compliance, pilfering, feigned ignorance, slander, arson, sabotage, and so forth." In the "personal-strategic" quadrant of Lister's taxonomy are the ways in which people exhibit agency by "getting out of" their situation. The "collective-strategic" area refers to ways in which people act together and "get organized" to attempt to effect change.

This analysis of agency, which we apply to the narratives of Leah and Zawadi, can be usefully complemented by attention to intersectionalities of power relations. Intersectionality refers to "the relationships amongst multiple dimensions and modalities of social relations and subject formations" (McCall 2005, 1771). An intersectional approach to resettlement starts with the view that refugees' experiences of and within resettlement processes are a product of complex intersections of race, religion, gender, social age, ability, ethnicity, class, and many other factors.[4] These patterns of human relations are constructed by individual and collective agents but also form structural opportunities and constraints within which refugees individually and collectively exercise their agency. In this chapter, intersectionality is used to analyze the ways in which the *Handbook*'s resettlement categories—such as "women at risk"—problematically reduce complex human relationships into static "measurements" of vulnerability. In contrast, we highlight the ways in which McCall's notion of "intercategorical complexity" (2005, 1773) can be applied to understand how refugees navigate "the complexity of relationships . . . within and across analytical categories" (1786). Intersectional analysis, as applied to two different refugee narratives in this chapter, thus provides an alternative to homogenizing discourses in the *Handbook* by highlighting the multiple and intersecting ways in which individuals experience migration and actively engage in resettlement processes.

Methodology

This chapter is based on a two-pronged methodological approach. First, Clark-Kazak undertook discourse analysis to understand the ways in which refugees' roles in resettlement were presented in the *UNHCR Resettlement Handbook*. Discourse refers not simply to language but rather to a system that "governs the way that a topic can be meaningfully talked about and reasoned about" (Hall 1997, 44). Here we are interested both in the structural opportunities and constraints that the *Handbook* identifies as well as the way refugees are discursively constructed within these resettlement processes. The *Handbook* was selected because, since the first edition in 1996, it has been used by "hundreds of UNHCR staff and partners" (UNHCR 2011, 1) and forms a point of reference for key government and UNHCR decision makers in the refugee resettlement process. Clark-Kazak used grounded theory to identify themes that emerged from the text.

Next we present and analyze the narratives of two refugee women who have participated in resettlement from Uganda and Tanzania. While the *Handbook* discursively constructs refugees as passive objects of transfer and as members of static categories, Leah's and Zawadi's stories demonstrate the ways in which they exercised their agency within the settlement processes.[5] Leah is a Congolese refugee in Uganda who was selected for resettlement from the Kyaka II refugee settlement.[6] Uganda is a country of first asylum that hosted over 475,000 refugees in 2015 (UNHCR 2016b, 60). Most refugees live in rural, isolated settlements where they are provided with plots of land to farm in an effort to promote self-reliance. A small number have been granted permission to live in larger urban centers, like Kampala, if they have specific medical or legal needs or if they can prove self-sufficiency. Others live informally without official permission or documentation in border areas or urban centers. UNHCR protection officers process cases for resettlement both in the settlements as well as at UNHCR country headquarters in Kampala. Leah's narrative and other data from Uganda presented in this chapter were collected by Clark-Kazak using interviews, focus group discussion, and observations over two fieldwork periods from September 2004 to December 2005.

Zawadi is a Congolese refugee who lived in Nyarugusu refugee camp in Tanzania.[7] Tanzania hosted the largest refugee population in Africa for the second half of the twentieth century (UNHCR 2010, 36). For the past decade, however, the Tanzanian government has focused on durable solutions for the refugees living in their country. The government naturalized the Burundians who had been living in the settlements since 1972, but they have not offered local integration to refugees living in the camps. Since 2007 they have closed ten of their eleven UN camps; Nyarugusu is the only one that remains open. The government has adopted a paradoxical stance toward Congolese refugees, not repatriating them as they did the Burundians but not abiding by their prima facie policy for new Congolese arrivals either (Betts 2013). The camp closures and confusing policy implementation have created a sense of urgency for Congolese refugees seeking resettlement, who fear they may be repatriated or deported as they have witnessed happen to others. Zawadi's narrative is drawn from Marnie Jane Thomson's fieldwork in refugee camps and aid offices in Tanzania, where she has spent more than two years conducting ethnographic research. These two narratives are not intended to be representative of all refugees. Indeed, the complexity of the stories and particularities of the experiences of Leah, Zawadi, and their families underscores the impossibility of generalizing about refugees. Rather, these two stories were chosen as specific examples of the ways in which refugees who share some similar subject positions like gender and ethnicity exercise their agency in different ways to navigate the structural opportunities and constraints of resettlement.

Resettlement in Historical Context

To understand refugees' agency within resettlement processes, it is important to acknowledge the structural constraints within which their journeys are situated. This section sketches a brief history of and current trends in resettlement, with attention to the ways in which refugees' rights and roles are constructed in policies and discourses about resettlement. Here, we are interested in how and why resettlement processes provide structural opportunities and constraints for refugees to exercise their individual and collective agency. We demonstrate how refugees' roles have been systematically marginalized within the development of resettlement policies and programming. Given existing literature on resettlement (Aleinikoff 1992; Chimni 1999; Casasola 2001; Troeller 2002; Pressé and Thomson 2007; Jansen 2008; Hatoss and Huijser 2010; Mirza 2010; Sandvik 2010a; Thomson 2012), this section is not intended to be exhaustive but rather is an attempt to set the context for a more detailed exploration in the rest of the chapter of the ways in which refugees navigate this system. We also provide some background information on the two refugee resettlement contexts in which Leah and Zawadi migrated: Uganda and Tanzania.

UNHCR has identified three "durable solutions" for refugees: repatriation to their country of origin; local integration in the country of asylum; and resettlement—the relocation of refugees from a country of asylum to another country where they are offered more permanent protection. Bhupinder Chimni identifies two distinct phases in the history of durable solutions: "In the first phase, which lasted roughly from 1945 until 1985, the solution of resettlement was promoted in practice, even as voluntary repatriation was accepted in principle as the preferred solution" (2004, 55). It should be noted that during the phase from 1975 to the mid-1980s, there was a large-scale resettlement of Indochinese refugees to several countries.[8] According to Chimni's analysis, the second phase, beginning in 1985, focused on repatriation with a gradual discursive and policy shift from voluntary to involuntary repatriation (see also Troeller 2002). In the late 1990s and early 2000s, a renewed focus on resettlement came as Western countries began to consider resettlement from African refugee populations (Sandvik 2010a) and as UNHCR promoted the "strategic use of resettlement" under the Multilateral Framework of Understandings for Resettlement in 2004 (van Selm 2004; Pressé and Thomson 2007). Currently, the UN secretary-general has called for more resettlement places, a position supported by many nongovernmental organizations.

UNHCR has identified "three functions of resettlement," which have been incorporated into the *Handbook*. First and foremost, resettlement is intended to provide protection to individuals who demonstrate a specific need to be removed from a situation of asylum. For example, a human rights defender who is subject to continued threats within the host community could demonstrate that local integration is not a "durable solution" and that resettlement is necessary based on "legal and physical protection needs." As discussed below, the *Handbook* outlines a system to determine and prioritize these protection needs based on a combination of categories and indicators. Second, resettlement sometimes provides a "durable solution" to a whole group of people who are in protracted displacement. For example, Canada has used group processing to resettle Karen and Bhutanese refugees (Batarseh 2016). Resettlement may also play a symbolic role as a foreign policy tool used by receiving states to express solidarity with countries of first asylum (van Selm 2004; see also Johansson, chapter 7, this volume), with recent discourses focusing on "responsibility-sharing." This symbolic role is a driving force behind Canada's recent commitment to resettle Syrian refugees.

It is important to note that UNHCR and key states—both individually through their foreign policy and collectively through their roles in multilateral fora in the United Nations—have been the main players in the development of these three functions of resettlement. Refugees themselves have not participated actively in the development of these policies and programmatic interventions. "The marginal role of refugees is not episodic but systemic, and has been guided by an understanding that resettlement needs are driven by the 'vulnerability' and 'passivity' of refugees."[9]

Resettlement processes are complex and resource intensive and are therefore open only to a minority of refugees. This, coupled with discretionary decision-making based on international legal principles or soft law (Sandvik 2011), means that refugees exercise their agency in certain ways to navigate the complex resettlement structures as well as to best position themselves as ideal candidates for resettlement (Jansen 2008; Sandvik 2010a; Thomson 2012). The next section focuses on the ways in which the resettlement structure managed by UNHCR discursively constructs refugees within these processes, and the following sections demonstrate how refugees exercise their agency within these structures.

Discursive Construction of Refugees within the *UNHCR Resettlement Handbook*

Before presenting a textual analysis of the *UNHCR Resettlement Handbook*, it is useful to provide a brief genealogy of the publication and its revisions. The first version of the *Handbook* was released in 1997 to specify "UNHCR recommendations on refugee selection criteria and resettlement practices in resettling states" (Garnier 2014, 945). It emerged from the experiences with and critiques of the Indochinese Comprehensive Plan of Action (Robinson 2004). A revised edition, released in 2004, was largely in response to allegations of fraud and abuse in the resettlement process in certain field offices (UN/OIOS 2001) as well as the security concerns of resettlement countries post-9/11 (Juma and Kagwanja 2003). The current edition (2011), analyzed here, was updated following an evaluation of UNHCR's resettlement program in the mid-1990s. As part of a renewed focus on resettlement, UNHCR also "started a resettlement staff-training drive, made a more concerted effort at international cooperation, actively promoted UNHCR's resettlement policy among existing resettlement countries, and sought out new countries with which to become involved in resettlement" (Casasola 2001, 76).

The *Handbook* defines resettlement in a state-centric way, with refugees themselves as passive subjects of transfer: "Resettlement involves the selection and transfer of refugees from a State in which they have sought protection to a third State which has agreed to admit them—as refugees—with permanent residence status" (UNHCR 2011, 3). While the subsequent sentences in the resettlement definition refer to protection, rights, and citizenship, resettlement is first and foremost framed as an activity of states, not refugees themselves. Refugees involved in resettlement are even less important in strategic resettlement, which, by definition, "maximizes the benefits, directly or indirectly, other than those received by the refugee being resettled" (UNHCR 2011, 40).

Similarly, the section on partnerships focuses primarily on the roles of the UNHCR, states, international organizations, and nongovernmental organizations, with refugees mentioned last, as in the recent UN resolution cited above: "Finally, of course, refugees are themselves partners in the process, and—with the appropriate integration measures in place and support from receiving communities—eventually prove to be an asset for the resettlement State, through their contribution to society at large" (UNHCR 2011, 5). Here the *Handbook* focuses mainly on refugees' roles *after* resettlement—as future contributors to their countries of resettlement rather than in the present as actors in the resettlement process. Refugees are not specifically mentioned in the membership of the Working Group on Resettlement and the Annual Tripartite Consultations on Resettlement.

Chapter 4 of the *Handbook*, which focuses on managing resettlement, is clearly oriented toward UNHCR resettlement and protection officers. What is striking here is how concerns about "combating fraud" discursively position as suspicious refugees who proactively seek out resettlement through "unsolicited requests."[10] Our reading of the *Handbook* resonates with Hyndman and Giles's (2011) claims that those who "wait patiently" are constructed as "good refugees" while those who exercise agency and make claims on states and UNHCR are seen as "deviant" and "problematic." The *Handbook's* concern with impartial management and "managing expectations" implies that resettlement processes should be distanced from refugees. Indeed, during Clark-Kazak's fieldwork in Kyaka II refugee settlement, some protection officers portrayed protection interviews as an adversarial court situation in which they were responsible for assessing which refugees have "legitimate" security claims. For example, in response to suggestions that refugees, particularly those in more remote areas of Kyaka II settlement, need more information on UNHCR's role in protection, assistance, and resettlement, UNHCR representatives argued that resettlement information sessions would simply provide refugees with the necessary details to manufacture stories so as to better fit protection criteria.[11]

Because there are more refugees requesting resettlement than there are resettlement places, the *Handbook* outlines the process by which UNHCR is "to prioritize among possible cases by assessing the urgency of their individual resettlement need and the applicability of the resettlement categories in order to identify the cases to be submitted to a resettlement country" (UNHCR 2011, 37). These resettlement categories, for which a full chapter (6) is reserved in the *Handbook*, are reproduced in full here (UNHCR 2011, 37):

Legal and/or Physical Protection Needs of the refugee in the country of refuge (this includes a threat of *refoulement*);

Survivors of Torture and/or Violence, where repatriation or the conditions of asylum could result in further traumatization and/or heightened risk; or where appropriate treatment is not available;

Medical Needs, in particular life-saving treatment that is unavailable in the country of refuge;

Women and Girls at Risk, who have protection problems particular to their gender;

Family Reunification, when resettlement is the only means to re-unite refugee family members who, owing to refugee flight or displacement, are separated by borders or entire continents;

Children and Adolescents at Risk, where a best interests determination supports resettlement;

Lack of Foreseeable Alternative Durable Solutions, which generally is relevant only when other solutions are not feasible in the foreseeable future, when resettlement can be used strategically, and/or when it can open possibilities for comprehensive solutions.

For each resettlement category, the *Handbook* provides a list of conditions that must be met to recommend resettlement. There are several points to highlight in relation to the resettlement categories. First, the list includes phenomena (e.g., family reunification) and issues (e.g., legal or physical protection needs) alongside categories of people: "women and girls at risk" and "children and adolescents at risk." This discursively objectifies human beings in these categories and can lead to essentialism. As argued previously in the context of UNHCR's "vulnerables" approach (Clark 2007), such essentialist language overlooks power relations because it assumes that women and girls are inherently "at risk" because of sex or age rather than focusing on the ways in which power relations related to social age and gender (and others) create contexts of vulnerability. This essentialist language also conceptually rules out the possibility of people in such circumstances exercising their agency to address the structures that render them vulnerable. Some recent web-based UNHCR documents suggest a more holistic approach to identifying and responding to vulnerability. For example, the UNHCR Europe office notes, "It is important to remember that a categories approach is illustrative rather than definitive" (2013, 34). However, the language of the *Handbook* categories remains fixed and essentialist,[12] and even the more inclusive categories are interpreted quite narrowly in practice, as demonstrated by Zawadi's experiences.

The second issue in relation to resettlement categories presented in the

Handbook is that "protection problems" related to "gender" are assumed to apply only to "women and girls." This overlooks gender norms that might pose risks for sexual minorities or for men and boys who do not conform to gender expectations. Third, the "at-risk" language attached to women and children discursively associates them with danger and protection needs. Finally, the categories identified in the *Handbook* limit the possibility of recognizing intersectionality of power relations. Here it should be noted that we are not adopting what McCall has described as an anticategorical approach to intersectionality (2005, 1773). Rather, we are exposing the limits of the categories that have been selected in the *Handbook*. In other words, we take issue with the ways in which complex analytical categories like gender and social age are reduced to "women at risk" and "children at risk." As we demonstrate in our analysis of Leah's and Zawadi's stories, we embrace McCall's (2005, 1773) call for "intercategorical complexity," which involves "provisionally adopt[ing] existing analytical categories to document relationships of inequality among social groups and changing configurations of inequality along multiple and conflicting dimensions." Here we use analytical categories of gender, social age, class, and ethnicity to demonstrate the ways in which these structures interact with refugees' expressions of agency.

These issues resurface in chapter 5 of the *Handbook*, which focuses on protection and identifying resettlement needs. Interestingly, in this chapter, "age" is conceived much more broadly than "children," and the *Handbook* explicitly states that "gender" does not just apply to women and that sexual minorities have specific protection concerns, despite the fact that references to gender in the chapter still pertain almost exclusively to "women and girls." Moreover, the chapter states, "as active participants in their own quest for solutions, refugees must be seen as persons with specific needs and rights, rather than simply as members of 'vulnerable groups'" (UNHCR 2011, 182). This chapter is thus much more nuanced and encompassing than implied by the settlement categories above. It provides a good point of departure for revising the problematic resettlement submission categories, as we discuss in our conclusion.

Leah's Story

Leah is a middle-aged Shi woman from Kisangani. She married a Bole man, who had two children—Lucie and Olivier—from a previous relationship. Leah's husband was a businessman dealing in diamonds, gold and other minerals. The family moved to Bukavu, where Leah's husband collaborated with the [Rassemblement congolais pour a démocratie] RCD, exchanging part of his wares for tax relief and protection. The business did well. Family photos show Leah's children and stepchildren dressed in smart clothes, posing at a computer and in front of a flat screen television. Leah describes their drop in living standards: "There in Congo we were at the top. Here, we find ourselves on the ground. Maybe we'll have the chance to get up again."

After the Kinshasa government re-established itself in the Kivus, Leah's husband's collaboration with the RCD became problematic. [Armed Forces of the Democratic Republic of the Congo] FARDC soldiers looked for him and threatened Leah and the children at their home. Leah fled with her children and stepchildren (3 girls and 5 boys, ranging in age from 3-year-old Diane to 17-year-old Olivier) to Goma, and then on to Beni, where they were assisted by a church. Leah and the children stayed for 1.5 months in Beni, but Leah had problems there because she is Shi. The church then facilitated their transport to Kampala. There, Leah registered as a refugee, with all the children as dependents. They were sent to Kyaka II, where Leah set up a household with another woman, Claudine, whom she had met at InterAid, a refugee organization in Kampala. They each had separate huts, but lived on a common plot of land and shared domestic duties and resources, until Claudine and her daughters returned to Kampala.

While all refugees in Kyaka II are supposed to live on designated land in rural parts of the settlement, Leah managed to convince the camp authorities to give her a plot right beside the camp offices, where she and her stepdaughter Lucie got employment in return for a "refugee incentive." Leah's wages were much lower than Ugandans working in the same position.

In early March 2005, Isaiah, a senior school official, encouraged Leah's stepdaughter Lucie to write a scholarship examination for schooling outside the settlement. He later reported that Leah had found her waiting to sit the examination and asked her to withdraw. Isaiah attributed this to the stepmother's jealousy: "These are the things that happen in Africa." However, Leah said that she was worried that any ties to Uganda, including funded schooling, would jeopardise the family's chances of resettlement. UNHCR protection officers felt that Leah had a good case for resettlement in the "women at risk" category. They invited her to fill in an application form and, together with her stepchildren, attend a resettlement interview. Eventually, they were resettled to the United States.[13]

Applying Lister's agency typology to Leah's experiences reveals many different ways in which she exercises her agency in relation to resettlement. Leah "gets by" through a series of relation-building actions with a church, with Claudine, and with camp authorities and UNHCR representatives. She leverages these latter relationships to "get at" access to strategic resources and decision-making: a plot of land closer to the center of administrative activity and jobs for her and Lucie with the camp administration so she does not have to farm her own plot. She also takes actions that will position her well to "get out" of her situation. She presents herself as a "woman at risk" and withdraws Lucie from the scholarship competition to make herself and her family better candidates for resettlement.

It is also important to interrogate the ways in which Leah and other refugees in Uganda interacted with the structures of resettlement outlined earlier in this chapter. Given prioritization of cases based on resettlement categories, those who were aware of these categories—like Leah—explicitly positioned themselves within them, adopting the language of "vulnerability" and "at risk" (Clark-Kazak 2010; see also Jansen 2008). Mats Utas coined the term "victimcy" to describe the expression of "individual agency by representing themselves as powerless victims" (2004, 209). Such exercise of agency is on the strategic axis of Lister's typology and can be both personal (in the case of individual claims for resettlement) and political (as whole groups adopt the "victim" label to advance strategic interests).

The static and essentialist nature of the "women and girls at risk" category led Leah to deny her daughter scholarship opportunities outside the settlement. An educated female is a powerful female, not someone who could be considered "at risk." This demonstrates how the categories themselves shape the understanding of vulnerability and need for refugees and aid workers alike. A reconceptualization of this category to account for both refugee agency and intersectional power dynamics would not only open up its understanding of genders that can be "at risk" but would also allow "at risk" to be evaluated as an intersectional category itself. This would deter refugees from denying themselves or their family members access to certain opportunities.

Leah's story also highlights structural barriers that prevent some refugees with protection concerns identified in the *Handbook* from accessing resettlement processes. In Kyaka II refugee settlement, protection interviews are conducted in the administrative center of Bujabuli—up to a four-hour walk from some parts of the settlement. Leah strategically convinced camp authorities to allocate her a plot of land on a nondesignated area close to the camp offices, and some other refugees with financial means rented rooms in Bujabuli. However, for most refugees, time and other resource constraints made access to protection officers limited if not impossible. Similarly, UNHCR's headquarters in Kampala is in the wealthy suburb of Kololo, and appointments must be booked through InterAid, UNHCR's implementing partner occupying a separate office (Sandvik 2011). These structural factors illustrate the importance of class, which intersects with other power relations but is often overlooked in discussions of protection and need.

Zawadi's Story

Zawadi was forty-seven years old in 2012. She came from Fizi, where her husband was a primary school teacher. Zawadi and her husband were ethnically Shi, but they traded salt, soap, kerosene, and oil in exchange for Mulenge's cows. They had four students from his school living with them who were Mulenge. The students came down from the mountain Minembwe to attend school, and, having established a trusting relationship with the Mulenge with whom they traded, Zawadi and her husband agreed to allow the students to stay with them.

One day in 1996, at the start of the first Congolese war, a neighbor found Zawadi in the marketplace. Mayi-Mayi, the local militia in the Kivu provinces that rose to defend Democratic Republic of Congo against the Burundian, Rwandan, and Ugandan troops that were invading, had killed everyone in her household that day. Zawadi's husband and children were at school, but her father, three of her sisters, and two brothers were killed. When Zawadi narrated this part of the story to UNHCR representatives, she explains that the Mayi-Mayi had killed her family members to punish her for living with Mulenge. The Mayi-Mayi assumed that the Mulenge, who were ethnically Tutsi, would automatically side with the Tutsi-led invading governments and thought anyone who associated with them to be traitors.

Zawadi immediately went to the school and told her husband that they must flee. The Mulenge students went back to live with their parents in Minembwe. Zawadi said the students made it safely because they were only children and people would assume they were Shi because "Shi and Banymulenge look alike." Zawadi, her husband, and her two children took a boat across Lake Tanganyika and arrived in Kibirizi in the Kigoma region of Tanzania. They built a house and lived there for about a year before their Tanzanian neighbors threatened to report them as undocumented immigrants. Worried about being deported, Zawadi's family registered with UNHCR and were taken to Nyarugusu camp.

In the refugee camp, Zawadi reported the persecution her family experienced in Congo to UNHCR protection officers. She also reported the problems they have faced in the camp. Many people there do not believe that they are Shi, believing instead that she and her family are Mulenge. She collected the rations for her family instead of giving her card to the village chief as most families in Nyarugusu camp do. "He [the chief] would just refuse to get our food," she said. Her daughter has a blood clotting disorder, and an expatriate resettlement officer, whom Zawadi knew by name, assured her that they were looking for medical cases like this for resettlement. Zawadi was frustrated, however, because she obtained the official medical certificate from a doctor at the camp hospital, who then forwarded it on to the UNHCR doctor. But they have seen no progress since then, so Zawadi sought ways to contact the UNHCR doctor, protection officers, and resettlement officers to remind them about the form. It took years, but she and her family have now been resettled.

Zawadi "gets by" by fleeing from Congo, building a new home in Kibirizi, registering with UNHCR after her neighbors threaten to report her family to the Tanzanian authorities, and collecting the rations for her family rather than partaking in the normal collection system headed by chiefs. Her refusal to wait and see what would happen if her Tanzanian neighbors did report her family could also be seen as "getting back at" both her neighbors and the Tanzanian authorities. Her refusal to hand her family's ration card to her village chief could also be interpreted as a form of "getting back at" the systems of authority and structures in the refugee camp.

Zawadi's strategies to qualify for resettlement also can be seen as a blending of Lister's taxonomy of refugee agency. In other words, Zawadi's quest to be resettled is an attempt to "get out" of the refugee camp, but it is also more than that. By reporting her stories of persecution in Congo and in the camp to UNHCR protection officers, Zawadi "gets at" the authorities who have the ability to forward her case to the resettlement officers. Likewise, by speaking with an expatriate resettlement officer, Zawadi framed her case as fitting within the "medical needs" resettlement category. She "gets at" the required documentation by consulting a doctor at the camp hospital. When her case stalls, Zawadi's follow-up with the camp authorities—including the camp hospital doctor, the UNHCR doctor, protection officers, resettlement officers—is an attempt to "get organized" within a chaotic aid bureaucracy (Dunn 2012). In the end, Zawadi cannot be certain which efforts by whom resulted in her resettlement, but she did all that she could to convince the relevant aid representatives that her family met multiple categories for resettlement, including legal or physical protection needs, medical needs, and lack of foreseeable alternative durable solutions.

While the first resettlement category, "legal and/or physical protection needs," appears to be broad and encompassing, Nyarugusu residents have found that in practice it is quite static and limited. They have learned that the UNHCR representatives treat the Mulenge ethnicity as a marker for vulnerability and, thus, resettlement. The many other ethnicities in the camp are not viewed in the same way. UNHCR has not officially identified Mulenge for group resettlement, as they have done for other ethnic groups such as the Somali Bantu. Unlike group resettlement schemes, Nyarugusu residents cannot demonstrate membership in a group to be eligible for resettlement. Rather, they must prove individual need for resettlement. One way to provide evidence for such claims, however, is to demonstrate membership or allegiance with a certain group. This is why Zawadi emphasized the relationship between her ethnic group, Shi, and Mulenge. Convincing UNHCR representatives that her family was persecuted because they were aligned with and often mistaken for Mulenge could afford her resettlement, while there was no room for individual need based on her ethnicity or other identifying factors.

While the first two resettlement categories, "legal and/or physical protection needs," and "survivors of torture and/or violence," and the final category, "lack of foreseeable alternative durable solutions," appear to be broad enough to account for intersectionalities of power, in practice they are not. For example, Zawadi could not use her family's experience with their Tanzanian neighbors as evidence for protection needs. Moreover, the murder of their family members, the violence of displacement, and life in a refugee camp were not recognized as vulnerabilities for resettlement unless they could be explained as the persecution of a specific ethnic group. Zawadi's individual need for resettlement rested on her ethnic group's allegiance with the Mulenge and her daughter's medical needs; there was no way to explain her case in terms of her own ethnicity, much less religion, gender, social age, class, or any other modality of social relations.

Conclusions and Recommendations

This chapter shows how refugees are actively involved in resettlement efforts but that the UNHCR *Handbook* and resettlement processes do not adequately take their agency into account. Indeed, resettlement is too often conceived of as a process involving UNHCR and states, with little attention to refugees' roles, decisions, and choices. By focusing in detail on the stories of Leah and Zawadi—two Congolese women in Uganda and Tanzania, respectively—this chapter attempts to shift the discussion. In so doing, it also provides an opportunity to offer recommendations for rethinking resettlement.

First, resettlement structures, processes, and documents, including the *Handbook*, should acknowledge the importance of refugees' actions and choices and more proactively include their experiences and perspectives. Documents could include narratives that demonstrate the complexity of refugees' choices and actions in contexts of constrained choices. Relatedly, dehumanizing and objectifying language—such as the reference to "transfer of refugees" in the resettlement definition—should be removed from current documents and avoided in the future. Attention needs to be paid to the objectifying tendency to include categories of people, especially "women and children," alongside inanimate objects and phenomena in lists of priorities.

Second, UNHCR's priority resettlement categories should be changed to come into greater alignment with its age, gender, and diversity mainstreaming policy. Here the focus should be on moving away from essentialist, fixed categories to a focus on intercategorical complexity by analyzing intersecting power relations that pose protection challenges. Leah's story demonstrates how the resettlement categories in and of themselves are rigid and limiting, and Zawadi's story shows how even apparently broad categories are still interpreted narrowly. Chapter 5 of the *Handbook* provides some points of departure for this conceptual and operational shift. In particular, "age" should not be conflated with "child," and "gender" should not be equated with "female." Furthermore, in practice, the broader resettlement categories should be treated as such and therefore allow for an intersectional analysis of power dynamics. Such an approach will not only release refugees from categorical constraints within the resettlement process, permitting them to tell fuller narratives; it will also free them from making choices, even squandering opportunities, based on meeting these essentialist categories. Recognizing refugees' agency requires much more nuanced attention to the multiple ways in which power relations intersect to provide structural opportunities and constraints within which refugees individually and collectively position themselves.

Third, UNHCR should acknowledge and address structural barriers that limit access to protection officers and resettlement processes. These in turn place constraints on refugees' exercise of agency and may result in refugees resorting to "getting back at" strategies. As Bram Jansen has argued, "the result is an environment that encourages refugees to cheat through claiming insecurity and negotiating vulnerability. Refugees come to believe that resettlement is something that can be actively achieved, rather than a benefit extended only to the genuinely vulnerable" (2008, 596). In other words, lack of attention to refugees' own resettlement priorities, needs, and activities may result in them circumventing and undermining official structures that are ostensibly in place to protect them and to prevent fraud.

Notes

1. "Refugee Nation: A Radical Solution," http://www.refugeenation.org/assets/refugeenationreport_final.pdf.

2. Notable exceptions include Bram Jansen's (2008), Kristin Bergtora Sandvik's (2010a) and Marnie Jane Thomson's (2012) work, which provide important insights into the ways in which refugees navigate resettlement structures in Kenya, Uganda, and Tanzania, respectively. Christoph Sévigny (2012) and Hyndman and Giles (2016) have focused on the "work" and strategies, respectively, of refugees resettled to Canada. This chapter builds on this existing research to explicitly bring notions of agency and intersectionality into the discussion.

3. This section draws extensively on Clark-Kazak (2014).

4. Social age refers to the socially constructed roles and meanings ascribed to age as well as to intra- and intergenerational power relations. See Clark-Kazak (2009).

5. We chose Leah's and Zawadi's stories as our case studies because even though these women share the same nationality, ethnicity, and gender, their stories of fleeing and navigating the resettlement process differ greatly. This not only demonstrates their individual agency in attempting to meet the criteria of the UNHCR categories of resettlement but also illustrates how an intersectional approach to power refuses to accept categories such as nationality, ethnicity, and gender as essential and static.

6. This is a pseudonym.

7. This is also a pseudonym.

8. For a detailed analysis of this resettlement, see the special issue of *Refuge: Canada's Journal on Refugees*, volume 32, no 2: http://refuge.journals.yorku.ca/index .php/refuge/issue/view/2311.

9. James Milner, email communication, March 24, 2017.

10. We acknowledge the contributions of James Milner to this section.

11. Clark-Kazak's interview data with UNHCR staff (pseudonyms used): "Emma," fieldnote 77, February 6, 2005, Kyaka II; "John," fieldnote 82, February 11, 2005, Kyaka II; and "Gloria," fieldnote 93, February 25, 2005, Kyaka II.

12. Although, as noted below and in the conclusion, chapter 5 of the *Handbook* does provide some openings for improvement.

13. Partially reproduced from Lucie's story in *Recounting Migration* (Clark-Kazak 2011).

12

Liberian Refugee Protest and the Meaning of Agency

Amanda Coffie

In November 2007 the governments of Ghana and Liberia and the Office of the United Nations High Commissioner for Refugees (UNHCR) were working to finalize the repatriation of Liberian refugees from Ghana and initiate the process of local integration for remaining refugees. Their work was motivated by a desire to bring to close some twenty years of exile, primarily through a successful repatriation program designed and implemented mainly by states and UNHCR. This process, however, began to unravel when a group of women describing themselves as Liberian Refugee Women with Refugee Concerns (or Concerned Women) emerged and demanded changes to the policies and practices of finding a durable solution for the remaining Liberian refugees in Ghana.

What emerged was a marked difference between the perspective of the states and UNHCR and the perspective of refugees on the question of durable solutions and how best to resolve what Ghana had referred to as its "Liberian Refugee Problem" (Dogbevi 2008). According to the governments of Ghana and Liberia, repatriation remained the preferred solution for refugees given the end of the Liberian civil war, the successful conduct of elections in 2005, and the presidential call for people and funds to aid with peacebuilding.[1] UNHCR also cited the decision of the Economic Community of West African States in favor of the return of refugees. In contrast, most remaining refugees preferred resettlement to third countries, such as the United States, and seemed unhappy about the repatriation program, especially the levels of assistance being offered to returning refugees (Essuman-Johnson 2011).

These differences in the preferences of refugees, UNHCR, and the government of Ghana came to the world's attention in March 2008, when refugees protested to UNHCR against the repatriation package and demanded a say in the range of solutions being offered to them. Beginning in November 2007, Concerned Women sent a communication to UNHCR headquarters in Geneva and to UNHCR-Ghana demanding repatriation cash grants of US$1,000. They also articulated their preference for resettlement to a Western country and opposition to local integration. UNHCR-Ghana explained to the refugees that their request could not be met due to budgetary constraints and that the official resettlement program had ended (UNHCR-Ghana 2008b). However, the refugees disagreed and continued with their protest within the camp, which lasted for six months.

Assessments of the nature and significance of the protest have varied, with some arguing that the protest was not a demonstration of agency on the part of refugees as they failed to achieve their objectives. UNHCR saw the action as a disruption caused by a small group of disgruntled refugees with misguided expectations about resettlement and repatriation. The government of Ghana described the protesters as unruly and held that the refugees through the leadership of ex-combatants engaged in subversive behavior that compromised the security of the state. Researchers have either agreed with the views of UNHCR and Ghana or have described the protests as a political failure. For example, Elizabeth Holzer, who has written extensively on this protest and had firsthand information as a researcher in the field during the protest, notes that the outcome of the action was negligible and does not compare with the achievements of other refugee protests, such as that of the Guatemalan refugees in Mexico, and can thus be characterized as a failure (Holzer 2012, 14).

In contrast, this chapter argues that the six-month protest is an important example of refugee agency, as discussed in the introduction to this volume. The protest empowered the refugees of Buduburam, especially women refugees, who found their voice and demanded recognition and participation in the search for solutions. In contrast with those who argue that agency is only present when those expressing agency are able to fundamentally alter the structures within which they operate, this chapter argues that the protest was a demonstration of agency by refugees because it contributed to the transformation of repatriation policies and practices enacted by states and UNHCR. In this way, the chapter emphasizes agency as the ability to effect change in policies and practices that condition lived realities rather than examining the protests through analytical frameworks of political failure, humanitarian crisis, and asylum state hostility. This choice allows for a discussion situated outside normative assumptions of what is politically correct or wrong action by refugees who are supposed to be apolitical. Additionally, conceptualizing refugees as actors with agency enables the study to transcend their portrayal as objects of intervention by states and UNHCR. Indeed, the goal of this chapter is to argue that discussions on the outcome of the Liberian refugee protest can usefully shift from a criminal/security and narrower assessment of successful or failed political action to an approach that considers expressions of agency in more incremental ways.

Thus, the chapter presents the protest as not just a single and isolated action but as an event rooted in the resource constraints and opportunities experienced by refugees as a result of their displacement and of the environment created by the policies of the host state and UNHCR and the top-down approach of institutional actors in the provision of solutions for refugees along with the silencing of refugees as actors in the processes. This presentation challenges both the institutional actors' account of the protest and the analyses of the protest as a political failure. In the end, the chapter claims that the protest was an expression of agency situated within particular resource constraints and opportunities, and the outcome was empowering for the refugees because the protesters were able to demonstrate their ability to make a choice in a context where they previously had no choice, and their action resulted in changes in the policies and practices of returning to Liberia from Ghana on terms negotiated between the range of actors involved, including refugees.

Methods

As a critical perspective of the Liberian refugee protest, the chapter investigates refugees as actors with agency through their interaction with the institutional actors, especially Ghana and UNHCR, and takes transformation as an outcome of the interaction. Examining the outcome of the refugee protest as either success or failure leads to a reductionist, zero–sum analysis where there are powerful winners and weaker losers. In contrast, by describing the outcome as transformational, the chapter reveals the agential capabilities of the refugees as well as the changes that accrued because of the action that otherwise might not have happened had they not acted. It also emphasizes the resource opportunities and constraints under which such actions occur, thereby shining a light on the empowering aspect of the refugee action. Thus, this study is both critical of the existing perceptions of the refugees as an incapable actor and aims at empowering the refugees.

To achieve these objectives, the chapter draws on the notion and operationalization of agency presented by Naila Kabeer (1999) and William H. Sewell (1992). Similar to Kabeer (1999, 438), the chapter argues that agency encompasses the meaning, motivation, and purpose that individuals bring to their activity. Furthermore, agency takes the form of bargaining and negotiation, deception and manipulation, and subversion and resistance as well as intangible, cognitive processes of reflection and analysis. For Sewell (1992) and Kabeer (1999, 438), agency "can be exercised by individuals as well as collectives," and its expression should not be limited to observable actions. Furthermore, Sewell (1992) cautions that "agency exercised by different persons is far from uniform, that agency differs enormously in kind and extent" (21). Also, Kabeer notes that agency is a process linked to resource opportunities and challenges resulting in outcomes and achievements, which are empowering. Empowerment according to Kabeer is the "process by which those who have been denied the ability to make strategic life choices acquire such ability" (1999, 436). Kabeer's conceptualization expands empowerment from just ends or changes to include the process of either individuals' or groups' ability to exercise choice(s). The ability to exercise choice, she notes, "can be thought of in terms of three interrelated dimensions: resources (preconditions) agency (process) and achievements (outcomes)" (1999, 437). On the contrary, "failure to achieve one's goal reflects some deep-seated constraint on the ability to choose and can be taken as a manifestation of disempowerment" (1999, 438).

This chapter draws on documents from UNHCR and the governments of Ghana and Liberia along with the literature on repatriation, generally, and specifically on the experience of Liberian refugees in Ghana. The chapter also draws on 2009 postprotest interactions with five women who participated in the protest and 2015 interviews at the Buduburam refugee camp.[2] The chapter begins with an overview of the resource conditions of the refugees in Buduburam, setting the resource context of the refugee protest. Next, the chapter outlines the policies and practices of repatriation as advanced and implemented by Ghana, Liberia, and UNHCR, which also highlights the constraints of such a top-down approach. Subsequently, the details of the refugee protest highlight the tactics and strategies of the protesters as a manifestation of their agency, the outcome of which was empowering for the refugees as it resulted in changes in the policies and practices of repatriation from Ghana to Liberia. Finally, the chapter examines the outcome of the refugee action, specifically the changes related to the return practices, which addressed some of the concerns of the refugees during the protest.

Resource Conditions of Buduburam: A "Model Refugee Camp"

The Buduburam refugee camp for Liberians who fled the fourteen-year civil war has been described as a model refugee camp (Coffie 2003, 2012; Kpatindé 2006; Dzeamesi 2008). The proximity of the camp to the capital, the free movement of refugees in the camp and around the country, and the open access to the international press, dignitaries, and volunteers contrast with the situation of refugees living in closed and isolated refugee camps elsewhere on the continent (Lischer 2005; Milner 2005). Others also note the resilience of refugees in the camps through their economic activities, which primarily contributed to the camp market growing into the largest market center in the Gomoa District in Ghana (Dick 2002; Coffie 2014).

As Ghana's first refugee camp, Buduburam opened in 1990 with a population of 6,800. As the Liberian war intensified and spread to other neighboring countries, the numbers increased. At the time of signing the 2003 Comprehensive Peace Accord (CPA) to end the civil war, the total Liberian refugee population in the camp was close to 42,500. The composition of the refugee population was likened to that of many other communities in Africa: it was a class society with rich, middle class, and poor (Porter et al. 2008). The Ghana Refugee Board managed the camp, and UNHCR administered the material assistance programs. Members of the welfare council, elected by the refugees, represented them in the administration of the camp (Owusu 2000). Additionally, there were some sociocultural, economic, and political organizations, more than a dozen churches, and two mosques in the camp (Coffie 2003). These organizations and associations helped relieve anxiety and boredom, promoted the well-being of refugees, and raised awareness and consciousness among refugees.

Other opportunities in the camp included the implementation of skills and training programs for refugees, especially for refugee women. This included the New Liberian Training Center and the Women Peace Movement that was at the forefront of the protest movement in Accra during the negotiations leading to the CPA and that included many Liberian refugee women (Coffie 2013; Holzer 2015). These initiatives, in addition to UNHCR-supported programs aimed at reducing gender-based violence and the insistence on female representation on the welfare council, effectively provided a fertile ground for the women to organize and make demands that challenged the position of UNHCR, Ghana, and Liberia regarding repatriation and solutions in general.

The security situation and the context of Ghana's transition from authoritarian regime to a consolidated democracy also provided the opportunities for refugees to protest and not accept the prescription of the state and UNHCR. The refugees witnessed the introduction of democracy and the rule of law in Ghana and the way this new form of governance was used to end the country's long history of human rights abuses and authoritarian regimes (Oquaye 1995; Coffie 2013). Ghana's political stability, its growing international reputation, and the internal security it enjoyed during the refugees' asylum period also increased other external actors' provision of opportunities for refugees. It is therefore not surprising that Liberian refugees in Ghana acquired higher education, training skills, and more resettlement numbers compared to their compatriots who lived in other countries in the subregion (Coffie 2014).

Regardless of these resource opportunities for refugee engagement in the camp, there is ample evidence the institutional arrangements did not allow for equal participation of all refugees. For example, "Buduburum did not have democratic elections, participatory budgeting or regular town hall meetings. The camp did not have any clear grievance procedures for the refugees to seek redress and/or impose limits on the powers of the authorities" (Holzer 2015, 142). Additionally, the channels of communication established by UNHCR in the camp did not allow for dialogue with those that dissented from the views of refugee representatives. Thus, it was not surprising that both UNHCR and the Ghanaian government, which had no effective means of recognizing this new group, saw Concerned Women as a problem. They insisted Concerned Women were not the legitimate representative of the refugees.

Structures of Repatriation to Liberia: Policies and Practices

The signing of the CPA in Accra, Ghana, on August 18, 2003, effectively ended a fourteen-year civil war and triggered the process of repatriation of the country's refugees located within West Africa. With the various warlords agreeing to end hostilities, the UN Peacekeeping Mission in Liberia was established on October 1, 2003, in conjunction with the National Transitional Government of Liberia, which began the process of disarmament, demobilization, repatriation, rehabilitation, and reintegration in December 2003. The CPA mandated that the transitional government must work with the international community in designing and implementing a plan to assist with the voluntary repatriation and reintegration of Liberian refugees (article 30 of the CPA).

Although the CPA did not identify the UNHCR as the main international agent for the return of refugees, the latter responded to the former's call for international assistance to support the process. UNHCR emphasized that the terms of the CPA required that repatriation must be voluntary and that the safety and dignity of the returnees had priority. To achieve this objective, UNHCR prepared and signed tripartite agreements with the transitional government and countries of asylum in the region governing conditions and modalities of voluntary repatriation. The agreements address "the rights of returning refugees and outlined specific protection guarantees in the implementation of the repatriation and reintegration programs" (UNHCR-Monrovia 2005, 9).

To facilitate the returnees' safety, UNHCR noted that the communities of return should have a UN peacekeeping presence and that the areas ought to be in the process of disarmament, free of hostility, and with preparations for elections in progress. Additionally, UNHCR demanded unhindered access to the population on the part of humanitarian agencies (UNHCR-Monrovia 2005, 9–10). The promotional campaigns of the repatriation exercise organized in the various asylum countries included UNHCR informing refugees about the conditions of the locations for return. The information campaigns focused on the modalities of the repatriation and reintegration operation, including the beneficiaries of the return and reintegration program; procedures and criteria for facilitated repatriation; the period for the process; registration procedures; transportation arrangements, including maximum luggage allowance; and predeparture health and examination requirements. These campaigns were imperative because, in all of the processes and agreements, refugees were not involved, yet the decision of whether to join the process was ultimately the refugees' own.

Finally, UNHCR instituted individual, family, and community programs to aid the process of return and (re)integration. It assisted in transportation from Ghana to a place of the refugees' choosing in Liberia. Also, each returnee was to receive a blanket, a sleeping mat, a bucket, and US$5 to cover the cost of internal transportation. Each family head also received one mosquito net, plastic sheets, a kitchen set, and a lantern. Women above twelve years of age also received two bars of soap of 250g each, two pairs of underwear, and one piece of Lapa (cloth) (UNHCR-Monrovia 2005, 24).

Government of Ghana and Repatriation of Liberian Refugees

The government of Ghana since the 1990s has been active in seeking both military and political solutions to the Liberian war. It sponsored the peace process and supported the ongoing peacebuilding process, of which the return of Liberian refugees is considered an important element. It is important to note that although the government of Ghana has provisions for local integration and resettlement in its 1992 Refugee Law, in practice it has followed its historical preference for repatriation (Coffie 2012, 187). Noting the security threat and resource burden, the government was reluctant to promote local integration as a long-term solution for Liberian refugees (Coffie 2013, 208). For example, "as of June 2004, when the second official repatriation program for Liberian refugees was set to begin, the Ghana

Refugee Board had no detailed official view on the local integration of refugees" (Coffie 2013, 209). Although the government offers resettlement as a solution to refugee situations, opportunities and decisions about access are usually between the individual refugee and the country offering resettlement. The government is limited to the provision of documents such as the status of the refugee applicant. Thus, the government of Ghana considered and promoted repatriation of Liberian refugees after the signing of the CPA as the most desirable solution.

The official repatriation of Liberian refugees from Ghana to Liberia began after the signing of a tripartite agreement between the governments of Liberia and Ghana and UNHCR in 2004. The agreement defined the procedures for the process and upheld the notion of noncoercion of the repatriation as stipulated by the global refugee regime. Furthermore, it set out guarantees for the refugees to return in safety and with dignity (UNHCR-Accra 2004). Although voluntary repatriation was strongly promoted prior to the 2005 Liberian presidential elections, very few refugees opted for this solution. At the end of 2005 less than 8 percent of the total Liberian refugee population in Ghana had returned.[3] Thus, in 2006, with just a year to end the official repatriation process, UNHCR and the governments of Ghana and Liberia embarked on another massive campaign to encourage the voluntary repatriation of Liberian refugees. The campaign included Liberian officials visiting the Buduburam refugee camp, explaining the need for the refugees to return, and exhorting them to do so to contribute to the rebuilding of Liberia. This included a visit of a Liberian delegation that included the minister of internal affairs to the Liberian refugee settlement in Ghana (UNHCR-Accra 2006). The governments of Liberia and Ghana and UNHCR also organized a "Go and Tell" program, where some selected returnees went back to the camp to showcase to the refugees the opportunities that exist in Liberia. According to the Liberian Refugee Returnee Resettlement Commission, a major outcome of this campaign was that 2007 recorded the highest numbers of Liberian refugees repatriating from Ghana, 14,641, representing 41 percent of the refugee population returned to Liberia.[4] Although the increase in returnee figures from Ghana was a boost for the repatriation exercise, it did not meet the 80 percent expectation of the governments of Liberia and Ghana and UNHCR (UNHCR-Accra 2006).

The Six-Month Protests: The Protesters and Their Strategies

As the 2007 deadline drew closer, attempts by UNHCR and the governments of Ghana and Liberia to accelerate the repatriation process and begin the transition to local integration were met with stiff opposition from the refugees. Resistance to the initiation of the local integration option became the foundation for the protest by Concerned Women. Over the next six months, the protesters made demands or "requests" on UNHCR and the governments of Ghana and Liberia to be heard and to change the rules around options available to refugees in finding a solution to their displacement.

While there were a range of protesters during this period, which raised concerns about events unfolding in the camp, a central group during this period was Concerned Women, which had identifiable leaders: Tomah, Isatta, Mary, Sia, and Mardea (Holzer 2015, 94). Apart from these leaders, other actors from the camp played an important role in motivating and sustaining the protests, although they did not necessarily actively participate in the protests themselves.[5] Among the members of the community leadership that acted in solidarity with Concerned Women were the leaders of Heads of the County, the Ministerial Council chair, the Elders Council chair, the Muslim Council chair, and members of the Hatai, the prominent intellectual club in the camp (Holzer 2015, 103). The categories of supporters who did not openly join in the protests but expressed support for Concerned Women, either in public or in private, referred to themselves as "stakeholders" (Holzer 2015, 103). Most of these stakeholders were opinion leaders of the camp and male. According to a respondent, early discussions among the protesters concluded that there was no need to include these opinion leaders in the actual protest as they were the leaders who had negotiated with UNHCR, supposedly on their behalf, but did not secure what Concerned Women believed to be their entitlement.[6]

The protest leaders argued that an all-female protest would likely result in a less hostile response from the security agencies in Ghana. Indeed, during an interaction, one of the respondents recalled a 2003 security sweep at the camp that targeted males.[7] On February 23, 2003, Ghanaian security agencies alleging that the camp had become a home to ex-rebel groups conducted a security exercise at the camp and focused exclusively on male refugees with the objective of removing armed elements from the camps and retrieving weapons. No arrests were made, but a small number of locally manufactured guns were retrieved from the camp, which the owners claimed were for hunting (Coffie 2015, 205). According to the respondent, based on that history, some of them argued that they should maintain the group as an all-female organization, and everyone, including some males who attended their meeting, agreed.

From the outset, the objective of Concerned Women was to be given a fair hearing by UNHCR in response to their concerns relating to the solutions being proposed for refugees (Holzer 2012). In their opinion, UNHCR had not sufficiently considered the concerns of refugees in developing a durable solutions strategy. It was this lack of consideration that led to the protests that ran from November 2007 to April 2008 (Holzer 2012), triggered specifically by UNHCR's announcement that local integration in Ghana was to be the solution for the remaining Liberian refugees in Buduburam camp. In response to the announcement, a group of women demanded that a public meeting should be held to discuss the change in policy and that "educated women" be included in the decision-making process (Holzer 2012, 9). It was the failure of UNHCR-Ghana to call such a meeting that ultimately triggered the response from refugee women to organize them and turn their gathering into a protest (Omata 2013). In this way, the protests were a response to UNHCR's (in)actions, not a planned strategy (Holzer 2015, 95).

In response to this initial concern, the first priority of the protesters was to ensure that their views were represented at meetings that discussed solutions for refugees, which were held either within or outside the Buduburam camp. To further this objective, the women began discrediting existing representatives, especially the women on the welfare council whom the protesters claimed had been selected by UNHCR and the Ghanaian government. According to Concerned Women, the representatives negotiating on their behalf were not informed on the issues and should not have been at the negotiating table. They referred to them as "illiterate women" (Holzer 2012, 9) who had been deliberately selected by UNHCR and the government as part of an effort to silence opposing voices from the camp.[8] However, in order not to antagonize and alienate the representatives, Concerned Women approached them and sought to make sure that the so-called illiterate representatives had what it took to resist the "internationals'" attempts at imposing solutions on refugees. In their opinion, they needed to train and reorient their representatives that they were not subservient to UNHCR and that the organizations could not impose local integration on refugees.[9] This strategy was not welcomed by the representative, who felt insulted by Concerned Women, and contributed to a disagreement between some of the members who either abandoned the group or threatened to leave.

After private efforts to "reeducate" and "train" women representatives received little attention and had limited impact, the women changed strategy at the end of November. On November 30, 2007, the women launched their first public protest in the camp. According to Holzer (2012, 10), about forty protesters marched through the open field in the camp to register their displeasure with the planning process and, in the words of one of the respondents, to "make their voices heard."[10] The decision to march in the open field, which is very close to the only highway connecting the middle section of Ghana to the capital, enabled the women to attract the public's attention without causing disorder or breaking the Public Order Act of Ghana (Act

491, 1994).[11] The act requires organizers of any event within a public place to notify police of their action and of the proposed route or place not less than five days before the action. The law also allows the police to request that protest organizers either postpone the date or relocate the place for the event, to safeguard the rights of others and public order (Act 491, Sections 1–7). Restricting themselves to the field kept them within the confines of the camp, so they did not need police permission or approval for their actions. This strategy was well thought out and helped them to evade the scrutiny of and potential threat from the police. For example, when the police were allegedly called by the camp manager in February 2008 to disperse the protesters, the police declined because the protesters had not violated the law, thus they could not prevent them from assembling in the open field.[12] Indeed, the commander of the camp police station is reported to have visited the protesters and encouraged them to pursue their agenda without breaking the laws (Holzer 2015, 101).

As protesters took turns walking around the field bearing their messages on placards, others also began writing and dispatching letters to UNHCR, the government, and the media. They communicated their grievances, recommendations, and demands to UNHCR office in Accra, UNHCR headquarters in Geneva, the US Embassy in Accra, the government of Ghana through the camp manager, and the government of Liberia through the embassy in Accra and directly to government agencies in Monrovia. The women continued the intermittent march through the camp from November 2007 to March 2008 and sometimes crossed over to block the main street, which caused traffic congestion and frustration for most of the users of the road, which is the only access route to Accra from the region. Nevertheless, for most of the protest, they remained in the field, waving placards inscribed with their grievances and demands, such as:

We know of the three (3) R's
Resettlement, Repatriation, Reintegration
We do not know about Local Integration!!!
Seventeen years of Silence is working against us.
No!! We must be heard!!!
GHANA-UNHCR
Please Resettle us for a better tomorrow. We are entitled to it!!!
It's a way forward
Yesterday of silence is dead and gone
Today is the day of speaking
(One of the writings on paper posters used by the refugee women protesters in 2008; cited in Holzer 2015, 96)

The protesters also took advantage of any meetings with UNHCR in the camp to present their views. One such occasion was on February 18, 2008, when UNHCR had scheduled a participatory planning session with elderly women of the camp to inform them about the durable solutions. Concerned Women, who did not meet the age requirement set by UNHCR to attend the meeting, sat in the audience and "heckled the speaker with questions with the aim of putting across their grievances" (Holzer 2015, 101–2). While this action led to the cancelation of a scheduled meeting with younger women the next day, the ultimate effect was to embolden Concerned Women to begin a sit-in in the offices of camp manager and UNHCR in response to UNHCR officials' actions or inactions and to attract the attention of the country representative in Accra (Holzer 2015, 101–2). The eventual escalation of the protest to the invasion of the offices by the women led to the proclamation of the camp as an insecure place and, hence, the closure of schools, the food distribution program, and nightclubs within the camp (Holzer 2012, 12).

While the strategies by the protesters in the first three months of the protest did not result in changes from UNHCR or government, the threat of a food boycott by sympathizers of the demonstration seemed to have drawn attention by making UNHCR respond (Holzer 2012, 11–12). The food distribution was "targeted at UN-designated most vulnerable persons," and as the protest escalated to a sit-down in the field and a boycott of camp activities such as schools and night clubs, registered recipients of the food aid also boycotted the program (Holzer 2012, 11–12). The food boycott seemed more efficient because the officials saw the approach as a threat to the well-being of some of the refugees. On many occasions, people who had food rations were the chronically ill persons, children with malnutrition, and so on. Therefore, a refusal to take food by such persons would not only result in negative media attention for UNHCR but in the words of UNHCR-Ghana would "cause stress for the majority of the recipient population" (quoted in Holzer 2015, 109).

Response to the Protest

The government of Ghana referred to the 2008 protest as a security threat, while both radio and newspaper commentary referred to the action as an act of ungratefulness by the refugees as well as an insult to the generosity and hospitality of Ghanaians who had hosted the refugees for almost two decades.[13] The government responded by arresting about six hundred protesters on March 17 and seventy more the next day. Of the latter group, sixteen were deported on March 23, allegedly because they were illegally present in the country and posed a national security threat. UNHCR afterward confirmed that thirteen of the sixteen deported individuals were registered refugees. The government argued that the deportees were a security threat because they were "ex-combatants" from the war in Liberia. The government provided no evidence for the allegation, but their justification was that Liberians were granted asylum based on war, and since the war had ended, they could go home. Addressing Ghanaians on April 1, 2008, the Ghanaian minister of the interior, Kwamena Bartels, repeatedly criticized the actions of refugees and announced the government's intention to invoke the cessation clause regarding refugees. He added that those refugees who could avail themselves of the protection of their home state but who continue not to do so could have their refugee status removed (Dogbevi 2008). Furthermore, to defuse the tension in the camp, some of the organizers of the protest were moved to a location about one hundred kilometers away from the camp for about three weeks (Essuman-Johnson 2011, 122).

The use of excessive force by the security personnel and the comments by and justifications from the government were condemned by UNHCR and other nongovernmental organizations and some individual Ghanaian citizens (UN-OCHA IRIN 2008). While the removal of status was legally permissible according to the procedures adopted by the government in granting refugee status to Liberians (Coffie 2012, 176), the government's action of arresting and subsequent deportation of refugees without trial was clearly against the rules and an abuse of the political and civil rights of the refugees under both international laws and the 1992 constitution of Ghana.

While UNHCR considered the actions of the protesters to be disruptive to their activities within the camp, it attempted to address the protests through several means. Its first response to the February–March 2008 sit-in was to withdraw all its personnel temporarily from the camp, claiming that the sit-in had created an insecure working environment. The organization also insisted that Concerned Women were not representative of the refugees and refused to meet with them. Instead they directed the protesters to channel their grievances through the welfare council, which was considered the legitimate representation of the people.

UNHCR later softened its stance after it received a letter from the stakeholders who categorically noted their support of the protest and, in light of the continuation of the protest, invited the protest organizers and the stakeholders to a meeting in Accra in March to "hold pragmatic discussions on the way forward" (Holzer 2015, 105). Ultimately, the meeting did not end the protest, as the refugees arrived at the meeting only to find that the Ghanaian minister of the interior was chairing the meeting and that the meeting was just an avenue for the minister to intimidate them to end the protest.

Responding to the refugees' accusation of the agency's deception, UNHCR stated that it had engaged and solicited the help and intervention of the Ghanaian authorities because of the food boycott. As noted by Holzer (2015, 109 and 130, quoted in UNHCR-Ghana 2008b), UNHCR became increasingly concerned as the situation is causing distress for the majority of the population which remains uninvolved." UNHCR therefore invited the Ghanaian authorities to address what they claim had become a security concern. The UNHCR's primary concern was for the safety of the refugees, and since it was not responsible for security in the camp, the UNHCR could maintain that, by inviting the Ghanaian authorities to intervene, it was merely discharging its responsibility to implement a humanitarian program in the camp.

However, this view is contested by one of the protesters. The respondents noted that in their view it was not their threat and boycotting of the food that made UNHCR-Ghana invite the authorities. Rather, their reaction was provoked by letters the protesters wrote to Geneva as well as the phone call that one of the leaders of Concerned Women made to UNHCR-Geneva.[14] According to Holzer (2012, 10), she observed the writing of the letters to Geneva but does not confirm if Geneva received and acted on them as noted by the current study's respondent. Regarding the phone call, Holzer (2015, 178) notes her role in helping one of the protesters to make the phone call and to navigate the complex switchboard access to Geneva, and she bears witness to how the person in Geneva, upon realizing the caller was a refugee, insisted that the caller instead file her complaint at the local UNHCR. However, the refugee persisted and questioned Geneva's logic of filing a complaint against the local office within the same office. Eventually she was provided a fax number to Geneva to send the written complaint. Contradicting the account of the protester, officials of UNHCR-Ghana insist that they were not pushed by Geneva but that their action was based on their concerns for security in the camp and the threat posed by the protesters to others not involved in the protest, such as the recipients of the food program.[15]

The arrest of some of the protesters led others to abandon the protest, but some remained on the field through to the first week in April. The remaining protesters are noted to have left after the Liberian ambassador to Ghana visited the refugees and promised to speak on their behalf, pleading with them to leave the field (Holzer 2015, 112). Meanwhile, the president of Liberia sent the country's foreign minister to Ghana for discussion with the Ghanaian government. The meeting ended with a signing of another tripartite agreement declaring that all Liberian refugees should leave Ghana in six months. UNHCR-Ghana therefore returned to Buduburam and once again began the process of repatriation to Liberia.

Reflections on the Achievements of the Protest

Reflecting on the outcomes of the protest, Holzer (2012, 2015) argues that the protest was a political failure because it did not result in fundamental changes in the policies and practices of UNHCR or the governments of Ghana or Liberia.[16] In contrast, this chapter argues that such a conclusion is the result of an overly narrow conceptualization of refugee agency. Based on the conceptualization of agency presented by Kabeer (1999) and Sewell (1992), as outlined above, the protest may in fact be understood to be an important expression of refugee agency as it not only represented the ability of refugees to resist the policies of institutional actors and attempt to contest these policies but also resulted in some achievements, including modest changes to the policies and practices of repatriation advanced by the governments of Ghana and Liberia and UNHCR. Moreover, the protest was also empowering for the refugees because it demonstrated their ability to move from a position of unquestioning acceptance of the social order in the camp.

In response to the protests, the governments of Ghana and Liberia met in hopes of finding a lasting solution to the remaining Liberian refugee caseload in Ghana (LRRRC 2009). Both parties agreed that remaining Liberian refugees were required to leave Ghana within six months. Holzer notes (2012, 14) that "the time frame was impractical because UNHCR did not have the means to facilitate the repatriation of such large group in six months." Subsequently, Ghana agreed to reduce the numbers to 50 percent and extend the time to seven months. Although Ghana never enforced this agreement, a little over eight thousand Liberians returned to Liberia during this period. This number is significant because UNHCR had declared the end of its assisted repatriation in 2007, yet it reviewed its earlier decision and provided support to this higher number of returnees.

Another reform of the repatriation practices resulting from the refugee protest was UNHCR's extension of the repatriation period by another two years beyond what Ghana had demanded. This was achieved because the government of Ghana fired the minister of interior, which "diminished Ghana's position on enforcing the agreement" (Holzer 2015, 112), especially on the period of repatriation. Although the government of Ghana did not indicate the reason for the dismissal of the minister, it was reported that his response to the Liberian refugee protest might have contributed to him losing his job.[17] While the reason for the minister's dismissal is unclear, his exit gave UNHCR an opportunity to extend the period of the repatriation to 2009.

Another achievement of the protest was that UNHCR began distributing cash grants of US$100 per adult and US$50 per child. The amount received is short of the refugees' demand of US$1,000. However, it represents a shift in the UNHCR-assisted repatriation package of Liberian refugees. For example, refugees that repatriated before 2008 did not receive any cash grants. In fact, cash grants ultimately became part of the UNHCR standard returnee aid package to Liberian returnees from the various asylum countries in West Africa (UNHCR-Monrovia 2013).

Conclusion

This chapter examined the case of Liberian refugees' protest of the repatriation process to argue for a broader understanding of refugee agency that recognizes that refugees are not passive actors, even in cases of limited resource capabilities. It outlined how the protest empowered refugees by unpacking the agency (strategies of the protesters), resources (the opportunities and constraints of their asylum experience particularly as existed in the camp), and by highlighting the refugees' achievements through protest. During the planning phase of the repatriation process, UNHCR and the governments of Ghana and Liberia assumed the refugees were a passive, unresponsive, and unfortunate group requiring their mercy and protection. In other words, they took as a given the refugees' grateful acceptance of decisions about their fate by others. The refugees, therefore, were not consulted during the negotiations that led to the CPA, which outlined the process of repatriation and the signing of the tripartite agreement between the host states, the home country, and UNHCR. However, the refugees were far from passive actors and demonstrated their agency in various forms and capacities during the process of return.

For example, Concerned Women made demands for things they believed would better meet their needs and interests; this group should have formed part of the initial negotiations leading to the peace agreement as well as the consultations for the tripartite agreement repatriation. This act is an indication of their agency because they demonstrated knowledge of the structures of repatriation, they sent protest letters not only to the involved governments and to UNHCR in Accra but also to UNHCR headquarters in Geneva, and they phoned to lodge a complaint against the local UNHCR. Getting through the switchboard was challenging, but the protester did not give up in the face of intimidation, persisting to narrate her story. Because the protesters mobilized themselves into a collective group, they increased their resource pool and further enhanced their grievances to demonstrate that their protest was not about a few ungrateful individuals seeking to threaten the security of their host. This reflects what Sewell (1992, 21) describes as the social aspect of agency. For him, agency entails an ability to coordinate one's action with others' and against others to form collective projects, to persuade, to coerce, and to monitor the simultaneous effect of one's action as well as that of the others. Thus, although the refugees' capabilities and resources pale in comparison to that of the governments and UNHCR, their actions demonstrate their agency in forms that "[encompass] the meaning, motivation and purpose" (Kabeer 1999) they brought to the process of repatriation. Among the other forms, the refugees reflected on the process, bargained, negotiated, resisted, and sometimes used deception to change the policy content and practice (structures) of the process.

Second, the chapter notes the marginal achievements of the protest mainly through the changes in repatriation policies and practices. The first outcome was the increase in the returnee aid package. They were able to push for a bigger returnee aid package, which included an increase in the cash amount from US$5 to US$100 that was eventually increased to US$375. Moreover, they were able to extend the period of repatriation by another two years; thus, the official return exercise ended in 2009 rather than the originally intended date of 2007. These changes are an indication of the refugees' attempt to shape the policy choices and practices of UNHCR and governments by their refugee experiences and expectations of the future. The role of the refugees in effecting these changes challenges both the notion of a lack of agency on the part of the refugees and a lack of capacity to transform repatriation structures.

Finally, the discussions in this chapter align with Sewell's (1992, 20) assertion that the exercise of agency is far from uniform and that it differs in both kind and extent. The kinds of desires the refugees could have had in their intentions and their creativity in the presentation/opposition to the policies and practices of repatriation can vary dramatically from one refugee situation to another. In short, refugees are different, with varying degrees of resources and capabilities. We should not expect the same achievements across all refugee cases even if their strategies are similar. Therefore, we need to avoid the narrow frames of success and failure as they do not account for the resource variations in the context of the forced migration experiences of refugees.

Notes

1. See Ellen Johnson-Sirleaf, Inaugural Address, January 16, 2006, *available at* https://awpc.cattcenter.iastate.edu/2017/03/09/inaugural-address-jan-16-2006/

2. I conducted the interviews with the five women during the field work in Liberia in 2009 for my PhD dissertation. While these interviews did not form part of the research for the dissertation, I took the opportunity to listen to and record their stories over a period of about two weeks (August 6–17, 2009). Although the interviews were conducted a year after the protest and the interviewees had returned to Liberia, we agreed that I would not use their names, because they were concerned

for their security and feared that families and friends in Ghana might be picked up by security and deported. Thus, they are referenced only by their gender. I conducted the interviews at Buduburam refugee camp as part of an ongoing study of the local integration of the Liberian refugees in Ghana (June–August 2015).

3. Computed by author using data from UNHCR Statistical Yearbooks from 2005 to 2010.

4. Computed by author using data from UNHCR Statistical Yearbooks from 2005 to 2010.

5. Interview with first female Liberian refugee returnee, Monrovia, Liberia, August 9, 2009.

6. Interview with first female Liberian refugee returnee.

7. Interview with second female Liberian refugee returnee, Monrovia, Liberia, August 9, 2009.

8. Interview with second female Liberian refugee returnee.

9. Interview with second female Liberian refugee returnee.

10. Interview with female Liberian refugee returnee, Monrovia, Liberia, August 12, 2009.

11. "The field" is an open space to the right at the entrance of the camp and opposite the marketplace. It served as the largest gathering place for activities such as soccer games and religious activities and as a place for UNHCR and government of Ghana events for the refugees and Ghanaians in the community. Public Order Act of Ghana (Act 491, 1994), http://laws.ghanalegal.com/acts/id/199/section/1/Notification_To_Police_Of_Special_Of_Event.

12. Interview with female Liberian refugee returnee, Monrovia Liberia, August 15, 2009.

13. For evidence of some of the public response to the protest, see this article written by a journalist formerly with the *Daily Graphic*, one of the two Ghanaian newspapers that have national coverage. The comment sections also provide evidence to this assertion. Aidoo (2008).

14. Interview with female Liberian refugee returnee, Monrovia, Liberia, August 12, 2009.

15. Interview with official of UNHCR-Ghana, Accra, Ghana, June 20, 2015.

16. For similar positions, see Agblorti (2011) and Essuman-Johnson (2011).

17. See "Kwamena Bartels Dismissed!," *GhanaWeb*, May 28, 2008, https://www.ghanaweb.com/GhanaHomePage/NewsArchive/Kwamena-Bartels-Dismissed-144284

13

From Roots to Rhizomes

Mapping Rhizomatic Strategies in the Sahrawi
and Palestinian Protracted Refugee Situations

Elena Fiddian-Qasmiyeh

The international community's three mandated durable solutions (local integration, resettlement, and repatriation) have proven inadequate to address the protection needs and rights of people living in protracted displacement situations, and alternative modes of analyzing and responding to these situations are constantly being explored and tested. These include models of South-South humanitarianism developed by state and nonstate actors from the Global South who are positioned on the margins of the hegemonic international humanitarian regime and by refugees through refugee-refugee humanitarianism (Fiddian-Qasmiyeh 2015a; 2016b).[1]

Many critics of the mainstream durable solutions framework take issue with its underlying sedentarist assumptions, including the widespread view that being "fixed" to a particular soil or territory is both "natural" and desirable and, thus, that "rerooting" displaced individuals, families, and communities is necessary to provide an anchor to end refugees' liminality and insecurity and to reconstitute the "national order of things" (Malkki 1995b). A concomitant process pathologizes displaced people by equating "uprootedness" with losing one's bearing or moral compass and with being on the threshold of death, whether social, physical, political, or existential (Malkki 1995a, 33). Liisa Malkki develops this line of argumentation through a critical analysis of arborescent and arbolic metaphors inspired by Gilles Deleuze and Félix Guattari (2013), among others. In arguing for new ways of mapping out the relationship between refugees and different spaces (and places) and in line with the broader poststructuralist and postcolonial framework guiding her analysis, Malkki shows how we can go beyond naturalized assumptions that have come to be "taken for granted."

In this chapter I explore Malkki's critique in more detail and extend her approach to displacement using Deleuze and Guattari's (2013, 1–27) concept of the rhizome. Unlike the vertical model of the root providing an anchor and succor to a plant, a rhizome is a network of subterranean lines that extend horizontally, sporadically erupting to the surface to create new shoots while the lines continue both to expand and interconnect. This chapter asks whether developing a rhizomatic analysis (a "rhizoanalysis") can prove fruitful when attempting to map out alternatives—or even challenges—to the three "rooted" and "rerooting" durable solutions.

The chapter's main aim is to examine what a rhizoanalysis of protracted displacement might entail (or produce), highlighting the extent to which "thinking through" rhizomes challenges us to develop alternative conceptualizations of "solutions" to refugees' problems.[2] While "solutions" are often viewed as providing an endpoint for refugees' liminality, a rhizome, by definition, has "no beginning or end; it is always in the middle" (Deleuze and Guattari 2013, 26). Rhizoanalysis thus prompts us to trace and to analyze the ways in which refugees negotiate the process of always being "in the middle" of displacement.

The chapter is divided into two main parts. Part one explores the application of rhizoanalysis to protracted displacement settings. Part two examines whether rhizomatic strategies can provide refugees with a means to navigate protracted displacement on a combination of individual, family, and collective levels. It does so through the case studies of two long-standing displacement situations in which the traditional durable solutions are out of reach for a clear majority of refugees. In particular, I examine Sahrawi and Palestinian refugees' experiences of leaving their refugee home-camps in southwest Algeria and Lebanon to complete their primary-, secondary-, and tertiary-level studies in Cuba and Libya and of subsequently leaving Cuba and Libya (under different circumstances) to live and work in their home-camps upon graduation. The discussions and analysis presented below are informed by my multi-sited ethnographic research since 2005 with and about Sahrawi refugees in Cuba and in the desert-based Sahrawi refugee camps in Algeria, Libya, Syria, and Spain, and with Palestinians educated in Cuba and Libya and currently based in seven urban refugee camps across Lebanon.[3]

The South-South educational migration programs underpinning both of these case studies are particularly informative. Although the Cuban and Libyan initiatives implemented from the 1970s to the early-2010s officially aimed to maximize refugees' "self-sufficiency" in protracted displacement contexts, they ultimately perpetuated different forms of dependence on externally provided aid and provided few guarantees against the possibility of refugees' imminent rejection and expulsion. In such cases, where refugees are always already at risk of renewed displacement, models of providing "solutions" clearly require reconceptualization beyond the scope of traditional frameworks. With this in mind, the chapter examines the extent to which educational (and postgraduation) migration could be seen as tracing lines for refugees to develop rhizomatic strategies that transcend the modes of action (and boundaries) established by international agencies such as United Nations High Commissioner for Refugees (UNHCR) and UN Relief and Works Agency for Palestine Refugees in the Near East (UNRWA). Inter alia, it considers whether educational migration enables individuals and families to achieve legal or socioeconomic self-sufficiency (i.e., providing key opportunities for growth for the refugee self at the micro or meso levels) if not political self-determination through modes of refugee-refugee solidarity that help refugees navigate new and overlapping processes of displacement in shared spaces of dispossession (Fiddian-Qasmiyeh 2015a; cf. Landau, chapter 8, this volume).

Through this focus on rhizomes, the chapter simultaneously echoes and critiques discussions pertaining to "mobility" as a fourth durable solution (Long 2014), highlighting the relevance of mobile, translocal, and transnational frameworks for increasing refugee self-sufficiency on different scales, and stressing the challenges and dangers that arise through participation in migration processes. Crucially, the processes and routes taken to seek protection and self-sufficiency often expose refugees to new or renewed forms of violence or dispossession. This suggests the need to reconceptualize "solutions" as intermediate, multidirectional, and fluctuating processes that enable refugees to negotiate and manage constantly evolving disequilibrium rather than as events or statuses to be resolutely achieved. Rhizoanalysis offers one way of imagining and evaluating alternative modes of responding to processes of protracted and overlapping displacement. I conclude that while rhizomatic strategies may facilitate the development of important individual and familial approaches to building meaningful lives in displacement, these strategies are (by definition) unable to lead to "solutions," durable or otherwise.

Refugees and Rhizoanalysis

The empirical and analytical distinctions between roots and rhizomes underpin Deleuze and Guattari's (2013) retheorization and critique of diverse modes of analysis and action. Roots draw nutrients up from the soil to the plant such that an uprooted plant or a plant with broken roots will ultimately die unless rerooted in the right soil at the right time (i.e., a specific spatiotemporal context). In contrast, Deleuze and Guattari celebrate—or, some decry, romanticize—the seemingly limitless adaptability of rhizomes, which sustain, recreate, and redefine life and living through horizontal subterranean "lines" characterized by multiple connections and multiplications. Sporadic eruptions create new shoots in new places, thereby changing the rhizome's very "nature as it expands its connections" (Deleuze and Guattari 2013, 7); at the same time, a rhizome "may be broken, shattered at a given spot, but it will start up again on one of its old lines, or on new lines" (8). In this way, a rhizome is always in a process of becoming: it is "a model that is perpetually in construction or collapsing" and is characterized by "a process that is perpetually prolonging itself, breaking off and starting up again" (21).

The concept of the rhizome enables us to consider the conditions under which refugees may develop and implement strategies and modes of adaptability and flexibility in diverse "shattering" processes, an exercise guided by Deleuze and Guattari's proposition that we "reverse the orientation of our thinking, from a verticalist imaginary where things are grounded and rooted to the metaphor of the endless and limitless 'plateau'" (Navaro-Yashin 2009, 13). Such a reversal of thinking—rhizoanalysis—"redirects analysis away from identifying stable meanings of interactions to mapping possibilities produced through interactions" (Lowry 2013, 26), including interactions produced by, and producing, instability and overlapping processes of displacement.

By examining how rhizomatic rather than rooted approaches might help us reconsider the future of displaced people in contexts of increasingly protracted and overlapping contexts of displacement, I do not mean to imply that refugees do not have an attachment to different places, nor do I propose that political solutions should not be developed that lay the foundations for refugees to have the right to return in safety and dignity to places to which they feel a strong attachment.[4]

Indeed, Deleuze and Guattari remind us of this coexistence—rather than duality—and mutually constitutive relationship between territorialization and deterritorialization: "Every rhizome contains lines of segmentarity according to which is it stratified, territorialized, organized, signified, attributed, etc., as well as lines of deterritorialization down which it constantly flees. There is a rupture in the rhizome whenever segmentary lines explode into a line of flight, but the line of flight is part of the rhizome. These lines always tie back to one another" (Deleuze and Guattari 2013, 8–9). The conceptualization of territorialized, segmentary lines of a rhizome "constantly flee[ing]" and "explod[ing]" into deterritorialized lines of flight that are essential constitutive parts of the rhizome is relevant to my reflection on contexts of protracted displacement that are characterized by simultaneous or overlapping displacements.

Deleuze and Guattari's (2013, 581–82) concepts of "territoriality" and "deterritoriality" are idiosyncratic and not necessarily consistent with many refugee studies scholars' usage of these concepts. However, some refugee scholars have implicitly endorsed key empirical and theoretical features of Deleuze and Guattari's conceptual distinction. For example, in explaining the relationship between territory, "terrain," and displacement, David Turton is careful to note that "when I speak of attachment to territory . . . I use the word 'territory' in the sense of an actually occupied 'terrain,' *from which the members of the group in question always see themselves as potentially in danger of being displaced*, rather than in the sense of an 'ancestral homeland' with which they have a 'natural' link and from which they see themselves as having become unnaturally 'uprooted'" (Turton 1999, 421, emphasis added). As with Deleuze and Guattari's distinction between "territoriality" and "deterritoriality," Turton's assertion reminds us that being displaced should not (only) be defined in terms of having been forcibly removed from a nurturing homeland but as the perpetual risk of being displaced from a broader terrain across which one has multiple and yet at times paradoxical attachments and affinities. In light of the specific focus of this chapter and book on rethinking durable solutions, it is particularly noteworthy that such a risk of ongoing displacement clearly resonates not only with refugees' experiences within their region of displacement but also in the places typically conceptualized as providing the solution to displacement.

Indeed, as I have discussed elsewhere regarding Palestinians in Europe (Fiddian-Qasmiyeh 2016c), even when holding "a" citizenship and thus having officially secured a durable "solution," many Palestinians continue to be on, or to embody, what I refer to as "the threshold of statelessness" (also see Qasmiyeh 2014). In effect, Palestinians' experiences of nationality have been fraught with insecurity, rather than offering security, whether in the context of the Middle East—where Palestinians who held Jordanian nationality have repeatedly been stripped of their nationality and rendered stateless once again (Wilcke 2010)—or in Europe. Even when not directly experienced, a process of "traveling fear" (following Said 1983; see also Fiddian-Qasmiyeh 2013) characterizes many experiences of "holding" a European nationality.

For instance, Marwa—a thirty-year-old born in a camp in Syria—referred to the constant fear of being stripped of her Swedish nationality, a fear that has traveled with her from the Middle East to Europe: "The fear becomes part of your identity because wherever you go, you are not fully accepted. Sweden can today be the perfect partner but still there is a fear that this relationship can change and end" (interview, Sweden, 2014; cited in Fiddian-Qasmiyeh 2016c). The potential for expulsion from the country that has granted you nationality while hosting you as a guest was also stressed by thirty-three-year-old Swedish citizen Faisal, who was born in a camp in Lebanon; he was concerned that there was no "guarantee that the next president or government will not do the same thing as previous governments. . . . Palestinians probably think that Sweden can one day have a racist government and can deport them" (interview, Sweden, 2014; cited in Fiddian-Qasmiyeh 2016c).

Such fears and insecurities are inherent to the geopolitical context of "durable solutions," which is always subject to ongoing shifts that continue to demonize and both figuratively and physically expel refugees from diverse national, regional, and international spaces. Indeed, for many refugees, the experience of displacement is best understood within the framework of a rhizome that has "no beginning or end; it is always in the middle, between things, interbeing, *intermezzo*" (Deleuze and Guattari 2013, 26), a middle "from which it grows and which it overspills," where the rhizome is "composed not of units but of dimensions, or rather directions in motion" (22). When viewed through this analytical lens, refugees are always already in the middle of displacement, never at the beginning or at the end. Recognizing that there is no "end" to "the refugee cycle" (Black and Koser 1999) does not undermine the significance of developing lines of segmentation and deterritorialization to continue life and living. Rather, it encourages us to examine protracted displacement from the perspective of an "always already" middle that focuses on "proceeding from the middle, through the middle, coming and going rather than starting and finishing" (Deleuze and Guattari 2013, 27) in order to identify rather than reify a sense of liminality that is often overlooked and to recognize the dual processes of territorialization and deterritorialization that characterize protracted displacement. To recognize that there are multiple attachments to multiple "plateaux" is to recognize that with each eruption into a line of flight, the rhizome itself changes and continues its process of becoming rather than reaching a (re)solution.

In effect, strong attachments to "certain places and territories" evidently characterize experiences of protracted displacement on an empirical level, including the Sahrawi and Palestinian cases below. In these instances, as I argue elsewhere, there is not only a strong attachment to the historic homeland (Western Sahara and Palestine, respectively) but also strong notions of attachment to home-camps and diverse urban hosting environments—even if such forms of attachment are ambivalent in nature, simultaneously attractive and yet repulsive (i.e., see Fiddian-Qasmiyeh 2013, 2019; Qasmiyeh and Fiddian-Qasmiyeh 2013; Gabiam and Fiddian-Qasmiyeh 2017). These multiple forms of attachment and the recognition that refugees, like rhizomes, "can act at a distance, come or return a long time after, but always under conditions of discontinuity, rupture, and multiplicity" (Deleuze and Guattari 2013, 16) require us to develop an alternative conceptualization of the modes through which refugees seek out and implement strategies to determine their own futures in contexts of ongoing and overlapping displacement.

Having briefly outlined this conceptual framework, I now examine the extent to which international scholarships and educational migration programs have created opportunities for Sahrawi and Palestinian refugees—as individuals, families, communities, and members of nations-in-waiting—to develop rhizomatic strategies that enable them to adapt to ongoing shifts, challenges, and opportunities in the context of multiple "eruptions" across time and space. I begin by offering a brief overview of UNHCR's approach to the relationship between higher education and "solutions" in protracted displacement contexts. I then examine Sahrawi and Palestinian refugees' experiences of leaving their refugee camp homes to study in Cuba and Libya free of charge with the understanding that they will return to work in their home-camps—and therefore support their communities—upon graduation.

Refugees' Educational Migration and Self-Sufficiency

It is widely recognized that "refugees often see the education of their children as a principal way of ensuring a better future" (Dryden-Peterson 2003, 1). Complementing its intrinsic and existential value, education is often seen as enhancing refugees' access to one of the three traditional durable solutions (UNHCR 2007) and to successful postconflict nation building (UNESCO 2011). For instance, educational access and outcomes are identified as indicators of refugees' local integration in their host countries (Ager and Strang 2008), and education is increasingly recognized as facilitating the development of refugees' self-reliance. As a programmatic approach and as a key indicator of successful local integration, "self-reliance" is defined by UNHCR as referring "to developing and strengthening livelihoods of persons of concern, and reducing their vulnerability and long-term reliance on humanitarian/external assistance" (UNHCR 2006, 1). Elsewhere, the UN defines "self-reliance" much more narrowly as "providing . . . a professional qualification geared towards future employment" (UNHCR 2007, 7).

UNHCR has sought to measure the success of higher education programs for refugees through a limited number of studies by examining refugee-graduates' professional and economic "self-reliance" and their contributions both to their refugee community pending a durable solution and their country of origin upon repatriation (i.e., UNHCR 2007, 8). However, quantitative snapshots of successful outcomes should be reevaluated through a more nuanced and comprehensive understanding of refugees' experiences of such initiatives. These reevaluations must be sensitive to the spatial and temporal delimitations of "success": for example, the early return of DAFI graduates to Afghanistan and their subsequent role in civil administration was viewed by UNHCR as a sign of the programs' success (see Morlang and Stolte 2008, cited in Dryden-Peterson 2011, 52). However, the UNHCR study did not account for ongoing displacement within and from Afghanistan during their initial evaluation, and it did not anticipate displacement beyond the study's own narrow time frame. To do so would require us to consider how success and self-sufficiency can be conceptualized in contexts of overlapping displacement and ongoing precarity. Such analyses must also acknowledge that there are diverse understandings of self-reliance beyond institutionalized definitions. Indeed, the relationship between higher education and self-reliance depends on whose definition (e.g., professional, economic, political) and which level (i.e., individual, familial, collective, or national) is prioritized, why, and to what effect.

The potential to promote professional self-sufficiency in Sahrawi and Palestinian students' home-camps via educational migration has been particularly significant in light of infrastructural limitations in both the desert-based Sahrawi refugee camps in Algeria and the urban Palestinian refugee camps in Lebanon and given these camps' dependence on externally provided humanitarian and political aid. However, while the promotion of self-sufficiency has long been officially espoused both by Cuba and Libya and by the Sahrawis' and Palestinians' political representatives (including the Polisario Front and the Palestine Liberation Organization, respectively), a core question I have explored through my multi-sited ethnographic research is how these and other educational migration programs have actually been experienced and navigated by individuals and communities both during their studies abroad and upon return to their home-camps (Fiddian-Qasmiyeh 2011, 2012, 2013, 2015a, 2015b).

Educational Migration and Navigating Rhizomatic Refugee "Maps"

In the context of this chapter, I read the broader South-South educational migration programs that have provided support to Sahrawi and Palestinian refugees as one dimension of a rhizomatic map that Sahrawi and Palestinian refugees use to navigate their protracted displacement landscapes while their respective quests for national self-determination or any meaningful durable solution remain on the distant horizon.[5] This rhizomatic map—which is constantly changing in light of (inter alia) geopolitical and diplomatic shifts—encompasses a broader set of lines and connections, including refugees' homelands (the Western Sahara and Palestine, respectively), home-

camps (the Sahrawi refugee camp complex in southwest Algeria and Palestinian refugee camps and informal settlements across Lebanon, Jordan, Syria, the
Occupied Palestinian Territories), and other "host-home" spaces across both
the Global South and Global North (see also Gabiam and Fiddian-Qasmiyeh
2017). In this context, while a diasporic reading would prioritize refugees'
connections (emotional, physical, existential, political) with their homeland
as their common "root," a rhizomatic reading allows/requires us to acknowledge the multiple origins underpinning refugees' identities and diverse strategies alike (Maalouf 2008). As I have argued elsewhere (Fiddian-Qasmiyeh
2013, 2019; Qasmiyeh and Fiddian-Qasmiyeh 2013; Gabiam and Fiddian-
Qasmiyeh 2017), refugee camps are not merely "reservoirs of memory" of
the homeland but are themselves spaces of belonging and longing; they are
both a symptom of displacement and an "original" space and space of origin
when viewed from the "middle" of displacement. In the next section, I examine to what extent certain lines of movement between the Sahrawi and
Palestinian refugee camps and Cuba and Libya have provided a form of "rhizomatic strategy" for refugees.

Sahrawi-Palestinian-Cuban Lines of Movement

From 1975 onward, thousands of Sahrawi children as young as six years old
left their refugee camp homes to study in Libya. Between 1977 and the early
2000s an estimated four thousand Sahrawi refugees left the camps at the age
of (approximately) eleven to complete their primary-, secondary-, and tertiary-level studies in Cuba.[6] As a result, both countries play a prominent role
in Sahrawi children's imaginary landscapes and futures, and each country has
arguably become part of "the Sahrawi rhizome." Out of forty-six seven- to
twelve-year-old Sahrawi children interviewed in 2005 (Crivello and Fiddian-Qasmiyeh 2010), sixteen reported that family members including their
parents, siblings, uncles/aunts, or cousins had studied in Cuba; thirteen, in
Libya. Seven children directly expressed their desire to study in Cuba in the
near future, while six children indicated their intention to study in Libya
(see Fiddian-Qasmiyeh 2015b). The expectation of retracing their relatives'
lines of movement by traveling to Cuba or Libya to study has long perme-
ated children's desires for the future. Indeed, educational migration to Cuba
can be understood as a key rhizomatic strategy for the children and adolescents who left their home-camps to spend long periods living and studying
in the Cuba, where they "enjoy[ed] equal educational opportunities as well
as slightly more advantageous treatment in terms of material and health support provided in Cuban schools" (UNHCR 2005, 5). Sahrawi and Palestinian
refugees' temporary "local integration," while impermanent, was nonethe-

less "durable," typically lasting between ten and eighteen years before their return to their home-camps.

However, as some interviewees pointed out, prolonged periods of separation from family members (often during formative years of childhood), caused considerable anguish, leading to the emergence (eruption) of a new problem, and in turn requiring a new line of flight. Thus, while educational migration to Cuba and Libya provided spaces and opportunity for growth, these were also spaces imbued with a sense of loss, especially for youth who longed to return "home" to the camps. This longing was itself characterized simultaneously by attraction and repulsion: the desire to rejoin their families and to work for the benefit of their entire refugee community—also an official aim of the Cuban educational migration program—was countered by the anticipation of the complex social, humanitarian, political, and security situations "at home." Cuban-educated Sahrawi returnees in particular experienced a wide range of difficulties upon their return to the camps, including alienation from family members, marginalization for perceived violations of key cultural and religious norms while in Cuba, and different forms of discrimination on the basis of linguistic differences and unfamiliarity with the camps' sociocultural and religious norms.

Nonetheless, upon graduation from Cuban universities, all Sahrawi and Palestinian students did indeed return to their respective home-camps. In the Sahrawi context, a large proportion of Cuban-educated returnees currently occupy positions of authority in the camps, with one member of the Sahrawi camp-based political leadership (the Polisario Front) estimating that in the mid-2000s, around two thousand Cuban-trained Sahrawis occupied the most important political, social, administrative, and professional roles in the refugee camps, including as doctors and nurses (ACN 2006). Sahrawis who completed undergraduate and postgraduate dissertations on the Western Sahara conflict (Fiddian-Qasmiyeh 2014) accrued the necessary political and linguistic training to work in Sahrawi institutions (where Spanish and Arabic are the official languages) and to represent the Sahrawi "cause" in the camps and in the Sahrawi state-in-exile's diplomatic missions around the world. As the "official face" of the Sahrawi camp-based political establishment, and as the main point of contact for thousands of Spanish-speaking visitors who travel to the camps both to express their solidarity and deliver humanitarian aid every year, these graduates in essence embody the benefits of Cuba's educational migration program, demonstrating the high degree of professional self-sufficiency that parallels the camps' material dependence on externally provided assistance (Fiddian-Qasmiyeh 2009; 2014).

However, while female graduates have typically remained within the camps to work, increasing numbers of male graduates from Cuba have emigrated to Spain to seek opportunities in professions unavailable in the camps.[7] Concurrently, an increase in paid jobs resulting from the arrival of foreign nongovernmental organizations (NGOs) after the declaration of a cease-fire in the early 1990s has also led to the phenomenon of emigration referred to by the camp-based National Union of Sahrawi Women as "a cancer devouring the Sahrawi [refugee] body" (Arabic document on file with author, author's translation). The emergence of opportunities for paid employment with NGOs in the camps (as opposed to "voluntary" and unremunerated work for the Sahrawi state-in-exile, as had previously been the case) has reinforced socioeconomic inequalities between camp inhabitants. Many graduates who are unable to obtain NGO or Polisario jobs, as well as many who *have* secured such positions, decide to leave the camps in order to send remittances to their families from Spain. Ironically, medical training designed to ensure self-sufficiency and to combat the legacies of Spanish colonialism has led ever-increasing numbers of Cuban-trained refugee doctors to leave the camps to work in the former colonial state, thereby increasing the presence of Sahrawi doctors in Spain while decreasing numbers of doctors in the camps. As a result, more Spanish doctors now travel to the camps to treat Sahrawi patients there via *comisiones médicas* (medical commissions). In response, in the 2000s the Cuban government rescinded scholarships for Sahrawi youth, contributing (along with broader geopolitical shifts) to a rupture in this line of movement and thereby ending Sahrawi refugee youth's participation in Cuba's South-South educational migration program.

Such a rupture not only changes the structure and directionalities of the Sahrawi rhizome, with existing and new lines of flight continuing to grow or erupt across time and space. It also exposes a tension that evidently exists between securing individual and family-based self-sufficiency through onward migration to Spain and ensuring that the refugee camps are locally managed with minimal interventions from non-Sahrawi humanitarians.

Any adequate evaluation of the success of the Cuban-Sahrawi educational migration system must consider many points of view over time, including retrospective evaluations of the transnational program from the perspectives of Sahrawis, Cubarauis, and non-Sahrawis alike. However, certain long-term implications of prioritizing individual and family-based self-sufficiency appear to be clear: future generations of Sahrawi children and youth will no longer be able to complete their secondary and tertiary educations in Cuba. Nonetheless, irrespective of the *actual* end of this program, Cuba's educational legacy will continue to play a significant role both in Sahrawi refugees' imaginary landscapes and in sociopolitical frameworks in the camps in the foreseeable future.

While the Cuban-Sahrawi connection has now ended, Cuba's education program for Palestinian refugees has taken on an intergenerational dimension. Indeed, Palestinian refugee camps across the Middle East are now home to a relatively large number of Palestinian-Cuban families,[8] and Palestinian-Cuban youth have reportedly been prioritized for the scholarship program since the early 2000s. These youth embody overlapping legal and political statuses even as they navigate and (re)create new and interconnecting rhizomatic lines of movement: they are simultaneously Cuban citizens and Palestinian refugees while, ideologically, it is assumed (if not desired) that they should be, become, and remain "revolutionaries" both at "home" and "away."

Palestinian graduates of Cuban universities interviewed in seven urban refugee camps in Lebanon agreed that the clear majority of Palestinian refugees had returned upon graduation "to serve our people." As with interviews conducted in Cuba and in the Sahrawi camps, the specializations offered through the scholarship program (in particular, gynecology, internal medicine, obstetrics, and pediatrics) were perceived to be "perfect" to enhance the medical self-sufficiency of the Palestinian camps and to meet the Cuban goal of benefiting the "local community." Interviewees' responses reproduced Cuba's official justification for the educational migration program almost verbatim. However, despite this stated desire, interviewees such as Ahmed stressed that "although Palestinians did decide to return to the camps, Lebanese legislation vis-à-vis Palestinians and the bad economic situation in Lebanon forced some Palestinians to leave the camps."[9] Indeed, although not necessarily successful, some graduates have attempted to leave the Palestinian camps because of the precarious socioeconomic conditions and discriminatory laws faced by Palestinians in Lebanon. Despite limited opportunities for employment within the camps, it is illegal for Palestinian refugees to seek work outside of the camps in at least twenty-five professions, including as doctors and engineers (Hanafi and Tiltnes 2009; also see Qasmiyeh and Fiddian-Qasmiyeh 2013). Thus, while structural conditions within the camps, in Lebanon more broadly, and in the international arena writ large ensure that the majority of Cuban-educated Palestinians continue to work within the camps so that Palestinian refugees are, indeed, the direct beneficiaries of the education program, the absence of legal avenues to migrate to the European Union prevents Palestinian graduates (so far) from following in Sahrawi graduates' footsteps.

Nonetheless, returning to and remaining in the refugee camps in Lebanon does not necessarily mean that Palestinian refugees' individual and collective needs have been met by these graduates in the way envisaged by Cuba. On the one hand, while they are not administratively "independent" or self-sufficient in the way that the Sahrawi camps are run (with international support) by the Sahrawi's political leadership (the Polisario Front and the Sahrawi Arab Democratic Republic), the Palestinian refugee camps are nonetheless independent spaces beyond Lebanese jurisdiction. For example, medical centers are not directly controlled by the Palestine Liberation Organization (PLO); rather, it is UNRWA and related NGOs that provide medical, educational, and other social services and who manage key camp infrastructure. On the other hand, although the Cuban education system has not enabled the development of self-sufficient camps on a collective level, Palestinian graduates have clearly benefited on an individual and, arguably, familial level. Indeed, all but one of the graduates interviewed as part of my research hold professional jobs as doctors, engineers, and lab technicians (Fiddian-Qasmiyeh 2015b). Importantly, however, not all graduates embody the Cuban aim of providing self-sufficient health care as envisaged by Cuba. While many graduates have been employed by UNRWA, others have established their own private medical clinics within the camps. The emergence of camp-based private clinics has in effect been instigated (and in many ways monopolized) by Cuban-educated Palestinians not employed by UNRWA. These graduates have thus taken a further step toward *individual* professional and socioeconomic self-sufficiency despite Cuba's official policy of offering scholarships to students to maximize professional "work that would be directed toward the national good and national development rather than the individual's upward mobility" (Breidlid 2013, 158).

In this context, it is evident that "the Sahrawi rhizome" or "the Palestinian rhizome" does not necessarily develop in isolation. Thus, it is essential in rhizomatic analyses to trace how, why, where, and when refugees' lines of movement intersect and connect with those of "other" refugees' (i.e., the Sahrawi-Cuban-Palestinian rhizome), which may tie back to one another to change the very nature and directionality of the rhizome(s) (Fiddian-Qasmiyeh 2016a, 2016b; on the Palestinian-Lebanese-Syrian rhizome, see Fiddian-Qasmiyeh 2019). These intersections highlight the importance of examining refugee-refugee relationality (Fiddian-Qasmiyeh 2016a). In the context of the discussion above, they also highlight the extent to which Lebanese and European Union policies have blocked the eruption of new lines of flight and movement outside of the confines of the Palestinian camps, arguably influencing the multiplication of lines of movement and contact within and between the camps. At the same time/place, UNRWA and other UN agencies and NGOs have "erupted" into the camps in ways that intersect with, block, and redirect particular lines of movement and action within, across, and beyond "the Palestinian rhizome." These "external" actors' own lines of movement intersect with and thus constitute the nature, growth, and directionalities of the Palestinian rhizome and the ways in which

Palestinians' rhizomatic strategies that aim to address individual, familial, and collective priorities can develop across time and space.

Mapping Sahrawi-Libyan-Palestinian Rhizomes

Until the 1980s, Libya offered scholarships for Sahrawi children as young as six to travel to Libya and later supported the education of older Sahrawi children and adolescents from the 1990s until 2011. Although Libya offered few scholarships to Palestinian refugees, a series of broader policies facilitated the South-South migration of tens of thousands of Palestinian students and workers to Libya, who in turn became part of an extensive and well-established Libyan-Palestinian community. Unlike the formal scholarships institutionalized by Muammar Gaddafi for Sahrawi refugees, Palestinians' migration to form part of Libya's transnational "eduscape" can perhaps be best conceptualized as a process of "self-service" insofar as Palestinians were encouraged to "help themselves" by migrating to Libya (Fiddian-Qasmiyeh 2015b, 6).[10]

Providing Palestinians with access to the Libyan labor market and national education system alike were notable policies in light of the broader regional insecurity faced by Palestinians, including discrimination, occupation, wars, and expulsions that have affected Palestinians across North Africa, the Middle East, and the Persian Gulf.[11] Such experiences remind us that throughout the region Palestinians continue to face violence and precarious conditions in spite of declarations of support for Pan-Arabism in general and the Palestinian cause and people in particular.[12] This is a theme I return to in more detail below, after providing a brief reflection on Sahrawi and Palestinian students' experiences of traveling to study or work in Libya.

Importantly, while Cuban-educated Sahrawis' experiences of alienation, discrimination, and marginalization are typically paralleled by high degrees of professional visibility and political audibility in the Sahrawi camps, Libyan-educated Sahrawis have in many ways remained on the margins in the camps following their return. A number of high-profile Sahrawi figures have, of course, studied in Libya (Fiddian-Qasmiyeh 2014), and yet Libyan-educated Sahrawi in the camps repeatedly informed me that refugees who had been educated in Libya and spoke only Arabic were rarely interviewed or listened to by Western visitors to the camps. This draws attention to the fact that attending school in Libya enabled/required Sahrawi children and youth to study in Modern Standard Arabic (Fus-ha) in addition to learning the Libyan dialect, with a view to either continuing their studies in Libya or following further lines of movement via educational migration within the region (i.e., to study in Algeria or Syria). These students could speak and understand multiple dialects of Arabic but were effectively monolingual upon their return to the camps and therefore had fewer opportunities to engage directly with European and North American visitors, NGOs, or researchers than their bilingual or trilingual counterparts. In turn, they had fewer opportunities to access professional employment with NGOs in the camps, to share their experiences with non-Sahrawi visitors, or to pursue onward migration to Spain.

Indeed, educational migration to Libya has not enhanced the professional or political self-sufficiency of the Sahrawi or Palestinian home-camps to the same degree as the Cuban scholarship system. On the one hand, within Libya, Palestinian refugee migrants who engaged in paid employment were not only self-sufficient but were often even prosperous and thus were able to support the socioeconomic well-being of their families in the refugee camps in Lebanon and elsewhere by sending remittances from Libya. On the other hand, however, the self-sufficiency of those Palestinians who studied and taught in Libya has not "traveled" with them upon their return to their home-camps in Lebanon. Indeed, the relatively poor employment outcomes experienced by these Palestinians following their return to Lebanon are all the more noticeable given that many of my interviewees had worked as teachers in Libyan schools during their time in North Africa. Hence, the program promoted an inverse form of self-sufficiency: Palestinian teachers enhanced Libya's educational self-sufficiency but were ultimately unable to support themselves upon their return to the camps in Lebanon.

Also paradoxical, and in contrast with the Cuban state's intergenerational support for Palestinians, Gaddafi sporadically implemented discriminatory policies, variously constituting Palestinians as part of the Libyan Self or as the quintessential Other including uneven mechanisms for the allocation of course subjects, (reportedly) banning Palestinians from starting university in the first term, and excluding Palestinians from undertaking specific courses at all (in particular, medicine or engineering) in order to strengthen his position vis-à-vis Libyan citizens (see Fiddian-Qasmiyeh 2015b). More dramatically, and linking back to the concepts of "lines of flight" and overlapping displacements outlined above, on at least three major occasions Sahrawi and Palestinian refugees faced mass expulsion from Libya on Gaddafi's orders, including in the 1980s and 1990s when Gaddafi's political relations with the Polisario and with the PLO were particularly fraught as well as, more recently, as a result of the 2011 Libyan uprising. These instances demonstrate that, even if a form of "self-reliance" in Libya had been secured via educational or labor migration, such rhizomatic strategies can be characterized by new and renewed forms of vulnerability to violence and displacement. For instance, as a means of protesting the PLO's signing of the Oslo Accords, in September 1995 Gaddafi expelled an estimated thirty thousand Palestinian refugees from Libya. This was justified by Gaddafi as an effort to support the Palestinians, to "try to secure their return to Gaza and Jericho. If Israel would not let them in, while Egypt does not allow them to pass through its territories, then I shall set a great camp [Al-Awda Camp] for them on the Egyptian-Libyan borders [Salloum border]" (Gaddafi, quoted by Sirhan in *Al-Majdal* 2010, 46).[13] In this notable example, individuals, families, and communities were simultaneously forcibly displaced and rendered immobile in sacrifice for the greater good: to force "the" durable solution of Palestinians' right to return to Palestine.

Subsequently, the outbreak of the 2011 Libyan war affected an estimated 100 Palestinian refugee scholarship holders and over 50,000–70,000 Palestinians who were working and studying in Libya at the time, as well as over 900 Sahrawi secondary- and tertiary-level students (Fiddian-Qasmiyeh 2015b). By the first week of March, the Palestinian ambassador in Tripoli announced that all 104 Palestinian refugee scholarship holders had been "evacuated" (Fiddian-Qasmiyeh 2015b), while the broader members of the Palestinian community in Libya experienced both mass-conflict-induced displacement and enforced immobility. Several thousand Palestinians were left "stranded" on the Libyan-Egyptian border, including at the Salloum crossing, where Gaddafi had created Al-Awda Camp in 1995. The eventual closure of Al-Awda Camp may have temporarily suppressed the "Palestinian" camp, a "shoot" that Gaddafi had forced to the surface of the Libyan-Egyptian border in the 1990s; however, a new line of flight in 2011 led to a camp's re-eruption in the same place at another time. This re-eruption reconnected both the new border camp and the trace of Al-Awda Camp to an ever-evolving Palestinian rhizome that is constituted through a multiplication of (current, past, future) places and spaces. The camp(s) for Palestinian refugees on the Salloum border were clearly not "solutions" for the people displaced and forcibly emplaced by the conflict in that country; simultaneously, it is clear that the "erasure" or "closure" of a camp at a particular time does not mark its end since traces remain, even as camps *in potentia*.

In contrast, refugees' home-camps have often been conceptualized and positioned as points of origin to which Palestinians and Sahrawi could and should be returned from the conflict in Libya as a "solution" to their ongoing precariousness within and on the borders of that country. In the Sahrawi case, on March 5, 2011, the Sahrawi minister of education, Mariem Salek Hmada, asserted that "all the Sahrawi students in Libya, including girls, arrived safe and healthy in the Sahrawi refugee camps. . . . The students have been repatriated under good conditions and without incident" (El-Hafed 2011). The "repatriation" of Sahrawi children from Libya to the refugee camps in (and by) Algeria highlights the fact that camps are neither merely points of departure in the Sahrawi rhizome nor places from which solutions must be sought; rather, the camps in Algeria have been positioned as the Sahrawi "home" and a point of "origin." Although return to the refugee camp-origin in such a context may well have been a "solution" for these Sahrawi adolescents, it was far from a durable solution as traditionally understood. Nonetheless, in the context of the collapse of the Libyan component of "the Sahrawi rhizome" and the Sahrawis' inability to return to the "original" *patria* (the Western Saharan homeland), such lines of flight to this "origin" demonstrate the rhizomatic nature of Sahrawi protracted displacement: rather than follow a linear process (displacement–protraction–solution), Sahrawi refugees, like so many others, are always already in the middle of displacement, where the camp is simultaneously the space of refuge and of danger, a point of origin and of departure, neither fully one nor the other.[14] This experience of simultaneity has regularly been expressed by Palestinians during my ongoing research in North Lebanon's Baddawi refugee camp. Formerly based in besieged (and now destroyed) camps and cities such as Yarmouk in Damascus, these refugees repeatedly indicated that, in fleeing Syria to Lebanon, they "arrived in the camp" and just "passed through Lebanon" (see Fiddian-Qasmiyeh 2016a, 2016b, 2019). Having crossed the Syrian-Lebanese border, my interlocutors explained that they had traveled directly to and arrived in Baddawi camp, where "established" refugee-residents offered them shelter, food, and clothes.[15] Baddawi refugee camp was identified as their intended destination point from the very outset of their journey(s), through which they retraced the lines of movement and segmentation that constitute Palestinian refugees' rhizomatic maps from their "original" home-camps in Syria to "solutions" in other Palestinians' home-camps.

Conclusion

In this chapter I argue that Sahrawi and Palestinian refugees' educational migration to Cuba and Libya can be conceptualized as one of many rhizomatic strategies embodied and enacted by refugees who are "always and already" in the middle of displacement. As such, these scholarship programs are one dimension of an ever-changing rhizomatic map that Sahrawi and Palestinian refugees use to navigate their protracted displacement landscapes while their respective quests for national self-determination remain on the distant horizon.

These educational migration programs were intentionally designed with the expectation of maximizing refugees' self-sufficiency on individual, collective, and national levels, including by fomenting diverse professional opportunities for refugees' self-reliance in their home-camps. As the case studies explored above demonstrate, although rhizomatic strategies potentially constitute a form of temporally and spatially bounded "middling solution," such processes can and do also create new ruptures and shocks that are themselves constitutive of Sahrawi and Palestinian experiences of protracted displacement. In essence, whether living in protracted home-camps, studying in (un)welcoming host states, or experiencing overlapping and new processes of displacement resulting from new and ongoing conflicts, Sahrawi and Palestinian refugees draw on rhizomatic strategies to (re)trace multidirectional lines of flight as a means of managing—and trying to thrive within, across, and beyond—constantly evolving disequilibrium.

I argue that a rhizomatic approach encourages us to identify and explore the ways in which refugees develop means both to stay alive and to develop meaningful lives for themselves and others through complex lines of movement across diverse spaces and places to which they are variously attached and yet from which their expulsion is always already imminent. While displacement is primarily a non-camp experience around the world, the Sahrawi and Palestinian cases explored here show that the experience of displacement often includes camps (past, present, and future) that serve as spaces of origin, departure, transit, and destination.

Furthermore, I suggest that, in precarious contexts, rhizomatic strategies can both provide the means for refugees to negotiate the uncertainties of life on individual, familial, and collective levels (i.e., within refugees' respective home-camps) and to support Other (or Self-Other) refugees who flee in search of safety (Fiddian-Qasmiyeh 2016a, 2016b). In this sense, Palestinian and Sahrawi refugees' ever-changing rhizomatic maps provide and develop lines of movement through which refugees can or must develop forms of refugee-refugee solidarity in contexts of overlapping processes of displacement in shared spaces of dispossession, even when such rhizomatic strategies cannot, and should not, be conceptualized as "durable solutions": the "return" or journey to the home-camp is a middling solution at best, and refugees always already embody a traveling fear of expulsion from different home and host spaces alike.

Notes

1. On the hegemonic features of the refugee regime and related discourse, see Fiddian-Qasmiyeh (2015b, 1–4, 18, 82–89).

2. For critiques and counter readings of rhizoanalysis, see Gedalof (2000) and Navaro-Yashin (2009).

3. For a related discussion, see Fiddian-Qasmiyeh (2019).

4. Malkki's critique of the sedentarist bias/basis of the traditional durable solutions

through this mode of analysis has in turn itself been subject to counter critiques, with Kibreab (1999), for instance, arguing that Malkki reifies an artificial deterritorialization of refugees' identity; in his critique he thus highlights a range of empirical "facts" that demonstrate the various forms of attachment that refugees have to their country of origin. Nonetheless, Stepputat disagrees with Kibreab's critique precisely by drawing attention to the significance of Malkki's intervention on both empirical and theoretical grounds. He argues that the need to denaturalize the links that we take for granted is entirely consistent with the acknowledgment that "displacement and migration are often accompanied by the development of a strong notion of attachment to certain places or territories" (Stepputat 1999, 418). In her own words, Malkki's approach does "not deny the importance of place in the construction of identities" (Malkki 1992, 38). Indeed, what is essential is to "examine how power works through the organization and conceptualization of space and movement" (Stepputat 1999, 416), and a rhizomatic analysis requires us to "simultaneously challenge and redefine locatedness," not deny the significance of locatedness (Gedalof 2000).

5. In the Sahrawi context, these South-South programs enabled, or even required, children as young as six to leave their refugee camp homes to complete their primary-, secondary-, and tertiary-level studies in countries including Cuba and Libya but also Algeria, the former-USSR, Mexico, Syria, and Venezuela.

6. Accurate figures do not exist of the total number of Sahrawi or Palestinian students who have studied in Libya or Cuba (see Fiddian-Qasmiyeh 2015b). According to a Polisario representative who studied in Cuba, in 2003 there were "2,000 students in Libya, 3,000 in Algeria, and 1,400 in Cuba" (Coggan 2003). On the recruitment strategies underpinning the Sahrawi and Palestinian educational migration programs, see Fiddian-Qasmiyeh (2015b).

7. On the gendered dynamics of these educational-migration programs, see Fiddian-Qasmiyeh (2014, 2015b).

8. These families are the result of relationships that began in Cuba when (primarily male) Palestinian students married (primarily female) Cuban nationals during their studies.

9. Interview in Lebanon, 2014; cited in Fiddian-Qasmiyeh (2015b).

10. I use the term "eduscape" in line with the application of Appadurai's analytic of "-scapes" (which he applies to info-, techno-, finance-, media-, and ideo-scapes) within the context of transnational education studies. See Madge, Raghuram, and Noxolo (2014).

11. Regarding access, Palestinians were exempted from visa requirements to enter and remain in Libya. On the benefits of these programs accrued by Libya, see Fiddian-Qasmiyeh (2015b).

12. On official and popular forms of "hostipitality" (following Derrida 2000a, 2000b), a term that recognizes that "hospitality inherently bears its own opposition, the ever-present possibility of hostility towards the Other who has, at one time, been welcomed at the threshold," see Fiddian-Qasmiyeh (2016b) and Fiddian-Qasmiyeh and Qasmiyeh (2016).

13. The name of the "great camp," Mukhayyam Al-Awda (the Return Camp)—

which Gaddafi established in September 1995 on the Salloum border between Libya and Egypt—clearly highlights the Palestinian right of return, as enshrined in UN Resolutions 194 and 3236.

14. Indeed, the then "unprecedented" violence in Libya in 2011 clearly demonstrates the ongoing vulnerability faced by Palestinians in the region, for whom the parallel processes of conflict-induced displacement and immobility could be conceived as part of an ongoing Nakba (catastrophe). While Sahrawi students' return to their home-camps was the "clear" solution to their vulnerability in Libya, seeking a path to safety for Palestinian refugees proved to be particularly complex. Jordan ultimately evacuated Palestinian scholarship-holders alongside their own citizens, even if these refugees did not hold Jordanian travel documents and had never lived in Jordan (see *Ma'an* 2011). These students included Palestinians who had formerly been resident in Syria, which as early as June 2011 had witnessed Syrian forces attacking Palestinian refugee camps in Yarmouk, Hama, and Latakia (Fiddian-Qasmiyeh 2015b).

15. It is notable that those Palestinians who had studied or taught in Cuba and Libya are now among the established refugees who are hosting refugees displaced by the ongoing conflict in Syria in camps across Lebanon (Fiddian-Qasmiyeh 2016a, 2016b, 2019).

Conclusion

Where Do We Go from Here?

James Milner, Megan Bradley, and
Blair Peruniak

The chapters in this volume illustrate the diverse and sometimes surprising ways that refugees and other forced migrants engage with resolution processes. Across contexts and time, refugees have often demonstrated a remarkable capacity to navigate or influence complex structures and institutional arrangements designed and implemented with the stated intention of providing assistance and solutions. Frequently, these efforts can contribute to refugees advancing solutions to their own displacement or to resolving the conditions that forced refugees to flee. These responses may be in tension—real or perceived—with the solutions being pursued by institutional actors, such as states and international organizations. In some instances, refugees may seek to influence institutional responses. In others, they may resist or contest programs or categories, seek to subvert these processes, or bypass institutional responses altogether. In a range of other instances, they may be prominent in institutional processes but often in only symbolic and performative ways.

This book has not sought to develop a single, generalizable theory on refugees' roles in displacement processes. However, the work underscores refugees' clear, if also complex and heterogeneous, capacities to shape resolution processes. The chapters suggest that institutional behaviors and policies pertaining to resolution processes cannot be neatly distinguished from the individual and collective efforts and influence of refugees themselves, as if they are discrete "levels of analysis." Rather, much more focused and sustained work is needed to understand this relationship more fully and to map more systematically the moments and pathways through which refugees influence and contest resolution processes.

The chapters in this volume have engaged with the role of refugees in resolution processes from different methodological and disciplinary perspectives across cases and in different contexts. In this way, they illustrate that no single approach has a monopoly on understanding and explaining the complexities of refugee engagement. As such, this book does not propose a single disciplinary or methodological approach to future research on these issues. Instead, this conclusion identifies certain moments, processes, and dynamics that can usefully serve as the focus of future research while also suggesting important insights for future policy and practice. These relate to: the participation of refugees in institutional processes, the construction and significance of categories, the scope and meaning of agency, and the mechanisms of representation.

Participation and Mechanisms

Institutional actors frequently assume that forced migrants want to participate in institutional processes, that the forms of this participation can be prescribed by institutional actors, and that these prescribed forms can ensure that refugees' perspectives can be substantively reflected in institutional processes. In contrast, the preceding chapters outline some of the various ways that refugees may participate that are outside the scope of institutional frameworks, highlighting how they may also avoid participation in processes as prescribed by institutional actors. What are the challenges raised by these forms of participation, and what are the alternatives? A recent experience from the United Nations provides a helpful context in which to begin answering this question.

Largely in response to the European refugee and migration crisis in 2015, the UN secretary-general at the time, Ban Ki-moon, initiated a process to develop more predictable responses to major movements of refugees and migrants. These efforts included the 2016 report from the secretary-general, *In Safety and Dignity: Addressing Large Movements of Refugees and Migrants*, and preparations for a UN High-Level Summit on September 19, 2016. The summit concluded with the UN General Assembly adopting the New York Declaration, a statement of principles intended to serve as the basis for negotiating two global compacts by 2018: the Global Compact on Refugees and the Global Compact on Safe, Orderly and Regular Migration.

At the opening plenary of the summit, refugee Mohammed Badran and migrant Eni Lestari Andayani Adi offered statements alongside the UN secretary-general, heads of UN agencies, and other institutional actors. Some pointed to this as a demonstration of a commitment to include refugees' perspectives, but the text of the New York Declaration had been negotiated by states months earlier and sent for translation weeks before the summit. In fact, the negotiation of the declaration had states as the central actors, with international organizations and civil society groups involved only indirectly. While refugees were invited by the president of the UN General Assembly to submit statements and videos describing their experiences, these statements were circulated only after the declaration had been concluded. The inclusion of a refugee and a migrant in the formal meeting was a symbolic recognition of the need for their perspectives to be integrated, but the process did not include opportunities for their substantive engagement.

This tension is not unique to institutional responses to refugees. In the area of international development, for example, Patrick Bond (2006) describes how the negotiation of global development targets, such as the Millennium Development Goals, are typically the domain of institutional actors, conducted in capitals, and involve limited substantive engagement by the supposed beneficiaries of such targets, namely the global poor. While recognizing the clear practical limitations to the participation of a billion individuals in such institutionalized processes, Bond notes that the lack of participation should, at minimum, condition the claims made about the legitimacy and representativeness of such agreements. Likewise, more active and substantive participation may be expected in the process of implementing global programs in local contexts.

Understanding the distinctive nature of the implementation process may be especially important in future research on the roles of refugees in resolution processes, especially given recent work that illustrates the contestation inherent in the processes of implementation and localization of international norms and peacebuilding initiatives (Autesserre 2010; Betts and Orchard 2014). Indeed, a useful focus of future research and practice in this area could be on the implementation process. Given that global institutional processes are highly choreographed and privilege institutional actors, and given the diversity of contexts and dynamics illustrated by the contributions to this volume, efforts to understand and encourage participation may usefully be concentrated on (among other concerns) the processes by which global standards are implemented in diverse local contexts (Milner 2014b; Milner and Wojnarowicz 2017). Indeed, the rich empirical examples of refugee involvement and innovation in resolution processes detailed in this book are in contexts where the global meets the local, which is the context in which implementation occurs.

Institutional actors such as UNHCR have reaffirmed the importance of refugee participation in the planning and delivery of programs. One of

UNHCR's "five core directions" for 2017 to 2021 is to empower displaced persons, pledging (UNHCR 2017, 24) that "we will take all possible steps to ensure that people of concern can participate in decisions that affect them and thereby gain better control over their own destinies. We will build on the resilience, knowledge, and skills of displaced and stateless people, recognizing them as agents with the potential to determine and build their own future and contribute to the development of the communities where they live." Likewise, paragraph 106 of the Global Compact on Refugees includes the provision that "States and relevant stakeholders will facilitate meaningful participation of refugees . . . [in follow-up meetings], ensuring the inclusion of their perspectives on progress."[1]

While potentially important, proponents of such forms of participation must be critically aware of the issues of power, capacity, and choice highlighted throughout this book. Such forms of engagement do not occur in neutral contexts but in environments where there are substantial asymmetries of power between individuals and institutions.[2] Participation in institutional processes of implementation needs to include scope for contesting and adapting global policies and programs being implemented in local contexts while accounting for the complex and often conflicting relationships between individuals and institutional actors. While UNHCR's recent emphasis on empowerment is encouraging, if it is to be anything more than idealistic rhetoric or tokenism, it must address the long-standing tendency for institutional actors to see their work as providing and prescribing solutions to displaced populations. Empowerment, in brief, must mean that institutional actors are willing to design and significantly adapt policies and programs starting from the interests and perspectives of refugees. Likewise, empowerment also needs to involve conversations with refugees on how their active involvement can be supported in terms of creating conditions favorable to substantive, sustained, and meaningful dialogue.

Notwithstanding such emphases on empowerment and engagement, various contributors to this book suggest that refugees may still eschew active involvement in institutional processes, favoring forms of engagement that are not easily inserted into formal structures or institutional frameworks. In this sense, nonparticipation in institutional processes may be equally or more significant than formal participation. Avoiding contact with institutional actors may be a conscious and considered strategy as it precludes the need to conform to categories and requirements of institutional programs. This has long been recognized in the context of refugees who prefer the anonymity of living in urban spaces, notwithstanding the associated precarity, or those who move outside of the conditions of established migration, repatriation, or resettlement programs. While institutional actors often deem such behavior "deviant" (Hyndman and Giles 2011), it is important for future work on the roles of refugees in resolution processes to not privilege certain forms of participation in the search for solutions over others.

Categories

In a similar way, the contributions to this book illustrate the importance of not privileging the use of certain categories and the need for continued, critical reflection on the meaning and consequences of the use of categories. As illustrated by Roger Zetter (1991), and Michael Barnett and Martha Finnemore (2004), among many others, categories are a central tool of institutional actors to manage and organize populations in the context of developing responses to social challenges. Such categories, however, can produce a range of consequences and serve as a basis of exclusion as much as inclusion. Several chapters in this book illustrate how refugees resist or contest these categories and their consequences, both in terms of the pursuit of durable solutions—from repatriation and local integration to resettlement—and in the context of peacebuilding and reconstruction following natural disasters.

This underscores the importance of at least two challenges for research and practice. The first relates to the need for ongoing critical analysis of the interests that contribute to the construction of categories. If institutional actors, such as UNHCR, are indeed committed to more actively helping to empower those who are displaced, as suggested above, it will be necessary to more critically understand the roles that categories play in both enabling and constraining this process. If participation is predicated on the inclusion of certain categories of individuals, it will be necessary to consider more fully how these categories are constructed, by whom, and to what end. This speaks to the need to further understand the productive power of international organizations, the consequences of the categories produced, and the various forms of contestation and resistance that are demonstrated by refugees in response to the often constraining and conditioning force of categories (Milner and Wojnarowicz 2017).

The second challenge relates to the use of institutional categories to delineate and determine, both practically and analytically, what forms of action are to be included in scholarly and policy-focused understandings of resolution processes. Traditionally, "durable solutions" for refugees consist of the trinity of voluntary repatriation, local integration, and resettlement. Often the search for these solutions unfolds as part of distinct categories of activity that constitute "peacebuilding." These areas have their own processes and moments around which the activities of institutional actors are convention-ally understood and examined. But as the empirical chapters of this book make clear, the engagement of refugees themselves does not always fall neatly into these categories and moments. A privileging of the categories and pro-cesses employed by institutional actors can efface the various forms of en-gagement demonstrated by refugees and inadvertently exclude them from understandings of what has been achieved and what might be possible vis-à-vis resolution processes. As outlined in the introduction, "displaced per-sons' self-styled strategies to resolve displacement or grapple with the chal-lenges and opportunities it presents often unfold under the radar of states and humanitarian agencies' managerial efforts."An important lesson that emerges from this book is the recognition of just how wide a range of strategies do unfold both under the radar and in plain sight.

Agency

The contributions to this collection all highlight the need for ongoing re-flection on the meaning and manifestations of refugee agency. Despite the significant variation in methods, theoretical frameworks, and the contexts considered in the book, the chapters all highlight the central importance of critical reflection on the agency of refugees and the relationship between that agency and the structures that refugees navigate. Many contributions to this book highlight the importance of intersectional analysis to understand how the ability of individuals to express their agency is conditioned by the intertwining of a diverse range of identities, interests, and power relations. In the introduction, we note that we use the term "refugee agency" as an "im-perfect shorthand for the ability of displaced individuals (and, in some cases, communities) to make and enact choices that potentially affect outcomes, particularly of resolution processes, recognizing that the extent to which dis-placed persons can exercise agency generally and in certain circumstances will depend on complex, shifting political, socioeconomic, cultural, histori-cal, and institutional structures." Many chapters in this volume illustrate how challenging yet necessary it is to further develop understandings of the mean-ings and manifestations of refugee agency, along with appreciation of the role of structures and diverse forms of power that may condition expressions of agency. Ultimately, however, as the chapters in this volume underscore, refu-gees often act to shape resolution processes, even in the context of highly re-strictive structures. The challenge remains for scholarship, policy, and practice to continue to become sufficiently honed and analytically aware to identify, better understand, and more effectively respond to refugees' diverse expres-sions of agency, including in their more surprising forms.

Conclusion

The preceding chapters illustrate the diversity of refugees' experiences in resolution processes and perspectives on their roles. Together they call for much more research on these issues, but research that is critically self-aware of the potential limitations of the analytical categories that have tradition-ally informed scholarship in this area. They call for methodological mod-esty in our efforts to generalize findings and point to the potential benefits of more participatory approaches to future research. For policy and practice, the chapters reaffirm the long-standing view that the participation of ref-ugees must involve the meaningful adaptation of global programs to local contexts and refugees' own perspectives and strategies. But the volume also points to the need to explore and appreciate the evolving consequences of categories in resolution processes and recognizes that helping to empower refugees may involve a greater willingness on the part of institutional actors to recognize, analyze, and adapt to nonparticipation, resistance, and contesta-tion of institutional responses. As the chapters of this book make clear, these are often considered strategies adopted by individuals who face seemingly impossible choices.

Notes

1. "Global Compact on Refugees, Draft Two," UNHCR, April 30, 2018, para. 109, http://www.unhcr.org/5ae758d07.

2. The Network for Refugee Voices has found that refugee participation in the development of the Global Compact on Refugees has been facilitated by refugee representatives speaking to the agenda established by states and learning to use lan-guage and behavior that replicates the performance of states in such settings rather than expecting institutional actors to create alternative approaches to engage with the perspectives and priorities of refugees. See "Should Refugees Shape Global Refugee Policy?," Network for Refugee Voices website, n.d., http://www.network forrefugeevoices.org/, accessed May 15, 2018.

References

Abu-Lughod, Lila. 1990. "The Romance of Resistance: Tracing Transformations of Power through Bedouin Women." *American Ethnologist* 17 (1): 41–55.

Adelman, Howard. 2002. "Refugee Repatriation." In *Ending Civil Wars: The Implementation of Peace Agreements*, edited by Stephen John Stedman, Donald Rothchild, and Elizabeth M. Cousens, 273–302. Boulder, CO: Lynne Rienner.

Afghanistan Independent Human Rights Commission (AIHRC). 2005. *A Call for Justice: Conclusion of National Consultation on Transitional Justice in Afghanistan*. Kabul: Afghanistan Independent Human Rights Commission.

Agamben, Giorgio. 1998. *Sovereign Power and Bare Life*. Palo Alto, CA: Stanford University Press.

Agblorti, Samuel K. M. 2011. *Refugee Integration in Ghana: The Host Community's Perspective*. Geneva: UNHCR Policy Development and Evaluation Service.

Agencia Cubana de Noticias (ACN) (2006). "Sahara: 30 años de exilio y lucha." *Agencia Cubana de Noticias*, February 22. http://www.rebelion.org/noticia.php?id=27171.

Ager, Alastair, Wendy Ager, and Lynellyn D. Long. 1995. "The Differential Experience of Mozambican Refugee Women and Men." *Journal of Refugee Studies* 8 (3): 265–87.

Ager, Alastair, and Alison Strang. 2008. "Understanding Integration: A Conceptual Framework." *Journal of Refugee Studies* 21 (2): 166–91.

Agier, Michel. 2011. *Managing the Undesirables: Refugee Camps and Humanitarian Government*. Cambridge, UK: Polity.

Aguilera, Michael B., and Douglas S. Massey. 2003. "Social Capital and the Wages of Mexican Migrants: New Hypotheses and Tests." *Social Forces* 82 (2): 671–701.

Ahonen, Pertti. 2003. *After the Expulsion: West Germany and Eastern Europe, 1945–1990*. Oxford: Oxford University Press.

Aidoo, Ata. 2008. "A Refugee's Dilemma: Biting the Fingers That Feed You." *Ghana Web*, March 22. https://www.ghanaweb.com/GhanaHomePage/features/A-refugee-s-dilemma-Biting-the-hands-that-feed-you-140974

Al Husseini, Jalal. 2007. "The Arab States and the Refugee Issue: A Retrospective View." In *Israel and the Palestinian Refugees*, edited by Eyal Benvenisti, Chaim Gans, and Sari Hanafi, 435–63. Dordrecht: Springer.

Aleinikoff, T. Alexander. 1992. "State-Centered Refugee Law: From Resettlement to Containment." *Michigan Journal of International Law* 14 (120): 120–38.

Allan, Diana. 2014. *Refugees of the Revolution: Experiences of Palestinian Exile*. Palo Alto, CA: Stanford University Press.

Allen, Tim, ed. 1994. *In Search of Cool Ground: War, Flight and Homecoming in Northeast Africa*. Oxford: James Currey.

Allen, Tim, and Hubert Morsink. 1994. *When Refugees Go Home*. United Nations Research Institute for Social Development in association with James Currey. London: Africa World Press.

Al-Majdal. 2010. "The Palestinian Crisis in Libya 1994–1996: Interview with Professor Bassem Sirhan." *Al-Majdal*, no. 45: "Forced Secondary Displacement: Palestinian Refugees in the Gaza Strip, Iraq, Jordan, and Libya," http://www.badil.org/en/publication/periodicals/al-majdal/itemlist/category/197-issue-45.html.

Alsop, Ruth, Mette Frost Bertelsen, and Jeremy Holland. 2006. *Empowerment in Practice: From Analysis to Implementation*. Washington, DC: International Bank for Reconstruction and Development / World Bank.

Amnesty International. 2013. *Haiti: 15 Minutes to Leave: Denial of the Right to Adequate Housing in Post-Quake Haiti*. London: Amnesty International. https://www.amnesty.org/en/documents/amr36/001/2015/en/.

Andersson, Ruben. 2013. *Illegality, Inc.: Clandestine Migration and the Business of Bordering Europe*. Oakland: University of California Press.

Annan, Kofi. 2005. Address to the Executive Committee of the Office of the United Nations High Commissioner for Refugees. Geneva, October 6.

Arendt, Hannah. 2004. *The Origins of Totalitarianism*. New York: Schocken.

———. 2013. *The Human Condition*. Chicago: University of Chicago Press.

Autesserre, Séverine. 2010. *The Trouble with the Congo: Local Violence and the Failure of International Peacebuilding*. Cambridge: Cambridge University Press.

Azzam, Fateh, ed. 2006. *A Tragedy of Failures and False Expectations: Report on the Events surrounding the Three-Month Sit-In and Forced Removal of Sudanese Refugees in Cairo, September–December 2005*. Cairo: American University in Cairo.

Bailey, Sarah. 2014. *Humanitarian Crises, Emergency Preparedness and Response: A Strategy and Options Analysis of Haiti*. London: Overseas Development Institute. https://www.odi.org/sites/odi.org.uk/files/odi-assets/publications-opinion-files/8788.pdf

Baines, Erin K. 2007. "The Haunting of Alice: Local Approaches to Justice and Reconciliation in Northern Uganda." *International Journal of Transitional Justice* 1 (1): 91–114.

———. 2015. "'Today, I Want to Speak Out the Truth': Victim Agency, Responsibility, and Transitional Justice." *International Political Sociology* 9 (4): 316–32.

———. 2017. *Buried in the Heart: Women, Complex Victimhood and the War in Northern Uganda*. Cambridge: Cambridge University Press.

Barnett, Michael. 2011a. *Empire of Humanity: A History of Humanitarianism.* Ithaca, NY: Cornell University Press.

———. 2011b. "Humanitarianism, Paternalism, and the UNHCR." In *Refugees in International Relations*, edited by Alexander Betts and Gil Loescher, 105–32. Oxford: Oxford University Press.

———. 2012. "International Paternalism and Humanitarian Governance." *Global Constitutionalism* 1 (3): 485–521.

———. 2017. *Paternalism beyond Borders.* Cambridge: Cambridge University Press.

Barnett, Michael, and Raymond Duvall. 2005. "Power in Global Governance." In *Power in Global Governance*, edited by Michael Barnett and Raymond Duvall, 1–32. Cambridge: Cambridge University Press.

Barnett, Michael, and Martha Finnemore. 2004. *Rules for the World: International Organizations in Global Politics.* Ithaca, NY: Cornell University Press.

Baron, Nick. 2009. "Remaking Soviet Society: The Filtration of Returnees from Nazi Germany, 1944–49." In *Warlands: Population Resettlement and State Reconstruction in the Soviet-East European Borderlands, 1945–50*, edited by Peter Gatrell and Nick Baron, 89–116. Basingstoke, UK: Palgrave Macmillan.

Barutciski, Michael. 2008. "Lausanne Revisited: Population Exchanges in International Law and Policy." In *Crossing the Aegean: An Appraisal of the 1923 Compulsory Population Exchange between Greece and Turkey*, edited by Renee Hirschon, 23–38. New York: Berghahn.

Bassel, Leah. 2012. *Refugee Women: Beyond Gender versus Culture.* London: Routledge.

Batarseh, Robert C. 2016. "Inside/Outside the Circle: From the Indochinese Designated Class to Contemporary Group Processing." *Refuge: Canada's Journal on Refugees* 32 (2): 54–66.

Bauman, Zygmunt. 1998. *Globalization: The Human Consequences.* New York: Columbia University Press.

Bayat, Asef. 2009. *Life as Politics: How Ordinary People Change the Middle East.* Stanford, CA: Stanford University Press.

Beall, Jo, and Daniel Esser. 2005. *Shaping Urban Futures: Challenges to Governing and Managing Afghan Cities.* Kabul: Afghanistan Research and Evaluation Unit.

Beauchemin, Cris. 2014. "A Manifesto for Quantitative Multi-Sited Approaches to International Migration." *International Migration Review* 48 (4): 921–38.

Beck, Ulrich. 2009. "Imagined Communities of Global Risk." Lecture for the Risk Conference in Shanghai. First draft, uncorrected version.

Bellamy, Catheryne, Simone Haysom, Caitlin Wake, and Veronique Barbelet. 2017. "The Lives and Livelihoods of Syrian Refugees: A Study of Refugee Perspectives and Their Institutional Environment in Turkey and Jordan." *Humanitarian Policy Group.* London: Overseas Development Institute.

Betts, Alexander. 2013. *Survival Migration: Failed Governance and the Crisis of Displacement.* Ithaca, NY: Cornell University Press.

Betts, Alexander, and Paul Collier. 2017. *Refuge: Transforming a Broken Refugee System.* London: Allen Lane.

Betts, Alexander, and Will Jones. 2016. *Mobilising the Diaspora: How Refugees Challenge Authoritarianism.* Cambridge: Cambridge University Press.

Betts, Alexander, and Phil Orchard. 2014. *Implementation and World Politics: How International Norms Change Practice*. Oxford: Oxford University Press.

Beunza, Alfonso Calzadilla, and Ignacio Martin Eresta. 2011. "An Evaluation of the Haiti Earthquake 2010: Meeting Shelter Needs: Issues, Achievements, and Constraints." Commissioned by IFRC. adore.ifrc.org/Download.aspx?FileId=83619& .pdf.

Bikundo, Edwin. 2012. "The International Criminal Court and Africa: Exemplary Justice." *Law and Critique* 23 (1): 21–41.

Black, Richard, and Khalid Koser, eds. 1999. *The End of the Refugee Cycle? Refugee Repatriation and Reconstruction*. Oxford: Berghahn.

Blattman, Christopher. 2009. "From Violence to Voting: War and Political Participation in Uganda." *American Political Science Review* 103 (2): 231–47.

Bloch, Alice, Sigona Nando, and Roger Zetter. 2014. *Sans papiers: The Social and Economic Lives of Young Undocumented Migrants*. London: Pluto Press.

Bloche, Joseph, and Mitu Gulati. 2016. "Competing for Refugees: A Market-Based Solution to a Humanitarian Crisis." *Columbia Human Rights Law Review* 48 (1): 53–111.

Blue, Sarah A. 2005. "Including Women in Development: Guatemalan Refugees and Local NGOs." *Latin American Perspectives* 32 (5): 101–17.

Bond, Patrick. 2006. "Global Governance Campaigning and MDGs: From Top-Down to Bottom-Up Anti-Poverty Work." *Third World Quarterly* 27 (2): 339–54.

Bookman, Milica Zarkovic. 1997. *The Demographic Struggle for Power*. London: Frank Cass.

Bornat, Joanna. 2008. "Biographical Methods." In *The Sage Handbook of Social Research Methods*, edited by P. Alasuutari, L. Bickman, and J. Brannen, 244–56. London: Sage.

Bradley, Megan. 2008. "Back to Basics: The Conditions of Just Refugee Returns." *Journal of Refugee Studies* 21 (3): 285–304.

————. 2012. "Truth-Telling and Displacement: Patterns and Prospects." In *Transitional Justice and Displacement*, edited by Roger Duthie, 189–232. New York: Social Science Research Council.

————. 2013a. *Refugee Repatriation: Justice, Responsibility and Redress*. Cambridge: Cambridge University Press.

————. 2013b. "Rethinking Return: Defining Success in Refugee Repatriation." *World Politics Review*, 3.

————. 2014. "Rethinking Refugeehood: Statelessness, Repatriation, and Refugee Agency." *Review of International Studies* 40 (1): 101–23.

————, ed. 2015. *Forced Migration, Reconciliation and Justice*. Montreal: McGill-Queen's University Press.

Bradley, Megan, James Milner, and Blair Peruniak. 2015. "Beyond Beneficiaries: Exploring Displaced Persons' Roles in Resolution Processes." Background paper prepared for workshop on "Beyond Beneficiaries: Understanding Displaced Persons' Roles in Resolution Processes," McGill University, Montreal, December 14–15, 2015.

Braithwaite, John, Hilary Charlesworth, Peter Reddy, and Leah Dunn. 2010. *Reconciliation and Architectures of Commitment: Sequencing Peace in Bougainville*. Acton, ACT: Australian National University Press.

Bratman, Michael. 2014a. "Rational and Social Agency: Reflections and Replies." In *Rational and Social Agency: The Philosophy of Michael Bratman*, edited by Manuel Vargas and Gideon Yaffe, 294–335. New York: Oxford University Press.

———. 2014b. *Shared Agency: A Planning Theory of Acting Together*. Oxford: Oxford University Press.

Breidlid, Anders. 2013. *Indigenous Knowledge and Development in the Global South*. London: Routledge.

Breton, Albert, and Margot Breton. 1997. "Democracy and Empowerment." In *Understanding Democracy: Economic and Political Perspectives*, edited by Albert Breton et al., 176–83. New York: Cambridge University Press.

Brookings Institution. 2015. "What Lessons Can Be Drawn from the Work of the U.N. Special Rapporteur and the Brookings Project over the Past 22 Years?" Panel, Internal Displacement: Lessons Learned after 20 Years and Challenges Ahead, Washington, DC, June 26.

Brun, Cathrine. 2003. "Local Citizens or Internally Displaced Persons? Dilemmas of Long Term Displacement in Sri Lanka." *Journal of Refugee Studies* 16 (4): 376–97.

———. 2015. "Active Waiting and Changing Hopes: Toward a Time Perspective on Protracted Displacement." *Social Analysis* 59 (1): 19–37.

Brynen, Rex. 1990. "The Politics of Exile: The Palestinians in Lebanon." *Journal of Refugee Studies* 3 (3): 204–27.

Burgess, Katrina. 2014. "Unpacking the Diaspora Channel in New Democracies: When Do Migrants Act Politically Back Home?" *Studies in Comparative International Development* 49 (1): 13–43.

Burma Lawyers' Council. 2007. "Analysis on the Situation of the Refugee Camps from the Rule of Law Aspect." *LawKa Pala: Legal Journal on Burma* 26: 38–62.

Burma Partnership. 2012. *Nothing about Us without Us*. Video, www.burmapartnership.org/nauwu/.

Burma Partnership and Burma Link. 2015. *Voices of Refugees: Situation of Burma's Refugees along the Thailand-Burma Border*. Briefing paper, http://www.burmalink.org/briefing-paper-voices-of-refugees-situation-of-burmas-refugees-along-the-thailand-burma-border/.

Butler, Judith. 1997. *The Psychic Life of Power: Theories in Subjection*. Stanford, CA: Stanford University Press.

Cadge, Wendy, and Elaine Howard Ecklund. 2007. "Immigration and Religion." *Annual Review of Sociology* 33: 359–79.

Calhan, Greger. 2014. "Forced Evictions, Mass Displacement, and the Uncertain Promise of Land and Property Restitution in Haiti." *Hastings Race & Poverty Law Journal* 11 (1): 157–200.

Callamard, Agnes. 1994a. "Malawi Refugee Policy, International Politics and the One-Party Regime." *Journal of International Affairs* 47 (2): 535–56.

———. 1994b. "Refugees and Local Hosts: A Study of the Trading Interactions between Mozambican Refugees and Malawian Villagers in the District of Mwanza." *Journal of Refugee Studies* 7 (1): 39–62.

Campbell, Bryce. 2012. "Addressing Concerns about Transitional Justice in Displacement Contexts: A Humanitarian Perspective." In *Transitional Justice and Displacement*, edited by Roger Duthie, 65–67. New York: Social Science Research Council.

Campbell, Elizabeth H. 2006. "Urban Refugees in Nairobi: Problems of Protection, Mechanisms of Survival, and Possibilities for Integration. *Journal of Refugee Studies* 19 (3): 396–413.

Campbell, Elizabeth, Jeff Crisp, and Esther Kiragu. 2011. *Navigating Nairobi: A Review of the Implementation of UNHCR's Urban Refugee Policy in Kenya's Capital City.* Geneva: UNHCR.

Carens, Joseph H. 2013. *The Ethics of Immigration.* New York: Oxford University Press.

Carmona, Magdalena Sepulveda, and Kate Donald. 2015. "Beyond Legal Empowerment: Improving Access to Justice from the Human Rights Perspective." *International Journal of Human Rights* 19 (3): 242–59.

Casasola, Michael. 2001. "Current Trends and New Challenges for Canada's Resettlement Program." *Refuge: Canada's Journal on Refugees* 19 (4): 41–53.

Castells, Manuel. 2002. "The Space of Flows." In *The Castells Reader on Cities and Social Theory*, edited by Manuel Castells and Ida Susser, 314–65. Oxford: Blackwell.

Chamberlayne, Prue, Janna Bornat, and Tom Wengraf, eds. 2000. *The Turn to Biographical Methods in Social Science.* London: Routledge.

Chandler, David. 2015. "Resilience and the 'Everyday': Beyond the Paradox of 'Liberal Peace.'" *Review of International Studies* 41 (1): 27–48.

Chatty, Dawn. 2010. "Palestinian Refugee Youth: Agency and Aspiration." *Refugee Survey Quarterly* 28 (2–3): 318–38.

Chimni, Bhupinder S. 1999. "From Resettlement to Involuntary Repatriation: Towards a Critical History of Durable Solutions to Refugee Problems." *New Issues in Refugee Research*, Working Paper No. 2. Geneva: UNHCR.

———. 2002. "Refugees and Post-Conflict Reconstruction: A Critical Perspective." *International Peacekeeping* 9 (2): 163–80.

———. 2004. "From Resettlement to Involuntary Repatriation: Towards a Critical History of Durable Solutions to Refugee Problems." *Refugee Survey Quarterly* 23 (3): 55–73.

Clark, Christina. 2007. "Understanding Vulnerability: From Categories to Experiences of Young Congolese People in Uganda." *Children and Society* 21 (4): 284–96.

Clark, Phil. 2014. "Bringing Them All Back Home: The Challenges of DDR and Transitional Justice in Contexts of Displacement in Rwanda and Uganda." *Journal of Refugee Studies* 27 (2): 234–59.

Clark-Kazak, Christina. 2009. "Towards a Working Definition and Application of Social Age in International Development Studies." *Journal of Development Studies* 45 (8): 1307–24.

———. 2010. "The Politics of Protection: Aid, Human Rights Discourse, and Power Relations in Kyaka II Settlement, Uganda." *Disasters* 34 (1): 55–70.

————. 2011. *Recounting Migration: Political Narratives of Congolese Young People in Uganda.* Montreal: McGill-Queen's University Press.

————. 2014. "'A refugee is someone who refused to be oppressed': Self-Survival Strategies of Congolese Young People in Uganda." *Stability: International Journal of Security and Development* 3 (1): Art. 13.

Coffie, Amanda. 2003. "Impact of Refugees on Their Host Community: The Case of Liberian Refugees in Ghana." Unpublished essay presented to the Department of Political Science, University of Ghana.

————. 2012. "Ghana's Asylum Policy and Practices since Independence." In *Public Policy Making in Ghana: How Politicians and Civil Servants Deal with Public Problems*, edited by Frank L. K. Ohmeng, Barbara W. Carroll, Joseph R. A. Ayee, and Alexander Bilson Darku, 157–89. New York: Edwin Mellen Press.

————. 2013. "Returning to Rebuild: Forced Migration, Resource Transformation and Reintegration of Liberian Returnees from Ghana and Guinea." PhD dissertation, Carleton University, Ontario.

————. 2014. "Filling in the Gap: Refugee Returnees Deploy Higher Education Skills to Peacebuilding." *Refugee Survey Quarterly* 33 (4): 1–28.

————. 2015. *Hidden Resources: Refugee Experience and the Politics of Peacebuilding.* Berlin: Lambert.

Coggan, Felicity. 2003. "Sahrawi Leader Tours New Zealand." *The Militant*, June 23.

Cohen, Roberta. 2007. "Response to Hathaway." *Journal of Refugee Studies* 3 (1): 370–76.

Cohen, Roberta, and Megan Bradley. 2010. "Disasters and Displacement: Gaps in Protection." *Journal of International Humanitarian Legal Studies* 1 (1): 95–142.

Cohen, Robert, and Francis Deng. 1998. *Masses in Flight: The Global Crisis of Internal Displacement.* Washington, DC: Brookings Institution Press.

Colic-Peisker, Val, and Farida Tilbury. 2003. "'Active' and 'Passive' Resettlement: The Influence of Support Services and Refugees' Own Resources on Resettlement Style." *International Migration* 41 (5): 61–91.

Collins, Patricia Hill, and Valerie Chepp. 2013. "Intersectionality." In *Oxford Handbook of Gender and Politics*, edited by Georgina Waylen, Karen Celis, Johanna Kantola, and S. Laurel Weldon, 60–85. Oxford: Oxford University Press.

Comaroff, Jean, and John L. Comaroff. 2012. *Theory from the South: Or, How Euro-America Is Evolving toward Africa.* Boulder, CO: Paradigm.

Conferencia Episcopal Colombiana. 1995. *Derechos humanos y desplazamiento interno en Colombia.* Bogota: Editorial Kimpres.

Connell, Raewyn. 2007. "The Northern Theory of Globalization." *Sociological Theory* 25 (4): 368–85.

Cooke, Bill, and Uma Kothari, eds. 2001. *Participation: The New Tyranny?* London: Zed.

Cooper, Dereck. 1992. *Urban Refugees: Ethiopians and Eritreans in Cairo.* Cairo: American University in Cairo Press.

Cooper, Elizabeth. 2007. "Praxis in a Refugee Camp? Meanings of Participation and

Empowerment for Long-Term Refugee Youth." *Children, Youth and Environments* 17 (3): 104–21.

Costy, Alexander. 2004. "The Peace Dividend in Mozambique, 1987–1997." In *Durable Peace: Challenges for Peacebuilding in Africa*, edited by Taiser Ali and Robert Matthew, 142–82. Toronto: University of Toronto Press.

Coulter, Chris. 2008. "Female Fighters in the Sierra Leone War: Challenging the Assumptions?" *Feminist Review* 88 (1): 54–73.

Crapanzano, Vincent. 2004. *Imaginative Horizons: An Essay in Literary-Philosophical Anthropology*. Chicago: University of Chicago Press.

Crawford, Nicholas, John Cosgrave, Simone Haysom, and Nadine Walicki. 2015. *Protracted Displacement: Uncertain Paths to Self-Reliance in Exile*. London: ODI Humanitarian Policy Group.

Crenshaw, Kimberle W. 1991. "Mapping the Margins: Intersectionality, Identity Politics, and Violence against Women of Color." *Stanford Law Review* 43 (6): 1241–99.

Cristo, J. F. 2012. *La guerra por las víctimas: Lo que nunca se supo de la Ley*. Bogota: Ediciones B.

Crivello, G., and Elena Fiddian-Qasmiyeh. 2010. "The Ties That Bind: Sahrawi Children and the Mediation of Aid in Exile." In *Deterritorialised Afghan and Sahrawi Youth: Refugees from the Margins of the Middle East*, edited by D. Chatty, 85–118. Oxford: Berghahn.

da Costa, Rosa. 2006. *The Administration of Justice in Refugee Camps: A Study of Practice*. Geneva: UNHCR, Division of International Protection.

Das, Veena. 2007. *Life and Words: Violence and the Descent into the Ordinary*. Berkeley: University of California Press.

Davis, Ian. 2012. "What Is the Vision for Sheltering and Housing in Haiti? Summary Observations of Reconstruction Progress following the Haiti Earthquake of January 12th 2010." https://reliefweb.int/sites/reliefweb.int/files/resources/Situation_Report_215.pdf.

Davis, J. 1992. "The Anthropology of Suffering." *Journal of Refugee Studies* 5 (2): 149–61.

De Boeck, Filip, and Marie-Françoise Plissart. 2004. *Kinshasa: Tales of the Invisible City*. Brussels: Luidon.

De Certeau, Michel. 1984. *The Practice of Everyday Life*. Berkeley: University of California Press.

de Greiff, Pablo. 2008. *The Handbook of Reparations*. Oxford: Oxford University Press.
———. 2013. "Transitional Justice and Development." www.developmentideas.info/website/wp-content/uploads/Ch24_TransitionalJustice_PablodeGreiff_2013.pdf.

Deleuze, Gilles, and Félix Guattari. 2013. *A Thousand Plateaus*. London: Bloomsbury.

Deneulin, Séverine. 2009. "Democracy and Political Participation." In *An Introduction to the Human Development and Capability Approach: Freedom and Agency*, edited by Séverine Deneulin and Lila Shahani, 185–202. London: Earthscan.

Deng, Francis. 1994. "Internally Displaced Persons: Report of the Representative of the UN Secretary-General, Francis Deng. Commission on Human Rights, January 1994." *International Journal of Refugee Law* 6 (2): 291–307.

Derrida, Jacques. 2000a. "Hostipitality." Translated by Barry Stocker with Forbes Morlock. *Angelaki: Journal of the Theoretical Humanities* 5 (3): 3–18.

———. 2000b. *Of Hospitality: Anne Dufourmantelle Invites Jacques Derrida to Respond.* Translated by Rachel Bowlby. Stanford, CA: Stanford University Press.

Deschamp, Bryan, and Sebastian Lohse. 2013. *Still Minding the Gap? A Review of Efforts to Link Relief and Development in Situations of Human Displacement, 2001–2012.* Geneva: UNHCR.

Deshingkar, Priya, and John Farrington. 2009. *Circular Migration and Multilocational Livelihood Strategies in Rural India.* Oxford: Oxford University Press.

De Waal, Thomas. 2009. "The Karabakh Trap: Dangers and Dilemmas of the Nagorny Karabakh Conflict." Occasional Papers, Conciliation Resources. http://www .c-r.org/resources/karabakh-trap-dangers-and-dilemmas-nagorny-karabakh -conflict-azerbaijani.

Dick, Shelly. 2002. "Liberians in Ghana: Living without Humanitarian Assistance." *New Issues in Refugee Research,* Working Paper No. 57. Geneva: UNHCR.

Dogbevi, E. 2008. "Liberian Refugees a Threat to Ghana's Security—Bartels." April 1, https://www.modernghana.com/news/161562/liberian-refugees-a-threat-to -ghanas-security-bartels.html.

Dolan, Chris. 2013. *Social Torture: The Case of Northern Uganda, 1986–2006.* New York: Berghahn.

Doraï, Mohamed Kamel. 2010. "Palestinian Refugee Camps in Lebanon: Migration, Mobility and the Urbanization Process." In *Palestinian Refugees: Identity, Space and Place in the Levant,* edited by Are Knudsen and Sari Hanafi, 67–80. London: Routledge.

Dryden-Peterson, Sarah. 2003. "Education of Refugees in Uganda: Relationships between Setting and Access." Refugee Law Project (RLP) working paper, Uganda.

———. 2011. *Refugee Education: A Global Review.* Geneva: UNHCR PDES.

Drydyk, Jay. 2005. "When Is Development More Democratic?" *Journal of Human Development* 6 (2): 247–60.

Dubernet, Cecile. 2001. *The International Containment of Displaced Persons: Humanitarian Spaces without Exit.* Aldershot, UK: Ashgate.

Dubois, Laurent. 2012. *Haiti: The Aftershocks of History.* New York: Henry Holt.

Duffield, Mark. 2008. "Global Civil War: The Non-Insured, International Containment and Post-Interventionary Society." *Journal of Refugee Studies* 21 (2): 145–65.

Dumper, Michael. 2007. *The Future for Palestinian Refugees: Toward Equity and Peace.* Boulder, CO: Lynne Rienner.

Dunn, Elizabeth. 2012. "The Chaos of Humanitarian Aid: Adhocracy in the Republic of Georgia." *Humanity* 3 (1): 1–23.

———. 2014. "Humanitarianism, Displacement, and the Politics of Nothing in Postwar Georgia." *Slavic Review* 73 (2): 287–306.

Duthie, Roger. 2012a. "Contributing to Durable Solutions: Transitional Justice and the Integration and Reintegration of Displaced Persons." In *Transitional Justice and Displacement,* edited by Roger Duthie. New York: Social Science Research Council.

————. ed. 2012b. *Transitional Justice and Displacement.* New York: Social Sciences Research Council.

Dzeamesi, Michael K. 2008. "Refugees, the UNHCR and Host Governments as Stakeholders in the Transformation of Refugee Communities: A Study into the Buduburam Refugee Camp in Ghana." *International Journal of Migration, Health and Social Care* 4 (1): 28–41.

Dzingirai, Vupenyu, Patience Mutopu, and Loren B. Landau. 2014. *Confirmations, Coffins and Corn: Kinship, Social Networks and Remittances from South Africa to Zimbabwe.* Migrating Out of Poverty Research Consortium Working Paper 18. Sussex: University of Sussex.

Eastmond, Marita. 2006. "Transnational Returns and Reconstruction in Post-War Bosnia and Herzegovina." *International Migration* 44 (3): 141–64.

El-Hafed, S. 2011. "Return to Sahrawi Refugee Camps of Sahrawi Students in Libya." *Sahrawi Press Service,* March 7.

El Tiempo. 2016. "Un total de 171.000 personas dejaron de ser pobres entre 2014 y 2015." *El Tiempo,* March 2. http://www.eltiempo.com/economia/sectores/cifra-de-pobreza-y-pobre-extrema-en-colombia-2016/16525815.

Elwood, Sarah, and Katharyne Mitchell. 2012. "Mapping Children's Politics: Spatial Stories, Dialogic Relations and Political Formation." *Geografiska Annaler: Series B, Human Geography* 94 (1): 1–15.

Enloe, Cynthia. 2011. "The Mundane Matters." *International Political Sociology* 5 (4): 447–50.

Erel, Umut. 2007. "Constructing Meaningful Lives: Biographic Methods in Research with Migrant Women." *Sociological Research Online* 12 (4): 1–14.

Essed, Philomena, Georg Frerks, and Joke Schrijvers. 2004. *Refugees and the Transformation of Societies: Agency, Policies, Ethics and Politics.* Oxford: Berghahn.

Essuman-Johnson, Abeeku. 2011. "When Refugees Don't Go Home: The Situation of Liberian Refugees in Ghana." *Journal of Immigrant & Refugee Studies* 9 (2): 105–26.

European Council on Refugees and Exile (ECRE). 2016. "NGOs Make Urgent Call: 'Dramatic increase in refugee resettlement urgently needed.'" Geneva, June 15. http://www.ecre.org/resettlement-urgently-needed/.

Fass, Simon. 1987. "Housing the Ultra-Poor: Theory and Practice in Haiti." *Journal of the American Planning Association* 53 (2): 193–205.

Fassin, Didier. 2011. *Humanitarian Reason: a Moral History of the Present.* Berkeley: University of California Press.

————, ed. 2012. *A Companion to Moral Anthropology.* Malden, MA: Wiley-Blackwell.

Fatton, Robert. 2002. *Haiti's Predatory Republic: The Unending Transition to Democracy.* Boulder, CO: Lynne Rienner.

Feldman, Ilana. 2012a. "The Challenge of Categories: UNRWA and the Definition of a 'Palestine Refugee.'" *Journal of Refugee Studies* 25 (3): 387–406.

————. 2012b. "The Humanitarian Condition: Palestinian Refugees and the Politics of Living." *Humanity: An International Journal of Human Rights, Humanitarianism, and Development* 3 (2): 155–72.

Ferris, Elizabeth G. 2011. *The Politics of Protection: The Limits of Humanitarian Action*. Washington, DC: Brookings Institution Press.

Fiddian-Qasmiyeh, Elena. 2009. "Representing Sahrawi Refugees' 'Educational Displacement' to Cuba: Self-Sufficient Agents or Manipulated Victims in Conflict?" *Journal of Refugee Studies* 22 (3): 323–50.

———. 2011. "Paradoxes of Refugees' Educational Migration: Promoting Self-Sufficiency or Renewing Dependency?" *Comparative Education* 47 (4): 433–47.

———. 2012. "Invisible Refugees and/or Overlapping Refugeedom? Protecting Sahrawis and Palestinians Displaced by the 2011 Libyan Uprising." *International Journal of Refugee Law* 24 (2): 263–93.

———. 2013. "The Inter-Generational Politics of 'Travelling Memories': Sahrawi Refugee Youth Remembering Home-Land and Home-Camp." *Journal of Intercultural Studies* 34 (6): 631–49.

———. 2014. *The Ideal Refugees: Gender, Islam and the Sahrawi Politics of Survival*. Syracuse, NY: Syracuse University Press.

———. 2015a. "Refugees Helping Refugees: How a Palestinian Refugee Camp in Lebanon Is Welcoming Syrians." *The Conversation*, November 4. http://thecon versation.com/refugees-helping-refugees-how-a-palestinian-camp-in-lebanon -is-welcoming-syrians-48056.

———. 2015b. *South-South Educational Migration, Humanitarianism and Development: Views from Cuba, North Africa and the Middle East*. Oxford: Routledge.

———. 2016a. "Refugees Hosting Refugees." *Forced Migration Review*, September.

———. 2016b. "Repressentations of Displacement in the East." *Public Culture* 28 (3): 457–73.

———. 2016c. "On the Threshold of Statelessness: Palestinian Narratives of Loss and Erasure." *Journal of Ethnic and Racial Studies* 39 (2): 301–21.

———. 2019. "Memories and Meanings of Camps (and More-than-Camps)." In *Refugee Imaginaries: Contemporary Research across the Humanities*, edited by D. Farrier, A. Woolley, L. Stonebridge, S. Durrant, and E. Cox. Edinburgh: Edinburgh University Press.

Fiddian-Qasmiyeh, Elena, and Yousif M. Qasmiyeh. 2016. "Refugee Neighbours and Hostipitality." *The Critique*, 1 December 2015.

Finnström, Sverker. 2008. *Living with Bad Surroundings: War, History, and Everyday Moments in Northern Uganda*. Durham, NC: Duke University Press.

Fitzgerald, Emmett, with the IASC Haiti E-Shelter/CCCM Cluster Returns Working Group. 2012. "Helping Families, Closing Camps: A Toolkit of Best Practice and Lessons Learned Haiti 2010–2012." Port-au-Prince: IASC Haiti E-Shelter /CCCM Cluster.

Fletcher, Laurel E., and Harvey M. Weinstein. 2002. "Violence and Social Repair: Rethinking the Contribution of Justice to Reconciliation." *Human Rights Quarterly* 24 (3): 573–639.

Frank, Matthew. 2008. *Expelling the Germans: British Opinion and Post-1945 Population Transfer in Context*. Oxford: Oxford University Press.

Freemantle, Iriann. 2010. "'You can only claim your yard and not a country': Exploring Context, Discourse and Practices of Cosmopolitanism amongst African Migrants in Johannesburg." PhD dissertation, University of the Witwatersrand, Johannesburg, South Africa.

Freire, Paulo. 1970. *Pedagogy of the Oppressed*. New York: Seabury Press.

Fresia, Marion, and Andreas Von Känel. 2016. "Beyond Space of Exception? Reflections on the Camp through the Prism of Refugee Schools." *Journal of Refugee Studies* 29 (2): 250–72.

Frischkorn, Rebecca. 2015. "Political Economy of Control: Urban Refugees and the Regulation of Space in Lusaka, Zambia." *Economic Anthropology* 2 (1): 205–23.

Gabiam, Nell, and Elena Fiddian-Qasmiyeh. 2017. "Palestinians and the Arab Uprisings: Political Activism and Narratives of Home, Homeland and Home-Camp." *Journal of Ethnic and Migration Studies* 43 (5): 731–48.

Garbin, David. 2012. "Marching for God in the Global City: Public Space, Religion and Diasporic Identities in a Transnational African Church." *Culture and Religion* 13 (4): 425–47.

García, Mauricio. 1993. *La eficacia simbólica del derecho*. Bogota: Ediciones Uniandes.

———. 2014. *La eficacia simbólica del derecho*. 2nd ed. Bogota: Editorial Planeta.

Gardiner, Michael E. 2000. *Critiques of Everyday Life*. London: Routledge.

Garnier, Adele. 2014. "Migration Management and Humanitarian Protection: The UNHCR's 'Resettlement Expansionism' and Its Impact on Policy-Making in the EU and Australia." *Journal of Ethnic and Migration Studies* 40 (6): 942–59.

Gatrell, Peter. 2013. *The Making of the Modern Refugee*. Oxford: Oxford University Press.

Gedalof, Irene. 2000. "Identity in Transit Nomads, Cyborgs and Women." *European Journal of Women's Studies* 7 (3): 337–54.

Geschiere, Peter. 2009. *The Perils of Belonging: Autochthony, Citizenship, and Exclusion in Africa and Europe*. Chicago: University of Chicago Press.

Gibney, Matthew J. 2015. "Refugees and Justice between States." *European Journal of Political Theory* 14 (4): 448–63.

Gilbert, Margaret. 2014. *Joint Commitment: How We Make the Social World*. New York: Oxford University Press.

Givens, Terri E., and Rahsaan Maxwell, eds. 2012. *Immigrant Politics: Race and Representation in Western Europe*. Boulder, CO: Lynne Rienner.

Global IDP Project. 2005. *IDPs from Kosovo: Stuck between Uncertain Return Prospects and Denial of Local Integration*. Geneva: Norwegian Refugee Council.

Gould, Chandré. 2011. "Trafficking? Exploring the Relevance of the Notion of Human Trafficking to Describe the Lived Experience of Sex Workers in Cape Town, South Africa." *Crime, Law and Social Change* 56 (5): 529–46.

Government of Canada. 2016a. "#WelcomeRefugees: The First 25,000—Phase 1." https://www.canada.ca/en/immigration-refugees-citizenship/services/refugees/welcome-syrian-refugees/first-2500-process/phase-1.html.

———. 2016b. "#WelcomeRefugees: Key Figures." https://www.canada.ca/en/immigration-refugees-citizenship/services/refugees/welcome-syrian-refugees/key-figures.html.

Gow, Greg. 2005. "Rubbing Shoulders in the Global City: Refugees, Citizenship and Multicultural Alliances in Fairfield, Sydney." *Ethnicities* 5 (3): 386–405.

Grabska, Katarzyna, and Martha Fanjoy. 2015. "'And When I Become a Man': Translocal Coping with Precariousness and Uncertainty among Returnee Men in South Sudan." *Social Analysis* 59 (1): 76–95.

Grace, Jeremy, and Erin Mooney. 2009. "Peacebuilding through the Electoral Participation of Displaced Populations." *Refugee Survey Quarterly* 28 (1): 95–121.

Granovetter, Mark S. 1973. "The Strength of Weak Ties." *American Journal of Sociology* 78 (6): 1360–80.

Gready, Paul, Jelke Boesten, Gordon Crawford, and Polly Wilding. 2010. "Transformative Justice: A Concept Note." Unpublished manuscript. https://www.wun.ac.uk/files/transformative_justice_-_concept_note_web_version.pdf.

Gready, Paul, and Simon Robins. 2014. "From Transitional to Transformative Justice: A New Agenda for Practice." *International Journal of Transitional Justice* 8 (3): 339–61.

Green, Penny. 2005. "Disaster by Design Corruption, Construction and Catastrophe." *British Journal of Criminology* 45 (4): 528–46.

Greenhill, Kelly M. 2008. "Strategic Engineered Migration as a Weapon of War." *Civil Wars* 10 (1): 6–21.

Gros, Jean-Germain. 2011. "Anatomy of a Haitian Tragedy: When the Fury of Nature Meets the Debility of the State." *Journal of Black Studies* 42 (2): 131–57.

Haider, Huma. 2014. "Transnational Transitional Justice and Reconciliation: The Participation of Conflict-Generated Diasporas in Addressing the Legacies of Mass Violence." *Journal of Refugee Studies* 27 (2): 207–33.

Häkli, Jouni, and Kirsi Kallio. 2014. "Subject, Action and Polis: Theorizing Political Agency." *Progress in Human Geography* 32 (2): 131–200.

Hall, Stuart. 1997. "The Work of Representation." In *Representation: Cultural Representations and Signifying Practices*, edited by Stuart Hall, 13–74. London: Sage.

Hallgrimsdottir, Helga Kristin, Rachel Phillips, and Cecilia Benoit. 2006. "Fallen Women and Rescued Girls: Social Stigma and Media Narratives of the Sex Industry in Victoria, BC, from 1980 to 2005." *Canadian Review of Sociology* 43 (3): 265–80.

Halliday, Timothy. 2006. "Migration, Risk, and Liquidity Constraints in El Salvador." *Economic Development and Cultural Change* 54 (4): 893–925.

Hanafi, Sari, and Åge Tiltnes. 2009. "The Employability of Palestinian Professionals in Lebanon." *Knowledge, Work and Society* 6 (1): 56–78.

Hansen, Thomas Blom, and Finn Stepputat. 2010. *States of Imagination: Ethnographic Explorations of the Postcolonial State.* Durham, NC: Duke University Press.

Harding, Joel, and Sheila Varadan. 2010. "A Community-Based Approach to Refugee Protection in a Protracted Refugee Situation." *Humanitarian Exchange Magazine* 46: 8–10.

Hargrave, Karen. 2014. "Repatriation through a Trust-Based Lens: Refugee-State Trust Relations on the Thai-Burma Border and Beyond." Refugee Studies Centre Working Paper Series No. 104, University of Oxford.

————. 2015. "Refugee-State Distrust on the Thai-Burma Border." *Forced Migration Review* 49: 95–97.

Harpviken, Kristian Berg. 2008. "From 'Refugee Warriors' to 'Returnee Warriors': Militant Homecoming in Afghanistan and Beyond." Global Migration and Transnational Politics Working Paper 5. Center for Global Studies, George Mason University, Arlington, VA.

Harrell-Bond, Barbara. 1989. "Repatriation: Under What Conditions Is It the Most Desirable Solution for Refugees? An Agenda for Research." *African Studies Review* 32 (1): 41–69.

————. 2002. "Can Humanitarian Work with Refugees be Humane?" *Human Rights Quarterly* 24 (1): 51–58.

Hathaway, James C. 2007. "Forced Migration Studies: Could We Agree Just to 'Date'?" *Journal of Refugee Studies* 20 (3): 349–69.

Hatoss, Aniko, and Henk Huijser. 2010. "Gendered Barriers to Educational Opportunities: Resettlement of Sudanese Refugees in Australia." *Gender and Education* 22 (2): 147–60.

Hayden, Bridget. 2006. "What's in Name: The Nature of the Individual in Refugee Studies." *Journal of Refugee Studies* 19 (4): 471–87.

Healey, R. L. 2006. "Asylum-Seekers and Refugees: a Structuration Theory Analysis of Their Experiences in the UK." *Population, Space and Place* 12 (4): 257–71.

Held, Virginia. 2006. *The Ethics of Care: Personal, Political and Global*. Oxford: Oxford University Press.

Hendrie, Barbara. 1991. "The Politics of Repatriation: The Tigrayan Refugee Repatriation, 1985–1987." *Journal of Refugee Studies* 4 (2): 200–218.

Hickey, Sam, and Giles Mohan. 2005. "Relocating Participation within a Radical Politics of Development." *Development and Change* 36 (2): 237–62.

Highmore, Ben. 2002. "Introduction: Questioning Everyday Life." In *The Everyday Life Reader*, edited by Ben Highmore, 1–34. London: Routledge.

Hirschmann, Nancy, and Christine Di Stefano. 1996. "Introduction: Revision, Reconstruction and the Challenges of the New." In *Revisioning the Political: Feminist Reconstructions of Traditional Concepts in Western Political Theory*, edited by Nancy Hirschmann and Christine Di Stefano, 1–26. Boulder, CO: Westview.

Hirst, Paul. 1994. *Associative Democracy: New Forms of Social and Economic Governance*. Cambridge, UK: Polity.

Holzer, Elizabeth. 2012. "A Case Study of Political Failure in a Refugee Camp." *Journal of Refugee Studies* 25 (2): 257–81.

————. 2015. *The Concerned Women of Buduburum: Refugee Activities and Humanitarian Dilemma*. Ithaca, NY: Cornell University Press.

Hornsby, Jennifer. 2004. "Agency and Actions." *Royal Institute of Philosophy Supplement* (55): 1–23.

Horst, Cindy. 2006a. "Buufis amongst Somalis in Dadaab: The Transnational and Historical Logics behind Resettlement Dreams." *Journal of Refugee Studies* 19 (2): 143–57.

————. 2006b. Refugee Livelihoods: Continuity and Transformations." *Refugee Survey Quarterly* 25 (2): 6–22.

————. 2006c. *Transnational Nomads: How Somalis Cope with Refugee Life in the Dadaab Camps of Kenya.* Oxford: Berghahn.

————. 2013. "The Depoliticization of Diasporas from the Horn of Africa: From Refugees to Transnational Aid Workers." *African Studies* 72 (2): 228–45.

————. 2017. "Implementing the Women, Peace and Security Agenda? Somali Debates on Women's Public Roles and Political Participation." *Journal of Eastern African Studies* 11 (3): 389–407.

Horst, Cindy, and E. Doeland. 2016. "Introducing a Women's Empowerment Agenda from Abroad? Gender and Stability in Somalia." PRIO Policy Brief 13. Oslo: PRIO.

Horst, Cindy, and Katarzyna Grabska. 2015. "Introduction: Flight and Exile: Uncertainty in the Context of Conflict-Induced Displacement." *Social Analysis* 59 (1): 1–18.

Horst, Cindy, and Anab Ibrahim Nur. 2016. "Governing Mobility through Humanitarianism in Somalia: Compromising Protection for the Sake of Return." *Development and Change* 47 (3): 542–62.

Horvath, Agnes, Bjørn Thomassen, and Harald Wydra. 2009. "Introduction: Liminality and Cultures of Change." *International Political Anthropology* 2 (1): 3–4.

Human Rights Foundation of Monland-Burma (HURFOM). 2014. "In Pursuit of Justice: Reflections on the Past and Hopes for the Future of Burma." Kanchanaburi, Thailand: HURFOM.

Hur, Mann Hyung. 2006. "Empowerment in Terms of Theoretical Perspectives: Exploring a Typology of the Process and Components across Disciplines." *Journal of Community Psychology* 34 (5): 523–40.

Hyndman, Jennifer. 1996. "Geographies of Displacement: Gender, Culture and Power in UNHCR Refugee Camps, Kenya." PhD dissertation, University of British Columbia, Vancouver.

————. 2000. *Managing Displacement: Refugees and the Politics of Humanitarianism.* Minneapolis: University of Minnesota Press.

Hyndman, Jennifer, and Wenona Giles. 2011. "Waiting for What? The Feminization of Asylum in Protracted Situations." *Gender, Place and Culture: A Journal of Feminist Geography* 18 (3): 361–79.

————. 2016. *Refugees in Extended Exile: Living on the Edge.* London: Routledge.

Inkeles, Alex, and Raymond Bauer. 1961. *The Soviet Citizen: Daily Life in a Totalitarian Society.* Cambridge, MA: Harvard University Press.

Inter-Agency Standing Committee (IASC). 2010. *IASC Framework on Durable Solutions for Internally Displaced Persons.* Washington, DC: Brookings Project on Internal Displacement.

Inter-American Commission on Human Rights (IACHR). 1999. "Internal Displacement." In *Third Report on the Human Rights Situation in Colombia.* OEA/Ser.L/V /II.102, February 26. http://www.cidh.org/countryrep/Colom99en/chapter-6 .htm.

————. 2007. *Follow-Up on the Demobilization Process of the AUC in Colombia: Digest of Published Documents (2004–2007)*. OEA/Ser.L/V/II CIDH/INF.2/07. https://www.cidh.oas.org/pdf%20files/Colombia-Demobilization-AUC%202008.pdf.

Inter-American Court of Human Rights. 2004. *Resolución de la Corte Interamericana de Derechos Humanons de 5 de julio de 2004*. Caso pueblo indígena Kankuamo.

Internal Displacement Monitoring Centre (IDMC). 2005. *Profile of Internal Displacement: Azerbaijan*. Geneva: IDMC.

————. 2014a. *Azerbaijan: After More than 20 Years, IDPs Still Urgently Need Policies to Support Full Integration*. Geneva: IDMC.

————. 2014b. *Global Overview 2014. People Internally Displaced by Conflict and Violence*. May. http://www.internal-displacement.org/library/publications/2014/global-overview-2014-people-internally-displaced-by-conflict-and-violence/.

————. 2015. *Global Overview 2015: People Internally Displaced by Conflict and Violence*. Geneva: IDMC.

International Center for Transitional Justice (ICTJ). 2009. "Impunity Prolonged: Burma and Its 2008 Constitution." New York: ICTJ.

————. 2014. "Navigating Paths to Justice in Myanmar's Transition." New York: ICTJ.

International Crisis Group (ICG). 2000. "Bosnia's Refugee Logjam Breaks: Is the International Community Ready?" May 30. https://www.crisisgroup.org/europe-central-asia/balkans/bosnia-and-herzegovina/bosnias-refugee-logjam-breaks-international-community-ready.

————. 2005a. "Nagorno-Karabakh: A Plan for Peace." *Europe Report* 167, October 11. https://www.crisisgroup.org/europe-central-asia/caucasus/nagorno-karabakh-azerbaijan/nagorno-karabakh-plan-peace.

————. 2005b. "Nagorno-Karabakh: Viewing the Conflict from the Ground." *Europe Report* 166, September 14. https://www.crisisgroup.org/europe-central-asia/caucasus/nagorno-karabakh-azerbaijan/nagorno-karabakh-viewing-conflict-ground.

————. 2007. "Nagorno-Karabakh: Risking War." *Europe Report* 187, November 14. https://www.crisisgroup.org/europe-central-asia/caucasus/nagorno-karabakh-azerbaijan/nagorno-karabakh-risking-war.

————. 2012. "Tackling Azerbaijan's IDP Burden." *Europe Briefing* 67, February 27. https://www.crisisgroup.org/europe-central-asia/caucasus/azerbaijan/tackling-azerbaijan-s-idp-burden.

————. 2014. "Bringing Back the Palestinian Refugee Question." *Middle East Report* 156, October 9. https://www.crisisgroup.org/middle-east-north-africa/eastern-mediterranean/israelpalestine/bringing-back-palestinian-refugee-question.

International Federation of Red Cross and Red Crescent Societies (IFRC). 2015. *Impact of the Regulatory Barriers to Providing Emergency and Transitional Shelter after Disasters: Country Case Study: Haiti*. Port-au-Prince. IFRC. https://www.ifrc.org/PageFiles/198142/Haiti%20Shelter%20Report%20EN%20Final2.pdf

International Organization for Migration (IOM) and ACTED. 2011. *Intentions des Deplaces Haïti*. Port-au-Prince. IOM and ACTED. http://reliefweb.int/report /haiti/overwhelming-majority-haitians-living-displacement-camps-want-leave -have-nowhere-go.

Isaac, Thomas, and Richard Franke. 2002. *Local Democracy and Development: The Kerala People's Campaign for Decentralized Planning*. Lanham, MD: Rowman and Littlefield.

Ivanovic, Mladjo. 2016. "The European Grammar of Recognition: Integrating Epistemic and Social Inclusion of Refugees in Host Societies." Paper presented at the Active Citizenship Today conference, June 1–2, University of Tromsø, Tromsø, Norway.

Jacobs, Jane. 1964. *The Death and Life of Great American Cities: The Failure of Town Planning*. Harmondsworth, UK: Penguin.

Jacobsen, Karen. 2017. "Camps or No Camps? Patterns of Refugee Distribution in Countries with and without Encampment Policies." Research note, Feinstein International Center, Tufts University, Medford, MA.

Jacobsen, Karen, and Susan Fratzke. 2016. *Building Livelihood Opportunities for Refugee Populations: Lessons from Past Practice*. Washington, DC: TransAtlantic Council on Migration and Migration Policy Institute.

Jacobsen, Karen, and Rebecca Furst. 2011. "Developing a Profiling Methodology for Displaced People in Urban Areas: Final Report." Feinstein International Center, Medford, MA.

Jansen, Bram J. 2008. "Between Vulnerability and Assertiveness: Negotiating Resettlement in Kakuma Refugee Camp, Kenya." *African Affairs* 107 (429): 569–87.

———. 2015. "'Digging Aid': The Camp as an Option in East and the Horn of Africa." *Journal of Refugee Studies* 29 (2): 149–65.

Jennings, Kathleen M., and Morten Bøås. 2015. "Transactions and Interactions: Everyday Life in the Peacekeeping Economy." *Journal of Intervention and Statebuilding* 9 (3): 281–95.

Johansson, Patrik. 2009. "Putting Peace to the Vote: Displaced Persons and a Future Referendum on Nagorno-Karabakh." *Refugee Survey Quarterly* 28 (1): 122–39.

———. 2010. "Peace by Repatriation: Concepts, Cases, and Conditions." PhD dissertation, Department of Political Science, Umeå University, Umeå, Sweden.

———. 2016. "Hit, men inte länge: Den internationella flyktingregimen och andra sätt att hantera ofrivillig migration." In *Krig/Fred. RJ:s årsbok 2016/2017*, edited by Jenny Björkman and Arne Jarrick, 39–53. Göteborg, Sweden: Makadam förlag.

Jolliffe, Kim. 2014. "Ceasefires and Durable Solutions in Myanmar: A Lessons Learned Review." *UNHCR New Issues in Refugee Research*, Research Paper No. 271.

Jones, Ayesha, ed. 2014. *Listening to Communities of Karen (Kayin) State, Myanmar*. Siĕmréab, Cambodia: Centre for Peace and Conflict Studies.

Jovanović, Miodrag A. 2005. "Recognizing Minority Identities through Collective Rights." *Human Rights Quarterly* 27 (2): 625–51.

Juergensen, Olaf Tataryn. 2000. "Repatriation as Peacebuilding and Reconstruction: the Case of Northern Mozambique, 1992–1995." *New Issues in Refugee Research*, Working Paper No. 31, October.

Juma, Monica K., and Peter M. Kagwanja. 2003. "Securing Refuge from Terror: Refugee Protection in East Africa after September 11." In *Problems of Protection: The UNHCR, Refugees, and Human Rights*, edited by Niklaus Steiner, Mark Gibney, and Gil Loescher, 225–36. New York: Routledge.

Kabachnik, Peter, Joanna Regulska, and Beth Mitchnek. 2010. "When and Where Is Home? The Double Displacement of Georgian IDPs from Abkhazia." *Journal of Refugee Studies* 23 (3): 315–36.

Kabeer, Naila. 1999. "Resources, Agency, Achievements: Reflections on the Measurement of Women Empowerment." *Development and Change* 30: 435–64.

Kälin, Walter. 2014. "Internal Displacement." In *The Oxford Handbook of Refugee and Forced Migration Studies*, edited by Elena Fiddian-Qasmiyeh, Gil Loescher, Katy Long, and Nando Sigona, 163–75. Oxford: Oxford University Press.

———. 2015. *Durable Solutions for Internally Displaced Persons: An Essential Dimension of Peacebuilding*. Washington, DC: Brookings Institution.

Kamal, Baher. 2016. "Now 1 in 2 World's Refugees Live in Urban Areas." Inter Press News Service, May 19, 2016. http://www.ipsnews.net/2016/05/now-1-in -2-worlds-refugees-live-in-urban-area/.

Kanaiapuni, Shawn Malia, Katharine M. Donato, Theresa Thompson-Colon, and Melissa Stainback. 2005. "Counting on Kin: Social Networks, Social Support, and Child Health Status." *Social Forces* 83 (3): 1137–64.

KANERE. 2012. "Refugee Protest Following Insecurity Situation." *Kakuma News Reflector* (blog), December 28. https://kanere.org/2012/12/28/refugee-protest -following-insecurity-situation/.

Kankonde, Peter. 2010. "Transnational Family Ties, Remittance Motives, and Social Death among Congolese Migrants: A Socio-Anthropological Analysis." *Journal of Comparative Family Studies* 41 (2): 225–43.

———. 2017. "Taking Roots in the Name of God? Super Diversity and Migrant Pentecostal Churches' Legitimation and Social Integration in Post-Apartheid South Africa." PhD dissertation, University of Göttingen, Göttingen, Germany.

Karadawi, Ahmed. 1999. *Refugee Policy in Sudan, 1967–1984*. Oxford: Berghahn.

KCBO. 2012. *Karen Community Based Organizations' Position on Refugees' Return to Burma*. Working paper, September 11. womenofburma.org/Statement&Release /11-09-2012-Karen-Community-Based-Organizations-Position-on-Refugees -Return-to-Burma-position-paper.pdf.

Keenan, Sarah. 2014. *Subversive Property: Law and the Production of Spaces of Belonging*. London: Routledge.

Kennedy, David. 2005. *The Dark Sides of Virtue: Reassessing International Humanitarianism*. Princeton, NJ: Princeton University Press.

Kermeliotis, Teo. 2013. "Africa's 'New Cities': Urban Future or Utopian Fantasies?" In *CNN: Future Cities*, May 30. http://edition.cnn.com/2013/05/30/business /africa-new-cities-konza-eko/index.html.

Khalidi, Walid, ed. 1992. *All That Remains: The Palestinian Villages Occupied and Depopulated by Israel in 1948*. Washington, DC: Institute for Palestine Studies.

Kibreab, Gaim. 1996. "Eritrean and Ethiopian Urban Refugees in Khartoum: What the Eye Refuses to See." *African Studies Review* 39 (3): 131–78.

———. 1999. "Revisiting the Debate on People, Place, Identity and Displacement." *Journal of Refugee Studies* 12 (4): 384–410.

Kihato, Caroline Wanjiku. 2011. "The City from Its Margins: Rethinking Urban Governance through the Everyday Lives of Migrant Women in Johannesburg." *Social Dynamics* 37 (3): 349–62.

———. 2013. *Migrant Women of Johannesburg: Everyday Life in an In-Between City*. London: Palgrave.

Kihato, C. W., and S. Muyeba. 2015. "The Challenges and Prospects of African Urbanization: Forging Africa's Economic Growth through Sustainable Urban Policies." Unpublished report for the Cities Alliance.

Kontogiorgi, Elisabeth. 2006. *Population Exchange in Greek Macedonia: The Rural Settlement of Refugees, 1922–1930*. Oxford: Clarendon Press.

Koser, Khalid. 1997. "Information and Repatriation: The Case of Mozambican Refugees in Malawi." *Journal of Refugee Studies* 10 (1): 1–17.

———. 2007. "Addressing Internal Displacement in Peace Processes, Peace Agreements and Peace-Building." *IDP Newsletter*.

Kpatindé, Francis. 2006. "A Tale of Two Camps: Bustling Buduburum and Quiet Krisan." UNHCR, July 26. http://www.unhcr.org/44c7783e4.html.

Krause-Vilmar, Jina, and Josh Chaffin. 2011. *No Place to Go but Up: Urban Refugees in Johannesburg, South Africa*. New York: Women's Refugee Commission.

Krznaric, Roman. 1997. "Guatemalan Returnees and the Dilemma of Political Mobilization." *Journal of Refugee Studies* 10 (1): 61–78.

Kuch, Amelia. 2016. "Naturalization of Burundian Refugees in Tanzania: The Debates on Local Integration and the Meaning of Citizenship Revisited." *Journal of Refugee Studies* 3 (1): 468–87.

Kukathas, Chandran. 2016 "Are Refugees Special?" In *Migration in Political Theory: The Ethics of Movement and Membership*, edited by Sarah Fine and Lea Ypi, 249–67. Oxford: Oxford University Press.

Kurze, Arnaud, Christopher Lamont, and Simon Robins. 2015. "Contested Spaces of Transitional Justice: Legal Empowerment in Global Post-Conflict Contexts Revisited." *International Journal of Human Rights* 19 (3): 260–76.

Kutz, Christopher. 2000. *Complicity: Ethics and Law for a Collective Age*. Cambridge: Cambridge University Press.

Lambourne, Wendy. 2009. "Transitional Justice and Peacebuilding after Mass Violence." *International Journal of Transitional Justice* 3 (1): 28–48.

Landau, Loren B. 2014. "Conviviality, Rights, and Conflict in Africa's Urban Estuaries." *Politics & Society* 14 (3): 359–80.

Landau, Loren B., and Marguerite Duponchel. 2011. "Laws, Policies, or Social Position? Capabilities and the Determinants of Effective Protection in Four African Cities." *Journal of Refugee Studies* 24 (1): 1–22.

Landau, Loren B., and Iriann Freemantle. 2010. "Tactical Cosmopolitanism and Idioms of Belonging: Insertion and Self-Exclusion in Johannesburg." *Journal of Ethnic and Migration Studies* 36 (3): 375–90.

———. 2016. "Beggaring Belonging in Africa's No-Man's Lands: Diversity, Usufruct and the Ethics of Accommodation." *Journal of Ethnic and Migration Studies* 42 (6): 933–51.

Lazar, Sian. 2013. *The Anthropology of Citizenship: A Reader.* Chichester, UK: Wiley.

Leader, Katelyn E. 2013. "Exploring the Significance of Urban to Rural Relocation." PhD dissertation, University of Oxford, Oxford.

Lebson, Mike. 2013. "Why Refugees Rebel: Towards a Comprehensive Theory of Refugee Militarization." *International Migration* 51 (5): 133–48.

Lecadet, Clara. 2016. "Refugee Politics: Self-Organized 'Government' and Protests in the Agamé Refugee Camp (2005–13)." *Journal of Refugee Studies* 29 (2): 187–207.

Leebaw, Bronwyn. 2011. *Judging State-Sponsored Violence, Imagining Political Change.* Cambridge: Cambridge University Press.

Leenders, Reinoud. 2009. "Refugee Warriors or War Refugees? Iraqi Refugees' Predicament in Syria, Jordan and Lebanon." *Mediterranean Politics* 14 (3): 343–63.

Lemaitre, Julieta. 2009. *El derecho como conjuro: Fetichismo legal, violencia y movimientos sociales.* Bogota: Siglo del Hombre Editores y Ediciones Uniandes.

———. 2013. "Diálogo sin debate: La participación en los decretos de la Ley de Víctimas." *Revista de Derecho Público* 31: 5–37.

———. 2016. "After the War: Displaced Women, Ordinary Ethics, and Grassroots Reconstruction in Colombia." *Social and Legal Studies* 25 (5): 545–65.

Lemaitre, Julieta, and Kristin Sandvik. 2015. "Shifting Frames, Vanishing Resources and Dangerous Legal Opportunities: Legal Mobilization among Displaced Women in Colombia." *Law and Society Review* 49 (1): 5–38.

———. 2016. "The Court and the Women: Structural Litigation and Grassroots Organizing for Internally Displaced People's Rights in Colombia." In *En/Gendering Governance: From the Local to the Global*, edited by Katherine Young and Kim Rubenstein. Cambridge: Cambridge University Press.

Lemaitre, Julieta, Kristin Sandvik, and Juliana Vargas. 2014. *Organización Comunitaria y Derechos Humanos.* Bogota: Ediciones Uniandes, Colección Documentos de Justicia Global.

Levine, Simon, S. Bailey, B. Boyer, and C. Mehu. 2012. "Avoiding Reality: Land, Institutions and Humanitarian Action in Post-Earthquake Haiti." Humanitarian Policy Group Working Paper, September. https://www.odi.org/sites/odi.org.uk/files/odi-assets/publications-opinion-files/7930.pdf.

Levinson, Hannah. 2010. "Refocusing the Refugee Regime: From Vagrancy to Value." *Res Cogitans* 1 (1): 143–55.

Liberian Refugee Repatriation and Resettlement Commission (LRRRC). 2008. Briefing Notes. Copy on file with the author.

Lindley, Anna. 2007. "Protracted Displacement and Remittances: The View from Eastleigh, Nairobi." *UNHCR: New Issues in Refugee Research*, Working Paper No. 114.

————. 2009. "The Early-Morning Phonecall: Remittances from a Refugee Diaspora Perspective." *Journal of Ethnic and Migration Studies* 35 (8): 1315–34.

Lischer, Sarah Kenyon. 2000. *Refugee Involvement in Political Violence: Quantitative Evidence from 1987–1998.* United Nations High Commissioner for Refugees (UNHCR), Working Paper No. 26, Center for International Studies, Cambridge, MA. http://www.refworld.org/docid/4ff583642.html.

————. 2005. *Dangerous Sanctuaries: Refugee Camps, Civil War, and the Dilemmas of Humanitarian Aid.* Ithaca, NY: Cornell University Press.

————. 2007. "Causes and Consequences of Conflict-Induced Displacement." *Civil Wars* 9 (2): 142–55.

Lister, Ruth. 2004. *Poverty.* Cambridge, UK: Polity Press.

Loescher, Gil. 2001. *UNHCR in World Politics: A Perilous Path.* Oxford: Oxford University Press.

Loescher, Gil, and James Milner. 2005. *Protracted Refugee Situations: Domestic and International Security Implications.* Adelphi Paper 375. London: International Institute for Strategic Studies.

————. 2008. "A Framework for Responding to Protracted Refugee Situations." In *Protracted Refugee Situations: Political, Human Rights and Security Implications*, edited by Gil Loescher, James Milner, Edward Newman, and Gary Troeller, 353–76. New York: United Nations University.

Long, Katy. 2014. "Rethinking 'Durable' Solutions." In *The Oxford Handbook of Refugee and Forced Migration Studies*, edited by Elena Fiddian-Qasmiyeh, Gil Loescher, Katy Long, and Nando Sigona. Oxford: Oxford University Press.

Lopez, Allison. 2014. "We Are Made for Peace, Not for War: Peace Proposals from Victims of Colombia's Armed Conflict, Luis Fernando Arias." Latin America Working Group, September 10. http://www.lawg.org/action-center/lawg-blog/69-general/1369-we-are-made-for-peace-not-for-war-peace-proposals-from-victims-of-colombias-armed-conflict-luis-fernando-arias.

Lowry, Carmen S. 2013. "Lines of Flight: A Rhizomatic Exploration of Transparency in Three International Humanitarian Sites." *Kaleidoscope: A Graduate Journal of Qualitative Communication Research* 12 (3): 19–33.

Lubkemann, Stephen C. 2008a. *Culture in Chaos: An Anthropology of the Social Condition in War.* Chicago: University of Chicago Press.

————. 2008b. "Involuntary Immobility: On a Theoretical Invisibility in Forced Migration Studies." *Journal of Refugee Studies* 21 (4): 454–75.

————. 2010. *Culture in Chaos: An Anthropology of the Social Condition in War.* Chicago: University of Chicago Press.

Lukes, Steven. 1973. *Emile Durkheim: His Life and Work.* London: Allen Lane.

————. 1974. *Power: A Radical View.* London: Macmillan.

Lumpp, Shoko Shimozawa, and Paul Stromberg. 2004. "Voluntary Repatriation to Afghanistan: Key Features." *Refugee Survey Quarterly* 23 (3): 149–73.

Lundahl, Mats. 2002. *Politics or Markets? Essays on Haitian Underdevelopment.* London: Routledge.

Lundy, Patricia, and Mark McGovern. 2008a. "Role of Community in Participatory Transitional Justice." In *Transnational Justice from Below: Grassroots Activism and the Struggle for Change*, edited by Kieran McEvoy and Lorna McGregor, 99–120. Oxford: Hart Publishing.

———. 2008b. "Whose Justice? Rethinking Transitional Justice from the Bottom Up." *Journal of Law and Society* 35 (2): 265–92.

Lyytinen, Eveliina, and Janosch Kullenberg. 2013. *Urban Refugee Research and Social Capital*. New York: IRC and WRC.

Maalouf, Amin. 2008. *Origins*. Translated by Catherine Temerson. London: Picador.

Ma'an. 2011. "Gadhafi Forces Detain Palestinian Students." *Ma'an News Agency*, March 2,.http://www.maannews.com/eng/ViewDetails.aspx?id=364160.

Madge, Clare, Parvati Raghuram, and Pat Noxolo. 2014. "Conceptualizing International Education: from International Student to International Study." *Progress in Human Geography* 39 (6): 681–701.

Madhavan, Sangeetha, and Loren B. Landau. 2011. "Bridges to Nowhere: Hosts, Migrants, and the Chimera of Social Capital in Three African Cities." *Population and Development Review* 37 (3): 473–97.

Madsen, Morten Lynge. 2004. "Living for Home: Policing Immorality among Undocumented Migrants in Johannesburg." *African Studies* 63 (2): 173–92.

Malauene, D. 2004. "The Impact of the Congolese Forced Migrants' 'Permanent Transit' Condition on Their Relations with Mozambique and Its People." Master's thesis, University of the Witwatersrand, Johannesburg, South Africa.

Malkki, Liisa H. 1992. "National Geographic: The Rooting of Peoples and the Territorialization of National Identity among Scholars and Refugees." *Cultural Anthropology* 7 (1): 24–44.

———. 1995a. *Purity and Exile: Violence, Memory and National Cosmology among Hutu Refugees in Tanzania*. Chicago: University of Chicago Press.

———. 1995b. "Refugees and Exile: From 'Refugee Studies' to the National Order of Things." *Annual Review of Anthropology* 24: 495–523.

———. 1996. "Speechless Emissaries: Refugees, Humanitarianism, and Dehistoricization." *Cultural Anthropology* 11 (3): 377–404.

Malley, Robert. 2001. "Fictions about the Failure at Camp David: A Year Later, Arabs and Israelis Must Remember the Truth." *New York Times*, July 8.

Maphosa, Sylvester, Laura DeLuca, and Alphonse Keasley, eds. 2014. *Building Peace from Within: An Examination of Community-Based Peacebuilding and Transitions in Africa*. Pretoria: Africa Institute of South Africa.

Mattei, Ugo, and Laura Nader. 2008. *Plunder: When the Rule of Law Is Illegal*. Malden, MA: Blackwell.

Mattingly, Carolyn. 2010. *The Paradox of Hope: Anthropology, Philosophy and Fijian Knowledge*. Stanford, CA: Stanford University Press.

Mbembé, J.-A., and Libby Meintjes. 2003. "Necropolitics." *Public Culture* 15 (1): 11–40.

Mbembé, J.-A., and Sarah Nuttall. 2004. "Writing the World from an African Metropolis." *Public Culture* 16 (3): 347–72.

McCall, Leslie. 2005. "The Complexity of Intersectionality." *Signs* 30 (3): 1771–1800.

McCallin, Barbara. 2012. *Restitution and Legal Pluralism in Contexts of Displacement. Case Studies on Transitional Justice and Displacement*. Brookings-LSE Project on Internal Displacement, August. https://www.ictj.org/sites/default/files/ICTJ-Brookings-Displacement-Restitution-Legal-Pluralism-CaseStudy-2012-English _0.pdf.

McConnachie, Kirsten. 2014. *Governing Refugees: Justice, Order and Legal Pluralism*. New York: Routledge.

McGarry, John. 1998. "'Demographic Engineering': The State-Directed Movement of Ethnic Groups as a Technique of Conflict Regulation." *Ethnic and Racial Studies* 21 (4): 613–38.

McHugh, Gerald. 2010. *Integrating Internal Displacement in Peace Processes and Agreements*. Washington, DC: United States Institute of Peace and Brookings Institution.

McKeown, Maeve Catherine. 2015. "Responsibility without Guilt: A Youngian Approach to Responsibility for Global Injustice." PhD dissertation, University College London.

Meyer, Sarah. 2006. "The 'Refugee Aid and Development' Approach in Uganda: Empowerment and Self-Reliance of Refugees in Practice." *UNHCR New Issues in Refugee Research* 131: 31.

Mezzadra, Sandro, and Brett Neilson. 2013. *Border as Method, or, the Multiplication of Labor*. Durham, NC: Duke University Press.

Mibenge, Chiseche Salome. 2013. *Sex and International Tribunals: The Erasure of Gender from the War Narrative*. Philadelphia: University of Pennsylvania Press.

Miller, David. 2016. *Strangers in Our Midst: The Political Philosophy of Immigration*. Cambridge, MA: Harvard University Press.

Milner, James. 2005. "The Militarization and Demilitarization of Refugee Camps in Guinea." In *Armed and Aimless: Armed Groups, Guns, and Human Security in the ECOWAS Region*, edited by Nicolas Florquin and Eric G. Berman, 145–80. Geneva: Small Arms Survey.

———. 2009. *Refugees, the State and the Politics of Asylum in Africa*. Basingstoke, UK: Palgrave Macmillan.

———. 2011. "Refugees and the Peacebuilding Process." *New Issues in Refugee Research*, Paper No. 224. Geneva: UNHCR. https://carleton.ca/polisci/wp-content/uploads/Milner-Refugees-and-the-peacemaking-process-2011.pdf.

———. 2013. "Two Steps Forward, One Step Back: Understanding the Shifting Politics of Refugee Policy in Tanzania." *New Issues in Refugee Research*, Paper No. 255. Geneva: UNHCR.

———. 2014a. "Can Global Refugee Policy Leverage Durable Solutions? Lessons from Tanzania's Naturalization of Burundian Refugees." *Journal of Refugee Studies* 27 (4): 553–73.

———. 2014b. "Introduction: Understanding Global Refugee Policy." *Journal of Refugee Studies* 27 (4): 477–94.

———. 2015. "Refugees, Peacebuilding, and Reconciliation: Lessons from Policy,

Practice and Research." In *Forced Migration, Reconciliation and Justice*, edited by Megan Bradley, 29–46. Montréal: McGill-Queens University Press.

Milner, James, and Krystyna Wojnarowicz. 2017. "Power in the Global Refugee Regime: Understanding Expressions and Experiences of Power in Global and Local Contexts." *Refuge* 33 (1): 7–17.

Ministerio de Interior. 2013. "Plan de salvaguarda del pueblo Kankuamo." http://siic .mininterior.gov.co/sites/default/files/p.s._kankuamo.pdf.

————. 2015. "'Sueño que el pueblo Kankuamo pueda vivir en paz': Jaime Enrique Arias." MinInterior, August 21. http://www.mininterior.gov.co/sala-de-prensa/no ticias/sueno-que-el-pueblo-kankuamo-pueda-vivir-en-paz-jaime-enrique -arias.

Mirza, Mansha. 2010. "Resettlement for Disabled Refugees." *Forced Migration Review* 35: 30–31.

Mitchell, Christopher. 2012. "Introduction: Linking National-Level Peacemaking with Grassroots Peacebuilding." In *Local Peacebuilding and National Peace: Interaction between Grassroots and Elite Processes*, edited by Christopher Mitchell and Landaon Hancock, 1–18. London: Continuum.

Molloy, Michael, John Bell, Nicole Waintraub, and Ian B. Anderson. 2015. "The Palestinian Refugee Issue: Intangible Needs and Moral Acknowledgement." In *Forced Migration, Reconciliation, and Justice*, edited by Megan Bradley, 298–322. Montreal: McGill-Queen's University Press.

Mora, Alexandra, Édgar Naranjo, Gloria Amparo Rodríguez, and Angela del Pilar Santamaría. 2010. *Conflictos y Judicialización de la Política en la Sierra Nevada de Santa Marta*. Bogota: Universidad El Rosario.

Morel, Michele. 2014. *The Right Not to Be Displaced in International Law*. Cambridge, UK: Intersentia.

Morlang, Claas, and Carolina Stolte. 2008. "Tertiary Refugee Education in Afghanistan: Vital for Reconstruction." *Forced Migration Review* 30: 62–63.

Morland, Paul. 2014. *Demographic Engineering: Population Strategies in Ethnic Conflict*. Farnham, UK: Ashgate.

Morris, Eric, and Stephen Stedman. 2008. "Protracted Refugee Situations, Conflict and Security: The Need for Better Diagnosis and Prescription." In *Protracted Refugee Situations: Political, Human Rights and Security Implications*, edited by Gil Loecher, James Milner, Edward Newman, and Gary G. Troeller, 69–84. Tokyo: United Nations University Press.

Moulin, Carolina. 2012. "Ungrateful Subjects? Refugee Protests and the Logic of Gratitude." In *Citizenship, Migrant Activism and the Politics of Movement*, edited by Peter Nyers and Kim Rygiel, 54–72. London: Routledge.

Moulin, Carolina, and Peter Nyers. 2007. "'We live in a country of UNHCR'—Refugee Protests and Global Political Society." *International Political Sociology* 1 (4): 356–72.

Mourelos, Yannis G. 1985. "The 1914 Persecutions and the First Attempt at an Exchange of Minorities between Greece and Turkey." *Balkan Studies* 26 (2): 389–414.

Muggah, Robert, ed. 2006. *No Refuge: The Crisis of Refugee Militarization in Africa*. London: Zed.

Mundy, Jacob A. 2007. "Performing the Nation, Pre-Figuring the State: the Western Saharan Refugees, Thirty Years Later." *Journal of Modern African Studies* 45 (2): 275–97.

Munshi, Kaivan. 2003. "Networks in the Modern Economy: Mexican Migrants in the US Labor Market." *Quarterly Journal of Economics* 118: 549–99.

Myers, Garth Andrew. 2011. *African Cities: Alternative Visions of Urban Theory and Practice.* Chicago: University of Chicago Press.

Nail, Thomas. 2015. *The Figure of the Migrant.* Redwood City, CA: Stanford University Press.

Nakata, Sana. 2015. *Childhood Citizenship, Governance and Policy: The Politics of Becoming Adult.* New York: Routledge.

Narayan, Deepa, ed. 2002. *Empowerment and Poverty Reduction: A Sourcebook.* Washington, DC: International Bank for Reconstruction and Development and World Bank.

Navaro-Yashin, Yael. 2009. "Affective Spaces, Melancholic Objects: Ruination and the Production of Anthropological Knowledge." *Journal of the Royal Anthropological Institute* 15 (1): 1–18.

Nordstrom, Carolyn. 1997. *A Different Kind of War Story.* Philadelphia: University of Pennsylvania Press.

North, L., and A. Simmons, ed. 1999. *Journeys of Fear: Refugee Return and National Transformation in Guatemala.* Montreal: McGill-Queen's University Press.

Norwegian Refugee Council (NRC). 2008. *While Waiting for Return: Achievements and Further Challenges in the National Response to IDP Needs in Azerbaijan.* Baku: NRC.

Nyers, Peter. 2006a. *Rethinking Refugees: Beyond States of Emergency.* New York: Routledge.

———. 2006b. "Taking Rights, Mediating Wrongs: Disagreements of the Political Agency of Non-Status Refugees." In *The Politics of Protection: Sites of Insecurity and Political Agency*, edited by Jef Huysmans, Andrew Dobson, and Raia Prokhovnik, 48–67. London: Routledge.

Nyers, Peter, and Kim Rygiel, eds. 2012. *Citizenship, Migrant Activism and the Politics of Movement.* London: Routledge.

Obura, Anna. 2002. *Peace Education Programme in Dadaab and Kakuma, Kenya: Evaluation Summary.* Geneva: UNHCR.

Okello, Moses Chrispus, and Lucy Hovil. 2007. "Confronting the Reality of Gender-Based Violence in Northern Uganda." *International Journal of Transitional Justice* 1 (3): 433–43.

Oliveira, Elsa, and Jo Vearey. 2015. "Images of Place: Visuals from Migrant Women Sex Workers in South Africa." *Medical Anthropology: Cross-Cultural Studies in Health and Illness* 34 (4): 305–18.

Oliver-Smith, Anthony. 2010. *Defying Displacement: Grassroots Resistance and the Critique of Development.* Austin: University of Texas Press.

Oloya, Opiyo. 2013. *Child to Soldier: Stories from Joseph Kony's Lord's Resistance Army.* Toronto: University of Toronto Press.

Omata, Naohiko. 2013. "The Complexity of Refugees' Return Decision-Making in a Protracted Exile: Beyond the Home-Coming Model and Durable Solutions." *Journal of Ethnic and Migration Studies* 39 (8): 1281–97.

Oquaye, Mike. 1995. "Human Rights and the Transition to Democracy under the PNDC in Ghana." *Human Rights Quarterly* 17 (3): 556–73.

Orchard, Phil. 2010. "Protection of Internally Displaced Persons: Soft Law as a Norm-generating Mechanism." *Review of International Studies* 36 (2): 281–303.

———. 2014. "Implementing a Global Internally Displaced Persons Protection Regime." In *Implementation and World Politics: How International Norms Change Practice*, edited by Alexander Betts and Phil Orchard, 105–23. Oxford: Oxford University Press.

Organización Nacional Indígena de Colombia (ONIC). 2015. "El Pueblo Kankuamo en Valledupar se moviliza por la Paz." *ONIC*, April 9. https://www.onic.org.co/noticias/659-movilizacion-por-la-paz-del-pueblo-kankuamo

Organization for American States (OAS). 2003. "Kankuamo Indigenous People, Colombia." http://www.oas.org/en/iachr/indigenous/protection/precautionary.asp.

Organization for Security and Co-Operation in Europe (OSCE). 2006. "Statement by the Minsk Group Co-Chairs, 6 July 2006." https://www.osce.org/mg/47496.

Ortner, Sherry B. 1995. "Resistance and the Problem of Ethnographic Refusal." *Comparative Studies in Society and History* 37 (1): 173–93.

———. 2006. *Anthropology and Social Theory: Culture, Power and the Acting Subject.* Durham, NC: Duke University Press.

Østergaard Nielsen, Eva, ed. 2003. *International Migration and Sending Countries: Perceptions, Policies and Transnational Relations.* Basingstoke, UK: Palgrave.

Owens, Patricia. 2009. "Reclaiming 'Bare Life'? Against Agamben on Refugees." *International Relations* 23 (4): 567–82.

Owusu, Maxwell. 2000. "Reluctant Refugees: Liberians in Ghana." *Journal of the International Institute* 7 (3).

Parnell, Susan, and Jennifer Robinson. 2012. "(Re)theorizing Cities from the Global South: Looking beyond Neoliberalism." *Urban Geography* 33 (4): 593–617.

Pascucci, E. 2016. "Transnational Disruptions: Materialities and Temporalities of Transnational Citizenship among Somali Refugees in Cairo." *Global Networks* 16 (3): 326–43.

p'Bitek, Okot. 1986. *Artist, The Ruler: Essays on Art, Culture and Values.* Nairobi: East African Publishers.

Perera, Suda. 2013. "Alternative Agency: Rwandan Refugee Warriors in Exclusionary States." *Conflict, Security and Development* 13 (5): 569–88.

Petrie, Charles, and Ashley South. 2013. "Mapping of Myanmar Peacebuilding Civil Society." Paper presented at the Civil Society Dialogue Network meeting, Supporting Myanmar's Evolving Peace Processes: What Roles for Civil Society and the EU?, Brussels, March 7.

Pettit, Philip. 2001. *A Theory of Freedom: From the Psychology to the Politics of Agency.* Oxford: Oxford University Press.

Phillips, Anne. 1995. *The Politics of Presence.* Oxford: Oxford University Press.

Polzer, Tara, and Laura Hammond. 2008. "Invisible Displacement." *Journal of Refugee Studies* 21 (4): 417–31.

Porter, Elisabeth. 2003. "Women, Political Decision-Making, and Peacebuilding." *Global Change, Peace and Security* 15 (3): 245–62.

Porter, Gina, Kate Hampshire, Peter Kyei, Michael Adjaloo, George Rapoo, and Kate Kilpatrick. 2008. "Linkages between Livelihood Opportunities and Refugee-Host Relations: Learning from the Experiences of Liberian Camp-Based Refugees in Ghana." *Journal of Refugee Studies* 21 (2): 230–51.

Portes, Alejandro, and Min Zhou. 1993. "The New Second Generation: Segmented Assimilation and Its Variants." *Annals of the American Academy of Political and Social Science* 530 (1): 74–96.

Posner, Daniel. 2004. "Civil Society and the Reconstruction of Failed States." In *When States Fail: Causes and Consequences*, edited by Robert Rotberg, 237–42. Princeton, NJ: Princeton University Press.

Potts, Deborah Helen. 2010. *Circular Migration in Zimbabwe and Contemporary Sub-Saharan Africa*. Oxford: James Currey.

Pressé, Debra, and Jessie Thomson. 2007. "The Resettlement Challenge: Integration of Refugees from Protracted Refugee Situations." *Refuge: Canada's Journal on Refugees* 24 (2): 94–99.

Pretty, Jules N. 1994. "Alternative Systems of Enquiry for Sustainable Agriculture." *IDS Bulletin* 2 (25): 37–41.

Pumarejo, María Adriana, and Patrick Morales. 2003. *La recuperación de la memoria histórica de los kankuamo: Un llamado de los antiguos. Siglos XX–XVIII*. Bogota: Universidad Nacional de Colombia.

Purdeková, Andrea. 2016. "'Barahunga Amahoro—They Are Fleeing Peace!' The Politics of Re-Displacement and Entrenchment in Post-War Burundi." *Journal of Refugee Studies* 30 (1): 1–26.

Purkey, Anna Lise. 2015. "Legal Empowerment for a Dignified Life: Fiduciary Duty and Human Rights-Based Capabilities in Protracted Refugee Situations." DCL thesis, McGill University Faculty of Law, oai:digitool.library.mcgill.ca:135319.

Qasmiyeh, Yousif M. 2014. "Thresholds." *Critical Quarterly* 56 (4): 67–70.

Qasmiyeh, Yousif M., and Elena Fiddian-Qasmiyeh. 2013. "Refugee Camps and Cities in Conversation." In *Rescripting Religion in the City: Migration and Religious Identity in the Modern Metropolis*, edited by Jane Garnett and Alana Harris, 131–43. Farnham, UK: Ashgate.

Rabinowitz, Dan. 2010. "The Right to Refuse: Abject Theory and the Return of Palestinian Refugees." *Critical Inquiry* 36 (3): 494–516.

Raj, Althia. 2016. "Canada's Private Refugee Sponsorship Program to Expand around the World." *Huffington Post*, September 20. https://www.huffingtonpost.ca/2016/09/20/canada-private-sponsorship-refugees-syria-un-george-soros_n_12102066.html.

Rajagopal, Balakrishnan. 2003. *International Law from Below: Development, Social Movements and Third World Resistance*. Cambridge: Cambridge University Press.

Ramsbotham, Oliver, Hugh Woodhouse, and Hugh Miall. 2016. *Contemporary Con-

flict Resolution: The Prevention, Management and Transformation of Deadly Conflicts. 4th ed. Cambridge, UK: Polity Press.

Reichel-Dolmatoff, Gerardo, and Alicia Reichel-Dolmatoff. 1971. *The People of Aritama.* Chicago: University of Chicago Press.

Reporteros Asociados del Mundo. 2015. "Avanza plan de salvaguarda del pueblo Kankuamo en Bogotá." August 17. http://www.reporterosasociados.com.co/2015 /08/avanza-plan-de-salvaguarda-del-pueblo-kankuamo-en-bogota/.

Resguardo Indígena Kankuamo. 2006a. "Documento de Autoprotección colectiva del pueblo Kankuamo." On file with authors.

———. 2006b. "MAKÚ JOGÚKI: ordenamiento educativo, del pueblo indígena kankuamo." https://datospdf.com/download/proyecto-etnoeducativo-del-pueblo -indigena-kankuamo-_5a4bc59eb7d7bc 74fca0426_pdf.

Robbins, Joel. 2013. "Beyond the Suffering Subject: Toward an Anthropology of the Good." *Journal of the Royal Anthropological Institute* 19 (3): 447–62.

Robinson, W. Courtland. 2004. "The Comprehensive Plan of Action for Indochinese Refugees, 1989–1997: Sharing the Burden and Passing the Buck." *Journal of Refugee Studies* 17 (3): 319–33.

Rodríguez, César. 2011. "Etnicidad.gov: los pueblos indígenas, la gobernanza global y el derecho a la consulta previa en los campos sociales minados." *Indiana Journal of Global Legal Studies* 18 (1): 1–44.

Rogge, John, and Joshua Akol. 1989. "Repatriation: Its Role in Resolving Africa's Refugee Dilemma." *International Migration Review* 23 (2): 184–200.

Rosenoff-Gauvin, Lara 2013. "In and Out of Culture: Okot p'Bitek's Work and Social Repair in Post-Conflict Acoliland." *Oral Tradition* 28 (1): 35–54.

Rosenthal, Gabriele. 2004. "Biographical Research." In *Qualitative Research Practice,* edited by Clive Seale, Gobo Giampietro Jaber F. Gubrium, and David Silverman, 48–64. London: Sage.

Roth, Abraham Sesshu. 2017. "Shared Agency." In *The Stanford Encyclopedia of Philosophy,* edited by Edward N. Zalta. Stanford University, Summer 2017 edition. https://plato.stanford.edu/archives/sum2017/entries/shared-agency/.

Rowlands, Jo. 1997. *Questioning Empowerment: Working with Women in Honduras.* Oxford: Oxfam.

Rozario, Santi. 1997. "Development and Rural Women in South Asia; The Limits of Empowerment and Conscientization." *Bulletin of Concerned Asian Scholars* 29 (4): 45–53.

Rubenstein, Jennifer. 2013 "Emergency Claims and Democratic Action." *Social Philosophy and Policy* 22 (2): 204–30.

Rubio-Marin, Ruth. 2000. *Immigration as a Democratic Challenge: Citizenship and Inclusion in Germany and the United States.* Cambridge: Cambridge University Press.

Said, Edward W. 1983. *The World, the Text, and the Critic.* London: Vintage.

———. 2001. *Reflections on Exile and Other Essays.* Cambridge, MA: Harvard University Press.

San Martin, Pablo. 2005. "Nationalism, Identity and Citizenship in Western Sahara." *Journal of North African Studies* 10 (3–4): 565–92.

Sandvik, Kristin Bergtora. 2010a. "A Legal History: The Emergence of the African Resettlement Candidate in International Refugee Management." *International Journal of Refugee Law* 22 (1): 20–47.

———. 2010b. "Unpacking World Refugee Day: Humanitarian Governance and Human Rights Practice?" *Journal of Human Rights Practice* 2 (2): 287–98.

———. 2011. "Blurring Boundaries: Refugee Resettlement in Kampala—between the Formal, the Informal, and the Illegal." *PoLAR: Political and Legal Anthropology Review* 34 (1): 11–32.

———. 2012. "The Politics and Possibilities of Victim Making in International Law / As Políticas e possibilidades da 'construção de vítimas' no direito internacional." *Revista da Faculdade de Direito do Sul de Minas* 27 (2): 237–58.

Sandvik, Kristin Bergtora, and Julieta Lemaitre. 2013. "Internally Displaced Women as Knowledge Producers and Users in Humanitarian Action: The View from Colombia." *Disasters* 37 (1): S36–S50.

———. 2015. "From IDPs to Victims in Colombia: A Bottom Up Reading of Law in Post-Conflict Transitions." In *International Law and Post-Conflict Reconstruction*, edited by Matthew Saul and James Sweeney, 252–71. London: Routledge.

Sanford, Victoria. 2003. "Eyewitness: Peacebuilding in a War Zone: The Case of Colombian Peace Communities." *International Peacekeeping* 10 (2): 107–18.

Sanyal, Romola. 2011. "Squatting in Camps: Building and Insurgency in Spaces of Refuge." *Urban Studies* 48 (5): 877–90.

Saunders, Doug. 2011. *Arrival City: The Final Migration and Our Next World*. New York: Knopf.

Schiller, Nina Glick, Ayşe Çaglar, and Thaddeus C. Guldbrandsen. 2006. "Beyond the Ethnic Lens: Locality, Globality, and Born-Again Incorporation." *American Ethnologist* 33 (4): 612–33.

Schuck, Peter H. 1997. "Refugee Burden-Sharing: A Modest Proposal." Faculty Scholarship Series Paper 1694. http://digitalcommons.law.yale.edu/fss_papers/1694.

Schuller, M. 2016. *Humanitarian Aftershocks in Haiti*. New Brunswick, NJ: Rutgers University Press.

Schultz, T. Paul. 1971. "Rural-Urban Migration in Colombia." *Review of Economics and Statistics* 53 (2): 157–63.

Schulz, Helena Lindholm. 2003. *The Palestinian Diaspora: Formation of Identities and Politics of Homeland*, with Juliane Hammer. London: Routledge.

Schulz, Philipp. 2015. Review of Evelyn Amony. *I Am Evelyn Amony: Reclaiming My Life from the Lord's Resistance Army*, by Evelyn Amany, *International Feminist Journal of Politics International Feminist Journal of Politics* 18 (2): 312–14.

Scott, James C. 1985. *Weapons of the Weak: Everyday Forms of Peasant Resistance*. New Haven, CT: Yale University Press.

———. 1990. *Domination and the Art of Resistance: Hidden Transcripts*. New Haven, CT: Yale University Press.

———. 1998. *Seeing like a State: How Certain Schemes to Improve the Human Condition Have Failed*. New Haven, CT: Yale University Press.

Segbers, Klaus, Simon Raiser, and Krister Volkmann. 2007. *The Making of Global City*

Regions: Johannesburg, Mumbai/Bombay, Sao Paulo, and Shanghai. Baltimore: Johns Hopkins University Press.

Sen, Amartya. 1993. "Capability and Well-Being." In *The Quality of Life*, edited by Martha Nussbaum and Amartya Sen, 30–53. Oxford: Oxford University Press.

Sengupta, Arjun. 2008. "The Political Economy of Legal Empowerment of the Poor." In *Rights and Legal Empowerment in Eradicating Poverty*, edited by Dan Banik, 31–32. Surrey, UK: Ashgate.

Sévigny, Christophe. 2012. "Starting from Refugees Themselves: Towards an Institutional Ethnography of Resettlement." *New Issues in Refugee Research* 247, UNHCR.

Sewell, William H. 1992. "A Theory of Structure, Duality Agency and Transformation." *American Journal of Sociology* 98 (1): 1–29.

Shapiro, Scott J. 2014. "Massively Shared Agency." In *Rational and Social Agency: The Philosophy of Michael Bratman*, edited by Manuel Vargas and Gideon Yaffe, 257–89. Oxford: Oxford University Press.

Sharp, Dustin N. 2011–12. "Addressing Economic Violence in Times of Transition: Towards a Positive-Peace Paradigm for Transitional Justice." *Fordham International Law Journal* 35 (3): 780–814.

Shaw, Rosalind. 2002. *Memories of the Slave Trade: Ritual and the Historical Imagination in Sierra Leone.* Chicago: University of Chicago Press.

Shefte, Whitney. 2015. "Western Sahara's Stranded Refugees Consider Renewal of Morocco Conflict." *Guardian*, January 6. https://www.theguardian.com/world/2015/jan/06/morocco-western-sahara-referendum-delay.

Sherwood, Angela, Megan Bradley, Lorenza Rossi, Rosalia Gitau, and Bradley Mellicker. 2014. *Supporting Durable Solutions to Urban, Post-Disaster Displacement: Challenges and Opportunities in Haiti.* Washington, DC: Brookings Institution / International Organization for Migration.

Simmel, Georg. 2004. "The Metropolis and Mental Life." In *The City Cultures Reader*, 2nd ed., edited by Malcolm Miles, Tim Hall, and Iain Borden, 12–19. London: Routledge.

Simone, AbdouMaliq. 2006. "Pirate Towns: Reworking Social and Symbolic Infrastructures in Johannesburg and Douala." *Urban Studies* 43 (2): 357–70.

———. 2010. *City Life from Jakarta to Dakar: Movements at the Crossroads.* New York: Routledge.

Singer, Audrey, Susan W. Hardwick, and Caroline B. Brettell. 2008. *Twenty-First Century Gateways: Immigrant Incorporation in Suburban America.* Washington, DC: Brookings Institution Press.

Skran, Claudena M. 1995. *Refugees in Inter-War Europe: The Emergence of a Regime.* Oxford: Clarendon.

Skrbis, Zlatko, Gavin Kendall, and Ian Woodward. 2004. "Locating Cosmopolitanism between Humanist Ideal and Grounded Social Category." *Theory, Culture and Society* 21 (6): 115–36.

Slaughter, Amy, and Jeff Crisp. 2008. "A Surrogate State? The Role of UNHCR in Protracted Refugee Situations." In *Protracted Refugee Situations: Political, Hu-*

man Rights and Security Implications, edited by Gil Loescher, James Milner, Edward Newman, and Gary Troeller. Tokyo: United Nations University Press.

———. 2009. "A Surrogate State? The Role of UNHCR in Protracted Refugee Situations." New Issues In Refugee Research, Research Paper No. 168. Geneva: UNHCR. http://www.unhcr.org/research/working/4981cb432/surrogate-state -role-unhcr-protracted-refugee-situations-amy-slaughter.html.

Smit, Anneke. 2012. *The Property Rights of Refugees and Internally Displaced Persons: Beyond Restitution*. London: Routledge.

Snyder, Anna. 2011. "Developing Refugee Peacebuilding Capacity: Women in Exile on the Thai/Burmese Border." *Critical Issues in Peace and Conflict Studies*, edited by Thomas Matyók, Jessica Senehi, and Sean Byrne, 177–98. Lanham, MD: Lexington.

Soguk, Nevzat. 1999. *States and Strangers: Refugees and Displacements of Statecraft*. Minneapolis: University of Minnesota Press.

South, Ashley, and Kim Jolliffe. 2015. *Forced Migration and the Myanmar Peace Process*. Geneva: UNHCR. http://www.unhcr.org/54f588cb9.pdf.

Sperl, Stefan, and Machtelt De Vriese. 2005. *From Emergency Evacuation to Community Empowerment: Review of the Repatriation and Reintegration Programme in Sierra Leone*. Geneva: UNHCR. http://www.unhcr.org/publ/RESEARCH/420b80384.pdf.

Standing, Guy. 2011. *The Precariat: The New Dangerous Class*. London: Bloomsbury Academic.

Stedman, Stephen John. 1997. "Spoiler Problems in Peace Processes." *International Security* 22 (2): 5–53.

———. 2003. "Conclusions and Policy Recommendations." In *Refugee Manipulation: War, Politics, and the Abuse of Human Suffering*, edited by Stephen John Stedman and Fred Tanner, 167–90. Washington, DC: Brookings Institution Press.

Stein, Barry N. 1986. "Durable Solutions for Developing Country Refugees." *International Migration Review* 20 (2): 264–82.

Stepputat, Finn. 1999. "Responses to Kibreab, 'Dead Horses?'" *Journal of Refugee Studies* 12 (4): 416–19.

Stewart, Richard B. 2014. "Remedying Disregard in Global Regulatory Governance: Accountability, Participation, and Responsiveness." *American Journal of International Law* 108 (2): 211–70.

Stølen, K.A. 2007. *Guatemalans in the Aftermath of Violence: The Refugees' Return*, Philadelphia: University of Pennsylvania Press.

Sumba, Florence, and Ken Wilson. 1993. "Returning Home in Northern Safala: A Review of Events since the Peace Agreement and Implications for Assistance Programmes." UN Archives S-0382-0003-0003.

Synge, Richard Synge. 1997. *Mozambique: UN Peacekeeping in Action*. Washington, DC: United States Institute for Peace.

Sznajder, Mario, and Luis Roniger. 2009. *The Politics of Exile in Latin America*. Cambridge: Cambridge University Press.

Taylor, David. 2014. "Victim Participation in Transitional Justice Mechanisms: Real Power or Empty Ritual?" Discussion paper prepared for Impunity Watch. www .impunitywatch.org/docs/IW_Discussion_Paper_Victim_Participation1.pdf.

Thomson, Marnie Jane. 2012. "Black Boxes of Bureaucracy: Transparency and Opacity in the Resettlement Process of Congolese Refugees." *Political and Legal Anthropology Review* 35 (2): 186–205.

Thomson, Susan. 2013. *Whispering Truth to Power: Everyday Resistance to Reconciliation in Postgenocide Rwanda*. Madison: University of Wisconsin Press.

Throop, Jason, and Douglas Hollan. 2008. "Whatever Happened to Empathy? Introduction." *Ethnos* 36 (4): 385–401.

Ticktin, Miriam I. 2011. *Casualties of Care: Immigration and the Politics of Humanitarianism in France*. Berkeley: University of California Press.

Tonkiss, Fran. 2003. "The Ethics of Indifference Community and Solitude in the City." *International Journal of Cultural Studies* 6 (3): 297–311.

Troeller, Gary. 2002. "UNHCR Resettlement: Evolution and Future Direction." *International Journal of Refugee Law* 14 (1): 85–95.

Turner, Simon. 2015. "What Is a Refugee Camp? Explorations of the Limits and Effects of the Camp." *Journal of Refugee Studies* 29 (2): 139–48.

Turner, Victor Witter. 1967. "Betwixt and Between: The Liminal Period in Rites De Passage." In *The Forest of Symbols: Aspects of Ndembu Ritual*, edited by Victor Turner, 93–111. Ithaca, NY: Cornell University Press.

Turton, David. 1999. "Response to Kibreab." *Journal of Refugee Studies* 12 (4): 419–22.

———. 2003. "Conceptualising Forced Migration." RSC Working Paper No. 12, October. University of Oxford. https://www.rsc.ox.ac.uk/files/files-1/wp12 -conceptualising-forced migration-2003.pdf.

Ulloa, Astrid. 2011. "The Politics of Autonomy of Indigenous Peoples of the Sierra Nevada de Santa Marta, Colombia: A Process of Relational Indigenous Autonomy." *Latin American and Caribbean Ethnic Studies* 6 (1): 79–107.

UN/OIOS. 2001. "Report of the Office of Internal Oversight Services on the Investigation into Allegations of Refugee Smuggling." Report at the Nairobi branch of the Office of the United Nations High Commissioner for Refugees. New York: UN General Assembly.

UNESCO. 2011. *The Hidden Crisis: Armed Conflict and Education*. EFA Global Monitoring Report. http://unesdoc.unesco.org/images/0019/001907/190743e.pdf.

United Nations (UN). 2009. "Report of the Secretary-General on Peacebuilding in the Immediate Aftermath of Conflict." June 11. A/63/881-S/2009/304. http:// www.un.org/en/ga/search/view_doc.asp?symbol=A/63/881.

United Nations Department of Economic and Social Affairs Population Division (UNDESA) 2014. *World Urbanisation Prospects: The 2014 Revision: Highlights*. New York: UNDESA.

United Nations Development Programme (UNDP). 2005. *Programming for Justice: Access for All—A Practitioner's Guide to a Human Rights-Based Approach to Access to Justice*. Asia-Pacific Rights and Justice Initiative. Bangkok: UNDP.

UN General Assembly. 2016. "New York Declaration for Refugees and Migrants, Statement of Financial Implications." Resolution A/71/L.1, September 19, 2016. http://www.un.org/en/ga/search/view_doc.asp?symbol=A/RES/71/1.

UN-Habitat. 2014. *African Cities 2014: Re-Imagining Sustainable Urban Transitions.* Nairobi: UN-Habitat. https://issuu.com/unpublications/docs/9789210 575614.

United Nations High Commissioner for Refugees (UNHCR). 1983. *UNHCR Guidelines on Reunification of Refugee Families* (July 1983). Geneva: UNHCR. http://www.unhcr.org/protection/globalconsult/3bd0378f4/unhcr-guidelines -reunification-refugee-families.html.

———. 1994. "Mozambique Repatriation Operation, 1994: Policy Objectives, Country Plan and Issues to Be Monitored: Summary: Document Prepared for the Representatives Meeting, Southern Africa Region, 6/7 March 1994." UN Archives S-0382-0003-0006.

———. 1997a. "Rebuilding a War-Torn Society: A Review of the UNHCR Reintegration Programme for Mozambican Returnees." *Refugee Survey Quarterly* 16 (2): 24–71.

———. 1997b. *The State of the World's Refugees: A Humanitarian Agenda.* Oxford: Oxford University Press.

———. 2004. *Handbook for Repatriation and Reintegration Activities.* Geneva: UNHCR.

———. 2005. *Handbook for Self-Reliance.* Geneva: UNHCR.

———. 2006. *UNHCR Handbook for Self-Reliance.* Operational Publications, July. Geneva: UNHCR.

———. 2007. *Tertiary Refugee Education: Impact and Achievements.* Geneva: UNHCR.

———. 2009. *UNHCR Policy on Refugee Protection and Solutions in Urban Areas.* September. Geneva: UNHCR.

———. 2010. *UNHCR Global Appeal 2010–2011.* Geneva: UNHCR.

———. 2011. *UNHCR Resettlement Handbook.* Rev. ed. Geneva: UNHCR.

———. 2012. *The State of the World's Refugees: In Search of Solidarity.* Oxford: Oxford University Press.

———. 2015. *UNHCR Urges CAR to Let Refugees Take Part in Elections,* https://www .unhcr.org/news/briefing/2015/7/55a4e87b6/unhcr-urges-car-refugees-part -elections.html

———. 2016a. "ACNUR insta a involucrar a los refugiados y los desplazados internos en las conversaciones de paz en Colombia." *UNHCR,* April 12. http:// www.acnur.org/noticias/noticia/2016/4/5af3065d1a/acnur-insta-a-involucrar -a-los-refugiados-y-los-desplazados-internos-en-las-conversaciones-de-paz-en -colombia.html?query="ACNUR%20insta%20a%20involucrar%20a%20los%20 refugiados%20y%20los%20desplazados%20internos%20en%20las%20conver saciones%20de%20paz%20en%20Colombia.

———. 2016b. *Global Trends: Forced Displacement in 2015,* June 20. http://www.un hcr.org/statistics/unhcrstats/576408cd7/unhcr-global-trends-2015.html.

———. 2016c. *Projected Global Resettlement Needs 2017,* June 13. https://reliefweb .int/report/world/unhcr-projected-global-resettlement-needs-2017.

———. 2017. *UNHCR's Strategic Directions: 2017–2021,* January 16. Geneva: UNHCR.

———. 2018. *Global Trends: Forced Displacement in 2017,* June 19. http://www.unhcr .org/statistics/unhcrstats/5b27be547/unhcr-global-trends-2017.html.

UNHCR-Accra. 2004. "First Voluntary Repatriation Movement Benefitting Liberian Refugees Takes Off from Accra," UNHCR Media Relations and Public Information Service, UNHCR Accra.

————. 2006. "High-ranking Liberian Delegation Impressed by Skills of Refugees
in Ghana." July 18. http://www.unhcr.org/news/latest/2006/7/44bcf45a4/high
-ranking-liberian-delegation-impressed-skills-refugees-ghana.html.

UNHCR Europe. 2013. "Response to Vulnerability in Asylum Project Report."
http://www.refworld.org/docid/56c444004.html.

UNHCR-Ghana. 2008a. "Update on the Liberia Refugee Situation in Ghana."
UNHCR Media Relations and Public Information Service, Accra.

————. 2008b. "UNHCR Condemns Disturbances at Buduburam Refugee Settlement." UNHCR Media Relations and Public Information Service Accra, March
11.

UNHCR-Monrovia. 2005. "Operations Plan for Sustainable Return and Reintegration of Displaced Populations in Liberia: A 4Rs Transitional Approach (2004–
2007)."

————. 2013. "UNHCR Completes Repatriation of 155,000 Liberians." http://
www.unhcr.org/news/makingdifference/2013/1/50e6af089/unhcr-completes
-repatriation-155000-liberians.html.

UNHCR and Mae Fah Luang Foundation (MFLF). 2014. "Displaced Persons in the
Temporary Shelters along the Thai-Myanmar Border: Future Hopes and Aspirations." http://data.unhcr.org/thailand/download.php?id=415.

Unidad de Víctimas. 2015. "Mejora la situación de la población desplazada en Colombia." https://reliefweb.int/report/colombia/encuesta-de-goce-efectivo-de
-derechos.

United Nations General Assembly (UNGA). 1948. Resolution 194 (III): Palestine—
Progress Report of the United Nations Mediator, A/RES/194 (III), December
11. https://www.refworld.org/docid/4fe2e5672.html.

United Nations High-Level Panel on Threats, Challenges, and Change. 2004. *A More
Secure World: Our Shared Responsibility*. UN Doc. A/59/565.

United Nations Secretary-General (UNSG). 1992. *An Agenda for Peace: Preventive
Diplomacy, Peacemaking and Peace-Keeping*. Report of the Secretary-General pursuant to the statement adopted by the Summit Meeting of the Security Council
on A/47/227. January 31.

————. 2005. *In Larger Freedom: Towards Security, Development, and Human Rights for
All. Report of the Secretary-General of the United Nations for Decision by Heads of State
and Government in September 2005*, UN Doc. A/59/2005. March 21.

————. 2009. *Report of the Secretary-General on Peacebuilding in the Immediate Aftermath
of Conflict*, UN Doc. A/63/881–S/2009/304. June 11.

————. 2011. *Policy Committee Decision No. 2011/20—Durable Solutions: Follow Up
to the Secretary-General's 2009 Report on Peacebuilding*. October 4.

United Nations Security Council Official Records (UNSCOR). 2004. *The Rule of
Law and Transitional Justice in Conflict and Post-Conflict Societies: Report of the Secretary
General*. UN Doc. S/2004/616, 3–4. https://www.un.org/ruleoflaw/blog/docu

ment/the-rule-of-law-and-transitional-justice-in-conflict-and-post-conflict-so
cieties-report-of-the-secretary-general/

UN News. 2004. "Colombia Has Biggest Humanitarian Crisis in Western Hemisphere." *UN News*, May 10. https://news.un.org/en/story/2004/05/103072-co
lombia-has-biggest-humanitarian-crisis-western-hemisphere-un-says

UN-OCHA IRIN. 2008. "Ghana-Liberia: Cessation Clause Invoked over Refugee
Demos," March 20, http://www.irinnews.org/report/77397/ghana-liberia-ces
sation-clause-invoked-over-refugee-demos

UN Operations in Mozambique, Office for Humanitarian Assistance Coordination
(ONUMOZ). 1993. "Post-War Population Movements in Mozambique." June.
UN Archives S-0382-0010-0004.

UN Population Division. 2016. "International Migration." http://www.un.org/en
/development/desa/population/theme/international -migration/.

Utas, Mats. 2003. *Sweet Battlefields: Youth and the Liberian Civil War*. Dissertations in
Cultural Anthropology, Uppsala University, Uppsala, Sweden.

———. 2004. "Fluid Research Fields: Studying Ex-Combatant Youth in the Aftermath of the Liberian Civil War." In *Children and Youth on the Front Line: Ethnography, Armed Conflict and Displacement*, edited by Jo Boyden and J. de Berry, 209–36.
Oxford: Berghahn.

———. 2005. "Victimcy, Girlfriending, Soldiering: Tactic Agency in a Young Woman's Social Navigation of the Liberian War Zone." *Anthropological Quarterly* 78 (2):
403–430.

van Bochove, Marianne, and Katja Rusinovic. 2008. "Transnationalism and Dimensions of Citizenship." *Journal of Ethnic and Migration Studies* 34 (8): 1337–43.

Van Gennep, Arnold. 1960. *The Rites of Passage*. Chicago: University of Chicago Press.

Van Hear, Nicholas. 1998. *New Diasporas: The Mass Exodus, Dispersal and Regrouping
of Migrant Communities*. Seattle: University of Washington Press.

Van Selm, Joanne. 2004. "The Strategic Use of Resettlement: Changing the Face of
Protection?" *Refuge: Canada's Journal on Refugees* 22 (1): 39–48.

Vecchio, Francesco. 2015. *Asylum Seeking and the Global City*. London: Routledge.

Vigh, Henrik E. 2006. *Navigating Terrains of War: Youth and Soldiering in Guinea-Bissau*.
Oxford: Berghahn.

———. 2008. "Crisis and Chronicity: Anthropological Perspectives on Continuous
Conflict and Decline." *Ethnos* 73 (1): 5–24.

Vincent, Marc, and Birgitte Refslund Sørensen. 2001. *Caught between Borders: Response Strategies of the Internally Displaced*. London: Pluto.

Voisin, Vanessa. 2007. "Retribute or Reintegrate? The Ambiguity of Soviet Policies
towards Repatriates: The Case of Kalinin Province, 1943–1950." *Jahrbücher für
Geschichte Osteuropas*, Neue Folge 55 (1): 34–55.

Wald, Kenneth D. 2008. "Homeland Interests, Hostland Politics: Politicized Ethnic
Identity among Middle Eastern Heritage Groups in the United States." *International Migration Review* 42 (2): 273–301.

Waldorf, Lars. 2013. "Legal Empowerment in Transitions: A Short Concept Note."
York, UK: Centre for Applied Human Rights, University of York.

Walker, Melanie. 2009. "Appendix 1: Teaching the Human Development and Capability Approach: Some Pedagogical Implications." In *An Introduction to the Human Development and Capability Approach: Freedom and Agency*, edited by Séverine Deneulin and Lila Shahani, 240–43. London: Earthscan.

Wallensteen, Peter. 2015. *Understanding Conflict Resolution*. 4th ed. London: Sage.

Watson, Vanessa. 2009. "Seeing from the South: Refocusing Urban Planning on the Globe's Central Urban Issues." *Urban Studies* 46 (11): 2259–75.

White, Louise. 1990. *The Comforts of Home: Prostitution in Colonial Nairobi*. Chicago: University of Chicago Press.

Wilcke, Christoph. 2010. *Stateless Again: Palestinian-Origin Jordanians Deprived of Their Nationality*. New York: Human Rights Watch.

Wilkinson, Iain, and Arthur Kleinman. 2016. *A Passion for Society: How We Think about Human Suffering*. Oakland: University of California Press.

Williams, Gareth. 2013. "Sharing Responsibility and Holding Responsible." *Journal of Applied Philosophy* 30 (4): 351–64.

Williams, Rhodri C. 2011. "Protracted Internal Displacement and Integration in Serbia." In *Resolving Internal Displacement: Prospects for Local Integration*, edited by Elizabeth Ferri, 82–104. Washington, DC: Brookings Institution.

Wirth, Louis. 1995. "Urbanism as a Way of Life" (1938). In *Metropolis: Centre and Symbol of Our Time*, edited by P. Kasinitz, 58–82. New York: New York University Press.

Wolf, Eric R. 1994. "Perilous Ideas: Race, Culture and People." *Current Anthropology* 35 (1): 1–12.

Worby, Eric. 2010. "Address Unknown: The Temporality of Displacement and the Ethics of Disconnection among Zimbabwean Migrants in Johannesburg." *Journal of Southern African Studies* 36 (2): 417–31.

World Bank. 2005. *Global Economic Prospects 2006: Economic Implications of Remittances and Migration*. Washington, DC: World Bank.

———. 2015. *The Welfare of Syrian Refugees: Evidence from Jordan and Lebanon*. Washington, DC: World Bank.

———. 2017. *Forcibly Displaced: Toward a Development Approach to Supporting Refugees, the Internally Displaced, and Their Hosts*. Washington, DC: World Bank.

Yassin, Nasser, Nora Stel, and Rima Rassi. 2016. "Organized Chaos: Informal Institution Building among Palestinian Refugees in the Maashouk Gathering in South Lebanon." *Journal of Refugee Studies* 29 (3): 341–62.

Ye, Junjia. 2015. "The Ambivalence of Familiarity: Understanding Breathable Diversity through Fleeting Encounters in Singapore's Jurong West." *Area* 48 (1): 77–83.

Young, Iris Marion. 2011. *Justice and the Politics of Difference*. Princeton, NJ: Princeton University Press.

Zapata-Barrero, Ricard, Lorenzo Gabrielli, Elena Sánchez-Montijano, and Thibaut Jaulin. 2013. "The Political Participation of Immigrants in Host Countries: An Interpretative Framework from the Perspective of Origin Countries and Societies." INTERACT RR 2013/07, Robert Schuman Centre for Advanced Studies. San Domenico di Fiesole (FI): European University Institute.

Zetter, Roger. 1991. "Labeling Refugees: Forming and Transforming a Bureaucratic Identity." *Journal of Refugee Studies* 4 (1): 39–62.

———. 2007. "More Labels, Fewer Refugees: Remaking the Refugee Label in an Era of Globalization." *Journal of Refugee Studies* 20 (2): 172–92.

Zetter, Roger, and George Deikun. 2010. "Meeting Humanitarian Challenges in Urban Areas." *Forced Migration Review* 34: 5–7.

Zetter, Roger, and Héloïse Ruaudel. 2016. "Refugees' Right to Work and Access to Labor Markets—An Assessment." KNOMAD Working Paper, World Bank Group.

Zulver, Julia. 2018. "Feasible Justice: Has Colombia Over-Promised and Under-Delivered Reparations for Its 8.6 Million Victims?" June 12. https://www.justiceinfo.net/en/reparations/37686-feasible-justice-has-colombia-over-promised-and-under-delivered-reparations-for-its-8-6-million-vic.html.

Zunes, Stephen, and Jacob Mundy. 2010. *Western Sahara: War, Nationalism, and Conflict Irresolution.* Syracuse, NY: Syracuse University Press.

Contributors

ERIN BAINES, associate professor, Liu Institute for Global Issues, University of British Columbia.

MEGAN BRADLEY, associate professor, Department of Political Science and Institute for the Study of International Development, McGill University.

CHRISTINA CLARK-KAZAK, associate professor, Graduate School of Public and International Affairs, University of Ottawa.

AMANDA COFFIE, research fellow, Legon Center for International Affairs and Diplomacy, University of Ghana.

FRANÇOIS CRÉPEAU, O.C., F.R.S.C., Ad.E., Trudeau Fellow, Hans & Tamar Oppenheimer Professor in Public International Law at McGill University, director of the McGill Centre for Human Rights and Legal Pluralism.

ELENA FIDDIAN-QASMIYEH, professor, Migration and Refugee Studies; director, Migration Research Unit, University College London.

CINDY HORST, research director and research professor, Migration and Refugee Studies, Peace Research Institute Oslo (PRIO).

KAREN JACOBSEN, Henry J. Leir Professor of Global Migration, Fletcher School of Law and Diplomacy, Tufts University.

PATRIK JOHANSSON, senior lecturer, Department of Political Science, Umeå University.

LOREN B. LANDAU, South African Research Chair in Human Mobility and the Politics of Difference, African Centre for Migration & Society, University of the Witwatersrand.

JULIETA LEMAITRE, Justice in the Special Jurisdiction for Peace (Chamber for the Recognition of Truth) and adjunct professor, Faulty of Law, Universidad de los Andes.

JAMES MILNER, associate professor, Department of Political Science, Carleton University.

BLAIR PERUNIAK, DPhil candidate, Department of International Development, University of Oxford.

ANNA PURKEY, assistant professor, Department of Sociology and Legal Studies, St. Jerome's University in the University of Waterloo.

KRISTIN BERGTORA SANDVIK, research professor, Humanitarian Studies, Peace Research Institute Oslo (PRIO) and Professor of Sociology of Law, Department of Criminology and Sociology of Law, University of Oslo.

ANGELA SHERWOOD, researcher, Amnesty International, and doctoral candidate, Queen Mary University of London.

MARNIE JANE THOMSON, scholar-in-residence, University of Colorado.

Index

CPSIA information can be obtained
at www.ICGtesting.com
Printed in the USA
BVHW030431270319
543812BV00001B/1/P